A Reading from Homer.

AN INTRODUCTION TO GREEK

HENRY LAMAR CROSBY

AND

JOHN NEVIN SCHAEFFER

DOVER PUBLICATIONS, INC.

MINEOLA, NEW YORK

Bibliographical Note

This Dover edition, first published in 2009, is an unabridged republication of the work originally published by Allyn and Bacon, Boston, in 1928. The original color frontispiece has been reproduced here in black and white. In the present edition, four full-page illustrations have been repositioned, and a map of the Greek peninsula has been omitted for space considerations.

Library of Congress Cataloging-in-Publication Data

Crosby, H. Lamar (Henry Lamar), b. 1880.
An introduction to Greek / Henry Lamar Crosby and John Nevin Schaeffer.
p. cm.
Includes index.
Previously published: Boston : Allyn and Bacon, c1928.
ISBN-13: 978-0-486-47056-6
ISBN-10: 0-486-47056-3
1. Greek language—Grammar. I. Schaeffer, John Nevin, 1882– II. Title.

PA258.C87 2009
488.2'421—dc22

2008051076

Manufactured in the United States by Courier Corporation
47056302 2015
www.doverpublications.com

PREFACE

"THE glory that was Greece" means little to a student whose first Greek book presents only grammar. This *Introduction to Greek* gives him an insight into the brilliant achievements of ancient Greece, and at the same time, in a logical, thorough, and interesting manner, it develops in him the power to read Greek.

Appropriate Greek mottoes at the head of each lesson indicate the universality of Greek thought. Selected passages for translation, with challenging titles, introduce the student to many notable writers and let him see how human and how much alive the ancient Greeks really were. Exercises on derivation and word-formation, together with the derived English words that occur in the lesson vocabularies, show him how vital a part Greek still plays in our English language and thought. Numerous beautiful pictures add to his interest and understanding of Greek achievement and influence.

All the readings are carefully adapted to the growing powers of the student. The vocabulary to be memorized is limited to 600 words, chosen from those most often used in the first four books of Xenophon's *Anabasis,* from those most useful in understanding English terms, and from cognates. All these words, except a few in the last group of lessons, appear at least four times in the exercises.

Special emphasis is given to syntactical constructions of most frequent occurrence in *Anabasis,* I–IV. To insure greater concentration upon what is vital, certain forms not needed in the early stage of Greek study are relegated to the Appendix. Every point of syntax to be mastered is used at least five times. The rules for the most part are phrased in the order in which the phenomena meet the eye of the reader of Greek and not as instructions for one translating from English into Greek.

Particular attention is called to the sentences for translation into Greek. These deal with the vocabulary, forms, and syntax of the previous lesson. Since students consider the English sentences the hardest and the least possible of improvisation, they often turn to them before finishing the necessary preliminary work. The present plan prevents this and assures adequate preparation.

Systematic reviews have been placed at intervals to follow successive groups of inflections. They have been so handled as to necessitate a rethinking of the matters under review and to prevent mere recitation by rote. Toward the end of the book a number of lessons are in part devoted to a review of case and mood forms and uses, so that the student may properly organize his knowledge into usable form. All through the book an effort has been made to stimulate consecutive thinking as against mere rote memory.

The authors acknowledge their indebtedness to the report of the Classical Investigation, whose findings and recommendations have been of great help, whether they concern Greek or Latin.

Thanks are due also Professor Shirley H. Weber, of Princeton University, and Dr. W. F. Dales, of Washington, D. C., for reading the manuscript of this book and for making valuable suggestions. Acknowledgment is due for permission to quote from the following: F. G. Allinson, *Greek Lands and Letters* (Houghton Mifflin Co.); John H. Finley, *The Prayer of Socrates* (The Outlook Co.); T. R. Glover, *Herodotus* (University of California Press); James Russell Lowell, *Address on Books and Libraries* (Houghton Mifflin Co.); E. S. McCartney, *Warfare by Land and Sea* (Longmans,

Green and Co.); H. G. Wells, *Tono-Bungay* (Duffield and Co.); A. F. West, *Value of the Classics* (Princeton University Press). The authors wish also to thank for the generous loan of photographs: Dr. Carl W. Blegen, of the University of Cincinnati; Dr. A. C. Schlesinger, of Williams College; Dr. R. S. Rogers, of Princeton University; Dr. Clarence Kennedy, of Smith College; and Mr. George R. Swain, of the University of Michigan.

HENRY LAMAR CROSBY
Professor of Greek, and
Dean of the Graduate School
University of Pennsylvania

JOHN NEVIN SCHAEFFER
Professor of Greek
Franklin and Marshall College

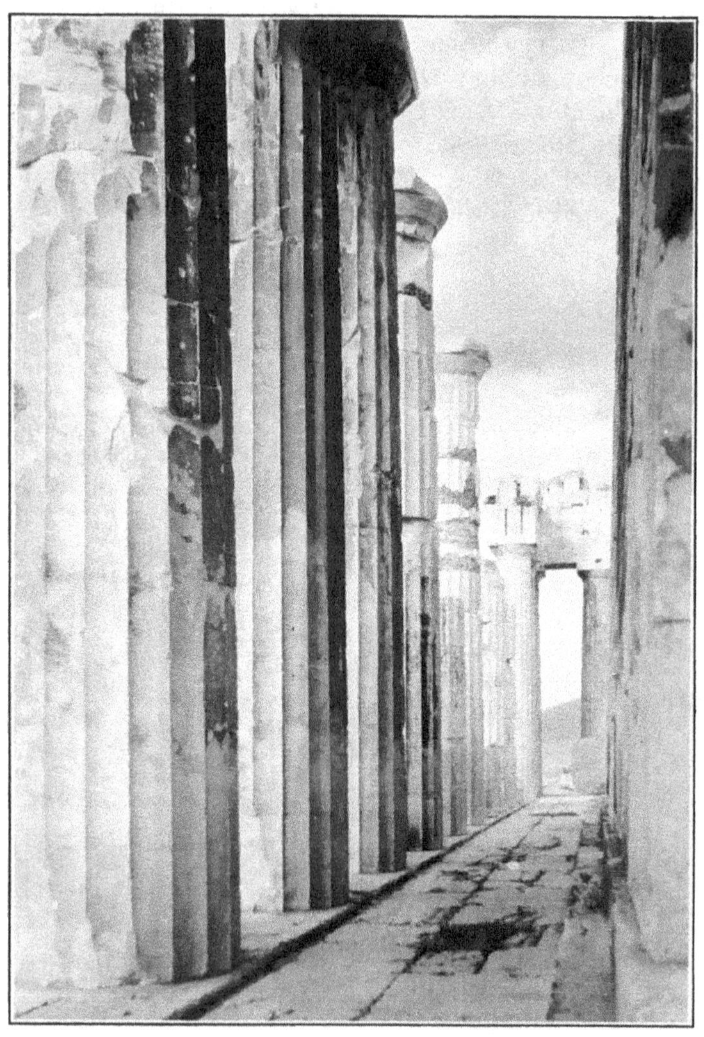

THE SOUTH COLONNADE OF THE PARTHENON

No mortar was used in Greek temples, but the joints in these columns are scarcely visible. (For a picture of the Parthenon, see page 97.)

CONTENTS

READING SELECTIONS

THE HERMES OF PRAXITELES

The ancients seem to have regarded the Hermes less highly than other works of Praxiteles. It is now the most famous statue in the world, since it is the only undoubted original by a known master of first rank.

ILLUSTRATIONS

AN INTRODUCTION TO GREEK

SHELTERED BY THE PARTHENON

The gleaming white of the familiar Erechtheum seen through these noble Doric columns reveals the brilliance of the Attic sun.

INTRODUCTION

We are all Greeks. Our laws, our literature, our religion, our art, have their root in Greece.[1]

If some magic carpet could whisk us back two thousand years or more to ancient Athens, how surprised we should be to see those early Greeks finding their chief delight, just as we do, in sports, fraternities, the theater, music, art, and literature!

The Metropolitan Museum of Art.

THE DISCOBOLUS

In any of the city's playgrounds we should find keen-eyed young men running, jumping, boxing, wrestling, throwing the discus and the javelin with as much zest as ourselves, and perhaps with more skill. Here they sought diversion after the business of the day. Here they trained for the great Olympic Games. An Olympic victor was welcomed home with all the enthusiasm and festivity that attends the winning of a World Series, and his fame was even more enduring.

[1] Shelley.

The Athenian did not feel it necessary to label his fraternity with Greek letters, as we do, but its interests and activities seemed to him quite as important. He was notably a social animal and held to the motto, *εἷς ἀνὴρ οὐδεὶς ἀνήρ*, "one man no man."

If our visit to Athens coincided with either of the two great dramatic festivals, we should find the whole city holding holiday. The great Dionysiac Theater seated about 17,000 spectators, and it was thronged all day long for the duration of the theater season. Here were performed some of the finest tragedies and comedies the world has ever known. But plays were not confined to Athens. Wherever Greeks were wont to congregate, they built theaters, even at Epidaurus, which was no town at all, but only a sanatorium.

Music was not only inseparably bound up with drama, it accompanied everything a Greek might do. As a schoolboy, he studied singing and the lyre. As a man, he honored his gods with song and dance. He sang at the banquet board, about the camp fire, or when about to charge the foe.

The arts of architecture, sculpture, and painting were no less honored. Even in their ruins, his public buildings and statues are the inspiration and the despair of modern artists. If his home was humble in comparison and but meagerly equipped when measured by present standards, it was because he found his keenest pleasure in public life. What furnishings he had were beautifully made and tastefully adorned.

Indeed, good taste was the mint mark of both work and play. Μηδὲν ἄγαν, "nothing too much," was the rule of life, which kept him from the vulgarity of the "barbarians" all about him, as well as from their extravagances in art.

If he did not devote much time to reading, it was because of his love of the open air. He took the keenest delight in literature, but it was a literature intended to be heard rather than to be read in private. The Greek seems to have invented nearly every form of composition and in none

Ewing Galloway.

THE THEATER AT EPIDAURUS

This is generally regarded as the most beautiful Greek theater now extant.

has he been surpassed. The roll of the immortals in the field of literature includes Homer in epic; Sappho and Alcæus in lyric; in drama the great triad, Æschylus, Sophocles, and Euripides; Herodotus, "the Father of History"; Demosthenes, whose name is synonymous with eloquence; Plato and Aristotle in philosophy and science.

The Study of Greek. Not everybody finds it convenient to visit Greece and to admire with his own eyes the visible remnants of Greek art. Too often we must get what we can from photographs or from the imitations all about us. But those of us who wish a first-hand acquaintance with what the Greeks thought and said may find our magic carpet in the study of the language. Translations are but a poor substitute at best and nowhere more disappointing than in the case of poetry, in which the Greek most excelled.

Greek and English. The best Greek is marked by a sense of proportion, by a striving for just the right word to convey the thought, and by a simplicity and directness of expression. With these qualities of good style we shall become familiar. More than that, we shall learn the fundamental meaning of a host of words that otherwise would seem strange and forbidding in the technical terminology of many fields of interest — in art, in science, in politics, and in the church. A distinguished scientist states that "In an experience of more than forty years as a teacher of medical students I easily distinguish among my auditors those who know Greek and those who do not, especially when I use scientific terms, such as 'toxicogenic bacillus' or a 'pathognomonic symptom.' I see the eyes of the former fill with the light of comprehension, while those of the latter are closed in ignorance and mystification."[1]

I. **The Greek Alphabet,** that is, ἄλφα-βητ(α), English "a-b-c's," is not the smallest item in our indebtedness to Greece. It was adopted by the Romans from their Greek neighbors at Cumæ, west of Naples, and handed on, with but slight modifications, to general European use.

---

[1] Victor C. Vaughan, Dean of the Medical School, University of Michigan, as reported in *Value of the Classics*, page 59.

The Greek Alphabet

Form [1]	Name	Trans-literated	Sound [2]	Greek Example
Α α	alpha	A a	drama	δρᾶ-μᾰ
Β β	beta	B b	bible	βι-βλί-ον
Γ γ	gamma	G g, ng	ganglion	γάγ-γλι-ον
Δ δ	delta	D d	decalog	δέ-κα
Ε ε	epsilon	E e	epic	ἔ-πος
Ζ ζ	zeta [3]	Z z	adze	ζώ-νη
Η η	eta	E e	they	ἤ-δη
Θ θ	theta	Th th	atheist	θε-ός
Ι ι	iota	I i	intrigue	ἐ-πῐ-πῑ-πτω
Κ κ	kappa	K k, C c	crisis	κρί-σις
Λ λ	lambda	L l	logic	λό-γος
Μ μ	mu	M m	meter	μέ-τρον
Ν ν	nu	N n	anti	ἀν-τί
Ξ ξ	xi	X x	axiom	ἀ-ξί-ω-μα
Ο ο	omicron	O o	obey	ἀ-πό
Π π	pi	P p	poet	ποι-η-τής
Ρ ρ	rho	Rh rh, r	catarrh	κα-τάρ-ρο-ος
Σ σ, ς	sigma	S s	spore	σπό-ρος
Τ τ	tau	T t	tone	το-νή
Υ υ	upsilon	Y y, u	abyss	ἄ-βῠσ-σος, Κῦ-ρος
Φ φ	phi	Ph ph	Philip	Φίλ-ιπ-πος
Χ χ	chi	Ch ch	character	χα-ρα-κτήρ
Ψ ψ	psi	Ps ps	apse	ἀ-ψίς
Ω ω	omega	O o	ocean	ὠ-κε-α-νός

[1] For centuries only capital letters were used by the Greeks. Although the small letters that later came into use are less like the Latin-English, we can easily trace their development from the capitals. The difference between the two types is no greater than that between capitals and small letters in English.

[2] The words used as illustrations represent as faithfully as is possible in English the best usage of modern scholars.

[3] Compare English *zed*.

Note that (*a*) **α, ι, υ** are sometimes long and sometimes short. When long, they will be marked **ᾱ, ῑ, ῡ**, unless they bear the circumflex accent (ˆ), which in itself indicates a long vowel: *στρατιᾱ́, στρατιᾶς.*

(*b*) Gamma is always hard. Before **κ, γ,** or **χ,** it is pronounced *ng*: *γάγγλιον.*

(*c*) Sigma is written **ς** at the end of words; elsewhere **σ**: *κρίσις.*

(*d*) Consonants are commonly classified as follows:

Mutes: 1. labial—**π, β, φ**; 2. guttural or palatal—**κ, γ, χ**; 3. dental or lingual—**τ, δ, θ.**

Liquids: **λ, μ, ν, ρ.**

Sibilant: **σ, ς.**

Double Consonants: **ζ, ξ, ψ.**

(*e*) The following table will be found useful for reference.

	VOICELESS MUTES	VOICED MUTES	ASPIRATE "ROUGH"
Labials	π	β	φ
Palatals	κ	γ	χ
Dentals	τ	δ	θ

In this table the mutes are grouped horizontally into *classes* (cognates) according to the organ of speech most prominent in their production, and vertically into *orders* (coördinates) according to the amount of force involved in their utterance. The significance of this grouping will become manifest in the study of inflection, each group having distinctive habits.

II. **Diphthongs** (*δί-φθογ-γοι*) represent the union of two vowels in one syllable. The second vowel is always either *ι* or *υ*.

Diphthong	Transliterated	Sound	Greek Example
αι	ae, e	ai in aisle	φαι-νό-με-νον
ει	ei, i, e	ei in freight	ἔκ-λει-ψις
οι	oe, i, e	oi in toil	Δελ-φοί
υι		we	υἱ-ός
αυ	au	ow in cow	αὐ-τός
ευ	eu	ĕh — oo	Εὐ-ρῑ-πί-δης
ηυ	eu	ēh — oo	ηὕ-ρη-κα
ου	u	ou in group	οὐ-ρα-νός

When a long vowel combines with iota, it forms an *improper* diphthong, the iota no longer affecting the sound. If the vowel to which it is attached is a capital, the iota is placed on the same line; otherwise it is placed beneath the letter to which it belongs and is called *iota subscript:* **Ηι, ῃ, Ωι, ῳ.**

III. **Breathings.** (*a*) The Athenians originally employed **H** as in English. When they adopted the Ionic alphabet, in which **H** was *eta*, it became necessary to invent a new symbol to take its place. That symbol (ʽ) is called the *rough breathing.* Words beginning with a vowel or diphthong without the h-sound receive the *smooth breathing* (ʼ).

(*b*) The sign of breathing precedes a capital but is placed above a small letter. In the case of a diphthong, the breathing is placed above the second member, unless the diphthong is improper: **Ἡ, ἡ, αἱ**; but **ᾗ, Ἅιδης.**

(*c*) Words beginning with *rho* (*ρ*) have the rough breathing.

(*d*) The rough breathing originally accompanied **φ, χ,** and **θ,** which are therefore called the "rough" forms of **π, β; κ, γ;** and **τ, δ,** respectively. See above I, *e*.

(*e*) When in inflection a voiced or voiceless labial or palatal[1] immediately precedes the aspirate **θ** of the ending, it is "roughened" to its corresponding aspirate.

IV. **Syllables.** (*a*) Every Greek word has as many syllables as it has vowels or diphthongs. There are no silent letters other than *iota subscript.*

(*b*) The final syllable is called *ultima;* the syllable preceding the ultima is called *penult;* the syllable preceding the penult is called *antepenult.*

(*c*) In dividing words into syllables, place with the following vowel or diphthong a single consonant or such combinations of consonants as can be pronounced together at the beginning of a word: ἄ-στρον, πῑ́-πτω, δεί-κνῡ-μι. But compound words, the first element of which is a preposition or δυσ-, are divided at the point of union: παρ-ῆν, δύσ-πο-ρος.

V. **Accent.** (*a*) A knowledge of quantity is essential in determining accent. A syllable is long by nature when it has a long vowel or a diphthong. The vowels **η** and **ω** are always long; **ε** and **ο** are always short; the others are sometimes short and sometimes long (§ I, *a*). The diphthongs **αι** and **οι**, when final, except in the optative and in the one word **οἴκοι**, are regarded as short in determining accent.

(*b*) There are three accents — *acute* (´), *grave* (`), and *circumflex* (῀). They do not affect the pronunciation, but they obey very strict laws and are at times the sole means of distinguishing between words otherwise identical in appearance: θερ-μός *hot,* θέρ-μος *bean,* εἶμι *I go,* εἰμί *I am.*

(*c*) The acute may stand only on one of the last three syllables of a word, the circumflex only on one of the last two, and the grave only on the last.

[1] A dental before another dental always becomes **σ**.

(*d*) The circumflex may stand only on a long vowel or a diphthong. Therefore, if a vowel has the circumflex accent, no other mark is needed to show that the vowel is long: Κῦρος *Cyrus*, but Κύρου *of Cyrus*.

(*e*) An accented antepenult takes the acute; but it must not have an accent if the last syllable is long by nature or ends in **ξ** or **ψ**: ἄνθρωπος *man*, ἀνθρώπου *of a man*.

(*f*) An accented penult takes the circumflex if it is long by nature and the last syllable is short; otherwise, the acute: δῶρον *gift*, but δώρου *of a gift*, λόγος *word*.

(*g*) An accented ultima, if short, takes the acute; if long, the acute or the circumflex: ποταμός *river*, ποταμῶν *of rivers*, ποταμούς *rivers*.

(*h*) An ultima that normally has an acute changes the acute to the grave when another word immediately follows without intervening punctuation: ποταμός *river*, but ποταμὸς καλός, *beautiful river*.

(*i*) A **proclitic** is a monosyllable that has no accent and is pronounced with the word that follows: ὁ ἄνθρωπος *the man*.

(*j*) An **enclitic** is a word that is pronounced with the preceding word and usually lacks an accent of its own: ἄνθρωποί τε (Latin *hominesque*). Enclitics are treated more fully in § 95.

VI. **Inflection:** Greek is a highly inflected language. It has three *genders* (masculine, feminine, and neuter), three *numbers* (singular, dual[1], and plural), and three *declensions* (called from their stems the **α**-declension, the **ο**-declension, and the consonant declension).

The Greek verb has three *voices* (active, middle, and passive), four *moods* (indicative, subjunctive, optative,

[1] Common only in poetry.

and imperative) and seven *tenses* (present, imperfect, future, aorist, perfect, pluperfect, and future perfect[1]). The present, future, perfect, and future perfect are called the *primary* tenses; the imperfect, aorist, and pluperfect are called the *secondary* tenses. The tenses are also divided into classes or *systems* according to their stems. Each system is composed of the tenses which have a common stem.

THE PLUNGE POOL AT DELPHI

This bath is a part of the equipment of the ancient gymnasium. (For a picture of the gymnasium. see page 295.)

EXERCISES

(*a*) Pronounce the Greek words of §§ I-II, stressing each syllable that bears an accent; then write in English letters.

---

[1] Rare.

(*b*) Write in Greek letters: nemesis,[1] asbestos,[1] chaos,[2] rhododendron,[1] hydrophobia,[2] diplōma,[1,3] zōnē,[2] Dēmosthenēs,[2] Ōrīōn,[2] Xerxēs,[2] Iōniā.[2]

(*c*) Accent the penult: Σωκρατης, Μουσα, δεκα, γραφοι (optative mood), κωνος, Μουσαι, κωνοι (noun). Accent the antepenult, if the quantity of the ultima permits: διαγνωσις, ὁριζων, ἀνθρωποι (noun), θεραπευοι (optative mood), φαινομενον.

(*d*) Mark the length of the ultima: γένεσις, ἀνθρώπων, νεκρόπολις, γυμνάσια, Κῦρος, ὧραι.

---

[1] Acute on antepenult. [2] Acute on penult.

[3] A long mark, *macron*, over ō or ē indicates that the Greek has ω or η; otherwise, *o* and *e* are ο and ε.

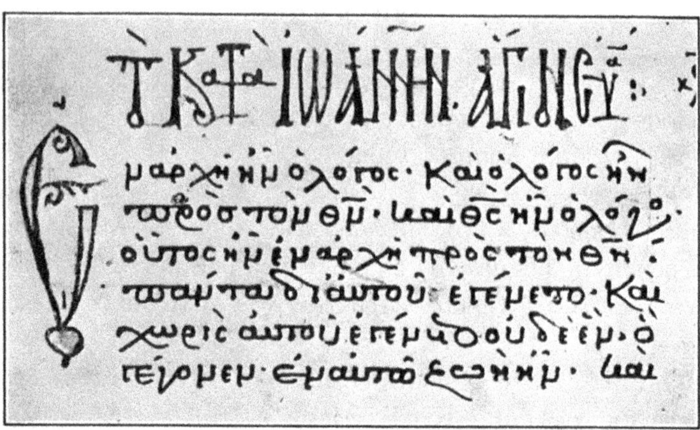

ΤΟ ΚΑΤΑ ΙΩΑΝΝΗΝ ΑΓΙΟΝ ΕΥΑΓΓΕΛΙΟΝ

᾿Εν ἀρχῇ ἦν ὁ λόγος, καὶ ὁ λόγος ἦν
πρὸς τὸν θεόν, καὶ θεὸς ἦν ὁ λόγος.
οὗτος ἦν ἐν ἀρχῇ πρὸς τὸν θεόν.
πάντα δι' αὐτοῦ ἐγένετο, καὶ
χωρὶς αὐτοῦ ἐγένετο οὐδὲ ἓν ὃ
γέγονεν. ἐν αὐτῷ ζωὴ ἦν, καὶ . . .

THE HOLY GOSPEL ACCORDING TO JOHN

In the beginning was the Word, and the Word was
with God, and the Word was God.
The same was in the beginning with God.
All things were made by him; and
without him was not anything made that was
made. In him was life; and . . .

The picture at the top of the page shows the opening lines of the gospel according to St. John, from a manuscript written 800 years ago. There are some variations from the letter forms you will study, for handwriting changes very rapidly. The same lines are given in modern Greek type directly below. These are followed by the King James Translation.

EAGER TO GO

LESSON I

DECLENSION OF O-STEMS

ἐν ἀρχῇ ἦν ὁ λόγος. — *In the beginning was the word.*[1]

---

1. Declensions. There are three declensions in Greek, instead of five as in Latin. To these, because of their general uniformity, the o-stems serve as a good introduction.

2. O-Stem Masculines. Nouns of the **o**-declension whose nominatives end in **-ος** are usually masculine.

ὁ ποταμός *the river*

	SINGULAR		PLURAL	
N.[2]	ὁ ποταμ ός	-us [3]	οἱ ποταμ οί	-ī [3]
G.	τ οῦ ποταμ οῦ	-ī	τ ῶν ποταμ ῶν	-ōrum
D.	τ ῷ ποταμ ῷ	-ō	τ οῖς ποταμ οῖς	-īs
A.	τ ὸν ποταμ όν	-um	τ οὺς ποταμ ούς	-ōs

In like manner inflect ὁ ἀδελφός.

3. Accents. (*a*) In nouns of the **o**-declension an acute (´) on the ultima in the nominative is changed to a circumflex (῀) in the genitive and dative of both numbers.

---

[1] St. John, I. 1.

[2] The letters *N G D A* prefixed to the various forms indicate respectively nominative, genitive, dative, accusative. Inasmuch as this will be the invariable order of presentation, it is thought unnecessary to print these letters in succeeding lessons. The vocative is not included in the forms to be memorized; nor is the dual.

[3] Endings of masculines of the *o*-declension in Latin.

(*b*) An acute on the ultima changes to a grave (\`) when a word follows without intervening punctuation:

ἀδελφὸν ἔχει *he has a brother.*

4. Cases. The endings of a noun tell its case and use.

(*a*) The **nominative** is the case of the *subject:*

οἱ στρατηγοὶ ἦσαν ἀδελφοί *the generals were brothers.*

(*b*) The **genitive** suggests relations like those expressed with *of* in English. It frequently denotes *possession:*

ὁ τοῦ στρατηγοῦ ἀδελφός *the brother of the general.*

(*c*) The **dative** suggests relations like those with *to* or *for* in English. It frequently denotes the *indirect object:*

τῷ στρατηγῷ πέμπει τὸν ἀδελφόν *he sends his brother to the general.*

(*d*) The **accusative** is the *direct object* of a transitive verb: ἀδελφὸν πέμπει *he sends a brother.*

5. The Article. (*a*) Like English, and unlike Latin, Greek has a definite article. This agrees with its noun in gender, number, and case. It often serves as a possessive pronoun, as *my*, *your*, *his*, etc. **ὁ** and **οἱ** are *proclitic* (page xxvii).

(*b*) Greek has no indefinite article. Many nouns having no definite article require *a* or *an* in translation:

ἔχει ἀδελφόν *he has a brother.*

6. VOCABULARY

ἀδελφός, -οῦ, ὁ[1]: *brother.*
PHILADELPHIA.[2]
ἔχει: *he, she,* or *it has.*
ἔχουσι: *they have.*
ἦν: *he, she, it,* or *there was.*
ἦσαν: *they* or *there were.*
παύει: *he, she,* or *it stops* (trans.).
παύουσι: *they stop.*
πέμπει: *he, she,* or *it sends.*
πέμπουσι: *they send.*
ποταμός, -οῦ, ὁ: *river.*
HIPPOPOTAMUS.
στρατηγός, -οῦ, ὁ: *general.*
STRATEGY.

[1] The definite article accompanies nouns in vocabularies to show gender.
[2] In the vocabularies derivatives and cognates are printed in small capitals.

7. **EXERCISES**

(*a*) What use of the noun do the heavy type endings suggest?

ἀδελφ **οῦ**	στρατηγ **ούς**	ποταμ **οῖς**	ποταμ **όν**
ἀδελφ **οί**	ἀδελφ **ός**	στρατηγ **ῶν**	στρατηγ **ῷ**

(*b*) Read aloud in Greek and translate into English:

1. *ἦν στρατηγός.* 2. *ἔχει ἀδελφούς.* 3. *παύουσι τὸν στρατηγόν.* 4. *οἱ στρατηγοὶ ἦσαν ἀδελφοί.* 5. *ἦν ποταμός.* 6. *τῷ στρατηγῷ πέμπει τοὺς ἀδελφούς.* 7. *παύει τοὺς στρατηγούς.* 8. *πέμπουσι τὸν τοῦ στρατηγοῦ*[1] *ἀδελφόν.*

(*c*) Complete these sentences, adding endings and accents:

1. *ὁ στρατηγ— ἔχει ἀδελφ—* (singular). 2. *ἦσαν ποταμ—.* 3. *τοῖς στρατηγ— πέμπουσι τοὺς ἀδελφ—.*

ὁ ποταμός

This lovely pass, the Vale of Tempe, between Mt. Ossa and Mt. Olympus, might have proven more troublesome to the Persians than Thermopylæ, had they not found an easier entrance into Greece. The Peneus River, which winds through it, is one of the few in Greece that never go dry.

[1] The possessive genitive normally follows the article of the noun it modifies.

LESSON II

DECLENSION OF O-STEMS — *Continued*

πόνος γὰρ, ὡς λέγουσιν, εὐκλείᾱς πατήρ.
Toil, so they say, is the father of fame.[1]

8. Persistent Accent. The accent of the nominative must be learned by observation. It will remain on the same syllable in the other cases if possible. An acute on the penult of a noun of the **o**-declension remains on that syllable throughout. An acute on the antepenult is drawn to the penult when the ultima is long (§ V, *e*). Final **-οι** of the nominative plural is considered short (§ V, *a*).

ὁ φίλος *the friend*

ὁ[2] φίλ **ος**	οἱ φίλ **οι**
τ **οῦ** φίλ **ου**	τ **ῶν** φίλ **ων**
τ **ῷ** φίλ **ῳ**	τ **οῖς** φίλ **οις**
τ **ὸν** φίλ **ον**	τ **οὺς** φίλ **ους**

ὁ δίκαιος[3] ἄνθρωπος *the just man*

ὁ δίκαι **ος** ἄνθρωπ **ος**[2]	οἱ δίκαι **οι** ἄνθρωπ **οι**
τ **οῦ** δικαί **ου** ἀνθρώπ **ου**	τ **ῶν** δικαί **ων** ἀνθρώπ **ων**
τ **ῷ** δικαί **ῳ** ἀνθρώπ **ῳ**	τ **οῖς** δικαί **οις** ἀνθρώπ **οις**
τ **ὸν** δίκαι **ον** ἄνθρωπ **ον**	τ **οὺς** δικαί **ους** ἀνθρώπ **ους**

In like manner inflect ὁ πόλεμος.

[1] Euripides, fragment.

[2] In the previous lesson you found singular and plural labeled. From now on you are given no labels, but you can readily tell which is which.

[3] As in Latin, adjectives agree with their nouns in gender, number, and case.

9. Genitive of Place from Which. The genitive with many prepositions denotes *place from which*:[1]

τὸν ἄνθρωπον πέμπει ἀπὸ τοῦ ποταμοῦ *he sends the man from the river;*
ἐκ τοῦ ποταμοῦ *out of the river.*

THE ARCADIAN GATE

The walls of Messene still testify to the engineering skill and daring of the victor of Leuctra. Note particularly the central doorpost of this great gate. It is nearly nineteen feet long.

10. VOCABULARY

ἄνθρωπος, -ου, ὁ: *man.* Lat. *homo.* ANTHROPOLOGY.

ἄξιος: *worthy, worth.* AXIOM.

ἀπό, prep. with G.: *from, away from.* Lat. *ab.* APOSTLE.

δίκαιος: *just.*

ἐκ (before consonants), ἐξ (before vowels), proclit. prep. with G.: *out of, from.* Lat. *ex.* ECLECTIC.

Ἑλλήσποντος, -ου, ὁ: *Hellespont, the Dardanelles.*

μακρός[2]: *long.* MACRON.

μῑκρός[2]: *small.* MICROSCOPIC.

πόλεμος, -ου, ὁ: *war;* πολέμιος: *hostile;* οἱ πολέμιοι: *enemy.* POLEMIC.

φίλος, -ου, ὁ: *friend.* PHILANTHROPIST.

---

[1] This is our second use of the genitive (§ 4). The use here given is like the Latin ablative in its *from* relations.

[2] Adjectives in **-ρος** usually have the acute on the last syllable.

11. **TRANSLATION HINTS**

1. Learn all words given in vocabularies.
2. Learn all forms as they are presented.
3. Note the significance of the various forms.
4. Read the Greek aloud, noting word groups.
5. Translate.

12. **EXERCISES**

PERICLES

The most brilliant period in Athenian history is justly called the Age of Pericles. His home was the haunt of sculptor and architect, poet and philosopher. To him we owe above all the planning and construction of the matchless Parthenon.

(*a*) Translate:

1. *τοὺς πολεμίους παύουσιν.*[1] 2. *τὸν ἄνθρωπον πέμπει ἀπὸ τοῦ Ἑλλησπόντου.* 3. *οἱ ἀδελφοὶ ἦσαν μῖκροί.* 4. *τοὺς φίλους πέμπουσιν*[1] *ἐκ τοῦ ποταμοῦ.* 5. *ὁ πόλεμος ἦν δίκαιος.* 6. *οἱ πολέμιοι ἀξίους στρατηγοὺς ἔχουσιν.*[1] 7. *ὁ στρατηγὸς τοὺς ἀνθρώπους πέμπει τῷ ἀδελφῷ.* 8. *οἱ ἄνθρωποι ἔχουσιν ἀξίους ἀδελφούς.*

(*b*) Complete:

1. *οἱ πολεμ— ἦσαν μακρ—.* 2. *τὸν ἀδελφ— πέμπει ἐκ τ— ποταμ—* (singular). 3. *οἱ στρατηγοὶ τοὺς φίλους πεμπ— τῷ ἀνθρωπ—.*

---

[1] **-ν** is usually added to words ending in **-σι** before a word beginning with a vowel or at the end of a sentence. This is called **ν-movable**.

LESSON III

PRESENT INDICATIVE AND INFINITIVE ACTIVE OF Ω-VERBS

οἱ γὰρ πόνοι τίκτουσι τὴν εὐανδρίᾱν. — *Labor begets manhood.*[1]

13. The Present Tense. This tense denotes action *occurring* or *continuing* or *repeated* in present time:

παύω *I stop, I am stopping, I keep stopping, I do stop.*

Present Indicative Active of **παύω** *I stop*

SINGULAR	PLURAL
παύ-ω	παύ-ο-μεν
παύ-εις	παύ-ε-τε
παύ-ει	παύ-ουσι (ν)

Present Infinitive Active παύ-ειν

In like manner inflect ἐθέλω.

14. Verb Structure. (*a*) In the inflection of a verb the *stem* is of fundamental importance. On it are built the various forms. **παυ-** is the stem of **παύω.**

(*b*) *Tense* is denoted by appropriate suffixes or prefixes. The tense suffix of the present is called the *variable vowel*, written ᵒ/ₑ, ο being used before μ or ν, ε elsewhere.

(*c*) *A personal ending* is attached to complete the verb. In the present indicative active the personal ending is clearly seen only in the first and second persons plural.

15. Verb Accent. In § 8 we saw that the accent of nouns was persistent. That of verbs is *recessive*, that is,

[1] Euripides, fragment. Literally: *For toils beget manhood.*

it goes back toward the beginning of the word as far as the quantity of the ultima will permit. This means that the accent stands on the antepenult if the ultima is short; on the penult if the ultima is long:

ἐθέλω, ἐθέλομεν.

16. Dative with Adjectives. The dative is used with many adjectives expressing *friendliness*, *hostility*, *association*, *fitness*, and the like:[1]

πολέμιος ἦν τῷ στρατηγῷ *he was hostile to the general.*

17. VOCABULARY

ἀγαθός: *good, brave.* AGATHA.
ἄγγελος, -ου, ὁ: *messenger.* ANGEL.
ἄγω: *lead.* Lat. *ago.*
γράφω: *write.* TELEGRAPH.
ἐθέλω: *wish, be willing.*
ἵππος, -ου, ὁ: *horse.* HIPPOPOTAMUS.
καί, conj.: *and, also, even.*
καλός: *beautiful, honorable, fine.*
κίνδῡνος, -ου, ὁ: *danger.*
λίθος, -ου, ὁ: *stone.* LITHOGRAPH.
λύω: *loose, break, destroy.* ANALYSIS.

18. EXERCISES

(*a*) What do the portions in heavy type tell as to the person and number of the subject?

ἄγ **ουσι** λύο **μεν** ἔχε **τε** ἐθέλ **ω** γράφ **εις**

(*b*) Translate:

1. ἔχομεν τοὺς καλοὺς λίθους. 2. ἐθέλω τῷ ἀγαθῷ ἀνθρώπῳ γράφειν.[2] 3. καὶ ὁ στρατηγὸς τὸν ἄγγελον ἄγει ἀπὸ τοῦ Ἑλλησπόντου. 4. οἱ ἀδελφοὶ ἐθέλουσι τοὺς ἵππους παύειν. 5. ὁ ἄγγελος ἔχει ἀγαθὸν ἵππον. 6. τοὺς φίλους ἐθέλομεν ἄγειν ἐκ τοῦ κινδύνου. 7. οἱ

[1] This is our second use of the dative (§ 4). Corresponding English adjectives are used with *to* or *for* and for the same reasons.

[2] Complementary infinitive, the object of ἐθέλω.

πολέμιοι λύουσι τοὺς τῶν στρατηγῶν ἵππους. 8. ὁ στρατηγὸς πολέμιος ἦν τοῖς ἀγγέλοις.

(c) Complete:

1. οἱ ἀδελφοὶ ἐθέλουσι γραφ—. 2. ἐθέλομεν τοὺς ἵππους ἀγ— ἐκ τοῦ ποταμ—. 3. οἱ ἄγγελοι πολέμιοι ἦσαν τ— στρατηγ— (singular).

AN IMMORTAL HORSE
This is one of the precious bits of sculpture from the eastern pediment of the Parthenon.

19. (a) **TRANSLATION HINTS**

1. Read the entire English sentence, noting how the words are related.

2. Call to mind Greek words with meanings like those in English.

3. Consider the changes in form needed to express the relations suggested by the English.

4. Form the Greek sentence mentally and say it aloud before starting to write.

5. Write the sentence, with accents and breathings.

(b) Write in Greek:

1. The brothers were small. 2. They are sending the man to the general. 3. The general is sending the enemy away from the river. 4. He sends the man out of the river. 5. They were brothers of the general.

20. Βρεκεκεκὲξ κοὰξ κοάξ. This is the famous refrain of the frog chorus in Aristophanes' comedy, *The Frogs.* In unison with this unceasing chant Dionysus rows Charon's boat across the Styx. It is the basis of Yale's well-known yell.

LESSON IV

DECLENSION OF O-STEM NEUTERS

πᾶν δένδρον ἀγαθὸν καρποὺς καλοὺς ποιεῖ.
Every good tree bringeth forth good fruit.[1]

21. O-Stem Neuters. These nouns have a nominative ending in **-ον**. They differ from masculines only in the nominative singular and the nominative and accusative plural.

As in Latin, nominative and accusative of neuters are identical in form. In the plural they end in **α** (Latin *a*).

τὸ ἄξιον δῶρον[2] *the worthy gift*

τ ὸ	ἄξι ον	δῶρ ον	-um[3]	τ ὰ	ἄξι α	δῶρ α	-a[3]
τ οῦ	ἀξί ου	δώρ ου	-ī	τ ῶν	ἀξί ων	δώρ ων	-ōrum
τ ῷ	ἀξί ῳ	δώρ ῳ	-ō	τ οῖς	ἀξί οις	δώρ οις	-īs
τ ὸ	ἄξι ον	δῶρ ον	-um	τ ὰ	ἄξι α	δῶρ α	-a

In like manner inflect τὸ καλὸν πεδίον.[2]

22. Agreement of Verb. A neuter plural subject regularly has its verb in the singular:

τὰ δῶρα ἦν ἄξια *the gifts were worthy.*

23. Dative of Place Where. The dative with most prepositions denotes *place where:*[4]

ἐν τῷ πεδίῳ *in the plain* (Latin : in oppido *in the town*);
παρὰ τῷ στρατηγῷ *at the side of the general.*

[1] St. Matthew, VII. 17.
[2] For accent of δῶρον and πεδίον see § V, *d* and *f*.
[3] Endings of neuters of the *o*-declension in Latin.
[4] This is our third use of the dative (§§ 4, 16). The use here given is like that of the Latin ablative in its *in* relations.

24. Accusative of Place to Which. The accusative with many prepositions denotes *place to which:*[1]

εἰς τὸ πεδίον *into the plain* (Latin: in oppidum *into the town*); παρὰ τὸν στρατηγόν *to the side of the general.*

25. VOCABULARY

δέ (δ' before vowels), postpos.[2] conj: *but, and.*

δένδρον, -ου, τό: *tree.* RHODODENDRON.

δῆλος: *plain, evident.*

δῶρον, -ου, τό: *gift.* THEODORE.

εἰς, proclit. prep. with A.: *into* (Lat. *in*).

ἐν, proclit. prep. with D.: *in* (Lat. *in*). ENCLITIC.

παρά, prep.: with G., *from the side of;* with D., *by the side of;* with A., *to the side of, to, alongside.* PARALLEL.

πεδίον, -ου, τό: *plain.*

στάδιον, -ου, τό: *stadium* (race course); *stade* (600 ft.).[3]

26. EXERCISES

(*a*) What probable use of the word is denoted by the heavy type endings?

πεδί **ου**	ἄξι **ον**
δῆλ **α**	δένδρ **ων**
δώρ **οις**	σταδί **ῳ**

(*b*) Translate:

1. ἐν τῷ πεδίῳ δῆλα ἦν τὰ δένδρα. 2. στάδιον ἦν παρὰ τῷ ποταμῷ. 3. καὶ εἰς τὸ στάδιον ἄγουσι δῶρα καλά. 4. οἱ δ' ἀδελφοὶ ἐθέλου-

"THE SCRATCH"

The Delphic stadium (page 12) still retains the row of flat stones whose double grooves, called by the Greeks ἡ γραμμή "the scratch," determined the position of the runners' feet.

[1] This is our second use of accusative (§ 4). It is the same in Latin.

[2] A postpositive word never stands first in its clause. It usually comes second.

[3] Used mostly in the plural, where it is inflected like ἄνθρωπος.

σιν ἵππους πέμπειν παρὰ τοὺς[1] φίλους. 5. παρὰ τοῦ στρατηγοῦ ἦν τὰ δῶρα. 6. ἐκ τοῦ πεδίου ἄγομεν τοὺς πολεμίους. 7. ὁ δ' ἄνθρωπος ἄξιος ἦν δώρων[2] καλῶν.

(*c*) Complete :

1. τὰ δὲ δένδρα —— (linking verb) μῑκρά. 2. ἵππους δ' ἄγετε εἰς τ— ποταμ— (singular). 3. ἐν τ— σταδι— (singular) ἦσαν οἱ ἀδελφ—.

(*d*) Write in Greek :

1. The stones were beautiful. 2. The brave messenger was hostile to the general. 3. The friends have fine horses. 4. He wishes to lead the men out of danger. 5. The brothers were hostile to the messenger.

τὸ ἐν Δελφοῖς στάδιον

This ancient Greek stadium, perhaps the best preserved of all, is located on the slopes of Parnassus, high above a lovely valley. Here every four years were held the famous Pythian Games in honor of Apollo.

---

[1] See § 5, *a*. [2] Genitive of price or value.

LESSON V

REVIEW

ἀρχὴ δέ τοι ἥμισυ παντός. — *Well begun is half done.*[1]

27. Importance of Vocabulary. If you wish to succeed in the study of any language, you must have above all else a good working vocabulary. The words assigned for study in this book have been chosen for their relative frequency and general utility. If you learn them, you should be able to figure out the meaning of many other words, and as a result be able to read with greater ease and pleasure.

ASSIGNMENTS

(*a*) Review all words thus far presented, observing spelling (including accent), inflection, meaning, and possible peculiarities of use. Study especially any words that seem unfamiliar. Test your knowledge by reference to the list in § 549.

(*b*) Name and define the Greek words suggested by: *apology, Francophile, dendrology, Dorothea, eccentric, evangelist, hippodrome, Mesopotamia, microcosm, misanthrope, monolith, paralysis, phonograph.* What other English derivatives can you add that belong to this group?

(*c*) What are the possible meanings suggested by the endings *ον*, *ῳ*, *ου*, *ους*, *οι*, *οις*, *α*?

(*d*) Give the Greek for: he is writing, you (singular) lead, we stop, they have, I am loosing, you (plural) wish, he sends.

---

[1] Greek maxim. Literally: *(The) beginning (is) half of everything.* Note these derivatives: ARCHAIC, HEMISPHERE, PANTOMIME.

28. EXERCISES

(*a*) Complete:

1. ὁ τ— στρατηγ— (singular) κίνδῡνος ἦν μῑκρ—.
2. δωρ— (plural) πέμπομεν παρὰ τ— φιλ— (plural).
3. οἱ δ' ἀδελφ— ἦσαν δικαι—.
4. ἐθέλετε γραφ—.
5. τὰ δενδρ— —— (linking verb) ἐν τ— πεδι— (singular).
6. ὁ ἄγγελος πολέμιος ἦν τ— ἀνθρωπ— (singular).

A Greek Boy's Tablet

Here we see half of a school tablet used by some Greek lad more than 2000 years ago. At the top the master has written two lines of verse, which the pupil has tried to reproduce twice in the space below. See if you can find mistakes in his work.

(*b*) Write in Greek:

1. But the messenger is leading the horses out of the Hellespont. 2. The trees in the plain were small. 3. And you (plural) wish to have beautiful gifts. 4. We are sending the men into the stadium. 5. The fine gifts were from (the side of) friends of the general.

LESSON VI

DECLENSION OF A-STEMS

σκηνὴ πᾶς ὁ βίος. — "*All the world's a stage.*"[1]

29. A-Stem Feminines. A-declension nouns whose nominatives end in **α** or **η** are *feminine*. Because the feminine article shows **η** in the singular, nouns and adjectives in **η** are presented first. Both types are the same in the plural.

ἡ καλὴ σκηνή *the beautiful tent*

ἡ	καλ **ὴ**	σκην **ή**[2]	**-a**[3]	**αἱ**	καλ **αὶ**	σκην **αί**	**-ae**[3]
τ **ῆς**	καλ **ῆς**	σκην **ῆς**	**-ae**	τ **ῶν**	καλ **ῶν**	σκην **ῶν**	**-ārum**
τ **ῇ**	καλ **ῇ**	σκην **ῇ**	**-ae**	τ **αῖς**	καλ **αῖς**	σκην **αῖς**	**-īs**
τ **ὴν**	καλ **ὴν**	σκην **ήν**	**-am**	τ **ὰς**	καλ **ὰς**	σκην **άς**	**-ās**

κώμη *village*

κώμ **η**[4]	κῶμ **αι**
κώμ **ης**	κωμ **ῶν**
κώμ **ῃ**	κώμ **αις**
κώμ **ην**	κώμ **ᾱς**

In like manner inflect ἡ φυγή and ἡ μάχη.[4]

What forms of the **α**-declension have the same ending as the corresponding form of the **ο**-declension? What have similar endings?

30. Adjectives. (*a*) Adjectives of the **ο**- and **α**-declensions have three endings, one for each gender, like the Latin *bonus*, *bona*, *bonum*.

---

[1] Greek Anthology. Literally: *All life is a tent* (See § 35).

[2] For the accent of ἡ, καλή, and σκηνή, see § V, *g*, *h*, and *i*.

[3] Endings of feminines of the *a*-declension in Latin.

[4] For the accent of all forms of κώμη and μάχη except the genitive plural, see § V, *f*. The genitive plural of **α**-stems originally ended in **-α(σ)ων**, Latin *-arum*. Therefore, words of this declension regularly circumflex the ultima of the genitive plural because of contraction of vowels.

(*b*) Such adjectives accent the feminine genitive plural like the genitive plural of the **o**-declension.

Inflect in all three genders ἀγαθός and δῆλος. Compare with paradigms, § 510, *a*.

31. Position of Adjectives. (*a*) When an adjective or an adjective phrase accompanies a noun with a definite article, the adjective usually stands between the article and the noun, as in English:

ὁ δίκαιος ἄνθρωπος *the just man.*

Note that (unlike English) even a prepositional phrase may stand in this position:

οἱ ἐν τῇ κώμῃ ἄνθρωποι or οἱ ἐν τῇ κώμῃ[1] *the men in the village.*

The adjective may also follow the noun and have the article repeated with it:

ὁ ἄνθρωπος ὁ δίκαιος *the just man.*

In the above instances the adjective or phrase is said to have the *attributive position.*

(*b*) When an adjective precedes the article or follows the article and the noun without the article being repeated, it is said to stand in the *predicate position:*

δίκαιος ὁ ἄνθρωπος or ὁ ἄνθρωπος δίκαιος *the man (is) just.*

32. Dative of Possession. In English we say *There is no lid to the box.* The Latin says *Puero est gladius, the boy has a sword.* So in Greek the dative is used to denote the *possessor*, while the thing possessed is subject of the verb *to be:*[2]

ἀγορᾶ οὐκ ἦν τῇ στρατιᾷ *the army had no market.*

[1] With an expression like this ἄνθρωποι is implied.
[2] This is our fourth use of the dative. What were the other three?

33. VOCABULARY

γάρ, postpos. conj.: *for.*
κώμη, -ης, ἡ: *village.*
μάχη, -ης, ἡ: *battle.* LOGOMACHY.
οὐ (before consonants), οὐκ (before smooth breathing), οὐχ (before rough breathing), proclit. adv.: *not.* UTOPIA.
σκηνή, -ῆς, ἡ: *tent.* SCENE.
σπονδή, -ῆς, ἡ: *libation;* pl., *treaty, truce.* SPONDEE.
φεύγω: *flee.* Lat. *fugio.* FUGITIVE.
φυγή, -ῆς, ἡ: *flight, exile.* Lat. *fuga.*
φυλακή, -ῆς, ἡ: *guard, garrison.* PROPHYLACTIC.
φυλάττω: *guard* (verb).

34. EXERCISES

(*a*) What use of the word do portions in heavy type suggest?

σπονδ **ῶν** φυγ **ῇ** μάχ **ην** κώμ **αις** σκην **ᾶς** φυλακ **ῆς** σπονδ **αί** σκην **ή**

(*b*) Translate:

1. οὐ φεύγομεν ἐν ταῖς μάχαις. 2. τῇ γὰρ φυλακῇ ἦν σκηνὴ καλή. 3. οἱ δ' ἐν τῇ κώμῃ φυλάττουσι τοὺς ἵππους. 4. οὐκ ἦσαν σπονδαὶ τοῖς ἐν τῷ πεδίῳ. 5. τῇ δὲ φυλακῇ πέμπεις δῶρα καλά. 6. ἡ τοῦ στρατηγοῦ φυγὴ οὐκ ἦν καλή. 7. ἐκ τῆς κώμης ἄγει τοὺς πολεμίους. 8. αἱ δὲ σκηναὶ δῆλαι ἦσαν.

(*c*) Complete:

1. τ— δὲ κωμ— ἦν φυλακή. 2. οὐκ ἦσαν σκην— τ— φυλακ—

THE DELPHIC THEATER
Every Greek settlement of any consequence had its theater. The one at Delphi is remarkably well preserved. Here in 1927 the *Prometheus Bound* of Æschylus was revived in great splendor.

(singular). 3. —— (article) ἐν τῷ πεδίῳ —— (negative adverb) ἐθέλουσι τὰς σπονδὰς λῡ—.

35. Word-formation. It is interesting to follow the changes in meanings of words. Words are living creatures and as such they constantly acquire new characteristics and new aptitudes as they adjust themselves to new conditions.

THE THEATER OF DIONYSUS

This is probably the earliest extant theater in the world. It is built on the southern slope of the acropolis at Athens. Here the great Greek dramas had their first performance. It seated about 17,000.

Thus σκηνή, *tent* or *booth*, was originally used of the tent or booth into which an actor withdrew to change his costume. When the theater became more elaborate, σκηνή referred to the wall that served as support for painted *scenery*. From this it was but a step to σκηνή meaning the *scene* of an action.

LESSON VII

DECLENSION OF A-STEMS — *Continued*

λύπης ἰᾱτρός ἐστιν ἀνθρώποις λόγος.
In reason men find a physician for their grief.[1]

36. Feminines in ᾱ. If ε, ι, or ρ immediately precedes the final vowel of the stem, words of the α-declension have ᾱ, not η, throughout the singular.[2]

ἡ μῑκρὰ στρατιά *the small army*

ἡ μῑκρ ὰ στρατι ά	αἱ μῑκρ αὶ στρατι αί
τ ῆς μῑκρ ᾶς στρατι ᾶς	τ ῶν μῑκρ ῶν στρατι ῶν
τ ῇ μῑκρ ᾷ στρατι ᾷ	τ αῖς μῑκρ αῖς στρατι αῖς
τ ὴν μῑκρ ὰν στρατι άν	τ ὰς μῑκρ ὰς στρατι άς

In like manner inflect ἡ φιλίᾱ χώρᾱ.

Inflect μῑκρός and ἄξιος in all genders (compare with paradigms, § 510, *a*).

37. Accusative of Extent. The accusative denotes *extent of space* or *duration of time:*[3]

διώξει τοὺς πολεμίους δέκα σταδίους (δέκα ἡμέρᾱς) *he will pursue the enemy ten stades (ten days).*

---

[1] Menander, fragment. Literally: *Reason is for men a physician of grief.*

[2] A few feminines have short α in the nominative and accusative singular. They will be treated later.

[3] This is our third use of the accusative. What were the other two?

38. **VOCABULARY**

ἀγορᾱ́, -ᾶς, ἡ : *market, market-place.* AGORAPHOBIA.

ἀρχή, -ῆς, ἡ : *beginning, rule, province.*

δέκα : *ten.* DECALOGUE.

διά, prep.: with G., *through ;* with A., *on account of.* DIAMETER.

ἐπιτήδειος, -ᾱ, -ον : *fit, suitable ;* τὰ ἐπιτήδεια[1] : *provisions.*

ἡμέρᾱ, -ᾱς, ἡ : *day.* EPHEMERAL.

στρατιᾱ́, -ᾶς, ἡ : *army.* Cf. **στρατηγός.**

φιλίᾱ, -ᾱς, ἡ : *friendship.* Cf. **φίλος.**

φίλιος, -ᾱ, -ον : *friendly.*

χώρᾱ, -ᾱς, ἡ : *country.*

39. **EXERCISES**

(*a*) Translate :

1. ἦν ἡ ἀγορὰ ἐπιτηδείᾱ τῇ στρατιᾷ ;[2] 2. αἱ φυλακαὶ φεύγουσι διὰ τοῦ πεδίου. 3. ἐθέλετε γὰρ τὴν στρατιὰν ἄγειν δέκα σταδίους. 4. τῇ δὲ κώμῃ οὐκ ἦν τὰ ἐπιτήδεια. 5. καὶ τὴν στρατιὰν ἄγομεν διὰ τῆς ἀγορᾶς. 6. διὰ τὴν φιλίᾱν ἔχουσιν ἀγορὰν καὶ τὰ ἐπιτήδεια. 7. ἡ δὲ στρατιὰ φιλίᾱ ἦν τῇ ἀρχῇ. 8. τὸν δ' ἀδελφὸν πέμπει εἰς τὴν χώρᾱν.

GATE OF ATHENA ARCHEGETIS

(*b*) Complete :

1. ἡ δὲ κώμη ἐπιτηδει— ἦν τ— στρατηγ— (singular). 2. δέκα ἡμερ— ἡ στρατιὰ ἦν

[1] Many Greek adjectives when preceded by the article are used as nouns. Compare English, *the blind*, a word to *the wise ;* and the Greek, οἱ πολέμιοι.

[2] As in English, Greek questions are sometimes introduced by an interrogative pronoun or adverb, but often the mark of interrogation at the end of a printed sentence is the only clue. This mark of interrogation in Greek is the same as the English semicolon (;).

ἐν τ— ἀγορ— (singular). 3. πέμπει δὲ τ— ἐπιτηδει— τ— φιλ— (plural).

(*c*) Write in Greek:

1. The messenger had (use ἦν) a horse. 2. The truce was long. 3. The men in the village are not guarding the tents. 4. The flight was not evident to the general. 5. The garrison did not have (use ἦν) tents.

THE ACROPOLIS

Although many Greek cities had a fortified hill, or acropolis, most people associate that word with the famous hill in the heart of Athens. At first the home of the early kings, it came to be devoted to the gods and heroes of the state. Its glorious temples were visible from the agora, as indeed for miles around in all directions.

40. Word-formation. (*a*) A very common means of forming adjectives is by adding to the stem of a noun the suffix **-ιος, -ιᾱ, -ιον,** which appears frequently in English as *-ian.* O-stems drop the **ο** before this suffix, **α**-stems retain the **α** to form the diphthong **αι**:

φίλος *friend,* φίλιος *friendly;*

but Ἀθῆναι *Athens,* Ἀθηναῖος *Athenian.*

(*b*) From δίκαιος and πολέμιος construct the corresponding nouns; from ἵππος and ἀγορά construct the corresponding adjectives.

LESSON VIII

IMPERFECT INDICATIVE ACTIVE OF Ω-VERBS

ἔργον δ' οὐδὲν ὄνειδος, ἀεργίη δέ τ' ὄνειδος.
Work is no disgrace, but idleness is.[1]

41. The Imperfect Tense. This tense denotes action *continued, repeated, customary,* or *attempted* in *past* time:

ἔπαυον *I was stopping, I kept stopping, I used to stop, I tried to stop.*

IMPERFECT INDICATIVE ACTIVE

παύω *I stop*	ἄγω *I lead*
ἔ-παυ-ο-ν	ἦγ-ο-ν
ἔ-παυ-ε-ς	ἦγ-ε-ς
ἔ-παυ-ε (ν)[2]	ἦγ-ε (ν)[2]
ἐ-παύ-ο-μεν	ἤγ-ο-μεν
ἐ-παύ-ε-τε	ἤγ-ε-τε
ἔ-παυ-ο-ν	ἦγ-ο-ν

42. Formation. **The imperfect tense** is built on the present stem showing the variable vowel (ο or ε). Being a secondary[3] tense, it differs from the present in having (1) augment, (2) secondary endings. It is found only in the indicative.

43. Augment. All secondary tenses of the indicative may be recognized by what is called *augment.* This is of two kinds:

1. *Syllabic.* Verbs with an initial consonant prefix ἐ by way of augment.

[1] Hesiod, *Works and Days*, 311.

[2] The ν in this form is not a personal ending. It is another use of ν-movable, page 6, note 1. [3] See page xxviii.

2. *Temporal.* Verbs with an initial vowel or diphthong lengthen the initial vowel. In so doing,

α	becomes	η	αι	becomes	ῃ
ε	"	η[1]	ᾳ	"	ῃ
ο	"	ω	αυ	"	ηυ
ι	"	ῑ	ευ	"	ηυ
υ	"	ῡ	οι	"	ῳ

Inflect the imperfect indicative active of πέμπω and ἀθροίζω.

44. Dative of Manner. The dative may denote *manner*:[2]

φεύγουσι σῑγῇ *they flee in silence.*

45. Balanced Structure. **μέν . . . δέ** are used with two words or phrases or clauses that are compared or contrasted: ὁ (ἡ, τὸ) **μέν** . . . ὁ (ἡ, τὸ) **δέ** *the one . . . the other;* οἱ (αἱ, τὰ) **μέν** . . . οἱ (αἱ, τὰ) **δέ** *some . . . others;* ὁ δέ, ἡ δέ, κ.τ.λ.[3] *but (and) he, she,* etc., indicating change of subject. **μέν** is rarely to be translated but is a valuable warning that a comparison or contrast is coming. It is one of the many little words, often untranslatable, that make Greek so effective for expressing important shades of meaning.

AN IONIC COLUMN

The delicate workmanship of the Erechtheum, to which this column belongs, awakens universal admiration.

---

[1] Certain verbs beginning with ε change ε to ει when augmented: ἔχω, εἶχον.

[2] This is our fifth use of the dative. What were the other four?

[3] κ.τ.λ. = καὶ τὰ λοιπά *and the rest.* Compare etc. = *et cetera.*

46. VOCABULARY

ἀθροίζω: *collect.*
ἀλλά, conj.: *but, however.* Stronger than δέ. Final **α** is often elided.
ἁρπάζω: *seize.* HARPY.
ἀρχαῖος, -ᾱ, -ον: *original, ancient.* Cf. **ἀρχή**. ARCHAIC.
βάρβαρος, -ου, ὁ: *foreigner, barbarian.*
ἔργον, -ου, τό: *work, deed.* ENERGY.
κραυγή, -ῆς, ἡ: *outcry, shout.*
λόγος, -ου, ὁ: *word, speech.* PROLOGUE.
σῑγή, -ῆς, ἡ: *silence.*

47. EXERCISES

(*a*) What do the portions in heavy type tell as to person and number of the subject?

ἦγο **ν** ἔλῡ **ε** ἐγράφο **μεν** ἤθροιζε **ς** ἠθέλε **τε**

Which personal endings of the imperfect are identical? Which resemble endings of the present?

(*b*) Translate:

1. ἤθροιζες λίθους παρὰ τὸν ποταμόν; 2. ἀλλ' ἐπέμπομεν τὴν φυλακὴν παρὰ τὸν ἀδελφόν. 3. ἡ στρατιὰ ἦν ἐν τῇ κώμῃ καὶ τὰ ἐπιτήδεια ἥρπαζεν. 4. οἱ μὲν γὰρ κραυγῇ ἐκ τῆς ἀγορᾶς ἔφευγον, οἱ δὲ σῑγῇ τὰς σκηνὰς ἐφύλαττον. 5. οἱ δὲ ἀρχαῖοι εἶχον[1] κώμᾱς μῑκράς. 6. καλὰ μὲν ἦν τὰ δῶρα, μῑκρὰ δέ. 7. τὰ μὲν ἔργα τὰ τοῦ βαρβάρου ἦν καλά, οἱ δὲ λόγοι φίλιοι.

(*c*) Complete:

1. ἠγ— (2d plural) τὸν ἱππ— ἐκ τ— πεδι— (singular). 2. καὶ τὸ ἐργ— δηλ— ἦν τ— πολεμι—. 3. ὁ δὲ κραυγ— ἐφευγ— εἰς τ— κωμ— (singular).

(*d*) Write in Greek:

1. The army was friendly to the country. 2. They guard the provisions for ten days. 3. On account of the treaty we do not wish to destroy the village. 4. The garrison flees ten stades.[2] 5. There were provisions in the tent.

[1] Page 23, note 1. [2] Page 11, note 3.

48. Greek as a World Language. (*a*) The international language of the first century of our era was Greek. To carry its message to the world, therefore, the New Testament was written in Greek. The following passage is from St. Luke, VI. 45:

ὁ μὲν ἀγαθὸς ἄνθρωπος ἐκ τοῦ ἀγαθοῦ θησαυροῦ (*treasure*) τῆς καρδίᾱς (compare CARDIAC) προ-φέρει (*brings forth*) τὸ ἀγαθόν,[1] ὁ δὲ πονηρὸς[1] (*evil*) ἐκ τοῦ πονηροῦ[1] τὸ πονηρόν.[1]

θησαυρὸς τῶν Ἀθηναίων

There was more wealth at Delphi than anywhere else in Greece. Many states maintained "treasuries" to house their offerings to Apollo and to display their own power.

(*b*) *Word-formation.* The Christian religion not only was transmitted through Greek. Its theology was shaped by Greek philosophy and its language and thought by Greek words.

Hundreds of ecclesiastical terms now in use came from Greek: *Christ*, *Bible*, *Episcopalian*, *anthem*, *hierarchy*, *cathedral*, *liturgy*, *Pentateuch*, *atheist*, *apostate*, *martyr*, *neophyte*, *hypocrite*, *laity*, *canon*, and the like.

How many similar derivatives can you supply from the Greek words that you have already had? Try these:

λόγος (combine with φίλος, and δέκα), ἀπό, ἐξ (combine with ὁδός *road*), παρά, ἄγγελος, διά.

---

[1] Page 20, note 1.

LESSON IX

FUTURE INDICATIVE AND INFINITIVE ACTIVE OF Ω-VERBS

καλὸν ἡσυχίᾱ. — *Leisure is a fine thing.*[1]

49. The Future Tense. This tense has the same personal endings as the present. It differs from the present only as to stem, which it forms by adding **σ** to the verb stem. In the case of verbs whose stem ends in a mute, the **σ** is the occasion of certain changes:

1. A labial (π, β, φ) unites with σ to form ψ (πς);
2. A palatal (κ, γ, χ) unites with σ to form ξ (κς);
3. A dental (τ, δ, θ) before σ is dropped:

πέμπω, πέμψω; ἄγω, ἄξω; ἀθροίζω(ἀθροιδ-), ἀθροίσω.

In most instances, the stem is readily recognized in the present tense, but verbs with stems in **ττ** are palatals and most verbs with stems in **ζ** are dentals. In case of doubt, consult the general vocabulary at the back of the book.

FUTURE INDICATIVE OF **παύω** *I stop*

παύ-σ-ω	παύ-σ-ο-μεν
παύ-σ-εις	παύ-σ-ε-τε
παύ-σ-ει	παύ-σ-ουσι(ν)

FUTURE INFINITIVE παύ-σ-ειν

In like manner inflect λῡ́ω, γράφω, ἄρχω, πείθω.

50. Indirect Discourse. (*a*) Verbs whose meaning implies mental action (*saying*, *thinking*, or the like) are used to introduce an indirect quotation: *the general sends* (*sent*)

[1] Periander.

may be stated indirectly *I believe the general to be sending (to have sent)*, or *I believe that the general is sending (sent)*.

(*b*) In Latin the main verb in the quoted statement is always infinitive. The same construction is frequently found in Greek.[1]

(*c*) In Latin, the subject of the infinitive in indirect discourse is always accusative. The same is true for Greek, unless the infinitive has the same subject as the introductory verb, in which case the subject of the infinitive is omitted and any word in agreement with that unexpressed subject is nominative:

νομίζω τὸν στρατηγὸν διώξειν *I think the general will pursue;*
νομίζω διώξειν *I think I shall pursue.*

THE PROPYLÆA
The gateway to the Acropolis.

(*d*) The tense of the infinitive in the quoted statement, regardless of the tense of the introductory verb, is the same as that used in the original statement:

οἱ πολέμιοι διώκουσι *the enemy are pursuing;*
νομίζει τούς πολεμίους διώκειν *he thinks the enemy are pursuing;*
ἐνόμιζε τοὺς πολεμίους διώκειν *he thought that the enemy were pursuing.*

[1] But in Greek other constructions appear, depending on the introductory verb employed.

51. **VOCABULARY**

ἄρχω, ἄρξω[1]: *begin, rule, command*, with G. ARCHBISHOP.

διώκω, διώξω: *pursue.*

θύρᾱ, -ᾱς, ἡ: *door;* αἱ θύραι: often used of *military headquarters* or of *the king's court* (compare Sublime Porte). THYROID.

ἰσχῡρός, -ά, -όν[2]: *strong.*

μέλλω, μελλήσω: *intend, delay*, usually with fut. inf.

νομίζω[3]: *believe, think*, with inf.

ὁδός, -οῦ, ἡ[4]: *road, route.* EXODUS.

πείθω, πείσω: *persuade.*

ὑπ-οπτεύω, ὑπ-οπτεύσω: *suspect* (ὑπό, *under* + ὀπτεύω, *look*), with inf. HYPODERMIC. OPTIC.

52. **EXERCISES**

(*a*) Identify the person and number of the following forms and give the corresponding forms of the present:

πέμψουσι, ἄξομεν, γράψει, φυλάξεις, ἀθροίσω, ἄρξετε, λῡ́σειν.

(*b*) Translate:

1. *οἱ βάρβαροι ὑπ-οπτεύσουσι τὰ ἔργα.* 2. *ἐνομίζομεν τοὺς βαρβάρους οὐχ ὑπ-οπτεύειν τὰ δῶρα.* 3. *μέλλει τῆς χώρᾱς ἄρξειν.* 4. *τὴν δὲ στρατιὰν πείσεις τὴν μακρὰν*[4] *ὁδὸν φυλάττειν.* 5. *οἱ δὲ πολέμιοι τὴν ἰσχῡρὰν φυλακὴν λῡ́σουσιν.* 6. *διώξομεν τὸν ἄγγελον παρὰ τὰς τοῦ στρατηγοῦ θύρᾱς.* 7. *ἀλλ' οἱ μὲν τοὺς πολεμίους παύσουσιν, οἱ δὲ τὰ ἐπιτήδεια ἀθροίσουσιν.* 8. *ὁ δὲ νομίζει καλὴν ὁδὸν ἄγειν διὰ τῆς ἀρχῆς.*

(*c*) Complete:

1. *ὑπ-οπτευσ—* *οἱ πολέμιοι τὸν στρατηγ—* *λῡ—* *τὰς σπονδάς.* 2. *μέλλεις λῡ—* *τὴν ὁδ—;* 3. *οἱ μὲν* —— (will pursue) *τοὺς πολεμίους, οἱ δὲ* —— (will seize) *τὰ ἐπιτήδεια.*

---

[1] From this point the future will regularly be listed in the vocabulary, because it constitutes one of the principal parts.

[2] For accent, see page 5, note 2.

[3] The future, which presents certain irregularities, will be given later.

[4] A few words of the o-declension are feminine. Of these, ὁδός is by far the most common.

(*d*) Write in Greek:

1. But the barbarians were collecting the horses in silence. 2. With a shout we were seizing the provisions. 3. The man

ὁδὸς ἀρχαίᾱ

This fine roadway, bordered with elevated sidewalks, led from the agora at Corinth to the harbor. The ancient Greeks did most of their travel by sea and so had few good roads.

used to write to his[1] brother. 4. The works were ancient, but beautiful. 5. They were brave in speech.

53. Word-formation. Many verbs with **ε** in the stem have cognate nouns or adjectives with **ο** instead of **ε**:

λείπω *leave*, λοιπός *left;*
λέγω *speak*, λόγος *word* or *speech;*
πέμπω *send* (*escort*), πομπή *procession;*
σπένδω *pour a libation*, σπονδή *libation.*

Compare Latin tego *I cover*, toga *cloak;* English *I sing*, *song.*

[1] See § 5, *a*.

LESSON X

FIRST AND SECOND AORIST INDICATIVE AND INFINITIVE ACTIVE OF Ω-VERBS

ὅ τι καλὸν φίλον ἀεί. — *A thing of beauty is a joy forever.*[1]

54. The Aorist. Aorist is the name of a tense of the Greek verb. The name is not used in the inflection of Latin or English verbs, but many of its functions are entirely familiar.

The aorist indicative in Greek expresses *a single act* (that is, not continued or repeated) in *past* time. It gives, as it were, a snapshot of past action, while the imperfect gives a motion picture:

ἔπαυον *I was stopping;* ἔπαυσα *I stopped.*

FIRST AORIST INDICATIVE OF **παύω** *I stop*

ἔ-παυ-σα	ἐ-παύ-σα-μεν
ἔ-παυ-σα-ς	ἐ-παύ-σα-τε
ἔ-παυ-σε(ν) [2]	ἔ-παυ-σα-ν

FIRST AORIST INFINITIVE παῦ-σαι

SECOND AORIST INDICATIVE OF **λείπω** *I leave*

ἔ-λιπ-ο-ν	ἐ-λίπ-ο-μεν
ἔ-λιπ-ε-ς	ἐ-λίπ-ε-τε
ἔ-λιπ-ε(ν) [2]	ἔ-λιπ-ο-ν

SECOND AORIST INFINITIVE λιπ-εῖν

55. Formation of the Aorist. (*a*) The aorist, in common with other secondary tenses, in the indicative has augment and secondary endings (§§ 42, 43).

[1] Euripides, *Bacchæ*, 881. Literally: *Whatever is beautiful is ever dear.*
[2] **ν-movable** (page 22, note 2).

(*b*) The distinguishing feature of the first aorist is the suffix **σα** (**σε** in the third singular), which obeys the same phonetic laws as the **σ** of the future (§ 49).

(*c*) The first aorist infinitive active is always accented on the penult:[1] ἀθροῖσαι, ἁρπάσαι.

(*d*) Some verbs lack a first aorist. Such verbs often have a second aorist, a distinguishing feature of which is a weakening of the vowel element of the stem. The second aorist indicative is inflected like the imperfect, and the corresponding infinitive has an ending like that of the present infinitive, but it is accented irregularly on the ultima:

λείπω, ἔλιπον, λιπεῖν;
φεύγω, ἔφυγον, φυγεῖν.

(*e*) The third form in the principal parts of a normal verb shows by the presence of **-σα** (**-α**)[2] or **-ον** whether the aorist is first or second.

Inflect λύω and φεύγω in the aorist indicative and infinitive.

56. There is usually **no difference of meaning** between first and second aorist, the terms signifying merely difference in formation:

ἔπαυσα (first aorist) *I stopped;* ἔλιπον (second aorist) *I left.*

57. Tenses of the Infinitive. The infinitive, except in indirect discourse,[3] has no time value. The present infinitive denotes *continuance* or *repetition* (a motion picture), while the aorist infinitive denotes *a single occurrence* (a snapshot):

ἐθέλει φεύγειν *he wishes to keep on fleeing;*
ἐθέλει φυγεῖν *he wishes to flee.*

---

[1] See § V, *f*.

[2] The type of verbs that have only **-α** and not **-σα** in the first aorist will be presented later.

[3] § 50, *d*.

THE ARCH OF HADRIAN

Hadrian, one of the "good" emperors of Rome, showed his love for Athens by beautifying the city. This arch bears on its western face the legend, "This is the Athens of Theseus, the former city," and on the eastern face, "This is the city of Hadrian, not of Theseus."

58. VOCABULARY

ἐνταῦθα, adv.: *there, at that place.*
ἐντεῦθεν, adv.: *from there, thence.*
ἐπιστολή, -ῆς, ἡ: *letter.* EPISTLE.
ἔχω, ἕξω: *have;* ἔσχον[1]: *got.*
λείπω, λείψω, ἔλιπον: *leave.* ECLIPSE.
λοιπός, -ή, -όν[2]: *left, remaining;* τὸ λοιπόν: *the future;* κ.τ.λ. (καὶ τὰ λοιπά): *etc.*
οἰκίᾱ, -ᾱς, ἡ: *house.* ECONOMY.
πύλη, -ης, ἡ: *gate;* pl., *pass.* PYLON. THERMOPYLÆ.

59. EXERCISES

(*a*) Translate:

1. *διὰ τὴν φιλίᾱν ὁ στρατηγὸς ἐθέλει ἐπιστολὴν γράψαι.* 2. *οἱ λοιποὶ ἄνθρωποι ὑπ-ώπτευσαν*[3] *τὸν ἄγγελον.* 3. *ἐνόμισα τοὺς λοιποὺς ὑπ-οπτεῦσαι τοὺς τοῦ ἀγγέλου λόγους.* 4. *ἔπεισε τοὺς φίλους τὰς οἰκίᾱς λῦσαι.* 5. *ἐνταῦθα ἐλίπετε τοὺς ἵππους.* 6. *ἐντεῦθεν ἐπέμψαμεν τὸν ἄγγελον παρὰ τὰς τοῦ στρατηγοῦ θύρᾱς.* 7. *ὑπ-οπτεύομεν τὴν φυλακὴν φεύγειν ἐκ τῶν οἰκιῶν.* 8. *διὰ τῶν πυλῶν ἔφευγον οἱ λοιποὶ πολέμιοι.*

(*b*) Complete:

1. *ἐνταῦθα ἐσχ—* (1st singular) *δωρ— ἀξι—.* 2. *οὐκ ἐθέλει ὁ στρατηγὸς τὰς πυλ— λιπ—.* 3. *τ— στρατι—* (singular) *ἐνομίσατε ἐν τ— μαχ—* (singular) *φυγ—.*

(*c*) Write in Greek:

1. We shall seize the horses in the country. 2. He thinks that the enemy are guarding the road. 3. Do you intend to pursue the guard? 4. I think that the messenger will persuade the general. 5. With a shout they will break the strong door.

---

[1] ἔσχον is aorist. Sigma was lost in the present and replaced by breathing in the future. [2] An example of vowel change (§ 53).

[3] The augment of compounds follows the prefix.

LESSON XI

REVIEW

σοφῷ γὰρ αἰσχρὸν ἐξαμαρτάνειν.
'Tis shameful for a wise man to make mistakes.[1]

60. ASSIGNMENTS

(*a*) Review all words in the vocabularies of Lessons VI–X. Follow suggestions given in § 27, *a*.

(*b*) Name and define the Greek words suggested by *scenic*, *spondaic*, *prophylaxis*, *logomachy*, *archangel*, *pylon*, *diaphanous*, *barbaric*, *archetype*, *erg*, *ecliptic*, *cathode*, *pyloric*, *energize*, *thyreotomy*.

(*c*) Add ten other derivatives to this group.

(*d*) Inflect παύω, διώκω, ἁρπάζω, and λείπω in all tenses of indicative and infinitive thus far studied.[2]

(*e*) Give the forms of ἄξιος and ἀγαθός that should be used with στρατηγῷ, χώρᾳ, δῶρα, φυγήν, φιλίᾱς (singular), φιλίᾱς (plural), ἀγγέλων, κώμαις.

(*f*) What time facts are indicated by the heavy type?

ἔπεμπε ἄ**ξ**ομεν **ἐ**λῡ**σα**μεν γρά**ψ**ειν **ἔ**λιπες

(*g*) What uses of the genitive have you thus far had? Of the dative? Of the accusative?

61. EXERCISES

(*a*) Complete:

1. τ— στρατηγ— (singular) ὑπ-ώπτευσαν λῡ— (present) τὰς σπονδάς. 2. πείσει τοὺς βαρβάρους τὰ ἐπιτήδεια

[1] Æschylus, *Prometheus*, 1039.

[2] Consult the vocabulary at the back of the book to see which of these verbs have first and which second aorist.

ἁρπα— (single act). 3. τὴν στρατιὰν ἐνόμιζε λειπ— τ— ἀγορ— (singular). 4. διὰ τ— χωρ— ἔφυγον δέκα σταδι—. 5. ἡ δὲ κώμη πολεμι— ἦν τ— στρατι— (singular). 6. οἱ μὲν σῑγῇ ἐφύλαττον τὰς σκηνάς, — δὲ κραυγ— ἔφευγον. 7. ἀγορὰ οὐκ ἦν τ— λοιπ— στρατι— (singular).

(*b*) Write in Greek: 1. They suspected that the garrison would not guard the pass. 2. The men from the country had the letters. 3. The village was not friendly to the foreigners. 4. On account of our[1] friendship we shall not break the truce. 5. Some were brave in deed, others in speech.

THE LINCOLN MEMORIAL

The influence of Greek architecture is visible throughout the world, but rarely with more pleasing effect than in this memorial at Washington, D. C.

[1] Use article.

LESSON XII

READING

ὦ ταὶ λιπαραὶ καὶ ἰοστέφανοι καὶ ἀοίδιμοι,
Ἑλλάδος ἔρεισμα, κλειναὶ Ἀθᾶναι.

City of light, with thy violet crown, beloved of the poets,
Thou art the bulwark of Greece; Athens, thy fame is for ay.[1]

62. The Value of Translation. "There is no better way for the student to train himself in the choice of the very word that will fit his thought than by translation from Latin and Greek. Thus he develops habits of analysis, habits of discriminating choice of words, habits of accurate apprehension of the meaning which another has sought to convey by written words, which lead to power of expression and to power of clear thinking. Such habits are worth more to the lawyer than all the information which a modern school may hope to impart."[2]

63. The Process of Translation. From the very beginning, cultivate right habits. The time thus saved will in the end repay you for any time that may seem to be lost at the start.

1. Read aloud and distinctly each Greek sentence as Greek, without conscious effort at translation.
2. Note familiar words; in unfamiliar words look for familiar roots or suggestions as to meaning contained in the context.

---

[1] Pindar, fragment. Literally: *O renowned Athens, brilliant, violet-crowned, and famed in song, stay of Greece.*

[2] Roscoe Pound, Dean of the Law School, Harvard University, as reported in *Value of the Classics*, page 49.

3. Note carefully word groups and relations of words as indicated by inflectional changes.

4. Do not jump about in the sentence, but try to grasp the thoughts as they follow in logical sequence, observing that emphatic words are likely to occur at the beginning or end of clauses or sentences.

5. If the meaning of any words is still unknown, consult the vocabulary.

6. If relations of words are still obscure, reread aloud until the entire thought is clear.

7. Translate into clear and accurate English.

64. VOCABULARY

Ἀθῆναι, -ῶν, αἱ: *Athens.*
Ἀθηναῖος, -ᾱ, -ον: *Athenian.*
ἀπ-έχω: *be distant, be away.*
δρόμος, -ου, ὁ: *a running, run, race, race course.* HIPPODROME.
ἐπί, prep.: with G., *on, upon;*[1] with D., *on, at, by;* with A., *upon, to, against.* EPIDERMIS.
ἑπτά: *seven.* HEPTAGON.
ἥκω, ἥξω:[2] *come, have come, arrive.*
ὀκτώ: *eight.* OCTOPUS.
σπεύδω, σπεύσω, ἔσπευσα: *hasten.*

65. MARATHON

"That man is little to be envied whose patriotism would not gain force upon the plain of Marathon."[3]

Δαρεῖος βασιλεὺς[4] (*king*) ἦν τῶν Περσῶν καὶ ἦρχε πάντων (*all*) τῶν ἐν τῇ Ἀσίᾳ ἀνθρώπων. τοὺς δὲ φίλους ἔπεμπε στρατηγοὺς σὺν (*with*) στρατιᾷ πολλῇ (*large*) καὶ πολλῷ ναυτικῷ (compare NAUTICAL) ἐπὶ Ἀθήνᾱς. οἱ δὲ στρατηγοὶ ἦγον τοὺς Πέρσᾱς εἰς τὸν Μαραθῶνα, εἰς ὃ (*which*) πεδίον καὶ οἱ Ἀθηναῖοι ἧκον. ἐνταῦθα οἱ μὲν Ἀθηναῖοι δρόμῳ ἔσπευσαν εἰς τοὺς βαρβάρους. ἀπ-εῖχον δὲ σταδίους ὀκτώ. οἱ δὲ Πέρσαι

---

[1] The difference between the genitive, dative, and accusative may be indicated by these phrases: *on horseback, a city on the sea, he marches on the town.* Compare παρά (§ 25).

[2] No aorist in use.

[3] Samuel Johnson.

[4] Predicate nominative in agreement with Δαρεῖος.

ἐνόμιζον μανίᾱν (compare MANIAC) εἶναι[1] τοῖς Ἀθηναίοις. ἡ μὲν μάχη ἡ ἐν τῷ Μαραθῶνι ἦν μακρά, τέλος (*finally*) δὲ τοὺς βαρβάρους οἱ Ἀθηναῖοι ἐδίωκον εἰς τὴν θάλατταν (*sea*) καὶ τῶν νεῶν (*ships*) ἥρπασαν ἑπτά.

Adapted from Herodotus,[2] Book VI.

THE FUNERAL MOUND AT MARATHON

This is an artificial knoll, about forty feet high, erected over the bodies of the Athenians slain at Marathon. No simpler memorial could be imagined for the most heroic exploit in Athenian history.

66. PRONUNCIATION OF ANGLICIZED GREEK PROPER NAMES

(*a*) Every educated person should know how to pronounce correctly the many Greek proper names that have passed into English literature and English speech. Especially is this to be expected of every person who has been privileged to study Greek.

(*b*) Here are a few simple rules which will help:

1. Because most Greek proper names have come into English *via* Latin, custom demands first that *the Greek letters shall*

[1] Present infinitive in Indirect Discourse (§ 50) = *to be*.

[2] For information regarding Herodotus and other personages referred to in this book, consult *Dictionary of Proper Names*, page 335.

be replaced by their Latin equivalents. These can be learned from §§ I and II, but note especially that **αι** passes into *æ* or *e*, **ει** into *ī* or *ē*, **οι** into *œ* or *ē* (when final, *οι* becomes *ī*), **ου** into *ū*, **υ** into *y* (except in diphthongs), **ος** into *us:*

Αἴσχυλος *Æschylus*, Αἰθιοπίᾱ *Ethiopia*, Ἀριστείδης *Aristides*, Θησεῖον *Theseum*, Φοῖβος *Phœbus*, Φοῖνιξ *Phœnician*, Φίλιπποι *Philippi*, Ἐπίκουρος *Epicurus*, Κύκλωψ *Cyclops*.

2. Use the ordinary English sounds for the letters, remembering that *c* (for *k*) and *g* are "soft" before *e* or *i* sounds.

3. Names that have become very common in English are likely to have lost or changed their inflectional endings:

Ἀθῆναι *Athens*, Συρᾱ́κουσαι *Syracuse*, Ὅμηρος *Homer*, Πλάτων *Plato*, Ἀλέξανδρος *Alexander*.

BRONZE BOY FROM MARATHON

This head belongs to a beautiful statue found in almost perfect condition by a fisherman in the Bay of Marathon in 1925.

4. The anglicized form is to be accented according to the Latin rules: two-syllabled words accent the penult; polysyllables accent the penult, if long, otherwise the antepenult: Ath′ens, Odys′seus, Penel′ope.[1]

(*c*) Transliterate into English and pronounce:

Κυθέρεια	Ἀγαμέμνων	Βορέᾱς	Κῦρος
Ἡρόδοτος	Ἀφροδίτη [1]	Θουκυδίδης	Ἀπόλλων
Ζεύς	Χάρων	Σωκράτης	Λυκοῦργος

(*d*) Words other than proper names have suffered still greater changes as to ending:

σπασμός *spasm*, φιλοσοφίᾱ *philosophy*, φιλόσοφος *philosopher*, ἄγγελος *angel*, ὠκεανός *ocean*.

[1] Final η, when transliterated into *ē*, is regularly sounded.

LESSON XIII

PRONOUNS

ἕτερος γὰρ αὐτὸς ὁ φίλος ἐστίν. — *A friend is another self.*[1]

67. The relative pronoun, ὅς, ἥ, ὅ *who, which*, presents nothing new in inflection. It is like ἀγαθός everywhere except in the neuter nominative and accusative singular, where it has the same endings as the article.

ὅς *who, which*

M.	F.	N.	M.	F.	N.
ὅς	ἥ	ὅ	οἵ	αἵ	ἅ
οὗ	ἧς	οὗ	ὧν	ὧν	ὧν
ᾧ	ᾗ	ᾧ	οἷς	αἷς	οἷς
ὅν	ἥν	ὅ	οὕς	ἅς	ἅ

68. αὐτός *self*, and **ἄλλος** *other*, are inflected similarly except that **ἄλλος** has the accent on the penult. Inflect them and compare with paradigms (§§ 519 and 520).

69. A relative pronoun, as in English and in Latin, agrees with its antecedent in gender, number, and person, but its case depends on the construction in its own clause:

> ὁ ἄγγελος ὃν ἔπεμψας ἐθέλει φυγεῖν *the messenger whom you sent wishes to flee.*

70. Uses of αὐτός. Following the article, it means *same;* modifying a noun or pronoun, but not following the article, it means *self;* standing alone, except in the nominative, it is a *personal pronoun of the third person:*

[1] Aristotle, *Nicomachean Ethics*, IX. 9. 10, 1170 B.

ἡ αὐτὴ κώμη	*the same village,*	ἡ κώμη αὐτή	*the village itself;*
Κῦρος αὐτός	*Cyrus himself,*	αὐτὸς ἔφυγεν	*he himself fled;*
αὐτῷ ἔγραψα	*I wrote to him,*	αὐτοὺς ἀθροίζει	*he collects them.*

71. VOCABULARY

ἀλλήλων:[1] *of one another.* PARALLEL.

ἄλλος, -η, -ο: *other, another;* if preceded by the article, *the other, the rest of.* ALLOPATHY.

αὐτός, -ή, -ό: *same, self, he, she, it, they,* etc. AUTOMATON.

βουλεύω, βουλεύσω, ἐβούλευσα: *plan.*

βουλή, -ῆς, ἡ: *plan.* BOULE.

ἐπι-βουλεύω: *plot against,* with D.

ἐπι-βουλή, -ῆς, ἡ: *plot.*

ἴσος, -η, -ον: *equal.* ISOSCELES.

κελεύω, κελεύσω, ἐκέλευσα: *order, command.*

ὅς, ἥ, ὅ, rel. pron.: *who, which, that.*

ὥρᾱ, -ᾱς, ἡ: *hour, season.* HOUR.

72. EXERCISES

(*a*) What does *αὐτός* mean in these phrases?

τὰ αὐτὰ δῶρα *αὐτοὺς ἄγει* *τὰς θύρᾱς αὐτάς*

(*b*) Translate:

1. *καὶ ἡ αὐτὴ στρατιὰ ἥρπαζε τὰς σκηνάς.* 2. *ἄλλος στρατηγὸς ἦγε βαρβάρους οἳ αὐτῷ ἦσαν φίλιοι.* 3. *ἀλλ᾽ ἐνόμιζεν αὐτοὺς ὑπ-οπτεύσειν τὴν βουλήν.* 4. *ὁ δρόμος αὐτὸς ἀπ-έχει ἀπὸ τῆς κώμης ὀκτὼ σταδίους.* 5. *οἱ ἐν Ἀθήναις ἀλλήλοις ἐπ-εβούλευσαν.* 6. *τῇ δὲ φυλακῇ ὥρᾳ ἦν αὐτὸν ἄγειν εἰς τὴν οἰκίᾱν ἐν ᾗ ἦσαν οἱ ἄλλοι φίλοι.* 7. *ἡ γὰρ φυγὴ δήλη ἦν αὐτοῖς τοῖς πολεμίοις.* 8. *ἡ ἄλλη ὁδὸς ἦγε παρὰ τὸν Ἑλλήσποντον.*

(*c*) Complete:

1. *τ— στρατηγ— ἐπ-εβούλευσαν οἱ βάρβαροι —— αὐτῷ ἦσαν πολέμιοι.* 2. *αὐτ—* (*them*) *πέμψομεν ἄλλο δῶρον —— ἔχομεν.* 3. *αὐτῇ ἦσαν ἀλλ— οἰκι—.*

---

[1] ἀλλήλων lacks the singular number and the nominative plural.

AN ANCIENT TIMEPIECE

This Horologium, or Tower of the Winds, stood in the Agora and served as both weather bureau and town clock. It was surmounted by a weather-vane. Sundials adorned the exterior, and within was a water clock. The figures beneath the cornice represent the eight winds.

73. SOME AXIOMS OF EUCLID[1]

1. τὰ τοῦ αὐτοῦ ἴσα καὶ ἀλλήλοις ἐστὶν (*are*) ἴσα.

2. καὶ ἐὰν (*if*) ἴσοις ἴσα προσ-τεθῇ (*be added*), τὰ ὅλα (*wholes*, compare HOLOCAUST) ἐστὶν ἴσα.

3. καὶ ἐὰν ἀπ' ἴσων ἴσα ἀφ-αιρεθῇ (*be taken*), τὰ λοιπά ἐστιν ἴσα.

4. καὶ ἐὰν ἀν-ίσοις (ἀν = *un-*) ἴσα προσ-τεθῇ, τὰ ὅλα ἐστὶν ἄν-ισα.

---

[1] Consult *Dictionary of Proper Names* for the facts about Euclid.

LESSON XIV

DEMONSTRATIVE PRONOUNS

σπεῦδε βραδέως. — *Make haste slowly.*[1]

74. The principal demonstrative pronouns are *οὗτος this* (Latin *hic*), *ὅδε this*, and *ἐκεῖνος that* (Latin *ille*).

οὗτος *this*

οὗτος[2]	αὕτη	τοῦτο	οὗτοι	αὗται	ταῦτα
τούτου	ταύτης	τούτου	τούτων	τούτων	τούτων
τούτῳ	ταύτῃ	τούτῳ	τούτοις	ταύταις	τούτοις
τοῦτον	ταύτην	τοῦτο	τούτους	ταύτᾱς	ταῦτα

ὅδε *this*

ὅδε	ἥδε	τόδε	οἵδε	αἵδε	τάδε
τοῦδε	τῆσδε	τοῦδε	τῶνδε	τῶνδε	τῶνδε
τῷδε	τῇδε	τῷδε	τοῖσδε	ταῖσδε	τοῖσδε
τόνδε	τήνδε	τόδε	τούσδε	τάσδε	τάδε

Note that **οὗτος** has the same endings as *αὐτός* (§ 68), that it has initial **τ-** only where the article ὁ, ἡ, τό has **τ-**, and that it has **ου** in the penult only when an o-sound occurs in the ultima, having **αυ** in the other forms.

Contrast *οὗτος* and *αὐτός* as to breathing, accent, and stem.

Note that the forms of *ὅδε* are the forms of the article with **-δε** added.

75. ἐκεῖνος has the same endings and accents as **οὗτος.** Inflect it, and compare with paradigm (§ 523).

[1] Suetonius, *Augustus*, 25. A favorite expression of Augustus.

[2] The three genders of pronouns and adjectives appear in parallel columns, like ὅς in the previous lesson.

76. Uses of the Demonstratives. (*a*) οὗτος and ὅδε both mean *this*, *this book*, etc.; but οὗτος usually refers to something already mentioned, and ὅδε to something yet to follow:

ταῦτα ἔγραψε *this* (just mentioned) *is what he wrote;*
ἔγραψε τάδε *he wrote as follows.*

(*b*) ἐκεῖνος refers to something more remote than do οὗτος and ὅδε and is translated *that.*

(*c*) All three may be used as emphatic personal pronouns, *he*, *she*, *it*, *they.*

(*d*) When used as demonstrative adjectives all three have the predicate position (§ 31, *b*):

αὕτη ἡ κώμη *this village;*
ἐκείνη ἡ κώμη *that village.*

77. Dative of Means. The dative indicates the *means* whereby an act is done:[1]

τὸν ποταμὸν διαβαίνει πλοίῳ *he crosses the river in* (by means of) *a boat.*

78. **VOCABULARY**

ἀ-διά-βατος, -ον[2]: *uncrossable.*
δια-βαίνω[3]: *cross.*
δια-βατός, -ή, -όν: *crossable.*
ἐκεῖνος, -η, -ο: *that.*
μεστός, -ή, -όν: *full, full of,* with G.
ὅδε, ἥδε, τόδε: *this* (as follows).
οὗτος, αὕτη, τοῦτο: *this* (as aforesaid).
πλοῖον, -ου, τό: *boat.*
σῖτος, -ου, ὁ: *grain, food.* PARASITE.
συμ-βουλεύω[4]: *advise,* with D. of the person.
σύν, prep. with D.: *with.* SYNOD.

---

[1] The dative has three distinct divisions as to use, corresponding to English phrases with *to* or *for*, *with*, and *in.*

[2] Masculine and feminine are alike in form. See paradigm (§ 510, *b*). Compare Latin *omnis.* [3] Future and aorist will be given later.

[4] συν- changes to συμ- before β for the sake of euphony.

79. **EXERCISES**

(*a*) Translate:

1. *ἐκεῖνο τὸ πλοῖον μεστὸν ἦν σίτου.* 2. *αἱ πύλαι αὐταὶ ἦσαν ἰσχῦραί.* 3. *ὑπ-ώπτευσε δὲ ταύτᾱς τὰς φυλακὰς δια-βαίνειν τὸ πεδίον.* 4. *αὕτη μὲν ἡ χώρᾱ αὐτοῖς ἦν φιλίᾱ, ὁ δὲ σῖτος οὐκ ἀγαθός.* 5. *οἱ σὺν αὐτῷ ταῦτα τὰ ἐπιτήδεια ἥρπασαν.* 6. *οἵδε οἱ ποταμοὶ δια-βατοὶ ἦσαν πλοίοις.* 7. *συμ-βουλεύομεν ἐκείνοις ἄγειν ταῦτα ταὐτά.*[1]

(*b*) Complete:

1. *οὗτοι τὸν πόλεμον παύσουσι τ— σπονδ—.* 2. *ἔπεμ-ψαν τ—* (description follows). 3. *ἐκεῖναι —— πύλαι ἦσαν ἀ-δια-βατ—.*

(*c*) Write in Greek:

1. The door itself was ancient. 2. The others will persuade him. 3. The messengers whom he sent are plotting against one another. 4. They had (*ἦν*) the same plan. 5. We ourselves shall leave Athens.

80. Dean Inge, of St. Paul's Cathedral, London, writes: "The Christian Church was the last great creative achievement of classical culture."[2] The *λόγος* of St. John's Gospel is one of many evidences of this.

ἐν ἀρχῇ ἦν ὁ λόγος, καὶ ὁ λόγος ἦν πρὸς[3] *τὸν θεόν* (compare THEOLOGY), *καὶ θεὸς ἦν ὁ λόγος. οὗτος ἦν ἐν ἀρχῇ πρὸς τὸν θεόν.*

St. John, I. 1–2.

---

[1] *τὰ αὐτά* usually blend into *ταὐτά*.

[2] *Legacy of Greece*, page 30.

[3] *in the presence of.*

LESSON XV

FEMININE NOUNS OF THE A-DECLENSION. PERSONAL PRONOUNS

θάλαττα, θάλαττα. — The sea, the sea![1]

81. Feminines in -ᾰ. Most nouns of the **α**-declension have **-ᾱ** or **-η** in the nominative and carry the same throughout the singular. A few nouns have **-ᾰ** in the nominative. These have **ᾱ** in the genitive and dative singular, if the preceding letter is **ι** or **ρ**; otherwise they have **η**.

ἅμαξα	*wagon*	**γέφῡρα**	*bridge*
ἅμαξα[2]	ἅμαξαι	γέφῡρα	γέφῡραι
ἁμάξης	ἁμαξῶν	γεφῡ́ρᾱς	γεφῡρῶν
ἁμάξῃ	ἁμάξαις	γεφῡ́ρᾳ	γεφῡ́ραις
ἅμαξαν	ἁμάξᾱς	γέφῡραν	γεφῡ́ρᾱς

Note that in the singular, nominative and accusative agree as to final vowel, quantity of final vowel, and accent; and that the genitive and dative show the same agreement.

In like manner inflect *θάλαττα* and *βασίλεια*.

82. The Personal Pronouns are *ἐγώ I*, *σύ you (thou)*, for the first and second persons. For the third person, ***αὐτός*** is used in all cases except the nominative.

ἐγώ *I*		**σύ** *you (thou)*	
ἐγώ	ἡμεῖς	σύ	ὑμεῖς
ἐμοῦ, μου[3]	ἡμῶν	σοῦ, σου[3]	ὑμῶν
ἐμοί, μοι	ἡμῖν	σοί, σοι	ὑμῖν
ἐμέ, με	ἡμᾶς	σέ, σε	ὑμᾶς

[1] Xenophon, *Anabasis*, IV. 7. 24.

[2] For accent, see § V, *e*, *f*, *g*.

[3] The unaccented forms are enclitic (§ V, *j*). When used, they show that no emphasis is intended. The accented forms are emphatic or are used with prepositions. The nominative is not used except when emphasis is desired.

83. Particular Conditions. (*a*) **εἰ** with a *present* or *past* tense of the *indicative* in the protasis [1] and the same tense of the indicative or its equivalent in the apodosis [1] states a particular condition without implying anything as to its fulfillment or non-fulfillment. This is called a *particular condition* in present or past time:

> εἰ τὴν γέφῡραν φυλάττει, τὰς σπονδὰς λῡ́ει *if he is guarding the bridge, he is breaking the treaty;*
> εἰ . . . ἐφύλαξε, . . . ἔλῡσε *if he guarded . . ., he broke. . . .*

(*b*) The regular negative of the protasis is μή, of the apodosis οὐ.

84. **VOCABULARY**

ἅμαξα, -ης, ἡ: *cart, wagon.*
βασίλεια, -ᾱς, ἡ: *queen.*
γέφῡρα, -ᾱς, ἡ: *bridge.*
ἐγώ: *I.* EGOTIST.
εἰ, proclit. conj.: *if.*
θάλαττα, -ης, ἡ: *sea.*
κακός, -ή, -όν: *bad, cowardly.* CACOPHONY.
μή, neg. adv.: *not.* Found instead of οὐ with most uses of the infinitive and in conditional clauses.
ὅπλον, -ου, τό: *implement, tool;* frequently pl., *arms* (in war). PANOPLY.
οὖν, post-pos. conj.: *therefore, then, accordingly.*
σύ: *thou, you.*

85. **EXERCISES**

(*a*) Translate:

1. ἡμῖν μὲν ἦσαν ἅμαξαι, ὑμῖν δ' οὔ.[2] 2. οἱ σὺν τῇ βασιλείᾳ τὴν γέφῡραν δι-έβαινον. 3. ἐγὼ δ' οὖν ἐνόμιζον σὲ τὴν οἰκίᾱν φυλάττειν. 4. ἐκείνη γὰρ οὐχ ὑπ-ώπτευσεν ὑμᾶς ἀλλήλοις ἐπι-βουλεύσειν. 5. τὰ αὐτὰ ὅπλα ἦν ἐμοὶ καὶ σοί. 6. εἰ μὴ ἐπὶ τὴν θάλατταν ἄγεις τὴν φυλακήν,

[1] The terms "protasis" and "apodosis" denote respectively the "if-clause" and the "conclusion" of conditional sentences.

[2] Proclitic οὐ takes an accent at the end of a sentence, because no word follows with which it may be pronounced.

οὐ λύεις τὰς σπονδάς. 7. οἱ μὲν κακοὶ ἐπὶ τῶν ἁμαξῶν ἔφυγον, ἡ δὲ βασίλεια οὐκ ἔλιπε τὴν γέφῡραν. 8. εἰ ὁ ποταμὸς ἦν δια-βατός, ἤθελον αὐτὸν δια-βαίνειν.

THE SEA GOD'S SHRINE

These columns of whitest marble, belonging to the temple of Poseidon, still welcome the seafarer to Attica as in the proud days of Pericles.

(*b*) Complete:

1. ὑμ— μὲν τῇ βασιλει— ἐπ-εβουλεύετε, ἡμ— δ' οὔ. 2. εἰ οὗτοι —— (linking verb) ἐπὶ τῇ γεφῡρ—, ἐφυλαξ— αὐτ— (that is, the bridge). 3. ὁ κακὸς ἄγγελος ἐμ— ἐγραψ— ταύτην —— ἐπιστολήν.

(*c*) Write in Greek:

1. That (man) plans as follows. 2. We shall advise him to seize the food. 3. This river was crossable in a boat. 4. These (things) were evident. 5. The grain was not in the boat itself.

86. Menander, the Athenian comic poet, by reason of his thorough acquaintance with human nature and his consummate literary art, has been almost as often quoted in later ages as Shakespeare. Even St. Paul (I Corinthians, XV. 33) repeats one of his lines:

φθείρουσιν ἤθη χρηστὰ ὁμῑλίαι κακαί *evil communications corrupt good manners.*

Translate the following characteristic utterance:

ἀρχὴ μεγίστη (*greatest*) τῶν ἐν ἀνθρώποις κακῶν ἀγαθά, τὰ λίαν (*excessive*) ἀγαθά.

Menander, fragment.

LESSON XVI

MASCULINE NOUNS OF THE A-DECLENSION. REFLEXIVE PRONOUNS

ἀγαπήσεις τὸν πλησίον σου ὡς σαυτόν.
Thou shalt love thy neighbor as thyself.[1]

87. Masculine Nouns of the A-declension. Most nouns of the **α**-declension are feminine. Masculines may be recognized not merely as referring to males but also as showing **-ης** or **-ας** instead of **-η** or **-α** in the nominative singular. Their genitive singular ends in **-ου**. Otherwise the inflection parallels that of the feminines.

στρατιώτης *soldier*		**Ξενίᾱς** *Xenias*
στρατιώτ **ης**	στρατιῶτ **αι**	Ξενί **ᾱς**
στρατιώτ **ου**	στρατιωτ **ῶν**	Ξενί **ου**
στρατιώτ **ῃ**	στρατιώτ **αις**	Ξενί **ᾳ**
στρατιώτ **ην**	στρατιώτ **ᾱς**	Ξενί **ᾱν**

Note the two indications of masculine gender in -ς of the nominative singular and -ου of the genitive singular, both of which occur in the **ο**-declension.

In like manner inflect ὁπλίτης.

88. Reflexive Pronouns are formed from the stems of the personal pronouns and the proper case forms of *αὐτός*. In the plural of the first and second persons both parts of the word are fully inflected. The pronoun of the third person, however, has the compounded form in the plural.

ἐμαυτοῦ *myself*

ἐμαυτοῦ[2]	ἐμαυτῆς	ἡμῶν αὐτῶν	ἡμῶν αὐτῶν
ἐμαυτῷ	ἐμαυτῇ	ἡμῖν αὐτοῖς	ἡμῖν αὐταῖς
ἐμαυτόν	ἐμαυτήν	ἡμᾶς αὐτούς	ἡμᾶς αὐτάς

[1] St. Matthew, XIX. 19.

[2] For obvious reasons the reflexive pronouns of the first and second persons have no neuter.

σεαυτοῦ *yourself*

σεαυτοῦ [1]	σεαυτῆς	ὑμῶν αὐτῶν	ὑμῶν αὐτῶν
σεαυτῷ	σεαυτῇ	ὑμῖν αὐτοῖς	ὑμῖν αὐταῖς
σεαυτόν	σεαυτήν	ὑμᾶς αὐτούς	ὑμᾶς αὐτάς

ἑαυτοῦ *himself, herself, itself*

ἑαυτοῦ [1]	ἑαυτῆς	ἑαυτοῦ	ἑαυτῶν	ἑαυτῶν	ἑαυτῶν
ἑαυτῷ	ἑαυτῇ	ἑαυτῷ	ἑαυτοῖς	ἑαυταῖς	ἑαυτοῖς
ἑαυτόν	ἑαυτήν	ἑαυτό	ἑαυτούς	ἑαυτάς	ἑαυτά

89. Reflexive Pronouns appear in the predicate and refer to the subject of the sentence or clause in which they stand. As such they are *direct reflexives.* Sometimes they appear in a dependent clause and refer to the subject of the main clause. They then are *indirect reflexives:*

ἧκον ἐπὶ τὴν ἐμαυτοῦ σκηνήν *I went to my own tent;*
ἔπεισαν ἐμὲ ἥκειν ἐπὶ τὴν ἑαυτῶν σκηνήν *they persuaded me to go to their (own) tent.*

90. **VOCABULARY**

ἑ-αυτοῦ, -ῆς, -οῦ : *of himself, herself, itself.*

ἐμ-αυτοῦ, -ῆς : *of myself.*

ἐξ-ελαύνω,[2] ἐξ-ήλασα : *drive out, march forth, march on.*

μένω :[2] *remain, wait for.*

Ξενίᾱς, -ου, ὁ : *Xenias,* an Arcadian general serving under Cyrus, the younger.

ὁπλῑ́της,[3] -ου, ὁ : *hoplite,* a heavy-armed soldier. Cf. **ὅπλα.**

πολῑ́της,[3] -ου, ὁ : *citizen.* POLITICS.

σατράπης, -ου, ὁ : *satrap,* a Persian viceroy.

σε-αυτοῦ, -ῆς : *of yourself.*

σταθμός, -οῦ, ὁ : *halting-place, day's march.*

στρατιώτης,[3] -ου, ὁ : *soldier.* Cf. **στρατιᾱ́, στρατηγός.**

---

[1] Contracted forms σαυτοῦ and αὑτοῦ are often used in place of σεαυτοῦ and ἑαυτοῦ.

[2] The future of this verb is irregular. It will be presented later.

[3] The suffix **-τα** (nominative **-της**) denotes the *agent* or *doer* of an action or the *person concerned.*

91. **EXERCISES**

(*a*) Translate:

1. *εἰ οὖν οἱ στρατιῶται μένουσιν ἐπὶ τῇ γεφύρᾳ, νομίζει αὐτοὺς τὰς σπονδὰς λύειν.* 2. *Ξενίᾱς καὶ οἱ σὺν αὐτῷ ὁπλῖται ἐξ-ελαύνουσι δέκα σταθμούς.* 3. *ἐγὼ μὲν ἔχω τὴν ἐμαυτοῦ ἀρχήν, σὺ δὲ τὴν σεαυτοῦ.* 4. *κελεύσουσι τούτους τοὺς στρατιώτᾱς φυλάττειν τὴν οἰκίᾱν.* 5. *ἐνόμισε δ' οὖν τὸν σατράπην οὐ γράψειν ἑαυτῷ τὰς ἐπιστολάς.* 6. *ὥρᾱ ἦν τῷ ἐκείνης τῆς χώρᾱς σατράπῃ τὴν πύλην φυλάττειν τοῖς ἑαυτοῦ.* 7. *αὐτοὶ μὲν οὐκ ἐθέλουσι τὰς σκηνὰς ἁρπάσαι, σοὶ δὲ συμ-βουλεύουσι ταῦτα.*

(*b*) Complete:

1. *ἡμῖν —— οἱ πολῖτ— ἦσαν φίλιοι, ὑμ— δὲ πολέμιοι.* 2. *Ξενίᾱς γὰρ οὐχ ὑπ-οπτεύσει τοὺς στρατιωτ— ἑαυτ— ἐπι-βουλεύειν.* 3. *ἐπὶ τὴν ἐμαυτ— σκηνὴν ἦγον τὸν σῖτον καὶ τὰ ἄλλα ἃ ἦν ἐμ—.*

(*c*) Write in Greek:

1. Accordingly the cowardly queen fled to the sea. 2. For you (singular) had (*ἦν*) a wagon, I did (omit) not. 3. They cross the river by a bridge. 4. If they are not guarding the arms, they are breaking the treaty. 5. Those arms were not on the wagon.

92. Review axioms given in § 73; then translate:

1. *καὶ ἐὰν ἀπ' ἀν-ίσων ἴσα ἀφ-αιρεθῇ, τὰ λοιπά ἐστιν ἄν-ισα.*
2. *καὶ τὰ τοῦ αὐτοῦ διπλάσια* (*doubles*) *ἴσα ἀλλήλοις ἐστίν.*
3. *καὶ τὰ τοῦ αὐτοῦ ἡμίση* (*halves*, compare HEMISPHERE) *ἴσα ἀλλήλοις ἐστίν.*

Euclid.

LESSON XVII

PRESENT AND IMPERFECT INDICATIVE AND PRESENT INFINITIVE OF εἰμί. ENCLITICS

ἄγροικός εἰμι· τὴν σκάφην σκάφην λέγω.
I am from the country; I call a spade a spade.[1]

93. The verb εἰμί *to be* is irregular, as are the corresponding verbs in English and Latin.

Present Indicative		Imperfect Indicative	
εἰμί	ἐσμέν	ἦν	ἦμεν
εἶ	ἐστέ	ἦσθα	ἦτε
ἐστί(ν)[2]	εἰσί(ν)[2]	ἦν	ἦσαν

Present Infinitive εἶναι

94. All forms of the present indicative of *εἰμί* except *εἶ* are enclitic. *ἔστι* when thus accented means *exists* or *is possible*, except that it is regularly so accented after *ἀλλά*, *καί*, *μή*, *οὐκ*, *τοῦτο*, *ὡς* and *εἰ* (*if*), whether it has this special meaning or not.

95. Enclitics. (*a*) If the preceding word has an accent on the ultima, the enclitic has no accent:

καλοί εἰσιν *they are beautiful.*

(*b*) If the preceding word has an acute on the antepenult or a circumflex on the penult, it receives an additional acute on the ultima and the enclitic has no accent:

ἄνθρωποί εἰσιν *they are men;*
στρατιῶταί εἰσιν *they are soldiers.*

[1] Comic Attic fragment. Literally: *I am a countryman; I call the tub a tub.*

[2] ν-movable.

(*c*) If the preceding word has an acute on the penult, an enclitic of one syllable has no accent but an enclitic of two syllables is accented on the final syllable:

ὁπλίτης τις *a certain hoplite;*
ὁπλίτης ἐστίν *he is a hoplite.*

96. Accent of Augmented Verbs. The accent cannot precede the augment. Therefore compound verbs are accented after the prefix:

ἐξ-άγω, ἐξ-ῆγον; ἄπ-ειμι, ἀπ-ῆν.

97. Contrary to Fact Conditions. **εἰ** with a *past* tense of the *indicative* in the protasis and a *past* tense of the *indicative* with **ἄν** in the apodosis implies that the condition is not or was not fulfilled. This is called a *contrary to fact condition.* The *imperfect* tense indicates *present* time; the *aorist* indicates *past* time:

εἰ τὴν γέφῡραν ἐφύλαττε, τὰς σπονδὰς ἂν ἔλῡεν *if he were guarding the bridge, he would be breaking the treaty;*
εἰ . . . ἐφύλαξε, . . . ἂν ἔλῡσεν *if he had guarded . . ., he would have broken. . . .*

Note carefully that the presence of **ἄν** in the apodosis distinguishes a contrary to fact from a past particular condition (§ 83).

98. **VOCABULARY**

ἄν, post-pos. particle belonging to certain types of conditional clauses but lacking an exact English equivalent.

ἄπ-ειμι: *be away, be absent.*

εἰμί,[1] enclit.: *be.*

ἔξ-εστι(ν),[2] impersonal: *it is possible.*

οὔ-πω, neg. adv.: *not yet.*

πάρ-ειμι: *be present.*

πέντε, indeclinable: *five.* PENTAGON.

στρατό-πεδον, -ου, τό: *camp.* Cf. **στρατιά** and **πεδίον**.

τόπος, -ου, ὁ: *place.* TOPOGRAPHY.

τότε, adv.: *then, at that time.*

φᾱσί(ν),[2] enclit.: *they say.*

φησί(ν),[2] enclit.: *he* or *she says.* PROPHET.

---

[1] The future will appear later. εἰμί has no aorist.

[2] ν-movable.

99. EXERCISES

(*a*) Translate:

1. τότε δὲ οὐκ ἐξ-ῆν ἡμῖν παρ-εῖναι. 2. καὶ διὰ φιλίᾱν τοῦτόν φᾱσιν οὐκ ἀπ-εῖναι. 3. ἔστιν οὖν τῇ στρατιᾷ τοὺς ἵππους ἁρπάσαι; 4. ἀλλ' ἐκ τῆς αὐτῆς χώρᾱς εἰσίν. 5. εἰ μὴ συν-εβουλεύσατε ἐμοί, οὐκ ἂν ἔγραψα τὴν ἐπιστολήν. 6. οὔ-πω γάρ φησι τὴν ἐπιβουλὴν δήλην εἶναι. 7. ἐντεῦθεν ἐξ-ηλαύνομεν πέντε σταθμοὺς ἐπὶ τὴν θάλατταν. 8. ἀλλ' οὔ-πω ἂν παρ-ῆμεν, εἰ μὴ ὁ ποταμὸς δια-βατὸς ἦν πλοίῳ. 9. ἐμοὶ γράφει οὐκ εἶναι ὁπλῑ́τᾱς ἐν τῷ στρατοπέδῳ.

(*b*) Complete:

1. καὶ αὐτοῖς οὐκ ἂν ἦν τ— ἐπιτηδει—, εἰ μὴ ἐν καλῷ τόπῳ —— (linking verb) τὸ στρατόπεδον. 2. ἐκείνους τοὺς στρατιώτᾱς φησὶ παρ— ἐπὶ τ— γεφῡρ—. 3. εἰ ἐκέλευσεν ἡμᾶς, ἐξ-ηλασ— ἂν ὀκτὼ σταθμούς.

(*c*) Write in Greek:

1. The soldiers gathered their own provisions. 2. The citizens think that we will bring them the food. 3. We shall guard the bridge with our own men (§ 91, *a*, 6). 4. The satrap has his own province. 5. The hoplites made (*marched*) a ten days' march.

100. IN HOSTILE TERRITORY

ἐντεῦθεν ἐξ-ελαύνει διὰ τῆς Λυκᾱονίᾱς. ταύτην τὴν χώρᾱν δι-ήρπασεν[1] ὡς (*as*) πολεμίᾱν. ἐντεῦθεν Κῦρος τὴν Κίλισσαν (*the Cilician queen*) εἰς τὴν Κιλικίᾱν ἀπο-πέμπει τὴν ταχίστην (*quickest*) ὁδόν·[2] καὶ συν-έπεμψεν αὐτῇ στρατιώτᾱς οὓς Μένων εἶχε καὶ αὐτόν.

Adapted from Xenophon, *Anabasis*, I. 2. 19–20.

---

[1] δι(α) = thoroughly. [2] Adverbial Accusative.

The Stadium at Athens

Here the Olympic games were revived in 1896 after the lapse of centuries. In the lower picture you can see its marble seats beyond the grove.

View of Athens from the Acropolis

Above the housetops rises the Arch of Hadrian (page 32). To the right are the surviving columns of the lofty Olympieum (page 118). Beyond the Stadium looms Hymettus, famed for its honey. The glory of Hymettus' slopes at sunset won for Athens the title, "violet crowned."

LESSON XVIII

CONSONANT DECLENSION (K-STEMS)

δέσποινα γὰρ γέροντι νυμφίῳ γυνή.
An old man's bride, an old man's boss.[1]

101. The Consonant Declension includes nouns whose stems end in a consonant.

The stem appears when the ending **-ος** is dropped from the genitive singular. To this stem the endings for the other cases are added.

The ending for the nominative singular should be learned from the vocabulary. Sometimes it ends in **-ς**. The dative plural ends in **-σι**. The **σ** in each of these instances unites with **κ**, **γ**, or **χ** to form **ξ**.

κῆρυξ (ὁ) *herald*		**φάλαγξ** (ἡ) *phalanx*	
κῆρυξ	κήρῡκ **ες**	φάλαγξ	φάλαγγ **ες**
κήρῡκ **ος**	κηρῡ́κ **ων**	φάλαγγ **ος**	φαλάγγ **ων**
κήρῡκ **ι**	κήρυξι(ν)	φάλαγγ **ι**	φάλαγξι(ν)
κήρῡκ **α**	κήρῡκ **ας**	φάλαγγ **α**	φάλαγγ **ας**

In like manner inflect φύλαξ and σάλπιγξ.

102. Monosyllables of the consonant declension are accented on the ultima in the genitive and dative of all numbers, the circumflex occurring on long vowels or diphthongs, otherwise the acute.

Inflect **Θρᾷξ**. Compare with paradigm (§ 509, *a*).

[1] Euripides, fragment. Literally: *For to an aged bridegroom a wife is mistress.*

103. Genitive of Time. The genitive denotes the *time within which* an action occurs:[1]

γράψω πέντε ἡμερῶν *I shall write within five days.*

104. VOCABULARY

γυνή, γυναικός,[2] ἡ: *woman, wife.* MISOGYNIST.

δι-αρπάζω, -αρπάσω, -ήρπασα: *plunder, pillage, sack.*

Θρᾷξ, -ᾳκός, ὁ: *Thracian.*

κατά, prep.: with G., *down from*; with A., *down along, along, according to.* CATALOGUE.

κῆρυξ, -ῡκος, ὁ: *herald.*

πρός, prep.: with G., *from the side of, in the sight of*; with D., *near, beside, besides*; with A., *to the side of, toward.* PROSELYTE.

σάλπιγξ, -γγος, ἡ: *trumpet.*

φάλαγξ, -γγος, ἡ: *phalanx, battle-line.*

φύλαξ, -ακος, ὁ: *guard.* Cf. **φυλακή, φυλάττω.**

105. EXERCISES

(*a*) What do the portions in heavy type tell as to the probable use of γυναικ **ί**, φυλάκ **ων**, Θρᾳκ **ός**, φάλαγγ **ες**, σάλπιγ **ξι**, κήρῡκ **α**? Distinguish between φυλακῶν and φυλάκων, φύλακας and φυλακᾱ́ς.

(*b*) Translate:

1. οἱ δὲ φύλακες ἔφευγον κατὰ τὴν ὁδόν. 2. καὶ δέκα ἡμερῶν κήρῡκα πέμψει ἡμῖν. 3. τὴν δὲ γυναῖκα πρὸς τὸ στρατόπεδον ἄξει. 4. εἰ μὴ παρ-ῆν ἡ ἰσχῡρᾱ̀ φάλαγξ, οἱ πολέμιοι δι-ήρπασαν ἂν τὰ ἐν τῷ στρατοπέδῳ. 5. ἀλλὰ ταύτης τῆς ἡμέρᾱς οἱ φύλακες ὑπ-ώπτευον αὐτὸν διώκειν τὴν τῶν πολεμίων φάλαγγα. 6. τῇ δὲ σάλπιγγι ἐκελεύομεν τοὺς στρατιώτᾱς ἀθροῖσαι τοὺς ἵππους. 7. πρὸς δὲ τούτοις κατὰ τῶν πυλῶν ἦγον αὐτούς. 8. ὁ δὲ κῆρυξ καὶ οἱ σὺν αὐτῷ φυλάξουσι καὶ τὰς γυναῖκας καὶ τὰ ἐπιτήδεια.

---

[1] What relation of time is denoted by the accusative?

[2] γυνή, like monosyllables of the consonant declension, accents the ultima in the genitive and dative of all numbers. In the other forms it accents the last syllable of the stem.

(*c*) Complete:

1. *πρὸς ἡμ— ἄξει τὰ ἐπιτήδεια πέντε ἡμερ—.* 2. *ὑποπτεύω τοὺς φύλακ— φυγεῖν κατὰ ταυτ— τ— ὁδ—.* 3. *ἡ δὲ τοῦ Θρᾳκ— γυνὴ αὐτῷ ἔπεμψε τ— σαλπιγγ—* (singular).

(*d*) Write in Greek:

1. It was impossible to stop the plot. 2. If they had suspected the satrap, they would have guarded the bridge. 3. If he were not absent, the hoplites would not be remaining in the same place for five days. 4. These men are not yet in the camp.

106. THE PHALANX

By means of the phalanx, invented and developed by Greeks, Alexander the Great imposed his will upon most of the civilized world. In the hands of the Romans, who were quick to grasp its possibilities, it grew into the famous *legion*.

"The average depth of the phalanx was eight men, although it occasionally reached sixteen, even before the time of the Macedonians. Epaminondas made his left wing about fifty ranks deep. The spear might be twenty-one feet long, or even twenty-four in Hellenistic times. Five or six rows of spear points would project beyond the front rank making an impenetrable barrier. The spears of the rear ranks rested upon the shoulders of men in front with their points directed upward. The formation looked like a huge porcupine with the quills pointing in one direction. The Roman consul, Lucius Aemilius, a seasoned veteran, confessed to friends at Rome that he had never seen anything more terrible and alarming than the Macedonian phalanx of Perseus."

E. S. McCartney, *Warfare by Land and Sea*, pages 25–27.

LESSON XIX

CONSONANT DECLENSION (Δ- OR T-STEMS)

ἄριστον μὲν ὕδωρ. — *Water is best.*[1]

107. Stems in τ or δ with unaccented ι before the final consonant have ιν in the accusative singular. Other nouns with τ or δ stems are normal.

In the dative plural τ and δ drop out before σι. When the stem ends in ντ, both letters drop out and the ο of the stem lengthens to ου.

ἀσπίς (ἡ) *shield*

ἀσπί ς	ἀσπί δες
ἀσπί δος	ἀσπί δων
ἀσπί δι	ἀσπί σι(ν)
ἀσπί δα	ἀσπί δας

χάρις (ἡ) *favor*

χάρι ς	χάρι τες
χάρι τος	χαρί των
χάρι τι	χάρι σι(ν)
χάρι ν	χάρι τας

νύξ (ἡ) *night*

νύξ[2]	νύκτ ες
νυκτ ός	νυκτ ῶν
νυκτ ί	νυξί(ν)
νύκτ α	νύκτ ας

ἄρχων (ὁ) *ruler*

ἄρχων	ἄρχοντ ες
ἄρχοντ ος	ἀρχόντ ων
ἄρχοντ ι	ἄρχου σι(ν)
ἄρχοντ α	ἄρχοντ ας

ἅρμα (τό) *chariot*

ἅρμα	ἅρματ α
ἅρματ ος	ἁρμάτ ων
ἅρματ ι	ἅρμα σι(ν)
ἅρμα	ἅρματ α

In like manner inflect Ἑλλάς, πρᾶγμα.

---

[1] Pindar, *Olympian*, I. 1.

[2] For accent of νύξ, see § 102.

108. Result Clauses. *ὥστε* followed by the *indicative* denotes an *actual result;* followed by the *infinitive* it denotes a *natural* or *probable result:*

εἶχον χρήματα ὥστε ἠγόρασα τὰ ἐπιτήδεια *I had money and (so that I) bought provisions;*

εἶχον χρήματα ὥστε ἀγοράσαι τὰ ἐπιτήδεια *I had money (so as) to buy provisions.*

109. **VOCABULARY**

ἅρμα, -ατος, τό: *chariot.*
ἄρχων, -οντος, ὁ: *archon, ruler, commander.* Cf. ἄρχω, ἀρχή.
ἀσπίς, -ίδος, ἡ: *shield.*
δόρυ, -ατος, τό: *spear.* DORYPHOROS.
Ἑλλάς, -άδος, ἡ: *Hellas, Greece.*
νύξ, νυκτός, ἡ: *night.* Lat. *nox.*
παῖς, παιδός,[1] ὁ or ἡ: *boy, girl, child.* PEDAGOGUE.
πρᾶγμα, -ατος, τό: *fact, business;* pl., *trouble.* PRAGMATIC.
ὕδωρ, ὕδατος, τό: *water.* HYDRANT.[2]
χάρις, -ιτος, ἡ: *favor, gratitude.* χάριν ἔχω: *feel grateful,* with D.[3] EUCHARIST.
χρῆμα, -ατος, τό: *thing;* pl., *things,* i.e., *property, wealth, money.*
ὥστε, conj.: with ind., *so that;* with inf., *so as to.*

110. **EXERCISES**

(*a*) Translate:

1. ἀλλὰ οὐκ ἦν αὐτῷ χρήματα, ὥστε πέμπειν ἡμῖν καὶ ἀσπίδας καὶ δόρατα. 2. τῆς δὲ νυκτὸς ὁ ἄρχων ἐκ τῆς κώμης ἔπεμψε τοὺς παῖδας. 3. χάριν δ' ἕξετέ μοι, ὑμᾶς γὰρ ἄξω εἰς τὴν Ἑλλάδα. 4. ἐνταῦθα δ' οὐκ ἔστιν ὕδωρ τοῖς ἵπποις, ὥστε κελεύει σε ἄγειν αὐτοὺς πρὸς τὸν ποταμόν. 5. οὗτος οὖν ἐπὶ τοῦ ἅρματος ἤλαυνε παρὰ τὴν φάλαγγα. 6. οἱ δὲ στρατιῶται πράγματα οὐκ ἂν ἔσχον, εἰ μὴ τὴν σάλπιγγα ἔλῡσεν ὁ κῆρυξ. 7. ἀλλ' εἰ ἔξ-εστι τὸν κήρῡκα χρήμασι

---

[1] The accent of the genitive plural is on the penult, by exception to § 102.

[2] From a late by-form ὑδρ—.

[3] Compare Latin *gratiam alicui habere.*

πεῖσαι, συμ-βουλεύω ὑμῖν ἐνταῦθα μένειν. 8. ἡ δὲ γυνὴ καὶ οἱ παῖδες οἱ τοῦ ἄρχοντος ἐλαύνουσιν ἐπὶ τῆς ἁμάξης.

(*b*) Complete:

1. τῷ γὰρ παι— ἔστι πλοῖον, ὥστε δια-βαιν— τὸν ποταμόν. 2. χαρ— ἔχουσιν ὑμ—, ἄγετε γὰρ αὐτοὺς ἐκ κακοῦ τόπου. 3. τὰ δὲ χρημ— ἔπεμψεν, ὥστε οἱ ὁπλῖται ἤθελ— ἐλαύνειν.

(*c*) Write in Greek:

1. With the trumpet he will order the guards to march (on). 2. Within five days the heralds were present. 3. In addition to this they plundered the wagons of the queen. 4. The woman fled down that road. 5. If the phalanx were present, the enemy would not be pillaging the houses.

A HOCKEY MATCH

"There is nothing new under the sun." The stone on which this scene is carved was built into the city wall of Athens after the departure of the Persians in 480 B.C.

LESSON XX

REVIEW

αἱ δεύτεραί πως φροντίδες σοφώτεραι. — *The sober second thought.*[1]

111. ASSIGNMENTS

Ewing Galloway

καλὸν τὸ ὕδωρ

The sacred isle of Delos now lies in ruins, but "Cleopatra's Well" still cheers the thirsty.

(*a*) Review Vocabulary III, page 330, following the method indicated in § 27, *a*.

(*b*) Name and define the Greek words suggested by: *sympathy*, *isothermal*, *egoist*, *autonomy*, *epitaph*, *pedagogy*, *polity*, *topic*, *pentathlon*, *cacophony*, *anhydrous*, *horoscope*, *epigram*, *thalassic*, *charity*, *cataract*, *prophylaxis*, *orthopedic*, *pediatrist*.

(*c*) What other derivatives can you add to this group?

(*d*) Inflect the singular of **θάλαττα**, **βασίλεια**, **ὁπλίτης**, **χάρις**, **ὕδωρ**, **νύξ**.

(*e*) Give the dative plural of **φύλαξ**, **δόρυ**, **ἄρχων**.

---

[1] Euripides, *Hippolytus*, 436. Literally: *Second thoughts somehow are wiser.*

(*f*) Write the forms of *αὐτός*, *οὗτος*, and *ὅδε* that would be used with *πολίτῃ*, *ἀσπίδες*, *ἅρματα*, *νυκτῶν*, *φύλακα*, *ὁπλίτᾱς*.

(*g*) Inflect *εἰμί* in the present and imperfect indicative.

112. EXERCISES

(*a*) Complete:

1. *κατὰ ταυτ— τ— ὁδὸν ἔφυγον οἱ κήρῡκες πρὸς τ— στρατοπεδ—.* 2. *οἱ μὲν ἄλλοι ἄρχοντες ἤθροιζον τοὺς ἑαυτ— στρατιωτ—, ἐγὼ δὲ τοὺς ἐμαυτ—.* 3. *καὶ ὅδε —— ποταμὸς δια-βατός ἐστι πλοι—.* 4. *πλοῖα* —— (linking verb) *ὑμῖν, ὥστε τὸν ποταμὸν δια-βαιν—.* 5. *ἀλλὰ οἱ σὺν ἡμ— ἤθελον μένειν πέντε ἡμερ—.* 6. *ἐπὶ τοῦ ἁρμα—* —— (linking verb) *αἱ ἀσπίδες* —— (relative pronoun) *ἡρπάσαμεν ἐκ τῆς σκηνῆς.* 7. *εἰ ἔμελλε τὰ δορα— ἄξειν, παρ— ἄν.*

(*b*) Write in Greek:

1. The satrap himself wrote as follows. 2. Within seven days the ruler will bring the arms and the chariots. 3. If the queen had not brought a guard with her, the men from the village would have pursued her. 4. He says that the other men are at that bridge. 5. The guards destroyed eight boats, so that it was not possible to cross the river.

πένταθλον

LESSON XXI

PARTICIPLES

ἐλπὶς ἐν ἀνθρώποις μούνη θεὸς ἐσθλὴ ἔνεστιν.
Hope is man's one good deity.[1]

113. Present Participle. The masculine of the present participle is inflected like ἄρχων (§ 107). The neuter has the same endings except in the nominative and accusative singular, where it uses the mere stem with **τ** dropped (because **τ** cannot end a Greek word), and in the same cases in the plural, where it adds **-α** to the stem. The feminine is inflected like ἅμαξα (§ 81).

Present Participle of **εἰμί** *I am*

ὤν	οὖσα	ὄν	ὄντες	οὖσαι	ὄντα
ὄντος	οὔσης	ὄντος	ὄντων	οὐσῶν	ὄντων
ὄντι	οὔσῃ	ὄντι	οὖσι	οὔσαις	οὖσι
ὄντα	οὖσαν	ὄν	ὄντας	οὔσᾱς	ὄντα

114. The present and future active participles of **παύω** are inflected like ὤν with the accent on **παυ-** or **παυσ-**, except in the feminine genitive plural. The second aorist active participle is also inflected like ὤν and has the same accents.

Write out entire the inflection of **παύων, παύσων, λιπών.** Compare with paradigms (§ 514, *a*).

[1] Theognis, 1135.

115. First Aorist Active Participle of **παύω** *I stop*

παύσᾱς	παύσᾱσα	παῦσαν
παύσαντος	παυσᾱ́σης	παύσαντος
παύσαντι	παυσᾱ́σῃ	παύσαντι
παύσαντα	παύσᾱσαν	παῦσαν
παύσαντες	παύσᾱσαι	παύσαντα
παυσάντων	παυσᾱσῶν	παυσάντων
παύσᾱσι(ν)	παυσᾱ́σαις	παύσᾱσι(ν)
παύσαντας	παυσᾱ́σᾱς	παύσαντα

Note that the stem here used is that of the first aorist active. The endings are the same as those of the present participle, except in the nominative singular, where **-ς** has been added to the stem, causing **ντ** to drop out and lengthening **α**. In like manner inflect **κελεύσᾱς**.

116. Uses of Participles. (*a*) A participle, when used in the attributive position (§ 31, *a*), has the force of an attributive adjective. This is called the *attributive participle:*

ὁ δι-αρπάζων στρατιώτης *the plundering soldier.*

The attributive participle often has its noun implied and may be translated by a noun or a relative clause. This is the regular equivalent of the English *he who*, *those who:*

οἱ φεύγοντες *the fugitives* or *those who are fleeing.*

(*b*) A participle, when used without an article and in agreement with a noun or pronoun expressed or implied, is called the *circumstantial participle.* It may tell the *time*, *manner*, *means*, *cause*, *condition*, or *attendant circumstances* of an action.

φεύγοντες δια-βαίνομεν τὸν ποταμόν *in flight we cross the river;*
ἔχων χρήματα εἶχες ἂν φίλους *if you had money, you would have friends.*

117. Tenses of the Participle usually indicate time as *related* to that of the main verb:

φεύγων δια-βαίνει *while fleeing he crosses;*
φυγὼν δια-βαίνει *having fled he crosses.*

118. **VOCABULARY**

ἐλπίς, -ίδος, ἡ: *hope, expectation.*

κωλύω, κωλύσω, ἐκώλυσα: *prevent.* KOLYNOS.

λαμβάνω, ἔλαβον: *take, receive.* SYLLABLE. (Future, page 187.)

ὄνομα, -ατος, τό: *name.* ONOMATOPOETIC.

παρ-έχω, παρ-έξω, παρ-έσχον: *furnish, cause.*

πιστεύω, πιστεύσω, ἐπίστευσα: *trust,* with D.

τρέπω, τρέψω, ἔτρεψα: *turn.*

τρόπος, -ου, ὁ: *turn, "bent," manner, character.* TROPIC.

φυγάς, -άδος, ὁ: *exile, fugitive.* Cf. **φυγή.**

ὡς, conj. adv.: *as, as if, when.*

ELEUSIS

The Eleusinian Mysteries, unlike the ordinary Greek religion, gave hope of a real life after death. Cicero was initiated into these Mysteries.

119. **EXERCISES**

(*a*) Translate:

1. *λύσαντες δὲ τὴν γέφυραν πράγματα παρ-έξομεν ἐκείνῃ τῇ στρατιᾷ.* 2. *τοὺς δὲ παρ-όντας ἀπ-έπεμπεν ὡς φίλους*

ὄντας. 3. ἔχοντας οὖν χρήματα ἐκώλῡεν αὐτοὺς δι-αρπάζειν τὴν χώρᾱν. 4. ἡ δὲ βασίλεια χρήματα παρ-εῖχε τῷ Κύρῳ πιστεύουσα τοῖς τούτου τρόποις. 5. καὶ τοῖς φυγάσιν ἐλπίς ἐστιν. 6. τοὺς δὲ στρατιώτᾱς ἐκέλευεν τὰ ὅπλα λαβόντας παρ-εῖναι. 7. τῷ φεύγοντι ὄνομά ἐστι φυγάς. 8. ἀγορὰν δὲ παρ-έχων ἡμᾶς ἂν φίλους εἶχες.

(*b*) Complete:

1. οἱ διωκ— ἀπὸ τῶν φευγ— ἀπ-εῖχον ὀκτὼ σταδι—. 2. τρεψα— οὖν τοὺς πολεμίους σπεύσετε πρὸς τ— θαλαττ—. 3. τοῖς μὲν μεν— πιστεύσομεν, τοῖς δὲ ἐξ-ελαυν— οὔ. 4. οὗτος γὰρ λαβ— τὰ χρημα— ἤθροισε στρατιᾱ́ν.

TORCHES FROM ELEUSIS

Much of the ritual was performed by torchlight.

120. A TRAITOR CAUGHT

Ὀρόντᾱς ἐπι-βουλεύει Κύρῳ. οὗτος Κύρῳ εἶπεν (*told*) ὅτι (*that*) εἰ αὐτῷ δοίη (*should give*) στρατιώτᾱς κατα-κάνοι ἂν (*would slay*) τοὺς πολεμίους τοὺς τὴν χώρᾱν κάοντας (*burning*). τῷ δὲ Κύρῳ ἀκούσαντι (compare ACOUSTIC) ταῦτα ἐδόκει (*seemed*) καλὰ εἶναι, καὶ ἐκέλευσεν αὐτὸν λαμβάνειν στρατιώτᾱς. ὁ δ' Ὀρόντᾱς νομίσᾱς αὐτῷ εἶναι τοὺς στρατιώτᾱς γράφει ἐπιστολὴν παρὰ βασιλέᾱ (*king*) ὅτι ἥξοι (*he would come*) ἔχων στρατιώτᾱς. ταύτην τὴν ἐπιστολὴν δίδωσι (*he gives*) πιστῷ (compare **πιστεύω**) ἀνθρώπῳ, ὡς ᾤετο (*he thought*). ὁ δὲ λαβὼν Κύρῳ δίδωσιν.

Adapted from Xenophon, *Anabasis*, I. 6. 2–3.

LESSON XXII

πᾶς. READING

πάντων χρημάτων μέτρον ἄνθρωπος. — *Man is the measure of all things.*[1]

---

121. Inflection of πᾶς. πᾶς has the same endings as παύσᾱς. The genitive and dative plural of the masculine and neuter violate the rule for accent of monosyllables of the consonant declension (§ 102). The accent of the feminine is regular.

πᾶς *every, all*

πᾶς	πᾶσα	πᾶν	πάντες	πᾶσαι	πάντα
παντός	πάσης	παντός	πάντων	πᾱσῶν	πάντων
παντί	πάσῃ	παντί	πᾶσι(ν)	πάσαις	πᾶσι(ν)
πάντα	πᾶσαν	πᾶν	πάντας	πάσᾱς	πάντα

122. Uses of πᾶς. (*a*) πᾶς, when modifying a noun, usually has the predicate position (§ 31, *b*) and means *all*:

πᾶσαι αἱ ὁδοί *all the roads;*
πᾶσα ἡ ὁδός *all the road.*

(*b*) πᾶς in the attributive position (§ 31, *a*) means *the whole* (*the entire number* or *amount*):

ἡ πᾶσα ὁδός *the whole road, the entire road.*

(*c*) πᾶς without an article means *all* (conceivable) or *every*:

πᾶσαι ὁδοί *all roads;*
πᾶσα ὁδός *every road.*

---

[1] Protagoras.

123. EXERCISES

(*a*) Write in Greek:

Every bridge, the entire night, all the rulers, all spears, all the water.

(*b*) Write in Greek:

1. The hoplites will rout (*turn into flight*) the pursuers. 2. By destroying the seven boats they caused us trouble. 3. The exiles do not trust those who are remaining here. 4. Since we are hopeful (*having hope*) we intend to hasten to the camp.

THE GREAT GOD PAN

This uncouth deity of mountain and woodland was believed to have inspired the Persians with "panic" at Marathon and Salamis.

124. VOCABULARY

εἶτα, adv.: *then, next.*

οὕτω (before consonants), οὕτως (before vowels), adv.: *thus, so, as aforesaid.* Cf. **οὗτος.**

πᾶς, πᾶσα, πᾶν: sing., *every, whole;* pl., *all.* PANDEMONIUM.

πρῶτος, -η, -ον: *first;* πρῶτον, adv.: *at first.* PROTOTYPE.

φόβος, -ου, ὁ: *fear.* HYDROPHOBIA.

125. Precision of Thought. "The practice of translation, by making us deliberate in the choice of the best equivalent of a foreign word in our own language, has likewise the advantage of continually schooling us in one of the main elements of a good style, — precision; and precision of thought is not only exemplified by precision of language, but is largely dependent on the habit of it."[1]

[1] James Russell Lowell, *Address on Books and Libraries.*

126. **THE REVIEW OF AN ARMY**

ἐνταῦθα οὖν θεωρία (*review*) ἦν τῆς Κύρου στρατιᾶς.[1] καὶ πρῶτον μὲν παρ-ήλαυνον οἱ βάρβαροι. εἶτα δὲ τοὺς Ἕλληνας (compare Ἑλλάς) παρ-ήλαυνον ὁ Κῦρος ἐφ'[2] ἅρματος καί ἡ Κίλισσα ἐφ' ἁρμαμάξης (*carriage*). εἶχον δὲ πάντες ὅπλα καλά. παρ-ελάσας δὲ τούτους κήρυκα ἔπεμψε παρὰ τοὺς στρατηγοὺς τῶν Ἑλλήνων, ὃς ἐκέλευσεν αὐτοὺς ἐπι-χωρῆσαι (*advance*, trans.) πᾶσαν τὴν φάλαγγα. ἐκ δὲ τούτου οἱ στρατιῶται ἐλαύνοντες σὺν κραυγῇ ἀπὸ τοῦ αὐτομάτου (compare AUTOMATIC) ἔσπευσαν ἐπὶ τὰς σκηνάς, τοῖς δὲ βαρβάροις ἦν φόβος, ὥστε ἔφυγον καὶ ἡ Κίλισσα ἐπὶ τῆς ἁρμαμάξης καὶ οἱ ἐκ τῆς ἀγορᾶς τὰ χρήματα κατα-λιπόντες.[3] οὕτως οὖν οἱ Ἕλληνες σὺν γέλωτι (*laughter*) ἐπὶ τὰς σκηνὰς ἧκον.

Adapted from Xenophon, *Anabasis*, I. 2. 16–18.

---

[1] Objective genitive, being the *object* of the *action* involved in θεωρία.

[2] ἐπί. A word that suffers elision roughens its mute before a rough breathing.

[3] κατά in compound words often means *behind*.

A PANATHENAIC AMPHORA

LESSON XXIII

CONTRACT VERBS IN -έω

φιλεῖ δὲ τῷ κάμνοντι συσπεύδειν θεός. — *God helps him who helps himself.*[1]

127. Contract Verbs. (*a*) Two successive vowels are regularly contracted into one long vowel or diphthong :

ε + ω = ω ; ε + ο or ου = ου ; ε + ε = ει.

ε is always absorbed by a vowel or diphthong.

(*b*) If the first of the contracting syllables is accented, the resultant syllable receives a circumflex :

φιλέω, φιλῶ.

In other tenses than the present (and imperfect) the final ε of the stem is regularly lengthened to η :

φιλέω, φιλήσω, ἐφίλησα.

PRESENT INDICATIVE ACTIVE OF **φιλέω** *I love*

(φιλέ-ω)	φιλ **ῶ**	(φιλέ-ο-μεν)	φιλ **οῦμεν**
(φιλέ-εις)	φιλ **εῖς**	(φιλέ-ε-τε)	φιλ **εῖτε**
(φιλέ-ει)	φιλ **εῖ**	(φιλέ-ουσι)	φιλ **οῦσι(ν)**

IMPERFECT INDICATIVE ACTIVE OF **φιλέω**

(ἐφίλε-ο-ν)	ἐφίλ **ουν**	(ἐφιλέ-ο-μεν)	ἐφιλ **οῦμεν**
(ἐφίλε-ε-ς)	ἐφίλ **εις**	(ἐφιλέ-ε-τε)	ἐφιλ **εῖτε**
(ἐφίλε-ε)	ἐφίλ **ει**	(ἐφίλε-ο-ν)	ἐφίλ **ουν**

PRESENT INFINITIVE ACTIVE	(φιλέ-ειν)	φιλ **εῖν**
PRESENT PARTICIPLE ACTIVE	(φιλέ-ων)	φιλ **ῶν**
	(φιλέ-ουσα)	φιλ **οῦσα**
	(φιλέ-ον)	φιλ **οῦν**

In like manner inflect αἰτέω.

[1] Æschylus, fragment. Literally : *God loves to assist zealously the man who works.*

128. Genitive Absolute. A noun or pronoun in the genitive case with a circumstantial participle in agreement may stand grammatically independent of the rest of the sentence. This is called the *genitive absolute* and corresponds to the ablative absolute in Latin and the nominative independent (absolute) in English.

Like any other use of the circumstantial participle, the genitive absolute may express *time*, *cause*, and the like. It is usually best translated as a clause :

Κύρου κελεύσαντος ταῦτα ἐποίησαν *when Cyrus ordered, they did this ;*

τούτων πρᾶγματα παρ-εχόντων σπεύσομεν *if they cause trouble, we shall hasten ;*

τῶν φυλάκων διωκόντων ἔφυγεν *with the guards pursuing, he fled.*

129. VOCABULARY

ἀ-δικέω, ἀδικήσω, ἠδίκησα : *injure, wrong.*

αἰτέω, αἰτήσω, ᾔτησα : *ask for, demand.*

δή, post-pos. particle emphasizing preceding word : *now, then, accordingly, indeed*, etc. Often untranslated.

δοκέω, δόξω, ἔδοξα : *seem, seem best, think.* Often with inf. as subject. DOGMATIC.

καλέω,[1] καλῶ, ἐκάλεσα : *call, name.* CALENDAR.

ποιέω, ποιήσω, ἐποίησα : *make, do.* POET (**ποιητής**).

πολεμέω, πολεμήσω, ἐπολέμησα : *make war.* Cf. **πόλεμος.**

φιλέω, φιλήσω, ἐφίλησα : *love.* Cf. **φίλος.**

ὧδε, adv. : *thus, as follows.* Cf. **ὅδε.**

130. EXERCISES

(*a*) Translate :

1. *καὶ δὴ ταῦτα αἰτοῦντες ἀ-δικεῖτέ με.* 2. *οὐ γὰρ ἂν ἐπολέμουν αὐτῷ,*[2] *εἰ τὰ δίκαια ἐποίει.* 3. *πᾶσι τοῖς*

---

[1] The present and future of this verb are identical in form.

[2] Dative of Association (§ 236).

πολίταις ἐδόκει ὧδε πολεμεῖν. 4. πάντων τὰ αὐτὰ ποιούντων εἰς τὴν σκηνὴν τὸν ἄρχοντα ἐκάλει. 5. ἡμῖν δὴ ἔδοξε δόρατα αἰτεῖν. 6. ταύτης δὲ ἐπι-βουλὴν ὑπ-οπτευούσης οὐκ ἔστι φυγεῖν. 7. ἀγαθὸς γὰρ ὢν τοὺς ἀγαθοὺς φιλεῖς. 8. εἰ δὲ τὴν Ἑλλάδα ἐφιλεῖτε, τοῖς βαρβάροις[1] ἂν ἐπολεμεῖτε.

ORPHEUS AND EURYDICE

Love led Orpheus to seek Eurydice in Hades. On the way out, he turned to look at her too soon, and Hermes conducted her away.

(*b*) Complete:

1. φιλ—σα αὐτὸν ἡ βασίλεια οὐκ ἤθελεν ἀ-δικ—. 2. τούτου καλεσαντ— οἱ ὁπλῖται ἡκ— ἐπὶ τὴν οἰκίᾱν. 3. καὶ δὴ ταῦτα αἰτ— ἡμᾶς ἂν ἠ-δικ—ς.

(*c*) Write in Greek:

1. These (men) pillaged every house. 2. All the children wanted (*wished*) to ride to their friends' tents. 3. Along the entire Hellespont there is not a bridge. 4. First (of all) the foreigners marched by, then the others.

131. **HUMAN FRAILTY**

Πόθεν (*whence*) πόλεμοι καὶ πόθεν μάχαι ἐν ὑμῖν; οὐκ ἐντεῦθεν, ἐκ τῶν ἡδονῶν (*pleasures*) ὑμῶν . . . ; ἐπιθῡμεῖτε (*desire*), καὶ οὐκ ἔχετε· . . . μάχεσθε (*you fight*) καὶ πολεμεῖτε. . . . αἰτεῖτε καὶ οὐ λαμβάνετε, διότι (*because*) κακῶς[2] αἰτεῖσθε (= αἰτεῖτε) St. James, IV. 1–3.

[1] Dative of Association (§ 236). [2] Adverb.

THE ERECHTHEUM

On the spot where Athena contended with Poseidon for the guardianship of Athens, stands the most elegant of all Greek temples. Near one end grew the sacred olive of the goddess. Within the shrine was her ancient wooden image. Beneath the north porch are still shown the marks of Poseidon's trident. (See the pictures on page 334 and facing page 180.)

132. Word-formation. Verbs formed by adding **-έω** to noun (or adjective) stems denote action of a nature similar to that expressed by the noun (or adjective). They usually denote a *condition* or an *activity*:

φίλος *friend*, φιλέω *be a friend, love;*
πόλεμος *war*, πολεμέω *make war;*
ἄδικος *unjust*, ἀδικέω *be unjust, do wrong.*

This type of verb is to be found chiefly in connection with words of the **o**-declension.

A DETAIL FROM THE ERECHTHEUM

This honeysuckle pattern, justly famous for its exquisite workmanship, is an ever-recurring theme in the decoration of the temple.

LESSON XXIV

PRESENT AND IMPERFECT INDICATIVE, PRESENT INFINITIVE, AND PARTICIPLE OF παύω IN MIDDLE AND PASSIVE VOICE

ἀνάγκᾳ δ' οὐδὲ θεοὶ μάχονται. — *Not even gods fight against necessity.*[1]

133. Passive Voice. Like English and Latin, Greek has a *passive* voice, which shows the subject as *acted upon:*

παύομαι *I am being stopped.*

134. Middle Voice. Greek also has a *middle* voice, which shows that the subject so acts as *somehow to affect himself.*

(*a*) The subject may act *on himself:*

παύομαι *I am stopping myself, I am stopping* (intransitive).

(*b*) The subject may act *on* or *with something that belongs to him*, or in such a way as *to benefit, injure*, or *otherwise affect himself* or *his interests :*

παρέχομαι *I supply for myself;*
λύομαι τοὺς ἵππους *I loose my* (*own*) *horses.*

135. PRESENT INDICATIVE MIDDLE AND PASSIVE OF **παύω**

παύ-ο-μαι	παυ-ό-μεθα
(π α ύ - ε-σαι) παύ-ει	παύ-ε-σθε
παύ-ε-ται	παύ-ο-νται

136. IMPERFECT INDICATIVE MIDDLE AND PASSIVE OF **παύω**

ἐ-παυ-ό-μην	ἐ-παυ-ό-μεθα
(ἐ - π α ύ - ε-σο) ἐ-παύ-ου	ἐ-παύ-ε-σθε
ἐ-παύ-ε-το	ἐ-παύ-ο-ντο

PRESENT INFINITIVE MIDDLE AND PASSIVE παύ-ε-σθαι
PRESENT PARTICIPLE MIDDLE AND PASSIVE παυ-ό-μενος, -η, -ον

[1] Simonides.

137. There is no difference in appearance between the middle and the passive in the present and imperfect. As in the active voice, the vowel **ο** appears before **μ** or **ν** of the ending, while **ε** appears before other endings. The **σ** of the second person singular drops out between two vowels, which are then contracted.

The present and imperfect middle and passive have the same stem as the present active.

138. Deponent Verbs. Some verbs have forms only in the middle or passive voice but with active meanings. They are called *deponents* :

ἕπομαι *I follow.*

Inflect the present and imperfect indicative, and give the present infinitive and participle of **πορεύομαι.**

139. Genitive of Agent. ὑπό and the genitive when modifying a passive verb indicate the *agent* or *doer* of an action (compare with the Latin *a* or *ab* and the ablative):[1]

ἀθροίζεται ὑπὸ αὐτοῦ *it is being gathered by him.*

140. VOCABULARY

ἄχθομαι: *be burdened, vexed.*
βούλομαι: *wish, desire.*
ἕπομαι: *follow*, with D.
ἔρχομαι, ἦλθον (aor.): *come, go.*
ἥδομαι; *be pleased.* HEDONIST.
μάχομαι: *fight, give battle.* Cf. **μάχη.**
μετά, prep.: with G., *with*; with A., *after*; as a prefix, often denotes *change.* METAPHOR.
μετα-πέμπομαι: *send after, summon.*
πορείᾱ, -ᾱς, ἡ: *journey.*
πορεύομαι: *journey, march.*
ὑπό, prep.: with G., *from under, by* (agent); with D., *under, beneath* (with verbs of *rest*); with A., *under* (with verbs of *motion*). HYPOTHESIS.

[1] What uses of the genitive have you now had?

141. EXERCISES

(*a*) What do the portions in heavy type tell as to person, number, and voice?

βούλ **ει**	πέμπο **μεν**	ἕπε **σθε**	πορευό **μεθα**
φυλάττ **ουσι**	μεταπέμπε **ται**	ἔρχο **νται**	διώκ **ω**
συμβουλεύ **εις**	ἄχθο **μαι**	ἐμάχο **ντο**	ἔχε **τε**
ὑποπτεύ **ει**	ἡδό **μην**	ἤχθ **ου**	εἵπε **το**

(*b*) What is the probable meaning of the middle of the following verbs?

βουλεύω   φυλάττω   παρ-έχω   συμ-βουλεύω   τρέπω

(*c*) Translate:

1. τότε δὴ ἤχθοντο τῇ πορείᾳ. 2. τὰ δ' ἐπιτήδεια ὑπὸ τῶν πορευομένων ἀθροίζεται. 3. χρήματα οὖν ἔχοντες τὸν σῖτον παρ-εσχόμεθα. 4. οὐ γὰρ τῷ ἀγγέλῳ ἐπείθεσθε;[1] 5. ἐβούλετο μετὰ τῶν ἄλλων ἔρχεσθαι. 6. μετὰ ταῦτα οἱ φίλοι αὐτῷ εἵποντο[2] τῷ δώρῳ ἡδόμενοι. 7. πάντες μετα-πέμπονται ὑπὸ τοῦ σατράπου. 8. ἀλλ' οὐ βούλομαι τοῖς ἐμαυτοῦ φίλοις[3] μάχεσθαι. 9. τοῖς μὲν οὖν πειθομένοις ἥδεται, τοὺς δὲ μὴ[4] μετα-πέμπεται.

(*d*) Complete:

1. οἱ μὲν ἐπορευ— μετὰ τ— ἀρχοντ— (singular), οἱ δὲ ἐμεν— ἐν τῷ στρατοπέδῳ. 2. τῷ βουλο— ἔξ-εστιν Ἀθήνᾱς ἐκ-λιπεῖν. 3. οἱ πολῖται τοῖς μαχομεν— ἤχθοντο.

(*e*) Write in Greek:

1. If it did not seem best to have it, we should not be asking for it. 2. Since there was hope (*there being hope*), the general was making war on the Thracians. 3. The enemy

---

[1] πείθω in the middle and passive means *obey* and governs the dative (as in Latin).

[2] For augment, see page 23, note 1. [3] Page 72, note 2.

[4] § 84. πειθομένους is to be supplied and is conditional.

seized him as he was hastening to this place. 4. All being present, Cyrus himself called the messenger into the tent.

142. A HEAVY SNOWFALL

στρατοπεδευομένων (compare **στρατόπεδον**) *δ' αὐτῶν ἐν τῇ χώρᾳ ἦν τῆς νυκτὸς χιὼν* (*snow*) *πολλή* (*much, heavy*), *ὥστε ἀπ-έκρυψε* (compare CRYPTIC) *καὶ τὰ ὅπλα καὶ τοὺς ἀνθρώπους κατα-κειμένους* (*lying down*)· *καὶ ἡ χιὼν συν-επόδισεν* (*impeded*) *τοὺς ἵππους.*

Adapted from Xenophon, *Anabasis*, IV. 4. 11.

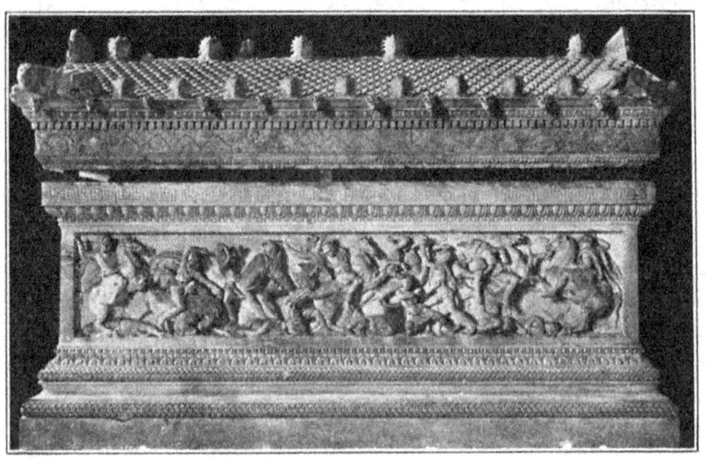

THE ALEXANDER SARCOPHAGUS

This beautiful coffin, now in Constantinople, may never have held the bones of the conqueror of the world, but he is depicted on it in battle.

LESSON XXV

MIDDLE AND PASSIVE OF VERBS IN -έω

ἄρχε πρῶτον μαθὼν ἄρχεσθαι. — *He who rules must first obey.*[1]

143. Contract Verbs. The principles already learned (§ 127) as to the contraction and accent of **φιλέω** in the present and imperfect active apply to its inflection in the middle and passive.

Write out the inflection of the present and imperfect indicative middle and passive of **φιλέω.** Give the present infinitive and participle middle and passive. Compare with paradigms (§ 534).

144. Temporal Clauses. (*a*) ἐπεί and ἐπειδή followed by an imperfect or aorist indicative often mean *when* and refer to a definite act or situation in past time :

ἐπεὶ ἦλθον ἐπὶ τὴν κώμην, αὐτὴν δι-ήρπασαν *when they came to the village, they pillaged it.*

(*b*) ἐπεί and ἐπειδή followed by any tense of the indicative may mean *because* or *since:*

ἐπεὶ δοκεῖ, ταῦτα ποιήσω *since it seems best, I shall do this.*

(*c*) πρίν accompanied by an *imperfect* or *aorist indicative* is usually translated *until.* It is so used only when the main clause contains a negative :

οὐ ταῦτα ἐποίησα πρὶν ἦλθεν *I did not do this until he came.*

[1] Solon, as quoted by Diogenes Laertius, I. 60. Literally: *Rule after having first learned to be ruled.*

(*d*) πρίν accompanied by an *infinitive* can only mean *before*, in which case there will be no negative in the main clause :

ἦλθε πρὶν αὐτοὺς ταῦτα ποιῆσαι *he came before they did this.*

145. **VOCABULARY**

αἱρέω, αἱρήσω, εἷλον: *take, seize, capture;* mid., *take for yourself, choose.* HERESY.

ἁλίσκομαι, ἁλώσομαι[1]: *be taken, be captured.* Frequently used as passive of αἱρέω.

ἀνά, prep. with A. only: *up, up along, up through;* as prefix, sometimes *back* or *according to.* ANABASIS, ANALOGY.

ἀφ-ικνέομαι, -ίξομαι, -ῑκόμην[1]: *reach, arrive.*

δεσπότης, -ου, ὁ: *master.* DESPOT.

ἐπεί, conj.: *when, because, since.*

ἐπειδή, conj.: *when, because, since.*

ἐπι-μελέομαι, -μελήσομαι[1]: *take care of, care for;* with G. or object clause.

ἡγέομαι, ἡγήσομαι, ἡγησάμην[1]: with G., *be leader of:* with D., *be leader for;* also with inf., *believe.* Cf. Lat. *duco.* HEGEMONY.

μόνος, -η, -ον: *only, sole.* Cf. μένω. MONOLOGUE.

περί, prep.: with G., *about, concerning, for;* with A., *about, around, near.* PERISCOPE.

πρίν, conj.: with ind., *until;* with inf., *before.*

146. **EXERCISES**

(*a*) Translate:

1. *καὶ δὴ ἄλλους στρατηγοὺς αἱροῦνται πρὶν ἐπὶ τὴν θάλατταν ἀφ-ικνεῖσθαι.* 2. *διὰ φιλίᾱς χώρᾱς ὑμῖν ἡγούμεθα, ἐπεὶ βούλεσθε σπεύδειν.* 3. *οὗτος ὁ στρατηγὸς μόνος πάντων τῶν στρατιωτῶν ἐπι-μελεῖται.* 4. *ἀλλ᾽ οὐκ ἐπολέμουν πρὶν πᾶσιν ἔδοξεν.* 5. *πρὶν εἰς τὸ στρατόπεδον φυγεῖν, ὑπὸ τῶν βαρβάρων ἡλίσκοντο.* 6. *ἐπεὶ ἀνὰ χώρᾱν πολεμίᾱν πορευόμεθα, αἱρούμεθα τούτους τοὺς ἄρχοντας.* 7. *οὕτως οὖν τῶν ἵππων ἐπι-μελούμενοι πρὸς τοὺς φίλους*

[1] Future and aorist middle are presented in the next lesson, at which time the forms will be more intelligible. They are given now for convenience.

ἦλθον. 8. ἀλλ' ἐπειδὴ ταῦθ' αἱρεῖσθε, ὑμῖν εἰς τὴν Ἑλλάδα ἡγοῦμαι.

(*b*) Complete:

1. οἱ ἐν τῇ κώμῃ ἥδοντο πρὶν τὸν δεσποτ— ἐλθ—. 2. πάντων τῶν σὺν αὐτῷ οὕτως ἐπι-μελ—ται ὥστε αὐτῷ —— (linking verb) φίλους. 3. ἐπεὶ ὁ σατράπης ἀνὰ τ— στρατοπεδ— ἦλθεν, ᾔτησε καὶ στρατιώτᾱς καὶ ἵππους. 4. περὶ τουτ— ὁ δεσποτ— λόγους ἐποι—το ὧδε.

καλαὶ αἱ ὀρχούμεναι

(*c*) Write in Greek:

1. You are being summoned by the boy. 2. Cyrus is coming with all his soldiers. 3. Does he want (*wish*) to give battle to those (who are) following? 4. Being vexed by the journey they stopped at that village for five days. 5. He stayed there under guard of (*being guarded by*) the hoplites.

147. A WISE CAMEL

κάμηλος κελευομένη ὑπὸ τοῦ δεσπότου ὀρχεῖσθαι (*dance*) ἔφη (*said*). 'Αλλ'[1] οὐ μόνον[2] ὀρχουμένη εἰμὶ ἄ-σχημος (*ungainly*), ἀλλὰ καὶ περι-πατοῦσα (*walking around*).

Adapted from Æsop, 182.

[1] Capital A indicates a direct quotation. [2] Adverb.

LESSON XXVI

FUTURE AND AORIST MIDDLE

χαλεπὸν τὸ ποιεῖν, τὸ δὲ κελεῦσαι ῥᾴδιον.
Commanding is easy, but performance is hard.[1]

---

148. The future middle uses the stem of the future active, but it has the same endings as the present middle.

FUTURE INDICATIVE MIDDLE OF **παύω** *I stop*

παύ-σο-μαι	παυ-σό-μεθα
(παύ-σε-σαι) παύσ-ει	παύ-σε-σθε
παύ-σε-ται	παύ-σο-νται

FUTURE INFINITIVE MIDDLE παύ-σε-σθαι

FUTURE PARTICIPLE MIDDLE παυ-σό-μενος, -η, -ον

In like manner inflect πέμπω, ἄγω, and πείθω (§ 49).

149. ἔσομαι, the future of εἰμί, is inflected like παύσομαι except in the third person singular of the indicative, where the variable vowel **ε** is wanting.

Write out the future indicative, infinitive, and participle of εἰμί. Compare with paradigm (§ 538).

150. The aorist middle uses the stem of the aorist active but it has the same endings as the imperfect middle. In the second person singular, as in the imperfect, the **σ** of the ending drops out between two vowels, **α + ο** becoming **ω** and **ε + ο** becoming **ου**.

---

[1] Philemon, fragment. Literally: *To do is hard, but to order is easy.*

151. First Aorist Indicative Middle of **παύω** *I stop*

ἐ-παυ-σά-μην	ἐ-παυ-σά-μεθα
(ἐ-παύ-σα-σο) ἐ-παύσ-ω	ἐ-παύ-σα-σθε
ἐ-παύ-σα-το	ἐ-παύ-σα-ντο

First Aorist Infinitive Middle παύ-σα-σθαι

First Aorist Participle Middle παυ-σά-μενος, -η, -ον

152. Second Aorist Indicative Middle of **λείπω** *I leave*

ἐ-λιπ-ό-μην	ἐ-λιπ-ό-μεθα
(ἐ-λίπ-ε-σο) ἐ-λίπ-ου	ἐ-λίπ-ε-σθε
ἐ-λίπ-ε-το	ἐ-λίπ-ο-ντο

Second Aorist Infinitive Middle λιπ-έ-σθαι[1]

Second Aorist Participle Middle λιπ-ό-μενος, -η, -ον

In like manner inflect πέμπω, διώκω, πείθω, ἀφ-ικνέομαι (§ 55).

153. Principal Parts of a Verb. Note that the first principal part gives the stem on which are built all forms of the present and imperfect; the second gives the stem for all forms of the future active and middle; the third gives the stem for all forms of the aorist active and middle. Consult *Grammatical Appendix* (§ 548) for further illustration of the function of the principal parts.

154. Future Participle of Purpose. The future participle expresses *purpose*, especially with verbs implying motion. This is another use of the circumstantial participle:

> ἔπεμψε στρατιώτᾱς ἀθροίσοντας τὰ ἐπιτήδεια *he sent soldiers to gather provisions.*

---

[1] The second aorist infinitive middle is always accented on the penult.

155. VOCABULARY

γίγνομαι, γενήσομαι, ἐγενόμην: *become, be born, be, prove to be,* etc. GENESIS.

δεξιός, -ά, -όν: *right, right-hand, clever;* ἡ δεξιά: *the right.* Lat. *dexter.*

δέχομαι, δέξομαι, ἐδεξάμην: *accept, await, receive.*

εἰμί, ἔσομαι: *be.*

ἕπομαι, ἕψομαι, ἑσπόμην: *follow,* with D.

θῡμός, -οῦ, ὁ: *spirit, temper, mind.*

ἱκανός, -ή, -όν: *sufficient, able, capable.*

νέος, -ᾱ, -ον: *new, young, fresh.* Lat. *novus.* NEOPHYTE.

ὀλίγος, -η, -ον: *little, few.* OLIGARCHY.

ὁμο-λογέω, -ήσω, ὡμο-λόγησα: *say the same thing, agree.* HOMOLOGOUS.

παρα-σκευάζω, -άσω, παρ-εσκεύασα: *prepare;* mid., *prepare oneself* or *for oneself.*

πρό-θῡμος, -ον [1]: *eager, ready.*

ὑπ-ισχνέομαι, ὑπο-σχήσομαι, ὑπ-εσχόμην: *undertake, promise.*

χαλεπός, -ή, -όν: *hard, severe.*

156. EXERCISES

(*a*) Translate:

1. *οἱ δὲ φύλακες ἱκανοὶ ἔσονται δέξασθαι τοὺς πολεμίους.* 2. *ὀλίγοι ὑπ-έσχοντο αὐτῷ ἕπεσθαι.* 3. *οὐ γὰρ χαλεπὸν ἔσται παρα-σκευάσασθαι τὴν οἰκίᾱν.* 4. *οἱ νέοι παρεσκευάσαντο ὡς τῷ δεσπότῃ ἑψόμενοι.* 5. *ἐντεῦθεν τῇ στρατιᾷ ἡγεῖτο τὸν ποταμὸν ἐν δεξιᾷ ἔχων.* 6. *ἐπειδὴ οὖν ὑμεῖς ἀγαθοὶ ἐγένεσθε, πρό-θῡμος ἐγὼ ἔσομαι οὐ μόνον δῶρα παρ-έχειν ἀλλὰ καὶ φίλους ὑμᾶς δέχεσθαι.* 7. *ὑπὸ πάντων δὴ ἀγαθὸς εἶναι ὡμο-λογεῖτο.*

(*b*) Complete:

1. *ἀγγέλους δ' οὖν πέμπει ἄξοντ— τὰς ἁμάξᾱς.* 2. *εἰ μὴ ἀφ-ίκεσθε, ὀλίγοι ἂν ἐνομισ— ὑμᾶς γεν— προ-θύμους.* 3. *ἐπεὶ ἐγεν— ἡ νύξ, ὀλιγ—* (indicate possession) *ἦν θῡμὸς ἕπεσθαι.* 4. *καὶ ἑλ— ἄρχοντα πάντες οἱ πολῖται ἐβούλοντο μένειν.*

---

[1] For inflection, see page 44, note 2.

(*c*) Write in Greek:

1. Before the master came, the guards took care of the fugitives. 2. When the spears were being taken, the men about us fled. 3. He was not willing to be their leader (*to be leader of them*), until the citizens persuaded him. 4. Since they are being captured, we think it best (*it seems best*) to choose other commanders.

157. DRAMATIS PERSONÆ

Δᾱρείου καὶ Παρυσάτιδος γίγνονται παῖδες δύο (Latin *duo*), *πρεσβύτερος* (*elder*, compare PRESBYTERY) *μὲν Ἀρτα-*

BOYS WILL BE BOYS

Hardly any sport or amusement known to-day is without its parallel in ancient Greece. Boys often took their pets to school with them.

ξέρξης, νεώτερος δὲ Κῦρος· ἐπεὶ δὲ ἠσθένει (*was ill*) *Δᾱρεῖος καὶ ὑπ-ώπτευε τελευτὴν* (*end*) *τοῦ βίου* (compare BIOLOGY), *ἐβούλετο αὐτοὺς παρ-εῖναι. ὁ μὲν οὖν πρεσβύτερος παρ-ῆν· Κῦρον δὲ μετα-πέμπεται ἀπὸ τῆς ἀρχῆς ἧς αὐτὸν σατράπην ἐποίησεν. καὶ δὴ καὶ στρατηγὸς ἦν πάντων τῶν εἰς Καστωλοῦ πεδίον ἀθροιζομένων.*

Adapted from Xenophon, *Anabasis*, I. 1. 1–2.

LESSON XXVII

REVIEW

δὶς ἐξαμαρτεῖν ταὐτὸν οὐκ ἀνδρὸς σοφοῦ.
To make the same slip twice is not (the part) of a wise man.[1]

158. **ASSIGNMENTS**

(*a*) Review Vocabulary IV, page 331, following the method indicated in § 27, *a*. Give for each verb such of the principal parts as have been presented.

(*b*) Name and define the Greek words suggested by these English derivatives: *anonymous*, *panacea*, *Anglophobia*, *trope*, *protagonist*, *pantheist*, *dogma*, *poem*, *protoplasm*, *orthodoxy*, *metabolism*, *analyze*, *monograph*, *poetic*, *metathesis*, *hypodermic*, *perimeter*, *eugenic*, *heretic*, *despotic*, *monarch*, *oligarch*, *heliotrope*, *paradox*.

(*c*) Add ten other derivatives to this group.

(*d*) Point out in the following words the clues to mood, tense, voice, person, and number:

δέξονται, γενέσθαι, φιλήσων, ἀφ-ιξόμενος, διῶξαι, ἐπεισάμην, ἐποιεῖτο, σπεύδομεν, ἐλάβετε, ὑπ-ισχνούμεθα, ᾔτουν, ἀθροίζομαι, μάχεσθε, ἐγένου, ἄγοντος.

(*e*) Give the third person singular of the present, imperfect, future, and aorist indicative active and middle of πέμπω, ἄγω, ἀθροίζω. Give the corresponding infinitives.

(*f*) Inflect the future and aorist active participles of πείθω.

[1] Menander, fragment.

(*g*) What vowels or diphthongs are contracted with **ε** to give **ου, ει, ω**? with **α** to give **ω**?

(*h*) Explain and illustrate the difference between attributive and circumstantial participles.

159. **EXERCISES**

(*a*) Complete:

1. *ἐχ— τὸ δόρυ ἐν τῇ δεξιᾷ ὁ ὁπλί̄της ἐπορευ— τὴν πᾶσ— ἡμέραν.* 2. *ἡμ— ἐστιν ἐλπὶς τοὺς φυγάδας ἀφ-ιξ— παρὰ τοὺς φίλους.* 3. *ὑπ-ώπτευσε τοὺς πολί̄τᾱς βουλ— ἑλ— ἄλλον ἄρχοντα.* 4. *ἀνὰ χωρ— φιλι— Ξενίας ἔπεμψ— ἀγγέλους ἀθροι— καὶ ἵππους καὶ ὅπλα.* 5. *ὑπὸ παντ— καλὸς εἶναι ὡμολογ—το.* 6. *τ— νυκτ— γενομεν— οἱ νέοι ἀφ-ῑκ— εἰς τὸ στρατόπεδον.* 7. *οἱ ἄρχοντας ἑλόμενοι μόνοι ἱκανοὶ* —— (*will be*) *μαχ—.* 8. *ταῦτα ὑπ-έσχετο πρὶν τοὺς πολεμίους πρᾱ́γματα παρα-σχ—.*

"Artemis" of Gabii
Many Greek statues exist only in Roman copies. The tree trunk often serves as a clue.

(*b*) Write in Greek:

1. He will not be able to receive the young men. 2. They are preparing (themselves) as if to march. 3. The general led them up through the plain (with) the enemy following. 4. There were few who were willing to promise this. 5. His fear did not cease until he reached Greece. 6. The guards prevented the pillagers from seizing the women and the children. 7. The exiles will arrive during the night.

LESSON XXVIII

WORD STUDY. READING

μέτρον ἄριστον. — Moderation is best.[1]

160. Common Sense in Translation. In learning to read our own language, we did not find it necessary to consult the dictionary for every new word. Had we done so, reading would have been an awful bore. The same is true of reading Greek. The meaning of the new word is often made unmistakable by the context.

Besides, words are likely to belong to "families." The vocabularies in this book have been so constructed as to stress that fact. We should cultivate the habit of recognizing family traits. For example, in the passage that you are about to read occur the two words *αὐλητὴν* (*αὐλητοῦ*) and *αὐλῆσαι*. Neither is important enough to deserve a place in a lesson vocabulary, and so the meaning of the former is supplied in the text. You should easily catch the family likeness to *αὐλῆσαι* and, recognizing the latter as manifestly an aorist active infinitive, arrive at the correct interpretation.

Not infrequently there exist related words in English. If we are wide awake, we may discover them for ourselves. But often such words are printed in parentheses as helps to translation (for example, MELODY).

The recognition of English derivatives is helpful also not only as a means of remembering the parent word in Greek

[1] Cleobulus, as quoted by Diogenes Laertius, I. 93.

but as shedding light upon the true meaning of the English word itself (for example, SCHEME).

If these hints are followed, translation will consume less time and produce more profit and enjoyment. There is a thrill in realizing that we are growing in the power to stand alone. Of course we must constantly ask ourselves, "Have I made sense without doing violence to words or inflections, and does my translation fit the passage?"

161. **VOCABULARY**

δεύτερος, -ᾱ, -ον : *second.* DEUTERONOMY.
ἔτι, adv. : *still, longer, yet.*
καλῶς, adv. : *well.* Cf. **καλός.**
κεφαλή, -ῆς, ἡ : *head.* CEPHALIC.
οὐκ-έτι, adv. : *not longer, no longer, never again.*
τράπεζα, -ης, ἡ : *table.* TRAPEZOID.
τρί-τος, -η, -ον : *third.* TRISYLLABIC.
ὦ, interj. : *O*, often preceding the name of the person addressed.

162. **Οὐ φροντὶς Ἱπποκλείδῃ**[1]

Scene: the banquet hall of Cleisthenes, tyrant of Sicyon. *Dramatis Personæ:* King Cleisthenes; Hippocleides, an Athenian dandy, favored suitor for the hand of the princess; other suitors, musicians, dancers, attendants. *Time:* about 575 B.C.

ὁ δὲ Ἱπποκλείδης ἐκέλευσε τὸν αὐλητὴν (*piper*) *αὐλῆσαι ἐμ-μέλειαν* (compare MELODY). *πειθομένου δὲ τοῦ αὐλητοῦ ὠρχεῖτο* (*danced*), *ὡς μὲν αὐτῷ ἐδόκει, καλῶς, ὁ δὲ Κλεισθένης πᾶν τὸ πρᾶγμα ὑπ-ώπτευεν. μετ' ὀλίγον δὲ ὁ Ἱπποκλείδης τράπεζαν μετ-επέμψατο, εἰσ-ελθούσης δὲ τῆς τραπέζης πρῶτον μὲν ἐπ' αὐτῆς ὠρχήσατο Λακωνικὰ σχημάτια* (*figures*, compare SCHEME), *εἶτα δὲ ἄλλα Ἀττικά, τὸ δὲ τρίτον* (adverbial) *τὴν κεφαλὴν ἐρείσᾱς* (*bracing*) *ἐπὶ τὴν τράπεζαν τοῖς σκέλεσι* (compare ISOSCELES) *ἐχειρο-νόμει* (*gesticulated*). *Κλεισθένης*

---

[1] This phrase became proverbial among the Athenians.

δὲ τοῖς μὲν πρώτοις καὶ τοῖς δευτέροις σχηματίοις ἀχθόμενος καὶ οὐκέτι βουλόμενος ἐκεῖνον γαμβρὸν (*son-in-law*) γενέσθαι διὰ τὴν ὄρχησιν καὶ τὴν ἀν-αιδείᾱν (*shamelessness*) ἐπ-εῖχεν (*waited*), οὐ βουλόμενος χαλεπὸς εἶναι πρὸς αὐτόν· ἐκείνου δὲ τοῖς σκέλεσι χειρο-νομήσαντος ἔφη· Ὦ παῖ[1] Τισάνδρου, ἀπ-ωρχήσω τὸν γάμον (*marriage*). ὁ δὲ Ἱπποκλείδης ἔφη· Οὐ φροντὶς (*care*) Ἱπποκλείδῃ.[2]

Adapted from Herodotus, VI. 129.

163. Word-formation. Words often change their meaning as they pass down the ages. The Greek ὀρχέομαι meant *I dance.* Its derivative ὀρχήστρᾱ meant *a dancing-place.* This then came to be applied to that part of the theater in which the chorus of the Greek drama went through its dances.

ORCHESTRA CHAIRS AT ATHENS

The space given over to this dancing was flat and circular, or nearly so. It had a σκηνή,[3] *a dressing-booth,* behind it and was surrounded elsewhere by rows of seats for spectators.

In Roman days the orchestra no longer suggested dancing, being occupied by the seats of the wealthy. It has a similar meaning to-day, but at times it refers to the place immediately in front of the stage occupied by the musicians. Most frequently it denotes such a group of musicians, no matter where they may be.

[1] As shown by ὦ and the general sense, παῖ is a vocative form of παῖς. As in Latin, the vocative is the case of direct address.

[2] Supply ἐστί.

[3] § 35.

LESSON XXIX

INTERROGATIVE AND INDEFINITE PRONOUNS

γηράσκω δ' ἀεὶ πολλὰ διδασκόμενος.
The older I grow, the more I learn.[1]

164. The chief interrogative pronoun is τίς, τί *who, what?* Except for the alternative forms τοῦ and τῷ, it always has an acute on the first syllable. This never changes to a grave in the monosyllabic forms.

τίς *who, what?*

(m. and f.)	(n.)	(m. and f.)	(n.)
τίς	τί	τίνες	τίνα
τίνος, τοῦ	τίνος, τοῦ	τίνων	τίνων
τίνι, τῷ	τίνι, τῷ	τίσι(ν)	τίσι(ν)
τίνα	τί	τίνας	τίνα

165. The indefinite pronoun τις, τι *some, any* is the same as τίς, τί in form but is always enclitic (§ 95).

Write out the inflection of τις, τι. Compare with paradigm (§ 524).

166. Write with proper accents:

τινες ἐστε ; τις ἐστιν ; ὁπλῖτᾱς τινας, κωμη τις, ἀγγελοι τινες, δωρον τι, δωρα τινα, ἁμαξων τινων.

167. The indefinite relative pronoun ὅστις, ἥτις, ὅ τι *whoever, whatever* is formed by combining the relative ὅς (§ 67) and the indefinite τις, each part being inflected. An exception appears in the alternative forms of the masculine and neuter genitive and dative singular ὅτου and

[1] Solon. Literally: *I grow old ever learning many things.*

ὅτῳ. In the neuter nominative and accusative singular ὅ τι is printed as two words to distinguish it from ὅτι (*that, since, because*). The accent of ὅς prevails, the τις being enclitic.

Write out the inflection of ὅστις, ἥτις, ὅ τι. Compare with paradigm (§ 525).

168. Note the following relationships in form and meaning. They will be helpful when other words of a similar nature appear.

INTERROGATIVE	INDEFINITE	INDEFINITE RELATIVE OR INDIRECT INTERROGATIVE
τίς (*who?*)	τις (*some one*)	ὅστις (*whoever*)
πότε (*when?*)	ποτέ ("*somewhen*," *once*)	ὁπότε (*whenever*)
ποῦ (*where?*)	που (*somewhere*)	ὅπου (*wherever*)
πῶς (*how?*)	πως (*somehow*)	ὅπως (*how*)

Where do πόσος and ὁπόσος fit in such a scheme?

169. **VOCABULARY**[1]

ἀεί, adv.: *always, ever.*

νῦν, adv.: *now.* Lat. *nunc.*

πόσος, -η, -ον, inter. adj.: *how large;* pl., *how many?*

ὁπόσος, indef. rel. adj.: *as much as;* pl., *as many as.*

πότε, inter. adv.: *when?*

ποτέ,[2] indef. adv.: "*somewhen*," *once.*

ὁπότε, indef. rel. adv.: *whenever.*

ποῦ, inter. adv.: *where?*

που, indef. adv.: *somewhere.*

ὅπου, indef. rel. adv.: *where, wherever.*

πῶς, inter. adv.: *how?*

πως, indef. adv.: *somehow, in any way.*

ὅπως, indef. rel. adv.: *how, that.*

τίς, τί, inter. pron.: *who, what?*

τί, sometimes = *why?*

τις, τι, indef. pron.: *some, any.*

ὅστις, ἥτις, ὅ τι, indef. rel. pron.: *whoever, whichever, whatever.*

χρόνος, -ου, ὁ: *time.* CHRONOMETER

[1] Not all the words in this vocabulary will be used in the lesson, but because of their interrelation it seems wise to group them here.

[2] Enclitic.

170. **EXERCISE**

Translate:

1. τίνες τὰς σκηνὰς δι-ήρπασαν; 2. ταῦτα νῦν φᾱσί τινες ἐκεῖνον παρὰ τοῦ ἀδελφοῦ λαβεῖν. 3. τί ταῦτα ὑπ-έσχου; 4. εἴ τι ἐκέλευον, ἄγγελον ἂν ὑμῖν ἔπεμπον. 5. πότε γενήσεται ἡ μάχη; 6. καὶ δή ποτε διὰ τοῦ πεδίου πορευόμενος εἰς κώμην τινὰ ἦλθεν ἐν ᾗ οὐκ ἦν ὕδωρ. 7. πόσους ἵππους καὶ παρὰ τίνος ἀθροίσεις; 8. ὑπ-ωπτεύομεν γάρ που βαρβάρους τινὰς ἡμῖν ἕπεσθαι. 9. καί ποτε λόγοι ἐγένοντο περὶ τῆς πορείᾱς.

SOPHOCLES

171. **TIME THE HEALER**

πάντων ἰᾱτρὸς (*healer*) τῶν ἀναγκαίων (*necessary*) κακῶν χρόνος ἐστίν. οὗτος καὶ σὲ νῦν ἰάσεται.

Menander, fragment.

172. **THE KEYNOTE OF GREEK GENIUS**

Ὦ Σόλων, Σόλων, Ἕλληνες ἀεὶ παῖδές ἐστε, γέρων δὲ Ἕλλην οὐκ ἔστιν. νέοι γάρ ἐστε τὰς ψῡχὰς [1] (*spirit*) πάντες.

Plato, *Timæus*, 22 B.

The Greeks were notably long-lived, but intellectual interest and activity kept them from going to seed with advancing years. Socrates was in his prime at seventy. Sophocles lived to be ninety and was producing masterpieces to the very end of his career.

---

[1] Accusative of specification.

LESSON XXX

SUBJUNCTIVE ACTIVE

ῥᾷον παραινεῖν ἢ παθόντα καρτερεῖν.
'Tis easier to give advice than to bear one's own ills.[1]

173. The **subjunctive** in all its tenses and voices uses the same endings as the present indicative. Its variable vowel is **ω** before **μ** or **ν**, elsewhere **η**.

174. The subjunctive uses the same stem as the corresponding tense and voice of the indicative.

PRESENT SUBJUNCTIVE ACTIVE

εἰμί	*I am*	**παύω**	*I stop*
ὦ	ὦμεν	παύ-ω	παύ-ωμεν
ᾖς	ἦτε	παύ-ῃς	παύ-ητε
ᾖ	ὦσι(ν)	παύ-ῃ	παύ-ωσι(ν)

AORIST SUBJUNCTIVE ACTIVE

παύω	*I stop*	**λείπω**	*I leave*
παύσ-ω	παύσ-ωμεν	λίπ-ω	λίπ-ωμεν
παύσ-ῃς	παύσ-ητε	λίπ-ῃς	λίπ-ητε
παύσ-ῃ	παύσ-ωσι(ν)	λίπ-ῃ	λίπ-ωσι(ν)

Inflect the present and aorist subjunctive active of πέμπω, ἄγω,[2] πείθω.

175. Contract Verbs in **-εω** have the **ε** absorbed before the long vowels **ω** and **η** (§ 127, *a*). The accent follows the principles laid down in § 127, *b*. Except for accent, **φιλέω** is like **παύω** in the present subjunctive active.

Write out the inflection of the present subjunctive active of **φιλέω**. Compare with paradigm (§ 534).

[1] Euripides, *Alcestis*, 1078. Literally: (*It is*) *easier to advise than having suffered to endure.*

[2] Consult *General Vocabulary*.

176. Uses of the Subjunctive. (*a*) The subjunctive as the main verb and in the first person (generally plural) denotes *exhortation.*

This independent usage always refers to *future* time. Present and aorist differ in that the present denotes *continued* or *repeated action* (motion picture), while the aorist denotes *simple occurrence* (snapshot):

παύωμεν *let us be stopping;*
παύσωμεν *let us stop.*

The negative is μή.

(*b*) ἵνα (ὡς or ὅπως) may introduce a subjunctive to express *purpose.* The tense values are as in § 176, *a.* This is the regular construction after a present or future tense:

ταῦτα ποιοῦσιν ἵνα σπεύδωσι πρὸς τὴν κώμην *they do this that they may be hastening to the village;*

ταῦτα ποιοῦσιν ἵνα σπεύσωσι πρὸς τὴν κώμην *they do this that they may hasten to the village.*

The negative is μή.

177. **VOCABULARY**

ἀναγκάζω, ἀναγκάσω, ἠνάγκασα: *compel.*

ἀνάγκη, -ης, ἡ: *necessity.*

ἵνα, conj. adv.: *that, in order that, to.*

μη(κ)-έτι,[1, 2] adv.: *no longer, never again.*

μή-τε[2] . . . μή-τε, neg. conj.: *neither . . . nor.*

ὅπως, conj. adv.: *how, in order that,* etc.

οὔ-τε . . . οὔ-τε, neg. conj.: *neither . . . nor.*

πάσχω, πείσομαι, ἔπαθον: *be treated, experience, suffer.* SYMPATHY.

τε, enclit. conj.: *and.* Usually followed by καί: *both . . . and.*

φέρω, οἴσω, ἤνεγκα: *bear, carry.* CHRISTOPHER.

ὡς, conj. adv.: *how, in order that, that,* etc.; also *as.*

---

[1] κ is due to analogy with οὐκ-έτι (§ 161).

[2] The distinction between the compound forms of μή and οὐ is the same as that between μή and οὐ themselves.

178. **EXERCISES**

(*a*) Translate:

1. *ἀλλὰ πιστεύωμεν τῷ ἀνθρώπῳ ὃν ἔπεμψαν.* 2. *ταῦτα ποιοῦμεν, ἵνα ἡμᾶς φιλῇς.* 3. *μηκέτι*[1] *οὖν δι-αρπάζωμεν μήτε*[1] *τὰς οἰκίᾱς μήτε*[1] *τὰς σκηνάς.* 4. *τῶν δὲ στρατιωτῶν ἀεὶ ἐπι-μελεῖται, ὅπως ἱκανοὶ ὦσιν.* 5. *ἐπιστολὴν δὲ πέμψουσι τῷ σατράπῃ, ὡς μὴ τοὺς φυγάδας αἱρῇ.* 6. *μὴ κατα-λίπωμεν τὰ ὅπλα.* 7. *τοῦτον δὴ αἱροῦνται στρατηγόν, ἵνα σπεύσωσι πρὸς τὴν Ἑλλάδα.* 8. *αἵ τε γυναῖκες καὶ οἱ παῖδες φεύγουσιν εἰς τὸ στρατόπεδον, ὅπως μὴ κακὰ πάθωσιν.*

THE MOSCHOPHOROS

This ancient marble statue from the Acropolis is called the calf-bearer. Compare Christophoros, Christopher, the Christ-bearer (§ 177).

(*b*) Complete:

1. *ἀνάγκη*[2] *δὲ τρόπῳ τιν— δια-βαίνειν τόνδε τὸν ποταμόν, ἵνα —κετι κακὰ παθ—μεν.* 2. *φύγωμεν εἰς χώρᾱν φιλίᾱν ἐχ— τάς τε γυναῖκας —— τοὺς παῖδας.* 3. *ἐκείνᾱς —— ἐπιστολὰς γράφει, ὅπως αὐτοὺς πεισ—.*

(*c*) Write in Greek:

1. Where are you? 2. Once there was talk about the water. 3. There were some tables in the house. 4. A certain soldier came on the run to demand food. 5. What were the gifts that you received from your friends?

---

[1] The heaping up of negatives is very frequent in Greek and serves only to strengthen the general negative idea.

[2] Supply *ἐστί.*

179. **THE BETTER PART OF VALOR**

δένδρον ὑπὸ τοῦ ἀνέμου (compare ANEMOMETER) εἰς ποταμὸν ἐρρίφθη (*was thrown*). φερόμενον δὲ κατὰ τὸν ποταμὸν τοῖς καλάμοις (*rushes*) ἔφη· Τί ὑμεῖς λεπτοὶ (*slender*) ὄντες κακὸν οὐ πάσχετε; οἱ δὲ κάλαμοι ἔφασαν· Σὺ μὲν τοῖς ἀνέμοις μάχει καὶ διὰ τοῦτο καταβάλλει (*are thrown down*), ἡμεῖς δὲ εἴκομεν (*yield*) αὐτοῖς, ὥστε κακὸν οὐ πάσχομεν.

Adapted from Æsop, 179 *c*.

THE PARTHENON

Shattered by an explosion of Turkish gunpowder, this shrine of Athena still overwhelms the beholder with its matchless grace and beauty.

LESSON XXXI

PRESENT SUBJUNCTIVE MIDDLE AND PASSIVE. AORIST SUBJUNCTIVE MIDDLE

ΝΙΨΟΝΑΝΟΜΗΜΑΜΗΜΟΝΑΝΟΨΙΝ.[1]
Wash your sins, not only your face.

180. The present subjunctive middle and passive bears the same relation in form to the present indicative middle and passive that the present subjunctive active bears to the present indicative active, having **ω** and **η** instead of **ο** and **ε**.

Present Subjunctive Middle and Passive of **παύω** *I stop*

παύ-ω-μαι	παυ-ώ-μεθα
(παύ-η-σαι) παύῃ	παύ-η-σθε
παύ-η-ται	παύ-ω-νται

181. The aorist subjunctive middle bears the same relation in form to the present subjunctive middle that the aorist subjunctive active bears to the present subjunctive active.

Write the inflection of the aorist subjunctive middle of παύω and λείπω. Compare with paradigms (§§ 527, 530).

182. φιλέω, except for accent, is the same as παύω in the present subjunctive middle and passive, **ε** being absorbed before a long vowel.

Write the inflection of the present subjunctive middle and passive of φιλέω, observing the principles laid down in § 127. Compare with paradigm (§ 534).

[1] Νίψον ἀνόμημα μὴ μόναν ὄψιν, an inscription on the sacred font in the courtyard of Hagia Sophia. It reads the same backward as forward, being what is called a palindrome (πάλιν *back*, and δρόμος *run*).

Inflect the present and aorist subjunctive middle of *πέμπω*, *ἄγω*, *πείθω*, *ποιέω*.

183. The Subjunctive in Conditions. *ἐάν* with the *subjunctive* forms the protasis of either a present general or a future more vivid condition. If the apodosis has a *present indicative* or its equivalent, the condition is *present general*, that is, it expresses *continued* or *repeated action* in *present time* (compare with particular conditions, § 83, *a*, which refer to definite and usually single acts):

ἐὰν ταῦτα βουλεύηται, ἀδικεῖ *if he plans this, he does wrong.*

If the apodosis contains a *future indicative* or its equivalent, the condition is *future more vivid* (the Greek makes no distinction between particular and general conditions in future time):

ἐὰν ταῦτα βουλεύηται, ἀδικήσει *if he plans (shall plan) this, he will do wrong.*

184. VOCABULARY

δεῖ, δεήσει, ἐδέησε, impers.: *be necessary*. Usually followed by A. and inf.

διδάσκω, διδάξω, ἐδίδαξα: *teach.* DIDACTIC.

ἐάν (= εἰ + ἄν), conj.: *if*, with subjv.

ἤν (= ἐάν), conj.: *if*, with subjv.

μᾶλλον, adv.: *rather (than)*, *more (than)*.

πάλαι, adv.: *long ago.* PALÆOZOIC.

σοφός, -ή, -όν: *wise.* SOPHOMORE.

σοφίᾱ, -ᾱς, ἡ: *wisdom.* SOPHIA.

ὥσ-περ, intens. form of ὡς: *just as.*

ὠφελέω, -ήσω, -ησα: *aid, help, benefit.*

ὠφέλιμος, -η, -ον: *beneficial, useful.* ANOPHELES, OPHELIA.

185. EXERCISES

(*a*) Translate:

1. πότε φόβος ἐκώλῡσε τὸν σατράπην τῆς πορείᾱς;[1]
2. ἐὰν μὴ ὠφελῶνται ὑπὸ Κύρου, οὐκ ἔσονται αὐτῷ φίλοι.

[1] Genitive of Separation without a preposition.

3. ἀνάγκη δὲ παρα-σκευάζεσθαι ὡς δεξόμενοι τοὺς πολεμίους.
4. ἢν δὲ μὴ παρ-έχηται ἀγοράν, τὸν σῖτον ἁρπάζουσιν.
5. ἐὰν δὲ παρ-έχωνται ἀγοράν, τὰ ἐπιτήδεια οὐχ ἁρπάσομεν.
6. δεῖ ταῦτα παθεῖν, ἵνα ἔχωμεν σοφίᾱν.

HADRIAN'S LIBRARY

The Roman emperor showed his admiration for Athens and its learning by erecting in the Agora the huge library to which these columns belong.

(*b*) Complete:

1. ἐὰν —— (*not*) ἐχ—μεν χρήματα, οὐκ ἐχ—μεν φίλους. 2. ἢν ἡμᾶς διδαξ—σιν, ἡμῖν γενησ— ὠφέλιμοι. 3. ποῦ δεῖ δια-βαιν— ἵνα ἐκείνους φυγ—μεν;

(*c*) Write in Greek:

1. Let us choose rulers. 2. He is delaying in order that the children may not suffer harm. 3. Let us not be injuring our enemies. 4. Let us hasten so that they may not compel us to carry the arms.

186. PHILOSOPHER AND FRIEND

ὁ δὲ Σωκράτης πρὸς ταῦτα ἔφη· Ἐγὼ δ' οὖν καὶ αὐτός, ὥσπερ ἄλλος τις ἵππῳ ἀγαθῷ ἥδεται, οὕτω καὶ ἔτι μᾶλλον ἥδομαι φίλοις ἀγαθοῖς, καὶ ἐάν τι ἔχω ἀγαθόν, διδάσκω τοὺς φίλους· καὶ τοὺς θησαυροὺς (*treasures*) τῶν πάλαι σοφῶν, οὓς ἐκεῖνοι κατ-έλιπον ἐν βιβλίοις γράψαντες, σὺν τοῖς φίλοις δι-έρχομαι, καὶ ἐάν τι ὁρῶμεν (*see*) ἀγαθὸν, ἐκ-λεγόμεθα (compare ECLECTIC)· καὶ μέγα (compare MEGAPHONE) νομίζομεν κέρδος (*gain*), ἐὰν ἀλλήλοις ὠφέλιμοι γιγνώμεθα.

Adapted from Xenophon, *Memorabilia*, I. 6. 14.

LESSON XXXII

OPTATIVE ACTIVE

τίς δὲ βίος, τί δὲ τερπνὸν ἄτερ χρῡσῆς Ἀφροδίτης;
What life, what joy without golden Aphrodite?[1]

---

187. The optative has ι (sometimes ιη) as its mood sign; in the third person plural it has ιε. This sign is added to the variable vowel ο in the present and the second aorist. The secondary personal endings (as in the imperfect) are then attached, except in the first person singular, where -μι is used. Final -οι in the optative is always long (§ V, *a*).

188. Present Optative of παύω *I stop*

παύ-οι-μι	παύ-οι-μεν
παύ-οι-ς	παύ-οι-τε
παύ-οι	παύ-οιε-ν

Second Aorist Optative of λείπω *I leave*

λίπ-οι-μι	λίπ-οι-μεν
λίπ-οι-ς	λίπ-οι-τε
λίπ-οι	λίπ-οιε-ν

189. The future optative is the same as that of the present except for the stem. Inflect *παύω* in the future optative active and compare with paradigm (§ 526).

190. In the first aorist optative likewise the ι is added to the stem, but the longer forms given for the second and third persons singular and the third person plural are regularly used in Attic Greek. Final -αι in the optative is always long (§ V, *a*).

---

[1] Mimnermus.

First Aorist Optative of **παύω** *I stop*

παύ-σ αι-μι	παύ-σ αι-μεν
(π α ύ - σ αι-ς) παύσ ειας	παύ-σ αι-τε
(π α ύ - σ αι) παύσ ειε(ν)	(π α ύ - σ αιε-ν) παύσ ειαν

191. Contract Verbs have **ιη** as the sign of the optative in the singular. The regular rules for contraction and accent apply (§ 127). *εἰμί* also has **ιη** in the singular. It has **ε** as its stem.

Write the inflection of the present optative active of *φιλέω* and *εἰμί*. Compare with paradigms (§§ 534, 538).

Inflect the present, future, and aorist optative active of *πέμπω*, *ἄγω*, *πείθω*, *ποιέω*.

192. Uses of the Optative. (*a*) The optative when used alone or with *εἴθε* or *εἰ γάρ* expresses a *wish* that refers to the *future*. As in the subjunctive (§ 176, *a*), present and aorist respectively denote *continued* action (motion picture) and *mere occurrence* (snapshot) of an act:

φεύγοι *may he be fleeing;*
φύγοι *may he flee.*

The negative is *μή*.

(*b*) *ἵνα* (*ὡς* or *ὅπως*) may introduce an optative to express *purpose*. The tense values are as in § 176, *a*. The optative appears only after a past tense or its equivalent; but even then the subjunctive sometimes appears and shows that special emphasis rests on the purpose:[1]

ταῦτα ἐποίουν ἵνα σπεύδοιεν πρὸς τὴν κώμην *they were doing this that they might be hastening to the village;*

ταῦτα ἐποίουν ἵνα σπεύσειαν πρὸς τὴν κώμην *they were doing this that they might hasten to the village.*

The negative is *μή*.

---

[1] The mood of the verb in the purpose clause is the same as when the purpose was originally conceived and brings the original form and thought vividly to the attention of the hearer or reader.

193. VOCABULARY

ἀργύριον, -ου, τό: *silver, money.*
ARGYROL, French *argent* (from Latin).

βίος, -ου, ὁ: *life, living.*
BIOLOGY.

γε, enclit. particle of emphasis, rarely to be translated: *indeed, at least.*

θεός, -οῦ, ὁ: *god* (ἡ θεός: *goddess*).
THEOLOGY. Cf. **θεά**.

μισθός, -οῦ, ὁ: *pay.*

ξένος, -ου, ὁ: *stranger, guest* or *host, mercenary,* i.e., *hired soldier.*

πόνος, -ου, ὁ: *toil, labor, travail.*

πράττω, πράξω, ἔπρᾱξα: *do, fare.*
PRACTICAL. Cf. **πρᾶγμα**.

χρῡσίον, -ου, τό: *gold, money.*

χρῡσός, -οῦ, ὁ: *gold, gold metal.*
CHRYSANTHEMUM.

194. EXERCISES

(*a*) What mood is indicated by the portions in heavy type?

φεύγ **ειν**	φεύγ **οιεν**
φύγ **ῃ**	πείσ **ει**
πείσ **ειε**	ποι **οῖ** μεν
πείσ **οι**	ποιήσ **αι** μεν
ποι **ῶ** μεν	πράξ **ω** σι

(*b*) Translate:

1. ταῦτα ἔπρᾱττον οἱ ξένοι ἵνα μισθὸν ἔχοιεν. 2. εἰ γὰρ οἱ θεοὶ ἡμῖν ἀργύριόν τε καὶ χρῡσίον παράσχοιεν. 3. μήποτε νομίζοιμεν τούς γε θεοὺς ποιεῖν κακά. 4. εἰ γὰρ καλῶς πράξειαν ἃ ἐθέλουσιν. 5. ἀργύριον καὶ χρῡσίον οὐκ ἔστι μοι· ὃ δὲ ἔχω, τοῦτο ἔσται σοι. 6. καὶ ὠφέλει αὐτούς, ἵνα δόξειε φίλος εἶναι

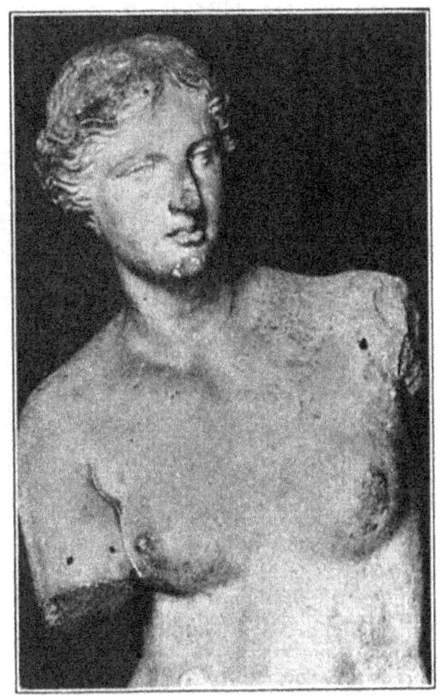

GOLDEN APHRODITE

This statue is popularly known as the Venus de Milo. Though unrecorded in antiquity and by an unknown artist, it has become the most famous of all Greek statues.

ἄξιος. 7. ἐν τῷ μακρῷ βίῳ οὐκ ὀλίγα πάσχουσι κακὰ καὶ οἱ δίκαιοι.

(c) Complete:

1. ἐπεὶ ὁ ξένος ἐδεξ— τὸ ἀργύριον, εἶχε χαρ—. 2. εἴθε μὴ οἱ πόνοι —— (linking verb) χαλεποί. 3. ταῦτά γε ἔπρᾱξαν ἵνα —— (*not*) κακὰ παθ—. 4. εἰ γὰρ ἡ χώρᾱ ἀνὰ ἣν πορευσόμεθα —— (linking verb) φιλίᾱ.

(*d*) Write in Greek:

1. (By) teaching this he becomes useful to you. 2. If you have money, you will have friends. 3. If he is pleased by anything, this man (always) is willing to teach us. 4. If you had not aided the exiles, they would not have felt grateful to you.

195. LOOSE LOGIC

ἡ γῆ (*earth*) μέλαινα (*dark*) πίνει (*drinks*),
πίνει δὲ δένδρε' (*trees*) αὐτήν.
πίνει θάλασσ' (θάλαττα) ἀναύρους (*streams*),
ὁ δ' ἥλιος (*sun*, compare HELIOGRAPH) θάλασσαν,
τὸν δ' ἥλιον σελήνη (*moon*).
τί μοι μάχεσθ', ἑταῖροι (*comrades*),
καὐτῷ (καὶ αὐτῷ) θέλοντι (ἐθέλοντι) πίνειν;

Anacreontic.

196. Q. E. D.

Διογένης ὁ φιλόσοφος ἔλεγε τῶν σοφῶν εἶναι πάντα· πάντα γὰρ τῶν θεῶν ἐστι· φίλοι δὲ τοῖς σοφοῖς οἱ θεοί· κοινὰ (*joint, common*) δὲ τὰ τῶν φίλων· πάντα ἄρα (*therefore*) τῶν σοφῶν.

Adapted from Diogenes Laertius, VI. 72.

LESSON XXXIII

PRESENT OPTATIVE MIDDLE AND PASSIVE. FUTURE AND AORIST OPTATIVE MIDDLE

ἐπὶ τούτῳ δέ τις ἂν μεγάλα διώκων τὰ παρ-όντ' οὐχὶ φέροι.
In pursuing great things you may miss things close at hand.[1]

197. The optative middle has the same stem as does the optative active in the present, future, and aorist (§§ 187–190). The regular imperfect endings of the middle are added, but σ drops out of the second person singular (§ 137).

Present Optative Middle and Passive of **παύω** *I stop*

παυ-οί-μην	παυ-οί-μεθα
(π α ύ-οι-σο) παύ οιο	παύ-οι-σθε
παύ-οι-το	παύ-οι-ντο

198. (*a*) Write the inflection of the optative middle of παύω in future and aorist; of λείπω in the aorist; and of φιλέω in the present (contracting ε with the endings of παυοίμην, § 127). Compare with paradigms (§§ 527, 530, 534).

(*b*) Write the inflection of the present, future, and aorist optative middle of πέμπω, ἄγω, πείθω, ποιέω.

199. The Optative in Conditions. (*a*) εἰ with the optative may state the protasis of a *past general* or a *future*

[1] Euripides, *Bacchæ*, 397–9. Literally: *And therefore a man pursuing great things might not gain the things present.*

less vivid condition. If the apodosis contains an *imperfect indicative* or its equivalent, the condition is *past general:*[1]

εἴ τι ὑπόσχοιτο, τοῦτο ἔπρᾱττε *if he ever promised anything, he always did it.*

If the apodosis contains an *optative* and ἄν, the condition is *future less vivid:*[2]

εἴ τι ὑπόσχοιτο, τοῦτο ἂν πρᾱ́ττοι *if he should promise anything, he would do it.*

(*b*) The optative with ἄν denotes a *future action* that is *qualified* by, or *dependent* upon, some circumstances or condition, whether expressed or implied:[3]

ἔλθοι ἄν *he might come* (that is, if nothing hinders).

This is called a *potential optative.* The negative is οὐ.

200. **VOCABULARY**

ἄ-δικος, -ον: *unjust.* Cf. **δίκαιος, ἀ-δικέω.**

ἀναγκαῖος, -ᾱ, -ον: *necessary.* Cf. **ἀνάγκη.**

δίκη, -ης, ἡ: *justice.*

ἐπι-θῡμέω, -ήσω, ἐπ-εθῡ́μησα: *desire,* with G. Cf. **θῡμός.**

ἤ, conj.: *or, than.*

οἶνος, -ου, ὁ: *wine.*

πάλιν, adv.: *again, back.* PALINODE.

πορίζω,ποριῶ, ἐπόρισα: *bring, supply.* Cf. **πορείᾱ, πορεύομαι.**

στρατεύω, στρατεύσω, ἐστράτευσα: *make campaign.* Usually mid. Cf. **στρατιᾱ́.**

τάττω, τάξω, ἔταξα: *order, arrange, station.* TAXIDERMIST, TACTICS.

τρέφω, θρέψω, ἔθρεψα: *nourish, support, rear, keep* (of animals). ATROPHY.

201. **EXERCISES**

(*a*) Translate:

1. ἀλλ᾽ εἴ τι ὑπ-ισχνοῖτο, τοῦτ᾽ ἐπ-εθῡ́μει πορίσαι. 2. εἰ δ᾽ αὐτοὺς διδάσκοις, ἥδοντο. 3. καὶ ἐκείνους οὐκ ἂν κωλῡ́οι

---

[1] What form does a present general condition assume? (§ 183.)

[2] What form does a future more vivid condition assume? (§ 183.)

[3] This is really a future less vivid condition with the conditional part omitted.

ὁ κίνδῡνος. 4. ὥστε ἐπ-εθύμουν στρατεύεσθαι μᾶλλον ἢ ἄ-δικοι γενέσθαι. 5. ἀλλ' ἔδει οἶνον καὶ σῖτον πορίζειν, ἵνα στρατευόμενοι τρέφοιντο. 6. οὗτος ἂν ὑμῖν πορίσειεν, εἴ του ἐπι-θῡμοῖσθε. 7. οὐκ ἂν φιλοίη τοὺς ἀ-δίκους δίκαιός τις ὤν. 8. πῶς γὰρ ἂν ἥδοισθε, εἰ μὴ βουλοίμεθα τὰ ταττόμενα πρᾱ́ττειν ;

Cupbearers to King Minos

(*b*) Complete :

1. εἰ ὁ σατράπης ἐπι-θῡμ— στρατεύεσθαι, τοὺς ἐν τῇ αὑτοῦ χώρᾳ κελευ— ἂν οἶνόν τε —— σῖτον πορίσαι. 2. οἱ δὲ ξένοι ἐν πόνοις καὶ κινδῡ́νοις ὄντες ἔφευγον —— (*that*) μὴ ἁλισκ—. 3. πᾶσαν τὴν ἡμέρᾱν ἤλαυν—, εἰ ἀναγκαῖον —— (linking verb) πρὸς ὕδωρ ἐλθεῖν.

(*c*) Write in Greek :

1. May he receive both silver and gold. 2. He taught them that they might be wise and might aid others. 3. Would that the soldiers might receive their pay. 4. May they fare well. 5. The mercenaries fled in order not to fare ill.

202. **PEACE AND WAR**

εἰρήνη (*peace*) γεωργὸν κἂν[1] πέτραις (*rocks*)
τρέφει καλῶς, πόλεμος δὲ κἂν πεδίῳ κακῶς.

Menander, fragment.

[1] κἄν = καὶ ἐν.

203. STRANGE DOCTRINE FOR A PAGAN

εἰ ἀναγκαῖον εἴη ἀ-δικεῖν ἢ ἀ-δικεῖσθαι, ἑλοίμην ἂν μᾶλλον ἀ-δικεῖσθαι ἢ ἀ-δικεῖν.

Socrates, as reported by Plato, *Gorgias*, 469.

204. A TRAITOR CAUGHT[1]

Τί[2] οὖν, ἔφη ὁ Κῦρος, ἀ-δικούμενος ὑπ' ἐμοῦ νῦν τὸ τρίτον ἐπι-βουλεύεις μοι; ὁμολογοῦντος δὲ τοῦ Ὀρόντᾱ[3] οὐκ ἀ-δικεῖσθαι, ὁ Κῦρος ἔφη· Ὁμολογεῖς οὖν περὶ ἐμὲ ἄ-δικος γενέσθαι; Ἀνάγκη γάρ,[4] ἔφη Ὀρόντᾱς· ἐκ τούτου πάλιν ὁ Κῦρος ἔφη· Ἔτι οὖν ἂν γένοιο τῷ ἐμῷ (*my*) ἀδελφῷ πολέμιος, ἐμοὶ δὲ φίλος; ὁ δ' ἔφη· Οὐ γὰρ[4] εἰ γενοίμην, ὦ Κῦρε, σοί γ' ἄν ποτε ἔτι δόξαιμι.

Adapted from Xenophon, *Anabasis*, I. 6. 8.

205. Word-formation. (*a*) **ἀ-** (before consonants), **ἀν-** (before vowels), known as *alpha privative*, when prefixed to noun or verb stems, form adjectives that have a negative meaning:[5]

ἀ-διά-βα-τος *not to be crossed, not crossable*, ἄ-δικος *unjust.*

(*b*) In like manner form adjectives meaning: (1) *unworthy;* (2) *obscure, doubtful;* (3) *godless, atheistic;* (4) *without gifts, incorruptible;* (5) *without war, unwarlike;* (6) *without place, out of the way, strange;* (7) *without food;* (8) *friendless.* Compare A-SEPTIC, AN-HYDROUS, AN-ARCHIC, A-PATHETIC.

---

[1] Continued from Lesson XXI.

[2] ἀδικέω admits of two accusatives, one of the person affected, the other of the thing done. If the verb is used in the passive, the former becomes subject, the latter is kept in the accusative.

[3] Doric genitive of the **α**-declension.

[4] Although γάρ usually may be translated *for*, not infrequently it is equivalent to the exclamatory *why*.

[5] These adjectives are of two endings and have recessive accent: ἀδιάβατος, ἀδιάβατον (§ 510, *b*).

LESSON XXXIV

CONDITIONAL RELATIVE CLAUSES

ὃν οἱ θεοὶ φιλοῦσιν ἀποθνῄσκει νέος. — *Whom the gods love dies young.*[1]

---

206. Conditional Relative Clauses. A relative pronoun or adverb may take the place of **εἰ** in the protasis of a condition. If **ἐάν** is the normal introductory word, the relative is accompanied by **ἄν**:

ὅστις = εἰ, ὅστις ἄν = ἐάν.

A relative used in this way has an indefinite antecedent, expressed or implied. The negative of the protasis is always μή.

The ἄν is often combined with an introductory relative adverb:

ἐπεὶ + ἄν = ἐπάν or ἐπήν, ἐπειδὴ + ἄν = ἐπειδάν, ὅτε + ἄν = ὅταν.

Review the various forms of conditional sentences (§ 547).

207. VOCABULARY

ἀπο-θνῄσκω, -θανοῦμαι, -έθανον: *die.*

ἐπάν or ἐπήν (ἐπεὶ + ἄν), conj.: *when, whenever.*

ἐπειδάν (ἐπειδὴ + ἄν), conj.: *when, whenever.*

θάνατος, -ου, ὁ: *death.*
THANATOPSIS.

μη-δέ, neg. conj. and adv.: *and not, nor, not even.*

ὅταν (ὅτε + ἄν), conj.: *when, whenever.*

ὅτε, conj.: *when.*

οὐ-δέ neg. conj. and adv.: *and not, nor, not even.*

σῴζω, σώσω, ἔσωσα: *save, bring safely, rescue.*
SOZODONT, CREOSOTE.

σωτηρίᾱ, -ᾱς, ἡ: *safety.*

---

[1] Menander, fragment.

208. **EXERCISES**

(*a*) Translate:

1. ὅστις δὲ Κύρῳ φίλος γένοιτο, δῶρα ἐλάμβανεν. 2. ὅστις δὲ ἄ-δικος γένοιτο, δῶρα οὐκ ἂν λαμβάνοι. 3. ὅστις δ' ἂν γένηται στρατηγός, ἕψομαι καὶ ἐπὶ θάνατον. 4. ὅντινα δ' ἂν χρόνον πορεύησθε, ὅδε ἀγορὰν παρ-έχει. 5. καὶ ἔσται αὐτοῖς ἀπ-ελθεῖν, ὅταν βούλωνται. 6. ἀλλ' ἐπειδὴ ἀπ-έθανεν ὁ Κῦρος, οἱ φίλοι οὐκέτι ἐλπίδα σωτηρίᾱς εἶχον. 7. τὸν δὲ βουλόμενον σώσω εἰς τὴν Ἑλλάδα. 8. οἱ δ' ἵπποι, ὁπότε τις διώκοι, ἔφευγον. 9. οὐδ' ἂν φιλοῖεν ὅστις μὴ καλὰ πράττοι.

MOURNING ATHENA

The dignified pathos of this bit of sculpture from the Acropolis is true to the spirit of Greek art. It is supposed to be a memorial to those slain in the Peloponnesian War.

(*b*) Complete:

1. ἐπεὶ οἱ ξένοι ἡμᾶς ὠφελοῖεν, αὐτοὺς —σῳζ— εἰς τὴν Ἑλλαδ—. 2. ὅστις ἂν βουλ— στρατευ—, Κῦρος κελεύσει παρ-εῖναι ὅπλα λαβόντα. 3. ὅταν τις ἀ-δικ—, κακὰ πασχ—.

(*c*) Write in Greek:

1. If they (ever) made a campaign, he (always) supported them by sending food and wine. 2. How much wine would the people in the village supply? 3. If it should be necessary to fight, their general would arrange them for (εἰς) battle. 4. If the rulers had not been unjust, the citizens would not have fared badly.

209. THEY THAT GO DOWN TO THE SEA IN SHIPS

One of the most notable features of Greek geography is the presence of the sea. Few countries with so limited a territory have had so extensive a coastline. The sea gave the people a livelihood, afforded the best means of access not only to their Greek neighbors but to the world at large, and both by its perils and by its rewards stimulated their intellect. No wonder, then, that their literature is filled with allusions to seafaring and to the beauty and the terrors of the deep.

THE ROCKY ROAD TO CORINTH

ἀεὶ καλὸς πλοῦς (*voyage*) ἔσθ',[1] ὅταν φεύγῃς κακά.

Sophocles, *Philoctetes*, 641.

ἂν (ἐὰν) καλὸν ἔχῃ τις σῶμα (*body*) καὶ ψῡχὴν (*soul*) κακήν, καλὴν ἔχει ναῦν (*ship*) καὶ κυβερνήτην (*pilot*) κακόν.

Menander, fragment.

210. Word-formation. (*a*) **-τικος** added to a verb stem makes an adjective that denotes *relation*, *fitness*, or *ability*. Many of these words have passed over into English with slight change:

πρᾱ́ττω (stem πρᾱγ-) *do*, πρᾱκτικός PRACTICAL;
ἀνα-λῡ́ω *analyze*, ἀναλυτικός ANALYTIC;
σήπω *decay*, σηπτικός SEPTIC.

[1] For ἐστι; in elision τ becomes θ before rough breathing.

(*b*) **-κος, -ικος** when added to noun stems make adjectives that denote *relation*, *fitness*, or *ability:*

φύσις *nature*, φυσικός PHYSICAL;
πολίτης *citizen*, πολῑτικός POLITICAL.

(*c*) Frequently in English *-al* (from Latin *-alis*) is added to *-ic* or *-tic*. Sometimes both forms occur: *comic*, *comical; electric*, *electrical.*

(*d*) The neuter plurals of these adjectives were used in Greek as names for the arts and sciences. Such words, when taken into English, have the English *-s* instead of *-a*:

φυσικά PHYSICS, πολῑτικά POLITICS, ἠθικά ETHICS.

(*e*) The Greeks sometimes also used the singular, which we have imitated in English. It was in agreement with an implied τέχνη *art*, or ἐπιστήμη *science:*

μουσική MUSIC, ἀριθμητική ARITHMETIC, ῥητορική RHETORIC.

(*f*) Give at least two English derivatives akin to each group above discussed. Consult an unabridged English dictionary and find the original Greek word. You will find that some apparent derivatives have no Greek original but are formed by analogy with words such as those given.

(*g*) Write the Greek original of the following words (ē = η, ō = ω): *apologētic*, *catēgoric*, *botanic*, *cathartic*, *optic*, *dynamic*, *theōrētic*, *mēchanics*, *dialectic.*

LESSON XXXV

INDIRECT DISCOURSE

χρήματα γὰρ ψῡχὴ πέλεται δειλοῖσι βροτοῖσι.
Money is the soul of craven men.[1]

211. Finite Moods in Indirect Discourse. λέγω (in active voice), εἶπον, ἀποκρῑ́νομαι, and certain other verbs of like meaning are followed by a clause introduced by ὅτι *that*, or ὡς (*how*) *that*. The verb in the subordinate clause has the same mood and tense that it would have if quoted directly; but after a secondary tense it may take the optative (tense always remaining the same). Retention of the original mood after a secondary tense produces vividness:

εἶπεν ὅτι παρέσοιτο *he said that he would be present.*

παρέσομαι *I shall be present*, was the original form and might remain as παρέσται, producing vividness.

212. Tenses in Indirect Discourse. The present tense in the subordinate verb indicates that its action is contemporaneous with that of the verb of *saying*, the future that the event is to follow, the aorist that the event has already occurred:

εἶπεν ὅτι	πρᾱ́ττοι	*he said that*	*he was doing;*
	πρᾱ́ξοι		*he would do;*
	πρᾱ́ξειε		*he had done.*

213. Infinitive in Indirect Discourse. φημί, λέγεται (passive), νομίζω, and certain other verbs are followed by

[1] Hesiod, *Works and Days*, 686.

the infinitive. The tenses have the same value as in § 212:

ἐνόμισεν αὐτοὺς	πρᾱ́ττειν	*he thought that*	*they were doing;*
	πρᾱ́ξειν		*they would do;*
	πρᾶξαι		*they had done.*

214. Participle in Indirect Discourse. *ὁράω, αἰσθάνομαι, ἀκούω, ἀγγέλλω*, and similar verbs denoting the operation of the senses[1] are often followed by a participle. The tenses have the same value as in § 212:

ἤγγελλεν αὐτοὺς	πρᾱ́ττοντας	*he was reporting that*	*they were doing;*
	πρᾱ́ξοντας		*they would do;*
	πρᾱ́ξαντας		*they had done.*

215. Some of these verbs, like *ἀκούω*, admit all three constructions. Others, like *πυνθάνομαι* and *αἰσθάνομαι*, have either the *ὅτι* construction or the participle.

216. If *ἄν* occurs, it shows that the original verb had *ἄν*:

ἀκούω	ὅτι ἂν ἔλθοι	*I hear that he may come.*
	αὐτὸν ἂν ἐλθεῖν	
	αὐτὸν ἂν ἐλθόντα	

The original form of this statement was:

ἔλθοι ἄν *he may come.*

217. Indirect Questions. A verb indicating a question is followed by an interrogative or an indirect relative and a verb in a finite mood.[2] An indirect question takes the same mood and tense as a direct question, but after a secondary tense it may take the optative (§ 212):

πυνθάνεται τί ἔσται αὐτῷ *he asks what he shall have;*
ἐπυνθάνετο τί ἔσοιτο (or ἔσται) αὐτῷ *he asked what he should have.*

---

[1] Such verbs are for the most part those meaning *to see, perceive, hear, learn, know, be ignorant of, remember, forget, show, appear, prove*, and *announce*.

[2] Note that the indirect question does not call for the subjunctive, as in Latin.

218. **VOCABULARY**

ἀγγέλλω:[1] *announce*. Cf. **ἄγγελος**.
αἰσθάνομαι, αἰσθήσομαι, ᾐσθόμην: *perceive*. ANESTHESIA.
ἀκούω, ἀκούσομαι, ἤκουσα: *hear*. ACOUSTIC.
γιγνώσκω,[2] γνώσομαι: *know*, *determine*. DIAGNOSIS. Cf. **γνώμη**.
εἶπον[3] (2d. aor.): *said*. EPIC.
εὑρίσκω, εὑρήσω, ηὗρον: *find*. EUREKA.
θαυμάζω, θαυμάσω, ἐθαύμασα: *wonder*, *marvel at*, *admire*. THAUMATURGY.
κλέπτω, κλέψω, ἔκλεψα: *steal*. KLEPTOMANIAC.
λέγω, λέξω, ἔλεξα: *say*, *tell*, *speak*. DIALECT.
ὅτι, conj.: *that*, *because*.
πυνθάνομαι, πεύσομαι, ἐπυθόμην: *inquire*, *learn* (by inquiry).
ὡς, conj. adv.: *that*.

219. **EXERCISES**

(*a*) Translate:

1. ὁ δ' ἄγγελος εἶπεν ὅτι ὁ ποταμὸς ἀ-διά-βατος εἴη. 2. ἐπύθετο γὰρ τοὺς πολεμίους τὴν γέφῡραν λῡ́σαντας. 3. θαυμάζω εἰ εὑρήσετε τὰ πλοῖα παρ-όντα. 4. ἀλλὰ γνώσεσθε τοὺς φύλακας ἱκανοὺς εἶναι τὸ στρατόπεδον φυλάττειν. 5. πεύσεσθε εἰ ἡ ὁδὸς μακρᾱ̀ ἔσται; 6. ἔλεγον ὅτι οὗτοι ἱκανοὶ ἔσοιντο. 7. ἤγγελλον δὲ τοὺς πολεμίους φυγόντας. 8. ταύτην εὑρήσεις κακὴν ὁδὸν οὖσαν. 9. ἀλλ' εἰ ῡ̔μᾶς ᾐσθόμην οὕτως ὀλίγους ὄντας, οὐκ ἂν ἔπεμψα ῡ̔μᾶς ἐπὶ τὴν κώμην. 10. τοῦ δὲ Κῡ́ρου[4] ἠκούσατε τοὺς βαρβάρους κραυγῇ μάχεσθαι. 11. ἀλλ' οὐ γιγνώσκομεν τίνα βουλὴν ποιεῖται. 12. εὑρίσκουσι δ' αὐτοὺς τὰ ὅπλα κλέπτοντας.

(*b*) Complete:

1. ἐνόμισαν δὲ τοὺς ἀρχοντ— κλεψ— (fut.) τό τε ἀργύριον —— τὸ χρῡσίον. 2. εἶπεν ὅτι οἱ στρατιῶται ἱκανοὶ

---

[1] Future and aorist to follow.
[2] Aorist to follow.
[3] Defective verb.
[4] **Genitive of source**, a variety of the genitive of separation.

ἐσ—ντο τὰς σκηνὰς δι-αρπα—. 3. εἰ μὴ ἡ βασίλεια ἤσθ— τοὺς ὁπλίτᾱς ταττο —, οὐκ ἂν —φυγ—. 4. ἐθαύμασαν εἰ οἱ ξένοι Κῦρ— ἐψ—.

THE LIONS' GATE

There are no live lions in Greece today, but they still exist abundantly in Greek art and literature. Those in this picture looked down on Agamemnon at his triumphant return from Troy.

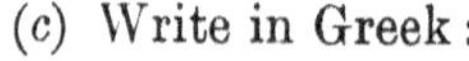

(c) Write in Greek:

1. Whomever they love, they will not wish to harm. 2. Whenever it shall no longer be necessary to keep (*have*) them, he will send to Greece those who so desire (*those wishing*). 3. When the commander died, his men turned (themselves) to flee (*into flight*). 4. Cyrus was a worthy friend to whomever he was a friend.

220. WHAT FOOLS THESE MORTALS BE!

βου-κόλος (*cowherd*) ποτὲ βοῦν ἀπ-οῦσαν ᾔσθετο. καὶ οὐχ ηὗρεν. ηὔξατο (*vowed*) οὖν τῷ θεῷ μόσχον (*calf*) θῦσαι (*sacrifice*), εἰ τὸν κλέπτην (compare **κλέπτω**) εὕροι. ἐλθὼν εἰς ὕλην (*forest*) τινά, λέοντα (*lion*) εὑρίσκει κατ-εσθίοντα τὴν βοῦν. Ὦ Ζεῦ, ἔφη, πρότερον (*before*) μὲν ηὐξάμην μόσχον θῦσαι, ἐὰν τὸν κλέπτην εὕρω, νῦν δὲ ταῦρον (compare TOREADOR) θύσω, ἐὰν τὸν κλέπτην ἐκ-φύγω.

Adapted from Æsop, 83.

LESSON XXXVI

REVIEW

μῑκροῖς πόνοις τὰ μεγάλα πῶς ἕλοι τις ἄν;
How could one by little toil achieve things great?[1]

221. **ASSIGNMENTS**

(*a*) Review vocabulary (§ 553), following the method indicated in § 27, *a*. Give the present, future, and aorist of each verb.

(*b*) Name and define the Greek words suggested by these English derivatives: *chronology*, *psychiatrist*, *didacticism*, *Xenia*, *chryselephantine*, *tact*, *euthanasia*, *agnostic*, *trilogy*, *paleography*, *semaphore*, *æsthetics*, *dialectic*, *hypertrophy*, *xenophobia*, *biographic*, *acousticon*, *dolichocephalic*, *pathology*, *pediatric*, *trapeze*, *praxis*, *lexicon*.

(*c*) What do the endings suggest as to meaning of the following: *magnetic*, *practical*, *graphic*, *cardiac*, *physics*, *linguistics*, *logic*, *dialectic*?

(*d*) Add ten other derivatives to each of these lists.

(*e*) Point out in the following words the portions that give clues as to mood:

πέμπητε, λέγοι, ἀκούσωσι, ἀκούσειε, ἁρπάσαιτο, πείθεσθαι, πείθηται, κελεῦσαι, εἶμεν, εἶναι, ὦμεν.

(*f*) Inflect the present subjunctive and optative active and middle of ποιέω; the aorist optative active of πράττω; the aorist optative of γίγνομαι.

(*g*) What may a subjunctive in a main clause indicate? in a subordinate clause after ἐάν, ἵνα, ὅπως? What may

[1] Euripides, *Orestes*, 694. The text has been modified slightly.

an optative indicate in a main clause without ἄν? with ἄν? in a subordinate clause after εἰ, ἵνα, ὅτι, ὡς?

Columns of the Olympieum

This, the largest temple in Greece, was begun about 530 B.C. and finished in 130 A.D.

(*h*) How do present general conditions differ from future more vivid? past general from future less vivid?

(*i*) Point out the interrogative and the indefinite pronouns:

τίνες εἰσίν, εἴ τις, τίνι στρατιώτῃ, λόγοι τινές, πρᾶγμά τι, τί πρᾶγμα, ἐκ τίνων.

222. EXERCISES.

(*a*) Complete:

1. *ὅστις ἂν γεν——— στρατηγός, οἱ σὺν ἐμ—* (personal pronoun) *ἑψ—.* 2. *ἐπύθοντο εἰ ἀναγκαῖον* ——— (linking verb) *τοὺς ἀδικ—ντας κακὰ παθ—.* 3. *μὴ οἱ ξένοι κλεπτ— τὰ χρήματα.* 4. *ἐθαύμασε πῶς ἂν ποι—τε πάντας τοὺς πόνους.* 5. *τοῦ γὰρ ἀγγέλου ἤκουσαν τὴν σωτηρίᾱς ἐλπίδα* ——— (linking verb) *καλ—.*

(*b*) Write in Greek:

1. They told us that because of the guards the bridge was uncrossable. 2. I wondered if he would learn that his brother was supporting an army. 3. Whoever delays will be captured. 4. Would that the mercenaries might receive their pay! 5. He drew up his men during the night, so that he might hasten to the village.

LESSON XXXVII

READING

τὰ μὲν διδακτὰ μανθάνω, τὰ δ' εὑρετὰ
ζητῶ, τὰ δ' εὐκτὰ παρὰ θεῶν ᾐτησάμην.
What may be taught I learn, what may be found I seek,
What may be prayed for I ask of the gods.[1]

---

223. VOCABULARY

εὔχομαι, εὔξομαι, ηὐξάμην: *pray, vow.*
θύω, θύσω, ἔθυσα: *sacrifice.*
λοχ-αγός, -οῦ, ὁ: *captain.* Cf. **στρατηγός.**
λόχος, -ου, ὁ: *company.*
μέν-τοι, postpos. adv.: *however.*
Ξενοφῶν, -ῶντος, ὁ: *Xenophon.*
πότερος, -ᾱ, -ον, pron.: *which* (of two); πότερον, adv.: *whether.* Often fol. by ἤ *or.*

224. THE DELPHIC ORACLE

Review carefully §§ 63 and 160.

The shrine of Apollo at Delphi was the most influential religious center in the ancient world. Belonging not to a single state but to all Greeks, it enjoyed their joint protection and patronage.

The god was supposed to make answer through the lips of his priestess, who, inspired by a vapor that issued from a fissure in the rock beneath the temple, uttered cries which were interpreted in verse by the attendant priests.

ἦν δέ τις[2] *ἐν τῇ στρατιᾷ Ξενοφῶν Ἀθηναῖος, ὃς οὔτε στρατηγὸς οὔτε λοχαγὸς οὔτε στρατιώτης ὢν εἵπετο, ἀλλὰ*

---

[1] Sophocles, fragment.

[2] Note the modesty of the writer who in this impersonal way introduces himself to the reader, and that not before Book III.

Πρόξενος αὐτὸν μετ-επέμψατο ξένος ὢν ἀρχαῖος· ὑπ-ισχνεῖτο δὲ αὐτῷ, εἰ ἔλθοι, φίλον αὐτὸν Κύρῳ ποιήσειν, ὃν αὐτὸς ἔφη οὐκ ὀλίγου ἄξιον εἶναι νομίζειν. ὁ μέντοι Ξενοφῶν ἀναγνοὺς[1] (*having read*) τὴν ἐπιστολὴν συν-εβουλεύετο Σωκράτει τῷ Ἀθηναίῳ περὶ τῆς πορείᾱς. καὶ ὁ Σωκράτης ὑπ-οπτεύσᾱς

WHERE ONCE APOLLO RULED SUPREME

In the foreground you see the orchestra of the ancient theater and close beside it all that now remains of the once glorious temple.

μὴ[2] οἱ Ἀθηναῖοι ἄχθοιντο, εἰ οὗτος φίλος γένοιτο τῷ Κύρῳ, ὅτι ἐδόκει ὁ Κῦρος προθύμως τοῖς Λακεδαιμονίοις ἐπὶ τὰς Ἀθήνᾱς συμ-πολεμῆσαι, συμ-βουλεύει τῷ Ξενοφῶντι ἐλθόντα[3] εἰς Δελφοὺς συμ-βουλεύεσθαι τῷ θεῷ περὶ τῆς πορείᾱς. ἐλθὼν δ' ὁ Ξενοφῶν ἐπ-ήρετο (*asked*) τὸν Ἀπόλλω τίνι ἂν θεῶν θύων καὶ εὐχόμενος εἰς τὴν Ἑλλάδα καλῶς πρᾱ́ξᾱς

---

[1] Aorist participle of ἀνα-γιγνώσκω.

[2] μὴ = *lest*, see § 314 *b*.

[3] In agreement with the implied subject.

ἀφ-ίκοιτο. καὶ εἶπεν αὐτῷ ὁ Ἀπόλλων τοὺς θεοὺς οἷς ἔδει θύειν. ἐπεὶ δὲ πάλιν ἦλθε, λέγει ταῦτα πάντα τῷ Σωκράτει. ὁ δ' ἀκούσᾱς οὐχ ἥδετο ὅτι οὐ τοῦτο πρῶτον ἐπυνθάνετο, πότερον δέοι πορεύεσθαι ἢ μένειν, ἀλλ' αὐτὸς νομίσᾱς δεῖν πορεύεσθαι ἐπυνθάνετο ὅπως ἂν καλῶς τοῦτο πρᾱ́ξειεν. Ἐπεὶ μέντοι οὕτως ἤρου (compare **ἐπ-ήρετο**), ταῦτ', ἔφη, δεῖ ποιεῖν ὅσα ὁ θεὸς ἐκέλευσεν.

Adapted from Xenophon, *Anabasis*, III. 1. 4–7.

225. Word-formation. (*a*) The names of certain sciences have been explained in § 210, *d* and *e*. Others are formed from γράφω and λέγω :

γέα (γῆ) *earth*, γεωγράφος *geographer*, γεωγραφίᾱ GEOGRAPHY;
ἄστρον *star*, ἀστρολόγος *astrologer*, ἀστρολογίᾱ ASTROLOGY;
θεός *god*, θεολόγος *theologian*, θεολογίᾱ THEOLOGY;
μῦθος *myth, story*, μῡθολόγος *story-teller*, μῡθολογίᾱ MYTHOLOGY.

Note carefully that the words in *-ology* are not derived from λόγος but from λέγω. The **-ιᾱ** denotes that *about which a particular person speaks.*

(*b*) Add two words in *-ography* and two in *-ology* to the above list, consulting an unabridged English dictionary to discover if the entire word comes from the Greek or whether it is a hybrid like *sociology.*

(*c*) From these compound nouns, verbs were formed in classic Greek by adding **-εω**. In later Greek **-ιζω** was so used, and in English we use this ending *-ize* (*-ise*) with great frequency, even attaching it to stems that have no connection with Greek :

ἀστρονομίζω *astronomize ;* in English CIVILIZE, ANGLICIZE.

(*d*) Add two words which an unabridged English dictionary shows are derived in this way.

LESSON XXXVIII

CONSONANT DECLENSION

τὸν καλὸν ἀγῶνα ἠγώνισμαι. — "*I have fought a good fight.*" [1]

226. Nouns with stems ending in a liquid (λ, μ, ν, ρ) are included in the consonant declension.

Review §§ 101, 107.

ἀγών (ὁ) *contest*		**ἡγεμών** (ὁ) *leader*	
ἀγών	ἀγῶνες	ἡγεμών	ἡγεμόνες
ἀγῶνος	ἀγώνων	ἡγεμόνος	ἡγεμόνων
ἀγῶνι	ἀγῶσι(ν)	ἡγεμόνι	ἡγεμόσι(ν)
ἀγῶνα	ἀγῶνας	ἡγεμόνα	ἡγεμόνας

Ἕλλην (ὁ) *Greek*		**ῥήτωρ** (ὁ) *orator*	
Ἕλλην	Ἕλληνες	ῥήτωρ	ῥήτορες
Ἕλληνος	Ἑλλήνων	ῥήτορος	ῥητόρων
Ἕλληνι	Ἕλλησι(ν)	ῥήτορι	ῥήτορσι
Ἕλληνα	Ἕλληνας	ῥήτορα	ῥήτορας

In like manner inflect μήν (§ 102), and χείρ (dative plural χερσί).

227. Adjectives in -ων with stems in **-ον** are declined like ἡγεμών, except for accent. The feminine is like the masculine (as in ἀδιάβατος and in Latin *omnis*). The neuter is like the masculine except in the nominative and accusative singular and plural. The accent is recessive (§ 15).

[1] II Timothy, IV. 7. Literally: *I have engaged in the noble contest.*

εὐδαίμων *prosperous*

(m. and f.)	(n.)	(m. and f.)	(n.)
εὐδαίμων	εὔδαιμον	εὐδαίμονες	εὐδαίμονα
εὐδαίμονος	εὐδαίμονος	εὐδαιμόνων	εὐδαιμόνων
εὐδαίμονι	εὐδαίμονι	εὐδαίμοσι(ν)	εὐδαίμοσι(ν)
εὐδαίμονα	εὔδαιμον	εὐδαίμονας	εὐδαίμονα

228. Dative of Time When. The dative denotes *time when.*[1] This use is akin to that of *place where* except that in Attic prose the latter requires a preposition:

ἐκείνῃ τῇ ἡμέρᾳ ἦλθεν *he came (on) that day.*

229. VOCABULARY

ἀγών, -ῶνος, ὁ: *contest, struggle.* AGONY, PROTAGONIST.
ἔδεισα[2] (aor.): *feared.*
Ἕλλην, -ηνος, ὁ: *Hellene, Greek.*
Ἑλληνικός, -ή, -όν[3]: *Hellenic, Greek.*
εὖ, adv.: *well.* EULOGY.
εὐ-δαίμων, εὔ-δαιμον: *lucky, prosperous.* EUDÆMONISM.
ἡγεμών, -όνος, ὁ: *leader, guide.* Cf. **ἡγέομαι.** HEGEMONY.
μήν, μηνός, ὁ: *month.* Cf. MOON.
πατρίς, -ίδος, ἡ: *fatherland.*
ῥήτωρ, -ορος, ὁ: *speaker, orator.* RHETORIC.
χείρ, χειρός, ἡ: *hand, arm.* CHIROPRACTOR.

230. EXERCISES

(*a*) Translate:

1. *ἐνταῦθα δὴ οἱ Ἕλληνες τῷ θεῷ ἀγῶνα δεύτερον ἐποίουν.* 2. *οὕτως οὖν εὐ-δαίμων ἐγένετο ἡ πατρίς.* 3. *ἐκείνῳ τῷ μηνὶ οἱ ῥήτορες τοῖς πολίταις συν-εβούλευσαν τάδε πράττειν.* 4. *ὧδε οὖν ἡ Ἑλληνικὴ στρατιὰ τούτους τοὺς μῆνας ὑπὸ Κύρου ἐτρέφετο.* 5. *ἐπεὶ ἐκέλευσεν αὐτοὺς μὴ δεῖσαι, ἡγεμόνα ἄλλον ᾔτησαν.* 6. *τοὺς δὲ ὠφελίμους γενομένους εὖ ἂν ποιοίη.* 7. *τοῖς Ἕλλησι πιστεύσᾱς ἐπὶ τὴν*

---

[1] What kinds of time relations are expressed by the genitive and the accusative (§§ 37, 103)? [2] Defective verb. [3] § 210.

πορείᾱν ἧκον. 8. τοῖς εὐ-δαίμοσί που πάντα εὖ γίγνεται. 9. οὐδὲ τῇ τρίτῃ ἡμέρᾳ ηὗρον τὰς ἁμάξᾱς ἐπὶ τῇ γεφῡ́ρᾳ.

(*b*) Complete:

1. τ— δευτερ— νυκτ— οἱ Ἑλλην— ἐδέξαντο σῖτον. 2. ὅντινα ἂν ἑλ—σθε ἀνάγκη ἔσται ἕπεσθαι. 3. τ— παντ— μην— ἡ Ἑλληνικ— στρατιὰ ἐπορεύετο ἀνὰ χώρᾱν χαλεπ—. 4. οἱ ἡγεμ— αὐτοὺς ἄξουσιν ἑπτὰ ἡμερ— εἰς τ— πατριδ—.

Ewing Galloway.

THE AREOPAGUS

St. Paul is thought to have spoken from the top of the Areopagus (Mars' Hill). Close beside the Acropolis it towered above the Agora and gave a view of many a temple and altar and sacred statue.

231. ON MARS' HILL

σταθεὶς (*standing*) δὲ Παῦλος ἐν μέσῳ (compare MESOPOTAMIA) τοῦ Ἀρείου Πάγου ἔφη· Ἄνδρες[1] Ἀθηναῖοι, κατὰ

[1] "*Men*," frequently joined to another noun as a set formula of address. Compare Ἄνδρες ἀδελφοί, *Acts* II. 29, mistranslated "Men and brethren."

πάντα ὡς δεισι-δαιμονεστέρους[1] *ὑμᾶς θεωρῶ* (*behold*)· *δι-ερχόμενος γὰρ καὶ ἀνα-θεωρῶν τὰ σεβάσματα* (*shrines*) *ὑμῶν εὗρον*[2] *καὶ βωμὸν* (*altar*) *ἐν ᾧ ἐπ-εγέγραπτο* (pluperfect passive) ΑΓΝΩΣΤΩΙ (compare **γιγνώσκω**) ΘΕΩΙ. *ὃ οὖν ἀ-γνοοῦντες* (compare ΑΓΝΩΣΤΩΙ) *εὐ-σεβεῖτε* (compare **σεβάσματα**), *τοῦτο ἐγὼ κατ-αγγέλλω ὑμῖν. ὁ θεὸς ὁ ποιήσᾱς τὸν κόσμον* (compare COSMOPOLITAN) *καὶ πάντα τὰ ἐν αὐτῷ, οὗτος οὐρανοῦ* (*heaven*) *καὶ γῆς* (compare GEOLOGY) *ὑπ-άρχων* (*being*) *κύριος* (*lord*) *οὐκ ἐν χειρο-ποιήτοις νᾱοῖς* (*temples*) *κατ-οικεῖ* (compare **οἰκίᾱ**) *οὐδὲ ὑπὸ χειρῶν ἀνθρωπίνων θεραπεύεται* (compare THERAPEUTIC).

Acts, XVII. 22–25.

232. The Greeks had many deities. When they offered prayer or sacrifice, they were careful to address the deity who had special charge over the particular locality or the matters involved. Sometimes they were in doubt as to the proper deities to address. On such occasions they named those who might be interested and uttered some kind of inclusive phrase, such as, "to whom it may concern." Again, they addressed the "Unknown God." It is to the latter that Paul refers.

233. The Greeks did not have a revealed religion. They had a strong religious bent and sought for the power that they felt was outside themselves. Some of their thinkers came very close to monotheism and many of their religious ideas and practices have passed into Christian theology and ritual (§ 48). (Consult Dean Inge in R. W. Livingstone's *The Legacy of Greece*, pages 25–56).

---

[1] Comparative of *δεισι-δαίμων rather god-fearing.*

[2] Equivalent to *ηὗρον*.

LESSON XXXIX

CONSONANT DECLENSION — *Continued*

κακῆς ἀπ' ἀρχῆς γίγνεται τέλος κακόν. — *A bad start means a bad finish.*[1]

234. Neuters with stems in -εσ drop the **σ** whenever it occurs between two vowels (§ 137) and contract the vowels in accord with the principles already learned for *φιλέω* (§ 127). In addition, note that **ε + α = η**. One **σ** is dropped in the dative plural.

γένος (τό) *birth*

γένος	(γένεσ α) γέν η
(γένεσ ος) γέν ους	(γενέσ ων) γενέ ων or γεν ῶν
(γένεσ ι) γέν ει	(γένεσ σι) γένε σι(ν)
γένος	(γένεσ α) γέν η

τριήρης (ἡ) *trireme*[2]

τριήρης	(τριήρεσ ες) τριήρ εις
(τριήρεσ ος) τριήρ ους	(τριηρέσ ων) τριήρ ων
(τριήρεσ ι) τριήρ ει	(τριήρεσ σι) τριήρ εσι(ν)
(τριήρεσ α) τριήρ η	τριήρ εις

In like manner inflect ὄρος and Σωκράτης (singular only).

235. Adjectives with stems in **-εσ** have endings like *τριήρης* in the masculine and feminine and like *γένος* in the

[1] Euripides, fragment. Literally: *From a bad beginning comes a bad end.*

[2] The few masculine and feminine nouns that are declined like *τριήρης* differ from *γένος* only in the nominative and accusative singular and plural. In the plural the accusative borrows the form of the nominative. The accent of the genitive plural is irregular.

neuter, except for the nominative and accusative singular, where the simple stem appears.

Inflect ἀληθής. Compare with paradigm (§ 512).

236. Dative of Association. The dative is used with words denoting friendly or hostile association. This is called the *dative of association:*[1]

μάχονται αὐτῷ *they are fighting (with) him;*
τῷ ἄρχοντι ἕπονται *they are following the commander.*

237. VOCABULARY

ἀ-ληθής, -ές : *true.* LETHE.
ἀ-σφαλής, -ές : *safe, sure.* ASPHALT.
γένος, -ους, τό : *birth, family, kind.* Lat. *genus.* Cf. **ἐγενόμην.** GENEALOGY.
εὖρος, -ους, τό : *breadth.*
Θεμιστοκλῆς, -έους, ὁ : *Themistocles.*
μέρος, -ους, τό : *part, share, rôle.*
ὄρος, -ους, τό : *mountain.* OREAD.
πλῆθος, -ους, τό : *fullness, quantity, multitude,* hence "*the masses.*" PLETHORIC.
Σωκράτης, -ους, ὁ : *Socrates.*
τεῖχος, -ους, τό : *wall* (of fortification).
τρι-ήρης, -ους, ἡ : *trireme, war vessel,* with three (τρι-) banks of oars.

238. EXERCISES

(*a*) Translate:

1. ὁ δὲ Κῦρος μέρος τι τῶν στρατιωτῶν σὺν ταῖς τριήρεσιν ἔπεμψεν. 2. πορευόμενοι δὲ διὰ τῶν ὀρέων εἰς πεδίον ἀφ-ίκοντο δένδρων[2] μεστόν. 3. θαυμάζομεν γὰρ εἰ ἀληθῆ εἶπεν ὁ ἄγγελος. 4. ἀδιάβατος οὖν ὁ ποταμός ἐστι τῷ εὔρει.[3] 5. τοῦτο δὲ τὸ γένος ἐμάχετο τῷ πλήθει. 6. τίνι τρόπῳ ἀπὸ τῶν τειχέων ἔφυγον; 7. μῖκρὰ μὲν ἦν Σωκράτει ἡ οἰκίᾱ, οἱ δὲ φίλοι ἀσφαλεῖς. 8. ἐκ τούτου

---

[1] What uses of the dative have you now had?
[2] Genitive of material or contents.
[3] Dative of cause.

τοῦ γένους ἦν Θεμιστοκλῆς. 9. *πρὸς ἐκεῖνον τὸν ποταμὸν ἀφ-ικόμενοι ἀλλήλοις σπονδὰς ἐποιήσαντο.*

(*b*) Complete:

1. *ἀεὶ γὰρ οἱ ἐπὶ τοῦ ὀρ— ἀλληλ— ἐμάχοντο.* 2. *εἰ αἰτοῖεν τριηρ—* (plural), *τὸ τειχ— οὐκ ἂν* —— (linking verb) *ἀσφαλ—.* 3. *Σωκρατ— οἱ παῖδες εἵποντο ὅπου ἐλθ—.*

(*c*) Write in Greek:

1. On the second day also the Greeks did not choose a leader. 2. The speaker announced that all was well. 3. That night there arose other struggles. 4. During that month the Greek soldiers kept asking for their pay. 5. They may reach their fatherland within ten months.

239. A PRACTICAL POLITICIAN

καὶ δὴ τῷ πλήθει ἐν-ήρμοττε (*fitted in with*) *Θεμιστοκλῆς λέγων μὲν τὸ ὄνομα ἑκάστου* (*each*), *κριτὴν* (*judge*) *δὲ ἀσφαλῆ περὶ τὰ συμβόλαια* (*contracts*) *παρ-έχων ἑαυτόν, ὥστε που καὶ πρὸς Σιμωνίδην τὸν Κεῖον εἰπεῖν, ἐπεὶ ἐδεῖτό τι οὐ μέτριον* (*moderate*) *αὐτοῦ στρατηγοῦντος, ὡς οὔτ' ἐκεῖνος ἂν γένοιτο ποιητὴς ἀγαθὸς ᾄδων* (*singing*) *παρὰ μέλος* (compare MELODY) *οὔτ' αὐτὸς ἀγαθὸς ἄρχων παρὰ νόμον* (compare AUTONOMOUS) *χαριζόμενος* (compare **χάρις**).

Adapted from Plutarch, *Themistocles*, V. 4.

240. The hero of H. G. Wells' *Tono-Bungay*, recounting the influences of his early life, says: "And I found Langhorne's 'Plutarch,' too, I remember, on those shelves. It seems queer to me now to think that I acquired pride and self-respect, the idea of a state and the germ of public spirit, in such a furtive fashion; queer, too, that it should rest with an old Greek, dead these eighteen hundred years. to teach me that."

LESSON XL

ADJECTIVES OF CONSONANT AND A-DECLENSIONS COMBINED. IRREGULAR ADJECTIVES

οὐ πολλὰ ἀλλὰ πολύ. — *Not quantity but quality.*[1]

241. Adjectives of the combined consonant and **α**-declensions present such irregularities in the masculine and neuter that detailed analysis is of little value. Learn the forms as given, noting that recognition of case, gender, and number is simple. The feminine is like γέφῡρα (§ 81).

242. **ταχύς** *swift*

ταχ ύς	ταχ εῖα	ταχ ύ	ταχ εῖς	ταχ εῖαι	ταχ έα
ταχ έος	ταχ είᾱς	ταχ έος	ταχ έων	ταχ ειῶν	ταχ έων
ταχ εῖ	ταχ είᾳ	ταχ εῖ	ταχ έσι(ν)	ταχ είαις	ταχ έσι(ν)
ταχ ύν	ταχ εῖαν	ταχ ύ	ταχ εῖς	ταχ είᾱς	ταχ έα

243. The irregular adjective πολύς has one **λ** and endings of the consonant declension where ταχύς has **υ**; elsewhere it has **λλ** and endings of the **ο**- and the **α**-declensions.

πολύς *much, many*

πολύς	πολλή	πολύ	πολλοί	πολλαί	πολλά
πολλοῦ	πολλῆς	πολλοῦ	πολλῶν	πολλῶν	πολλῶν
πολλῷ	πολλῇ	πολλῷ	πολλοῖς	πολλαῖς	πολλοῖς
πολύν	πολλήν	πολύ	πολλούς	πολλᾱ́ς	πολλά

244. Another irregular adjective, μέγας, has the stem μεγα- and endings of the consonant declension where ταχύς has **υ**; elsewhere it has the stem μεγαλ- and endings of the

[1] Greek maxim. Literally: *Not many things but much.*

ο- and the α-declensions. The accent of the feminine genitive plural is irregular, being influenced by the corresponding form of the masculine and neuter.

μέγας *big, great*

μέγας	μεγάλη	μέγα	μεγάλοι	μεγάλαι	μεγάλα
μεγάλου	μεγάλης	μεγάλου	μεγάλων	μεγάλων	μεγάλων
μεγάλῳ	μεγάλῃ	μεγάλῳ	μεγάλοις	μεγάλαις	μεγάλοις
μέγαν	μεγάλην	μέγα	μεγάλους	μεγάλᾱς	μεγάλα

245. Two Accusatives. (*a*) Two accusatives may occur with verbs meaning *appoint*, *choose*, *call*, *make*, and the like. One of these accusatives is the direct object, the other is a predicate accusative:

αὐτὸν ποιεῖ σατράπην *he makes him satrap.*

(*b*) Two accusatives may occur with verbs meaning *ask*, *deprive*, *teach*, *persuade*. One of these accusatives is usually a person, the other a thing:

αὐτοὺς αἰτεῖ ὅπλα *he asks them for arms.*

(*c*) Somewhat akin to this are the two accusatives, or accusative and adverb, with verbs meaning *do anything to* or *say anything of* :[1]

αὐτοὺς ἀγαθὰ (or εὖ) ποιεῖ *he treats them well.*

246. Omission of the Linking Verb. The linking verbs ἐστί and εἰσί must often be supplied in *general* or *proverbial* expressions, in expressions of *necessity* or *duty*, and with some adjectives:

ἀρχὴ ἥμισυ πάντων *(the) beginning (is) half of all* (that is, *well begun, half done*);
ἀνάγκη θύειν *sacrifice a necessity (it is necessary to sacrifice).*

---

1 What uses of the accusative have you now had?

247. **VOCABULARY**

εὐθύς, -εῖα, -ύ: *straight, direct;* εὐθύς, adv.: *straightway, immediately.*
ἡδέως, adv.: *gladly.*
ἡδύς, -εῖα, -ύ: *sweet, pleasant.*
μέγας, μεγάλη, μέγα: *great, large.* MEGALOMANIA.
πλήν, prep. with G.: *except.*
πολύς, πολλή, πολύ: *much;* pl., *many;* οἱ πολλοί: *the majority.* POLYGON.
πρό, prep. with G.: *before, in front of.* PROLOGUE.
ταχύς, -εῖα, -ύ: *swift.* TACHYMETER.
τέλος, -ους, τό: *end;* A. used as adv.: *finally.* TELEOLOGICAL.
ὑπέρ, prep.: with G., *above, in behalf of;* with A., *above, beyond.* HYPERBOLA, HYPERTROPHY.

248. **EXERCISES**

(*a*) Translate:

1. καὶ ἡ μὲν ἀρχὴ χαλεπή, τὸ δὲ τέλος ἡδύ. 2. ἐνταῦθα οὖν ἡδέως ἂν αὐτὸν αἰτησαίμην πολλά. 3. καὶ πρὸ τῆς μάχης ταχείαις τριήρεσιν ἀφ-ίκοντο ἐπὶ τὸ Κύρου στρατόπεδον. 4. τῇ δὲ τρίτῃ ἡμέρᾳ πάντες πλὴν τῶν ἐν τῇ ἀγορᾷ ἔφυγον. 5. τοὺς δὲ βαρβάρους διώξουσιν ὑπὲρ τὰ ὄρη. 6. ὑπὲρ γὰρ τῆς πατρίδος ἀναγκαῖον πολλοὺς κινδύνους ἔχειν. 7. τέλος δὲ πρὸς ἀδιάβατον ποταμὸν ἀφ-ικόμενοι ἐπαυσάμεθα. 8. ἐν τούτῳ τῷ ἀγῶνι τὸν ῥήτορα οἱ πολλοὶ εὐθὺς εἵλοντο ἡγεμόνα.

APOLLO WITH HIS LYRE

Every phase of Greek life had its deity. Apollo was the god of Music.

(*b*) Complete:

1. πρὸ δὲ τούτων τῶν ὀρῶν ἦν μεγ— πεδίον, ἐν ᾧ ἔμενε πολλ— ἡμέρᾱς. 2. ἀλλ' ἡ εὐθ— ὁδὸς οὐκ ἄγει πρὸς

σωτηρι—. 3. *καὶ πολ— χρόνον ἐθαυμάζομεν εἰ οἱ Ἕλληνες αὐτὸν ἡγεμον— ποιησ—.*

(*c*) Write in Greek:

1. They are fighting the Greeks on the mountain. 2. The companies will not reach the wall if they do not proceed in silence. 3. Since the triremes were safe, the Athenians vowed to sacrifice to all the gods. 4. The multitude was not willing to follow him. 5. That day each received his share.

249. To Callimachus, head of the great library at Alexandria (third century B.C.), famed as poet, philosopher, and literary critic, is attributed the saying:

μέγα βιβλίον μέγα κακόν.

The books were rolls and difficult to handle when large. (Ask your instructor to explain the nature of a roll.)

250. **EROS WINS**

θέλω λέγειν Ἀτρείδᾱς,	*I wish to hymn th' Atreidæ,*
θέλω δὲ Κάδμον ᾄδειν·	*I fain would sing of Cadmus;*
ἡ βάρβιτος δὲ χορδαῖς	*But when I touch my lyre,*
Ἔρωτα μοῦνον ἠχεῖ.	*All I can get is Eros.*
ἤμειψα νεῦρα πρώην	*I changed the strings but lately,*
καὶ τὴν λύρην ἅπᾱσαν,	*I even changed the lyre:*
κἀγὼ μὲν ᾖδον ἄθλους	*But when I would have chanted*
Ἡρακλέους· λύρη δὲ	*Great Heracles' labors,*
ἔρωτας ἀντ-εφώνει.	*The lyre returned me Eros.*
χαίροιτε λοιπὸν ἡμῖν,	*Farewell, then, noble heroes;*
ἥρωες· ἡ λύρη γὰρ	*No use to strive, for clearly*
μόνους Ἔρωτας ᾄδει.	*The lyre sings naught but Eros.*
Anacreontic.	

Who were the Atreidæ, Cadmus, Heracles?
With the verse rendering as an aid, translate.

LESSON XLI

REGULAR COMPARISON OF ADJECTIVES

χαλεπὸν τὸ μὴ φιλῆσαι. — *'Tis hard not to love.*[1]

251. Comparison of Adjectives. (*a*) The comparative degree of adjectives is commonly formed by adding **-τερος, -ᾱ, -ον** to the masculine stem of the positive.

(*b*) The superlative is formed by adding **-τατος, -η, -ον**.

(*c*) If the penult of an adjective in **-ος** contains a short vowel not followed by two consonants or a double consonant, the **ο** of the stem is lengthened to **ω** in forming the comparative and the superlative.

Positive	Comparative	Superlative
δίκαιος (δικαιο-)	δικαιότερος	δικαιότατος
μακρός (μακρο-)	μακρότερος	μακρότατος
πιστός (πιστο-)	πιστότερος	πιστότατος
ἀληθής (ἀληθεσ-)	ἀληθέστερος	ἀληθέστατος
εὐδαίμων	εὐδαιμονέστερος (as if stem were εὐδαιμονεσ-)	εὐδαιμονέστατος
ἄξιος (ἀξιο-)	ἀξιώτερος	ἀξιώτατος
φοβερός (φοβερο-)	φοβερώτερος	φοβερώτατος

252. Certain adjectives, chiefly those in **-υς** and **-ρος**, add to the root of the word **-ῑων, -ῑον** for the comparative and **-ιστος, -η, -ον** for the superlative.

ἡδύς	ἡδίων	ἥδιστος
ταχύς	(ταχίων) θάττων	τάχιστος
αἰσχρός	αἰσχίων	αἴσχιστος

[1] Anacreontic. The infinitive is here used as a neuter noun, as τό shows.

Give the comparative and superlative of δεινός, σοφός, ἀσφαλής.

253. Inflection of Comparatives and Superlatives. (*a*) Comparatives in **-τερος** are declined like μῑκρός; superlatives in **-τατος** and **-ιστος** are declined like ἀγαθός. The accent of all comparatives and superlatives is recessive (§ 15).

Inflect πιστότερος, πιστότατος, τάχιστος.

(*b*) Comparatives in **-ῑων** are inflected like εὐδαίμων, except that they have additional forms as given below. These additional forms come from a stem in **-οσ**, which drops the **σ** between two vowels and contracts: **ο + α = ω**, **ο + ε = ου**. The accusative plural has borrowed the form of the nominative.

ἡδίων *sweeter*

(m. and f.)	(n.)	(m. and f.)	(n.)
ἡδί **ων**	ἥδῑ **ον**	ἡδί **ονες** or ἡδί **ους**	ἡδί **ονα** or ἡδί **ω**
ἡδί **ονος**	ἡδί **ονος**	ἡδῑ **όνων**	ἡδῑ **όνων**
ἡδί **ονι**	ἡδί **ονι**	ἡδί **οσι(ν)**	ἡδί **οσι**
ἡδί **ονα** or ἡδί **ω**	ἥδῑ **ον**	ἡδί **ονας** or ἡδί **ους**	ἡδί **ονα** or ἡδί **ω**

254. Genitive of Comparison. A comparative, unless accompanied by ἤ, is followed by the genitive. This is called the *genitive of comparison:* [1]

Κῦρος νεώτερος ἦν τοῦ ἀδελφοῦ *Cyrus was younger than his brother.*

If ἤ is used, the persons or things compared usually are in the same case, and always so when used with the same verb (compare the Latin construction with and without *quam*):

τούτῳ οὖν ἐπίστευον μᾶλλον ἢ ἐκείνῳ *I therefore trusted this man more than that man.*

---

[1] What uses of the genitive have you now had?

255. VOCABULARY

αἰσχρός, -ά, -όν: *shameful, ugly.* Opposite of **καλός.**

αἴτιος, -ᾱ, -ον: *responsible, accountable;* with G., *responsible for.*

ἀ-πορέω, -ήσω, ἠ-πόρησα: *be at a loss, be troubled, be helpless.* Cf. **πορείᾱ, πορεύομαι.**

ἀ-πορίᾱ, -ᾱς, ἡ: *difficulty, helplessness, lack.*

ἄ-πορος, -ον: *helpless, needy, impassable.*

δεινός, -ή, -όν: *to be feared, terrible, skilful, clever.* Cf. **ἔδεισα.** DINOSAURUS.

ὅτι, adv. with superl. to denote the highest degree possible. Cf. Lat. *quam.*

πιστός, -ή, -όν: *faithful, loyal, trusty.*

φοβερός, -ά, -όν: *fearful, frightful.* Cf. **φόβος.**

ὡς, adv. with superl. to denote the highest degree possible. Cf. Lat. *quam.*

256. EXERCISES

(*a*) Translate:

1. τοῦτο ἔστιν αἴσχιστον, ὅτι ὑμεῖς αἴτιοι ἐγένεσθε τῆς φυγῆς. 2. πολὺν δὲ χρῡσὸν ὑπ-έσχετο αὐτοῖς, ὥστε ἦσαν ὅτι προθῡμότατοι. 3. ὁπότε δὲ κατὰ τῶν ὀρῶν πορευοίμεθα, τὰ δεινότατα ἐπάσχομεν. 4. ἀλλὰ νῦν οἱ πρὸ ταύτης τῆς μάχης ἀ-πορήσαντες ὡς φοβερώτατοι ἐγένοντο τοῖς πολεμίοις. 5. ταῖς ταχίσταις τριήρεσιν ἐξ-έσται διώκειν τε καὶ ἑλεῖν τοὺς αἰσχρούς. 6. νομίζει τοὺς Ἕλληνας πιστοτέρους εἶναι τῶν βαρβάρων. 7. Σωκράτης δίκην ἐφίλει μᾶλλον ἢ σωτηρίᾱν. 8. οἱ δὲ ποταμοὶ ἄ-poροι ἔσονται ἡμῖν, ἢν τὰς γεφύρᾱς λύσωσιν.

(*b*) Complete:

1. αἱ τριήρεις θᾶττ— ἦσαν τ— πλοι— (plural). 2. τῶν δ' οὖν Ἑλλήνων Κῦρος ἐπ-εμελεῖτο μᾶλλον ἢ τ— βαρβαρ—. 3. ἀλλ' ὀλίγοι ἄνθρωποί εἰσιν ὅτι εὐδαιμ—. 4. οἱ γὰρ πολλοὶ φοβερ—τατοι γίγνονται ἐπὰν σίτου —— (linking verb) ἀπορίᾱ.

(c) Write in Greek:

1. It is necessary to incur great danger in behalf of Greece. 2. Whomever the majority choose as leader, we shall gladly follow. 3. If the triremes were not swift, the commander would have saved few men. 4. Great was the breadth of the wall. 5. We might ask our friends for many things.

FRIGHTFUL MEDUSA

This very archaic bit of sculpture shows Perseus cutting off her head.

257. WISEST OF ALL

σοφὸς Σοφοκλῆς, σοφώτερος
δ' Εὐρῑπίδης,
ἀνδρῶν[1] *δὲ πάντων Σωκράτης*
σοφώτατος.

Ancient Oracle, quoted by Suidas under *σοφός*.

258. ARISTOTLE ON FRIENDSHIP

ἐρωτηθεὶς (*being asked*) *τί ἐστι φίλος, ἔφη, Μία* (*one*) *ψῡχὴ* (*mind*, compare PSYCHOLOGY) *δύο σώμασιν* (*bodies*) *ἐν-οικοῦσα* (compare **οἰκία**).

Diogenes Laertius, V. 21.

ὦ φίλοι, οὐδεὶς (*no*) *φίλος.*

Ibid., V. 21.

ἐρωτηθεὶς πῶς ἂν τοῖς φίλοις προσ-φεροίμεθα (*behave*), *ἔφη, Ὡς ἂν εὐξαίμεθα αὐτοὺς ἡμῖν προσ-φέρεσθαι.*

Ibid., V. 21.

---

[1] *Of men.* Partitive genitive, denoting the whole of which a part is mentioned.

LESSON XLII

IRREGULAR COMPARISON

χαλεπὸν δὲ καὶ φιλῆσαι. — *And hard as well to love.*[1]

259. Irregularities occur in the comparison of a number of adjectives.[2]

Positive	Comparative	Superlative
ἀγαθός *good, brave*, etc.	ἀμείνων *better, braver*	ἄριστος *best, bravest*, etc. ARISTOCRAT.
	βελτΐων morally *better*	βέλτιστος morally *best*
	κρείττων physically *stronger, preferable*	κράτιστος *strongest, best*
κακός *bad, ugly, cowardly*	κακΐων	κάκιστος
	χείρων *meaner*	χείριστος
	ἥττων *weaker, inferior*	[ἥκιστα, adv.: *least, by no means*]
καλός *beautiful, noble*	καλλΐων	κάλλιστος
μέγας *great, large*	μείζων	μέγιστος
μῑκρός *small*	μῑκρότερος	μῑκρότατος
	μείων; pl., *fewer*	
	ἐλάττων[3]	ἐλάχιστος
πολύς *much*; pl., *many*	πλείων or πλέων PLEONASM.	πλεῖστος

260. Some words lack a positive:

[πρό *before*]	πρότερος *former*	πρῶτος *first*
	ὕστερος *later, latter*	ὕστατος *last*

Inflect ἀμείνων (like ἡδΐων), πρότερος, πλεῖστος.

[1] Anacreontic.

[2] Only the more common adjectives are here given.

[3] Serves also as comparative for ὀλίγος *little, few*.

261. Dative of Degree of Difference. The dative, when used with expressions of comparison, denotes the *degree of difference* between the persons or things compared. This is a variety of the dative of means (compare with the Latin ablative of degree of difference) : [1]

Κῦρος πολλῷ ἦν νεώτερος *Cyrus was much younger* (that is, *younger by much*).

262. EXERCISES

Ἀριστίων
A warrior of Marathon.

(*a*) Translate :

1. τοῦ δὲ ἀγαθοῦ πολῑ́του [2] ἐστὶ τὰ ἄριστα καὶ λέγειν καὶ πρᾱ́ττειν. 2. οὐκ ἐλάχιστόν ἐστι σοφίᾱς μέρος σαυτὸν γιγνώσκειν. 3. ἐπορίσαντο δ᾽ οὖν σῖτον ὀλίγῳ πλείω. 4. τούτους μέντοι τοὺς σταθμοὺς πολλῷ μακροτέρους ἐποίει. 5. ἡ δὲ γυνὴ προτέρᾱ Κῡ́ρου ὀκτὼ ἡμέραις ἦλθεν. 6. ἐνόμιζε δὲ τοὺς Ἕλληνας ἀμείνους εἶναι πολλῶν βαρβάρων. 7. τί κάλλῑον ἢ ὑπὲρ τῆς πατρίδος ἀπο-θανεῖν; 8. ἀλλὰ σὺν μείζονι στρατιᾷ ἐπορεύετο ἢ ὡς ἐπ᾽ ἐκείνους. 9. ἐκέλευσε τοὺς στρατηγοὺς τὰ ἐπιτήδεια λαβόντας ὡς πλεῖστα παρ-εῖναι. 10. οὗτοι οἱ ἵπποι μῑκρότεροι μὲν ἦσαν, κρείττονες δέ.

(*b*) Write in Greek :

1. The Greeks were more faithful. 2. If the women reach the wall, they will be very safe. 3. The orators became more clever

[1] What uses of the dative have you now had?

[2] A possessive genitive used in the predicate with ἐστί may denote the person whose *characteristic* it is to do what is indicated by the infinitive subject.

than the rest of the citizens. 4. The barbarians were as frightful as possible. 5. They found the road through the mountains more impassable than that (use article) along the river.

263. **ESSE QUAM VIDERI**

οὐ γὰρ δοκεῖν ἄριστος, ἀλλ' εἶναι [ἐ]θέλει.

Æschylus, *Seven against Thebes*, 592.

λίθοι μέγιστοι

These columns from the temple of Zeus at Olympia are the largest in Greece. At the base they measure seven and one-third feet in diameter. (For a general view of Olympia see page 153.)

264. **OPTIMISM**

ἔλεξε γάρ τις ὡς τὰ χείρονα
πλείω βροτοῖσίν (*to mortals*) ἐστι τῶν ἀμεινόνων·
ἐγὼ δὲ τούτοις ἀντίᾱν (*opposing*) γνώμην ἔχω,
πλείω τὰ χρηστὰ (*good things*) τῶν κακῶν εἶναι βροτοῖς.

Euripides, *Suppliants*, 196–199.

265. ΓΝΩΜΑΙ ΜΕΝΑΝΔΡΟΥ

εἶτ᾽ οὐ μέγιστός ἐστι τῶν θεῶν Ἔρως
καὶ τῑμιώτατός (*most precious*) γε τῶν πάντων πολύ;

ἆρ᾽ ἐστὶν ἀγαθῶν πᾶσι πλείστων ἀξίᾱ
ἡ σύνεσις (*intelligence*), ἂν ᾖ πρὸς τὰ βελτίω σοφή.

κρεῖττον ὀλίγ᾽ ἐστὶ χρήματ᾽ ἀν-υπόπτως (*honestly*) ἔχειν
ἢ πολλὰ φανερῶς (*openly*) ἃ μετ᾽ ὀνείδους (*reproach*) δεῖ λαβεῖν.

ἀεὶ κράτιστόν ἐστι τἀληθῆ (= τὰ ἀληθῆ) λέγειν.

266. RIGHT IS MIGHT

κρεῖττόν ἐστι μετ᾽ ὀλίγων ἀγαθῶν πρὸς πάντας τοὺς κακοὺς ἢ μετὰ πολλῶν κακῶν πρὸς ὀλίγους ἀγαθοὺς μάχεσθαι.

Antisthenes, quoted by Diogenes Laertius, VI. 12.

A Greek Vase

LESSON XLIII

FORMATION AND COMPARISON OF ADVERBS

χαλεπώτερον δὲ πάντων ἀποτυγχάνειν φιλοῦντα.
But harder than all to love and lose.[1]

267. Adverbs may usually be formed by changing the **ν** of the genitive plural masculine of the adjective to **ς**. The accent remains as in the genitive plural. The comparative of the adverb is the neuter accusative singular of the comparative of the adjective; the superlative is the neuter accusative plural of the superlative of the adjective.

POSITIVE	COMPARATIVE	SUPERLATIVE
ἀσφαλῶς *safely, surely*	ἀσφαλέστερον	ἀσφαλέστατα
δικαίως *justly*	δικαιότερον	δικαιότατα
φοβερῶς *fearfully, frightfully*	φοβερώτερον	φοβερώτατα
ἡδέως *gladly*	ἥδῑον	ἥδιστα
καλῶς *beautifully*	κάλλῑον	κάλλιστα

Give the positive, comparative, and superlative of the adverbs corresponding to ἄξιος, μέγας, ἀληθής, ταχύς, κακός, δεινός.

268. Irregularities occur in the comparison of some adverbs.

ἐγγύς *near, nearly*	ἐγγύτερον or ἐγγυτέρω	ἐγγύτατα or ἐγγυτάτω
εὖ *well* (adv. of ἀγαθός)	ἄμεινον	ἄριστα
μάλα *very*	μᾶλλον *more, rather*	μάλιστα *most, certainly*
πολύ *much, by far*	πλεῖον or πλέον	πλεῖστα

[1] Anacreontic, concluding mottoes of XLI and XLII.

269. Cognate Accusative. A noun, adjective, or pronoun in the accusative may contain the *same idea as that of the verb*. This is called the *cognate accusative*:

μάχην μάχονται *they are fighting a battle;*
τάδε ὑπ-έσχετο *he made this promise* (that is, *he promised this*);
τὴν ταχίστην (ὁδὸν) πορεύεται *he is proceeding (by) the quickest road.*

270. Adverbial Accusative.[1] Many accusatives lose all obvious relation in idea to the verb and serve as its *adverbial modifiers*. This is called the *adverbial accusative*:[2]

τὴν ταχίστην (ὁδὸν) ἔπρᾱξαν ταῦτα *they did this the quickest way;*
τέλος ἦλθεν *finally he came;*
τί ἦλθεν; *why did he come?*
θᾶττον πορεύεται ἢ ἡμεῖς *he is proceeding more swiftly than we;*
τάχιστα πορεύεται *he is proceeding most swiftly.*

271. VOCABULARY

ἐπ-αινέω, ἐπ-αινέσω, ἐπ-ήνεσα: *praise.*
κρατέω, κρατήσω, ἐκράτησα: *overpower, conquer.* Cf. **κράτιστος**, DEMOCRATIC.
κράτος, -ους, τό: *power.*
ὄπισθεν, adv.: *from the rear, in the rear, behind.* Cf. **ἐντεῦθεν.**
πάνυ, adv.: *wholly, very.* Cf. **πᾶς.**
πρόσθεν, adv.: *from the front, in front, before.* Cf. **ὄπισθεν.**
ῥᾴδιος, -ᾱ, -ον: *easy.*
ῥίπτω, ῥίψω, ἔρρῑψα: *throw, cast aside.*
στόμα, -ατος, τό: *mouth, van* (of an army).

272. EXERCISES

(*a*) Translate:

1. ἐπεὶ γὰρ ἐγγύτερον ἐγένοντο, πολὺ θᾶττον ἐδίωκον τοὺς πολεμίους. 2. τέλος δὲ ταῦθ' ὡς ἥδιστ' ἂν ἐπ-αινοίην. 3. νῦν δὲ ἐὰν καλῶς πρᾱ́ξωμεν,[3] πολλῷ πλέον ἕξομεν κράτος. 4. ὑμεῖς δὲ εὖ παθόντες[4] ὑπ' αὐτοῦ δικαίως ἂν φύγοιτε τὴν

[1] This use, and that of adjectives as cognate accusatives, illustrates the suitability of the accusative case of the adjective as the form of the adverb.

[2] What uses of the accusative have you now had?

[3] *Fare.* Compare *How do you do?*

[4] πάσχω is often used as the passive of ποιέω and as such takes the constructions of a passive verb.

ὁ κράτιστος

This charioteer, found at Delphi, marks a victory in the Pythian Games. It is the most famous work in bronze remaining from the best period of Greek art.

αὐτὴν φυγήν. 5. ἀλλ' εἰ ὅτι μάλιστ' αὐτὸν ἐπαινοῖτε, οὐκ-έτι ἂν φίλους ὑμᾶς νομίζοι. 6. τούτου ἡγουμένου ῥᾴδιον ἔσται πάνυ ἀσφαλῶς πορεύεσθαι. 7. τὴν στρατιὰν μέντοι ἐγγὺς τοῦ ποταμοῦ εἶχεν, ἵνα μὴ ὄπισθεν γένοιντο οἱ πολέμιοι. 8. κρατήσαντες οὖν πολὺ προθῡμότερον ἐπορεύοντο ἢ τὸ πρόσθεν. 9. καὶ τοῦτ' οὐχ ἥκιστα αἴτιον τῆς φυγῆς ἐγένετο. 10. οἱ γὰρ ἐκ τοῦ στόματος τὰ ὅπλα ῥίψαντες ἀνὰ κράτος [1] ἔφυγον.

(*b*) Write in Greek:

1. As many as possible will be present. 2. These (persons) are much more cowardly than the Greeks. 3. His brother did not suspect that Cyrus was enlisting (*collecting*) as brave (men) as possible. 4. The mercenaries arrived a little later than we. 5. We must (*it is necessary*) have very swift triremes.

273. A SUPERLATIVE CHARACTER

Κῦρος μὲν οὖν οὕτως ἀπ-έθανεν, ὢν Περσῶν τῶν μετὰ Κῦρον τὸν ἀρχαῖον γενομένων βασιλικώτατός (compare **βασίλεια**) τε καὶ ἄρχειν ἀξιώτατος. πρῶτον μὲν γὰρ ἔτι παῖς ὤν, ὅτε ἐπαιδεύετο (compare PEDAGOGY) καὶ σὺν τῷ ἀδελφῷ καὶ σὺν τοῖς ἄλλοις παισί, πάντων πάντα [2] κράτιστος ἐνομίζετο. πάντες γὰρ οἱ τῶν ἀρίστων Περσῶν παῖδες ἐπὶ ταῖς βασιλικαῖς θύραις παιδεύονται. ἔνθα Κῦρος αἰδημονέστατος (*respectful*) μὲν πρῶτον τῶν παίδων ἐδόκει εἶναι, ἔπειτα δὲ φιλ-ιππότατος καὶ τοὺς ἵππους ἄριστα ἐλαύνειν. ἐνόμιζον δ' αὐτὸν καὶ τῶν εἰς τὸν πόλεμον ἔργων φιλο-μαθέστατον (*interested in*) εἶναι.

Adapted from Xenophon, *Anabasis*, I. 9. 1–6.

---

[1] ἀνὰ κράτος, *at full speed; κατὰ κράτος* would mean *in accordance with their power*.

[2] **Accusative of respect**, showing the thing or things in respect to which Κῦρος was κράτιστος.

LESSON XLIV

CONSONANT DECLENSION

φιλαργυρία μητρόπολις πάντων τῶν κακῶν.
The love of money is the root of all evil.[1]

274. Stems in ι, αυ, or ευ present such irregularities in their inflection that detailed analysis is of little value. Learn the forms as given, noting for purposes of case recognition those forms that seem peculiar.

πόλις (ἡ) *city*		**βασιλεύς** (ὁ) *king*	
πόλις	πόλεις	βασιλεύς	βασιλεῖς
πόλεως	πόλεων	βασιλέως	βασιλέων
πόλει	πόλεσι(ν)	βασιλεῖ	βασιλεῦσι(ν)
πόλιν	πόλεις	βασιλέᾱ	βασιλέᾱς

ναῦς (ἡ) *ship*	
ναῦς	νῆες
νεώς	νεῶν
νηί	ναυσί(ν)
ναῦν	ναῦς

Like πόλις, inflect ἀνάβασις; like βασιλεύς, inflect ἱππεύς.

275. Partitive Genitive. (*a*) The genitive may denote the *whole*, of which a part is mentioned. It may be used with any word that expresses or implies a part. This use is called the *partitive genitive*:[2]

μέρος τῆς στρατιᾶς *part of the army.*

(*b*) Any verb whose action affects the object *only in part* may take the genitive. This is true especially of verbs

[1] Diogenes, as quoted by Diogenes Laertius, VI. 50.

[2] What uses of the genitive have you now had?

meaning *share, take hold of, hit, miss, begin, hear*, and the like:

ἔλαβε τῆς στρατιᾶς *he took (part) of the army;*
ἦρχε τοῦ λόγου *he began his speech;*
ἤκουσαν τῆς σάλπιγγος *they heard the trumpet.*

276. Prepositions. (*a*) Prepositions at first were adverbs and in classic Greek they still occasionally retain that function. Usually they show adverbial force when used as prefixes to compound verbs. Often the preposition with the proper case is repeated in connection with the compound verb.

(*b*) Prepositions thus compounded sometimes have their literal meaning:

εἰσ-πίπτει εἰς τὴν ναῦν *he rushes (falls) into the ship;*
ἀπο-φεύγει *he flees away.*

Again, they often have a more or less figurative force:

αὐτὸν ἐκ-πλήττουσι *they strike him out* (of his senses), *they astound him;*
δια-φθείρει *he destroys th⟨o⟩rough⟨ly⟩.*

(*c*) You will not find in the lesson vocabularies of this book all the compound verbs used in the Greek sentences or passages. A little ingenuity will usually suggest the proper meaning of an unfamiliar compound.

277. VOCABULARY

ἀνά-βασις, -εως, ἡ: *a going-up* (from the sea), *inland march.* ANABASIS.

βασιλεύς, -έως, ὁ: *king.* Cf. **βασίλεια.** BASIL.

βασιλεύω, -σω, -σα: *be king:* aor., *became king.*

βοη-θέω, βοηθήσω, ἐβοήθησα: with D., *run to aid* (at a shout for help), *assist.*

θέω, θεύσομαι[1]: *run.*

ἱππεύς, -έως, ὁ: *horseman, knight.*

ναῦς, νεώς, ἡ: *ship.* NAUSEA.

πίπτω, πεσοῦμαι, ἔπεσον: *fall.*

πλήττω, πλήξω, ἔπληξα: *strike.* APOPLEXY ("stroke").

πόλις, -εως, ἡ: *city, state.* Cf. **πολίτης.** POLITICAL.

στενός, -ή, -όν: *narrow.* STENOGRAPHIC.

[1] Other forms are supplied by other verbs.

278. EXERCISES

(*a*) Translate:

1. ἀλλ' οὐκ ἔστι τοῖς φίλοις βοη-θεῖν. 2. πολλοὶ τῶν ἱππέων ἐξ-επλήττοντο, ὥστε ἀνὰ κράτος ἔθεον. 3. ἡ ἀνά-βασις ἦν ἐπὶ βασιλέᾱ.[1] 4. αἱ δ' οὖν βασιλέως νῆες οὔπω ἥκουσιν. 5. καὶ οἱ βάρβαροι, ὅταν πρὸς μάχην ἔρχωνται, κραυγῇ θέουσιν. 6. εἰς δὲ τὴν ναῦν εἰσ-πεσόντες πάντας πλήξομεν. 7. καὶ μάλα ἡδέως ὁ ῥήτωρ ἦρχε τοῦ λόγου. 8. εἰ μὴ ἐν τῇ ἀνα-βάσει ἀπ-έθανεν ὁ Κῦρος, ἐβασίλευσεν ἄν; 9. ποῦ τῆς πόλεως ἦσθα ὅτε τῆς σάλπιγγος ἤκουσας; 10. πότερον ἐβασίλευε πολὺν χρόνον ἢ οὔ; 11. τὸ τούτου τοῦ ποταμοῦ στόμα ἦν στενώτερον, ὥστε ταῖς ναυσὶν ἄ-πορον εἶναι. 12. τῷ δ' ἀδελφῷ, βασιλεῖ ὄντι, ἥξουσι πολλοὶ ἐκ τῶν πόλεων ὡς βοηθήσοντες.

(*b*) Write in Greek:

1. Why did the triremes not flee more rapidly? 2. They fought a very hard battle. 3. When there was (*there being*) danger, we proceeded (by) the quickest road. 4. The captain arranged his company as well as possible. 5. They were very near to the camp before they perceived that the enemy were no longer in their rear.

279. A HEADSTRONG YOUTH

ἔτι δὲ παῖς ὢν ἔπαιζεν (*was playing*) ὁ Ἀλκιβιάδης ἀστραγάλοις (*dice*) ἐν ὁδῷ στενῇ, τῆς δὲ βολῆς (*throw*) καθ-ηκούσης εἰς αὐτὸν ἅμαξα ἐπ-ήρχετο. πρῶτον μὲν οὖν ἐκέλευε παύσασθαι τὸν τὴν ἅμαξαν ἄγοντα· ὑπ-έπῑπτε γὰρ ἡ βολὴ τῇ παρ-όδῳ τῆς ἁμάξης. οὐ πειθομένου δ' ἐκείνου ἀλλ' ἐπ-άγοντος, οἱ μὲν ἄλλοι παῖδες ἔφευγον, ὁ δ' Ἀλκι-

[1] βασιλεύς, where it refers to the Great King of Persia, commonly omits the article.

βιάδης κατα-πεσὼν ἐπὶ στόμα πρὸ τοῦ ἵππου ἐκέλευεν οὕτως, εἰ βούλεται, δι-εξ-ελθεῖν, ὥστε ὁ μὲν ἄνθρωπος δείσᾱς ἀν-έκρουσε (*backed up*) τὸν ἵππον, οἱ δὲ παρόντες τῷ πράγματι ἐξ-επλήττοντο καὶ σὺν κραυγῇ ἐβοήθησαν αὐτῷ.

Adapted from Plutarch, *Alcibiades*, II.

ἱππεὺς Ἀθηναῖος

This slab from the Parthenon Frieze portrays a member of the City Troop about to mount for the Panathenaic procession.

280. Word-formation. (*a*) The suffix **-σις**, both in Greek and in English, denotes a *name of an action:*

ἀναλῡ́ω *analyze*, ἀνάλυσις ANALYSIS;
σήπω *decay*, σῆψις *a decaying*, SEPSIS;
διαβαίνω *cross*, διάβασις *a crossing:*
ἀναβαίνω *go up* (or *inland*), ἀνάβασις *an inland march*, ANABASIS.

(*b*) The suffix **-ευς** denotes the *agent* or *doer of an action:*

γράφω *write*, γραφεύς *writer;*
ἵππος *horse*, ἱππεύς *horseman;*
βασιλεύω *be king*, βασιλεύς *king*.

LESSON XLV

SYNCOPATED NOUNS OF THE CONSONANT DECLENSION

ἄνδρες γὰρ πόλις, καὶ οὐ τείχη οὐδὲ νῆες ἀνδρῶν κεναί.
Men make a state, not walls nor empty ships.[1]

281. Syncopated nouns of the consonant declension drop **ε** of the stem in the genitive and dative singular and dative plural. ἀνήρ substitutes **δ** for **ε** except in the nominative.

πατήρ (ὁ) *father*		**μήτηρ** (ἡ) *mother*	
πατήρ	πατέρες	μήτηρ	μητέρες
πατρός	πατέρων	μητρός	μητέρων
πατρί	πατράσι(ν)	μητρί	μητράσι(ν)
πατέρα	πατέρας	μητέρα	μητέρας

ἀνήρ (ὁ) *man*	
ἀνήρ	ἄνδρες
ἀνδρός	ἀνδρῶν
ἀνδρί	ἀνδράσι(ν)
ἄνδρα	ἄνδρας

282. Possessive adjectives are ἐμός *my* or *mine;* σός *your* or *yours* (singular); ἡμέτερος *our* or *ours;* ὑμέτερος *your* or *yours* (plural). They are formed from the stems of the personal pronouns and are declined like adjectives of the **ο**- and **α**-declensions. When these adjectives have the attributive position, they refer to a definite person or thing; used without the article, they refer to something indefinite:

ἡ ἐμὴ οἰκίᾱ *my house*, but οἰκίᾱ ἐμή *a house of mine.*

[1] Thucydides, VII. 77. 7.

283. VOCABULARY

ἀνήρ, ἀνδρός, ὁ: *man, husband.* PHILANDER, ANDREW (Ἀνδρέας).

γέρων, -οντος, ὁ: *old man.*

ἐμός, -ή, -όν: *my, mine.* Cf. ἐγώ.

ἡμέτερος, -ᾱ, -ον: *our, ours.* Cf. ἡμεῖς.

κέρας, κέρᾱτος or κέρως,[1] τό: *horn, wing* (milit.). Lat. *cornu.* RHINOCEROS.

μήτηρ, μητρός, ἡ: *mother.* Lat. *mater.*

πατήρ, πατρός, ὁ: *father.* Lat. *pater.*

πῦρ, πυρός, τό (sing. only): *fire.* PYROTECHNIC.

σός, -ή, -όν: *thy, thine, your* (sing.). Cf. σύ.

σῶμα, -ατος, τό: *body.* CHROMOSOME.

ὑμέτερος, -ᾱ, -ον: *your, yours* (pl.). Cf. ὑμεῖς.

284. EXERCISES

(*a*) Translate:

1. ἡ δὲ μήτηρ ἐφίλει Κῦρον μᾶλλον ἢ τὸν βασιλεύοντα Ἀρταξέρξην. 2. ἡ δὲ στρατιά μου οὕτως ἐτρέφετο. 3. τὸν δὲ γέροντα, πατέρα ὄντα αὐτοῦ, ἰσχῡρῶς ἐφίλει. 4. τούτῳ τῷ ἀνδρὶ συμ-βουλευσόμεθα, ἐπειδὰν εἰς τὴν ἐμὴν χώρᾱν ἀφ-ικώμεθα. 5. τοῦ δὲ πατρὸς κάλλιστα ἐπ-εμελεῖτο. 6. καὶ δὴ οἱ ἡμέτεροι πατέρες ἄνδρες ἀγαθοὶ γενόμενοι τὴν Ἑλλάδα ἔσωσαν ἡμῖν. 7. τοῦ δὲ δεξιοῦ κέρως[1] Κλέαρχος ἡγήσεται. 8. νυκτὸς γενομένης πρὸς τὸ πῦρ ἔθεον. 9. σώματα δ' ἔχομεν κρείττω τῶν ὑμετέρων. 10. εἰ μὴ ἥρπασαν τὰ ὅπλα τά τε ὑμέτερα καὶ τὰ ἡμέτερα, ἐδιώκομεν ἂν αὐτούς. 11. ἐν Θερμοπύλαις πάντες καὶ οὐχ ἥκιστα αὐτὸς βασιλεὺς ηὗρον τοὺς Μήδους πολλοὺς μὲν ἀνθρώπους ὄντας, ὀλίγους δὲ ἄνδρας.

(*b*) Write in Greek:

1. I began my speech as follows. 2. Where in (*of*) the city were the horsemen? 3. We heard a shout when the horseman fell from his horse. 4. They will aid the king

[1] κέρας has a stem κερασ- as well as κερατ-. The σ drops out between two vowels, as in γένος (§ 234), and the vowels contract (§ 509, *e*).

with money, but not with ships. 5. Some of the Greek cities used to fight much with one another.

285. **A FEARLESS STATESMAN**

εἰ γὰρ ἔροιτό (*ask*) *τις ὑμᾶς· Εἰρήνην* (*peace*, compare IRENIC) *ἄγετ', ὦ ἄνδρες Ἀθηναῖοι; Μὰ Δί'* (*No, by Zeus*) *οὐχ ἡμεῖς γ', εἴποιτ' ἄν, ἀλλὰ Φιλίππῳ πολεμοῦμεν. οὐκ ἐχειρο-τονεῖτε* (*vote* or *elect*) *δ' ἐξ ὑμῶν αὐτῶν δέκα ταξι-άρχους* (*τάξις* = *division*) *καὶ στρατηγοὺς καὶ φυλ-άρχους* (*φυλή* = *tribe*) *καὶ ἱππ-άρχους δύο; τί οὖν οὗτοι ποιοῦσιν; πλὴν ἑνὸς* (*one*) *ἀνδρός, ὃν ἂν*[1] *πέμψητ' ἐπὶ τὸν πόλεμον, οἱ λοιποὶ τὰς πομπὰς* (*processions*) *πέμπουσιν ὑμῖν μετὰ τῶν ἱερο-ποιῶν* (*ἱερά* = *sacrifices*)*· ὥσπερ γὰρ οἱ πλάττοντες* (compare PLASTIC) *τοὺς πηλίνους* (*of clay*), *εἰς τὴν ἀγορὰν χειρο-τονεῖτε τοὺς ταξι-άρχους καὶ τοὺς φυλ-άρχους, οὐκ ἐπὶ τὸν πόλεμον.*

DEMOSTHENES

Demosthenes, *First Philippic*, 25–26.

286. Demosthenes, the foremost orator of all time, achieved his greatest fame in his long struggle against Philip of Macedon and his yet more illustrious son, Alexander the Great. Although Demosthenes failed to repel the invader, it was not through lack of vision or courage or patriotic fervor, but because his countrymen were substituting private ease and gain for public honor. His *Philippics* mark the acme of oratorical ardor and unsparing vituperation. Cicero found them splendid models.

[1] Be sure you understand why ἂν and the subjunctive are used here.

LESSON XLVI

REVIEW

μελέτη τὸ πᾶν. — *Practice makes perfect.*[1]

287. ASSIGNMENTS

(*a*) Review vocabulary (§ 554), following the method indicated in § 27, *a*.

(*b*) Name and define the Greek words suggested by *demoniac, eugenic, Hellenist, tachometer, program, megalomania, teleology, polyandry, hypercritical, aristocracy, cosmopolitan, pyrite, hysteron proteron.*

(*c*) Add ten other derivatives to this list.

(*d*) Ask your instructor to show you how these words developed: *surgeon, apoplexy, agony, Agonistes, pliocene, nausea.*

(*e*) What indication as to meaning is given by *-ography, -ology, -ize*, -σις, -ευς?

(*f*) What forms of ταχύς and μέγας occur with τριήρη, ἀγώνων, νῆες, γένος? what forms of πολύς and πλείων, with ναῦν, λόχοι, ἡγεμόσι, ὄρη?

(*g*) Give the accusative singular and dative plural of Ἕλλην, μέρος, ἀνήρ, πατήρ, πόλις; the dative singular and accusative plural of μήτηρ, χείρ, εὖρος, βασιλεύς, ἡγεμών.

(*h*) Compare μέγας, ἀληθής, εὐδαίμων, κακός, αἰσχρός, ἡδέως, εὖ, μάλα.

[1] Periander, as quoted by Diogenes Laertius, I. 99. Literally: *Practice (is) everything.*

288. EXERCISES

(*a*) Complete:

1. ἀπὸ τοῦ ὀρ— ἀνὰ κρατ— ἀπ-ῆλθον οἱ πολλοὶ τ— Ἑλλην—. 2. ἡττ— ἐγένετο ὁ παῖς τ— πατρ—. 3. πολλ— θαττ— εἰσιν αἱ τριηρ— ἢ τ— πλοι— (plural). 4. Κῦρος ἀξι—τατος ἦν βασιλεύειν. 5. τὸν ἀνδρ— ἐποίησαν ἡγεμον— τ— κερ— (singular). 6. ὡς ταχ— πάντες πλὴν τ— γερ— εἰσ-έπεσον εἰς τὴν ναῦν. 7. ταύτῃ τῇ νυκτ— ἡ στενὴ ὁδὸς ἦν ἀ-πορ—.

General View of Olympia

The Olympic victor's prize was only a wreath of wild olive leaves, but he felt it an ample reward for his years of arduous preparation.

(*b*) Write in Greek:

1. As many as possible of the captains will come on (*by*) the ships. 2. Your father learned this many days later than you. 3. He reported that that day the fire was terrible. 4. Since the men on the wall were very few, it would have been most shameful if the Greeks had not captured the city. 5. May you always treat your mother well!

LESSON XLVII

READING

οὐδὲ τεθνᾶσι θανόντες. — *Though dead, they are not dead.*[1]

289. VOCABULARY

ἀντί, prep. with G.: *instead of, for;* as prefix, *against.* ANTITHESIS.

ἀπο-κτείνω:[2, 3] *kill off.*

βαίνω, βήσομαι:[2] *go.* ANABASIS.

βάλλω, ἔβαλον:[3] *throw;* εἰσ-βάλλω (milit.): *invade.* PROBLEM, BALLISTICS.

ἐλπίζω, ἐλπίσω, ἤλπισα: *expect, hope.* Cf. ἐλπίς.

ὑστεραῖος, -ᾱ, -ον: *later, following, second, next;* τῇ ὑστεραίᾳ (ἡμέρᾳ): *next day.* Cf. ὕστερος.

χωρίον, -ου, τό: *place, spot.* Dimin. of χώρᾱ.

290. THERMOPYLÆ

ἐπειδὴ ὁ Ξέρξης καὶ οἱ Μῆδοι[4] εἰσ-έβαλλον εἰς τὴν Ἑλλάδα, ὑπ-έμενον οἱ Ἕλληνες ἐν Θερμοπύλαις· τοῦτο τὸ χωρίον δί-οδον στενὴν παρ-έχει εἰς τὴν Ἑλλάδα. ἐστρατήγει δὲ Λεωνίδᾱς, βασιλεὺς ὢν τῶν Λακεδαιμονίων. ἐπεὶ δ' ἐγγὺς ἐγένετο ὁ Ξέρξης, προύπεμψεν (προ + πέμπω) ἱππέᾱ πευσόμενον ὅ τι ποιοῦσιν οἱ Ἕλληνες καὶ ὁπόσοι εἰσίν. οὗτος ἐθεώρησε (*viewed*, compare THEORY) τοὺς Λακεδαιμονίους τοὺς μὲν γυμναζομένους (compare GYMNASIUM) τοὺς δὲ τὰς κόμᾱς (*hair*) κτενιζομένους (*combing*). κοσμοῦνται (compare COSMETIC) γὰρ τὰς κεφαλάς, ὅταν κινδῡνεύειν μέλλωσιν.

μετὰ δὲ ταῦτα ὡς ἐπ-έπεσον τοῖς Ἕλλησιν οἱ Μῆδοι, πολλοὶ ἔπῑπτον. τῇ δὲ ὑστεραίᾳ πάλιν εἰσ-βαλόντες οὐκ

---

[1] Simonides.

[2] Aorist later.

[3] Future later.

[4] Μῆδοι = Persians.

ἄμεινον ἔπρᾱττον· τότε δὴ ἀ-ποροῦντος βασιλέως, Ἐφιάλτης Μηλιεὺς[1] ἀνὴρ ἀγγέλλει αὐτῷ ἀτραπὸν (*trail*) οὖσαν, ἣ διὰ τῶν ὀρέων εἰς τὸ ὄπισθεν τῶν Ἑλλήνων φέρει.

ὁ δὲ Λεωνίδᾱς πυθόμενος τοὺς βαρβάρους κατὰ ταύτην τὴν ἀτραπὸν δια-βαίνοντας τὰ ὄρη, τοὺς μὲν ἄλλους ἀπ-έπεμψεν, αὐτὸς δὲ καὶ τριακόσιοι (300) Σπαρτιᾶται ὑπ-έμενον. ταῦτα γὰρ ποιήσᾱς ἤλπιζε σώσειν τὴν Ἑλλάδα. εἶπε γὰρ ἡ Πυθίᾱ (Delphic Sibyl) ὅτι δέοι ἢ τὴν Λακεδαίμονα ἀπ-ολέσθαι (*perish*) ἢ τὸν βασιλέᾱ αὐτῶν. εἰσ-βαλλόντων οὖν τῶν βαρβάρων, πρῶτον μὲν ἀντ-εῖχον (intransitive) καὶ πολλοὺς ἀπ-έκτεινον, τέλος δὲ πάντες ἀπ-έθανον. ἐπὶ δὲ τῷ τάφῳ (compare EPITAPH) τοῦτο τὸ ἐπί-γραμμά ἐστιν·

IN MEMORY OF PLATÆA

Those who fell at Platæa would be immortal even without this tripod base and the brazen serpent that it once held to commemorate them.

ὦ ξεῖν',[2] ἀγγέλλειν[3] Λακεδαιμονίοις ὅτι τῇδε (*here*)
κείμεθα (*lie*) τοῖς κείνων[4] ῥήμασι (*orders*) πειθόμενοι.[5]

Condensed from Herodotus, VII. 201–228.

---

[1] Μηλίς = Malis, a district in southern Thessaly.

[2] Dialectic for ξέν(ε), vocative of ξένος.

[3] Infinitive as imperative.

[4] Dialectic for ἐκείνων.

[5] Cicero has translated this in the first Tusculan, 101:

Dic, hospes, Spartae nos te hic vidisse iacentis
Dum sanctis patriae legibus obsequimur.

291. Thermopylæ, Salamis, Platæa! What a story they make! The bare facts, the very names, are inspiration; but the art, the sympathy, the grace of Herodotus have given them such a setting as no other three battles in human history have had. . . . "Most Homeric of men," he has written an epic — the eternal epic of human freedom, never to be read without a deepening of our belief in man and his idealisms, and of our faith in the triumph of the highest.

T. R. Glover, *Herodotus*, page 254.

292. Word-formation. (*a*) Nouns that are formed from verb stems by adding **-ματ** (nominative **-μα**, English *-ma*) express the *result* or *effect* of an *action*. Their nominatives often pass directly into English; more often **α** is dropped:

δοκέω *seem best*, δόγ-μα DOGMA;
δράω *do* (*act*), δρᾶ-μα *deed*, *action*, DRAMA;
γράφω *write*, γράμ-μα *thing written*, EPIGRAM;
ποιέω *make*, ποίη-μα POEM.

This ending when added to stems of verbs in **-ιζω** drops **α** in passing into English:

σχίζω *split*, σχίσ-μα SCHISM;
σοφίζομαι *act cleverly*, σόφισμα SOPHISM.

(*b*) Nouns that are formed from verb-stems by adding **-τηρ** or **-τωρ** denote the *agent* or *doer* of an *act:*

δο- *give*, δο-τήρ *giver;*
ῥε- *speak*, ῥή-τωρ *orator*, RHETOR;
σῴζω *save*, σω-τήρ *savior.*

LESSON XLVIII

IMPERATIVE ACTIVE[1]

ἀμφότερον, βασιλεύς τ' ἀγαθὸς κρατερός τ' αἰχμητής.
Both a goodly king and a stalwart warrior.[2]

293. The imperative active has a formation that is regular and obvious except for the second person singular, which in the present and second aorist lacks an ending and in the first aorist has a peculiar ending.

PRESENT IMPERATIVE OF **παύω** *I stop*

παῦ-ε	παύ-ε-τε
παυ-έ-τω	παυ-ό-ντων

SECOND AORIST IMPERATIVE OF **λείπω** *I leave*

λίπ-ε[3]	λίπ-ε-τε
λιπ-έ-τω	λιπ-ό-ντων

FIRST AORIST IMPERATIVE OF **παύω** *I stop*

παῦ-σον	παύ-σα-τε
παυ-σά-τω	παυ-σά-ντων

PRESENT IMPERATIVE OF **εἰμί** *I am*

ἴσ-θι	ἔσ-τε
ἔσ-τω	ἔσ-των

[1] The perfect imperative active is not given in this lesson because of its great rarity.

[2] Homer, *Iliad*, III. 179. This was the favorite motto of Alexander the Great.

[3] A few second aorist imperatives accent the ultima of the second person singular: εἰπέ, ἐλθέ, εὑρέ, ἰδέ, λαβέ.

Inflect the present and aorist imperative active of *πράττω* and *λαμβάνω*.

Inflect the present imperative active of *φιλέω*, observing rules for contraction and accent (§ 127). Compare with paradigm (§ 534).

294. Uses of the Imperative. (*a*) The imperative denotes a *command*. The present imperative does not differ from the aorist imperative in *time*, all imperatives necessarily referring to the future. The difference is that to be found with the subjunctive (§ 176, *a*), the present denoting *continuance* or *repetition* (motion picture), the aorist *mere occurrence* (snapshot):

πρᾶττε *keep doing*, πρᾶξον *do*.

(*b*) μή and the *present imperative* or *aorist subjunctive* denote a *prohibition:*

μὴ βάλλετε *do not be continually throwing ;*
μὴ βάλητε *do not throw.*

Note that the present (not aorist) imperative and the aorist (not present) subjunctive are used here.

(*c*) How is exhortation expressed? (§ 176, *a*)

295. **VOCABULARY**

ἀμφότερος, -ᾱ, -ον (rare in sing.) : *both.*

ἐλευθερίᾱ, -ᾱς, ἡ : *freedom.* ELEUTHERISM.

ἐλεύθερος, -ᾱ, -ον : *free.*

ἕτερος, -ᾱ, -ον : *other* (of two); θάτερον = τὸ ἕτερον. HETERODOX.

Ζεύς, Διός,[1] **ὁ** : *Zeus.*

θαρρέω, -ήσω, -ησα : *have courage.*

μνῆμα, -ατος, τό : *memorial, monument.*

τείνω[2] : *stretch, reach.* Lat. *tendo.*

χρή, χρῆν,[3] **χρῇ,**[4] **χρείη, χρῆναι** : *be necessary, fitting.*

---

[1] D. Διί ; A. Δία.

[2] Future and aorist follow.

[3] Imperfect, seemingly for χρὴ ἦν.

[4] χρῇ = χρή + ᾖ.

296. EXERCISES

(*a*) What clues do the portions in heavy type afford?

εἴπ **έ**	εἶπ **ε**	κελ **εῦσ** ον	κέλ **ευσ** ον	**ἡ** ρπά **σα** τε
ἔσ **τω**	**ἔ** στε	ἐστ **έ**	λειπέ **τω**	**ἁ** ρπά **σα** τε

(*b*) Translate:

1. *καὶ ὅτῳ ταῦτα δοκεῖ, λαβὼν τὰ ὅπλα ἐλθέτω εἰς τὸ πρόσθεν.* 2. *μὴ ἀπ-άγγελλε τοὺς ἱππέᾱς ὄντας ἐλαχίστους.* 3. *λέξον δ', ἔφη, καὶ σύ, ὦ Ξενοφῶν, ἃ*[1] *καὶ πρὸς ἡμᾶς.* 4. *μὴ ἐλπίσητε ἐμὲ χείρονα ἔσεσθαι περὶ ὑμᾶς ἢ ὑμᾶς περὶ ἐμέ.* 5. *θαρρεῖτε δὲ πρὸς τὴν ἀνά-βασιν.* 6. *πρὸς δὲ τοὺς ἱππέᾱς ἔφη, Ἄνδρες ἀγαθοὶ ἔστε, ἵνα ἄξιοι γένησθε τῆς ἐλευθερίᾱς.* 7. *τῶν δὲ ἀμφοτέρων θἄτερον χρὴ ποιεῖν, ἢ ἕπεσθαί μοι ἢ μηκέτι νομίζειν με στρατηγὸν εἶναι.* 8. *ἀλλὰ μὴ ἐπ-αινέσῃς τοὺς αἰσχροὺς ῥήτορας.* 9. *ἀνα-τείνετε τὴν χεῖρα, εἰ ἐπ-αινεῖτε.*

297. SALAMIS

The battle of Salamis was the greatest sea fight in which the Greeks ever engaged. It marked the culmination of patriotic devotion on the part of Athens. Æschylus, in his play *The Persians*, gives a graphic description of the fight. The city had been abandoned to the invader. The old men, women, and children had been removed to places of safety, and the fighting men were with the fleet.

ὦ παῖδες Ἑλλήνων ἴτε (*go*),
ἐλευθεροῦτε (compare **ἐλεύθερος**) *πατρίδ', ἐλευθεροῦτε δὲ*
παῖδας, γυναῖκας, θεῶν τε πατρῴων ἕδη (*seats*),
θήκᾱς (*tombs*) *τε προ-γόνων* (compare **γίγνομαι**) · *νῦν ὑπὲρ πάντων ἀγών.*

Æschylus, *Persæ*, 402–5.

[1] Supply the proper form of λέγω.

298. POET AND PATRIOT

The epitaph of that same Æschylus, written by himself, is notable in that it contains no word of his supreme genius as a dramatist, but dwells wholly on his valor at Marathon.

Αἴσχυλον Εὐφορίωνος Ἀθηναῖον τόδε κεύθει
  μνῆμα κατα-φθίμενον πῡροφόροιο Γέλας·
Ἀλκὴν δ' εὐ-δόκιμον Μαραθώνιον ἄλσος ἂν εἴποι
  καὶ βαθυ-χαιτήεις Μῆδος ἐπιστάμενος.

F. G. Allinson thus translates the lines:

Æschylus, son of Euphorion, here an Athenian lieth,
  Wheatfields of Gela his tomb waving around and above;
Marathon's glebe-land could tell you the tale of his valor approvèd,
  Aye and the long-haired Mede knew of it, knew of it well.

299. "DRINK TO ME ONLY"

Εἰμὶ μὲν οὐ φιλό-οινος· ὅταν δ' ἐθέλῃς με μεθύσσαι (*make drunk*)
  πρῶτα σὺ γευομένη (*tasting*) πρόσ-φερε καὶ δέχομαι·
Εἰ γὰρ ἐπι-ψαύσεις (*touch*) τοῖς χείλεσιν (*lips*), οὐκέτι νήφειν (*be sober*)
  εὐμαρές (*easy*), οὐδὲ φυγεῖν τὸν γλυκὺν (*sweet*) οἰνο-χόον (χέω = *pour*).
Πορθμεύει (*brings*) γὰρ ἔμοιγε κύλιξ (*cup*) παρὰ σοῦ τὸ φίλημα,
  καί μοι ἀπ-αγγέλλει τὴν χάριν ἣν ἔλαβεν.

This six-line poem of an obscure poet in the Greek Anthology was the inspiration of Ben Jonson's famous *Drink to me only with thine eyes.* Compare the two.

LESSON XLIX

IMPERATIVE MIDDLE AND PASSIVE[1]

οὐδὲν γλύκῑον ἧς πατρίδος. — *Naught is sweeter than one's native land.*[2]

300. The imperative middle and passive has an entirely regular formation in the present tense, the **σ** of the second person singular, as usual, dropping out between two vowels, which then contract.

PRESENT IMPERATIVE MIDDLE AND PASSIVE OF **παύω** *I stop*

(παύ-ε-**σο**) παύ-**ου**	παύ-ε-**σθε**
παυ-έ-**σθω**	παυ-έ-**σθων**

Inflect the present imperative middle and passive of φιλέω, observing the rules for contraction and accent (§ 127). Compare with paradigm (§ 534).

301. The second aorist imperative middle has the same endings as the present, except that it has a circumflex on the ultima in the second person singular.

SECOND AORIST IMPERATIVE MIDDLE OF **λείπω** *I leave*

(λιπ-έ-**σο**) λιπ-**οῦ**	λίπ-ε-**σθε**
λιπ-έ-**σθω**	λιπ-έ-**σθων**

302. The first aorist imperative middle has a peculiar ending in the second person singular, as did the same form of the first aorist imperative active.

---

[1] The perfect imperative middle and passive is not given because of its great rarity.

[2] Homer, *Odyssey*, IX. 34.

First Aorist Imperative Middle of **παύω**

παῦ-σ **αι** [1]	παύ-σα-**σθε**
παυ-σά-**σθω**	παυ-σά-**σθων**

Inflect the present and aorist imperatives of *μετα-πέμπομαι* and *ἀφ-ικνέομαι*.

303. VOCABULARY

ἀλλάττω, ἀλλάξω, ἤλλαξα : *change*. PARALLAX, HYPALLAGE.

ἄνω, adv. : *up*. Cf. **ἀνά**.

αὖ, adv. : *again, on the other hand*.

ἐκεῖ, adv. : *there*.

ἔνθα, adv. : *there, then, where* (rel.).

ἤδη, adv. : *now, already*.

μέσος, -η, -ον : *middle ; τὸ μέσον : the middle*. MESOPOTAMIA.

στράτευμα, -ατος, τό : *army*. Cf. **στρατεύω**.

στρέφω, στρέψω, ἔστρεψα : *turn*. STREPTOCOCCUS, STROPHE.

304. EXERCISES

(*a*) What clues are afforded by the portions in heavy type?

λείπ **ου** **ἐ** λείπ **ου** λιπ **οῦ** **ἐ** λίπ **ου** κωλ **ῦ** σαι κ **ώ** λῦσαι κελευέ **σθω** κελευσά **σθων** κελεύ **σασθε** **ἐ** κελεύ **σασθε**

(*b*) Translate :

1. *καὶ νῦν, ἔφη, μὴ μέλλωμεν, ὦ ἄνδρες, ἀλλ' ἀπ-ελθόντες ἤδη αἱρεῖσθε οἵ δεόμενοι ἄρχοντας, καὶ ἑλόμενοι ἥκετε εἰς τὸ μέσον τοῦ στρατοπέδου.* 2. *ἀλλά, εἰ βούλει, μένε ἐπὶ τῷ στρατεύματι, ἐγὼ δὲ πορεύσομαι · εἰ δὲ βούλει, σὺ μὲν πορεύου ἐπὶ τὸ ὄρος, ἐγὼ δ' ἐθέλω μένειν.* 3. *ἀνα-στρεψάμενοι δὲ αὖ ἀπ-αλλάττεσθε ἀπὸ τούτου τοῦ χωρίου.* 4. *φύλαξαι δὲ μὴ κακίων δοκῇς τοῦ γέροντος.* 5. *μὴ ἔλησθε τὰ ἐκεῖ μᾶλλον ἢ τὰ παρ' ἐμοί.* 6. *ἵνα δὲ πύθῃ περὶ τῶν ἄνω, μετά-πεμψαι τὸν πιστὸν ἡγεμόνα.*

---

[1] A verb of three syllables has an accent on the antepenult in the second person singular, first aorist imperative middle : κέλευσαι. It must be carefully distinguished from κελεῦσαι, first aorist infinitive active, and from κελεύσαι, third person singular, first aorist optative active, which, however, is usually replaced by κελεύσειε.

(*c*) Write in Greek:

1. Do not rush (*fall*) into the ships. 2. If they wish to be free, let them be as brave as possible. 3. Let the old men do whatever seems best. 4. Let us take (*having*) courage (and) be worthy of our freedom. 5. Do not expect that the ships will aid any longer.

305. **PRO PATRIA**

Spartan has always been synonymous with the simplicity, hardihood, and devotion that characterize the true soldier.

"HOLLOW LACEDÆMON"

The lovely valley of Sparta needed no defense except its valiant soldiers.

Far inferior in number to their neighbors, many of whom they had reduced to serfdom, the Spartans were forced to maintain their status by threat of arms. They entered military school at an early age and their best years were spent in barracks or on campaign. Such an environment discouraged individualism and fostered patriotism. Their literature consisted chiefly of choral songs suited to the mess-hall or the campfire, or to religious gatherings.[1]

[1] An interesting picture of Spartan life is given in *The Coward of Thermopylæ* by C. D. Snedeker.

We hear of but few poets at Sparta. The best known, Tyrtæus, is said to have been a lame schoolmaster sent by the Athenians in a spirit of mockery. If the poet was really lame, his verses were not, and he succeeded remarkably well in giving expression to the ideals peculiar to the people among whom he dwelt. Two of his poems follow.

(The Attic equivalents of dialectic forms are indicated wherever necessary.)

I

τεθνάμεναι (*to die*) γὰρ καλὸν ἐν[ὶ] προ-μάχοισ[ι] πεσόντα
ἄνδρ' ἀγαθὸν περὶ ᾗ (*his*) πατρίδι μαρνάμενον (*fighting*).

. . . .

θυμῷ γῆς περὶ τῆσδε μαχώμεθα καὶ περὶ παίδων
θνῄσκωμεν ψῡχέων (ψῡχῶν) μηκέτι φειδόμενοι (*sparing*).
ὦ νέοι, ἀλλὰ[1] μάχεσθε παρ' ἀλλήλοισ[ι] μένοντες,
μηδὲ φυγῆς αἰσχρᾶς ἄρχετε μηδὲ φόβου,
ἀλλὰ μέγαν ποιεῖσθε καὶ ἄλκιμον (*valiant*) ἐν φρεσὶ (*breast*) θῡμόν,
μηδὲ φιλο-ψῡχεῖτ' ἀνδράσι μαρνάμενοι.

II

The stirring march-song that follows breathes pride of race and interest in military traditions. (Ask your instructor to read you these lively anapæsts.)

ἄγετ' (*up*), ὦ Σπάρτᾱς (-ης) εὐάνδρω (-ου)
κῶροι (*scions*) πατέρων πολιᾱτᾶν (πολῑτῶν)
λαιᾷ (*left hand*) μὲν ἴτυν (*shield*) προ-βάλεσθε,
δόρυ δ' εὐτόλμως (*courageously*) ἄν-σχεσθε
μὴ φειδόμενοι τᾶς (τῆς) ζωᾶς (compare ZOÖLOGY)·
οὐ γὰρ πάτριον (*customary*) τᾷ (τῇ) Σπάρτᾳ.

[1] Used with the imperative to give force and liveliness.

LESSON L

FUTURE OF LIQUID VERBS

μὴ κρίνετε ἵνα μὴ κριθῆτε. — *Judge not that ye be not judged.*[1]

306. Verbs whose stem ends in a liquid (λ, μ, ν, ρ) add **εσ** to form the future active and middle. The **σ**, as usual, drops out between two vowels, which then contract:

φαίνω, φανέ(σ)ω, φανῶ.

The future of such verbs is inflected in the same way as the present of *φιλέω*.

Inflect the future indicative, optative, infinitive, and participle active and middle of *φαίνω*. Compare with paradigm (§ 529).

307. Verbs in -ιζω that have more than two syllables form their future in **-ιεω** and are inflected like *φαίνω*:

νομίζω; νομιέω: νομιῶ, νομιεῖς, νομιεῖ, κ.τ.λ.

Similar forms appear in the future of a few verbs which drop the single **σ** between two vowels and contract the vowels:

καλέ(σ)ω: καλῶ, καλεῖς, καλεῖ, κ.τ.λ.;
μαχέ(σ)ομαι: μαχοῦμαι, μαχεῖ, μαχεῖται, κ.τ.λ.

Consult the general vocabulary for the future of the following verbs which have already been studied:

ἀγγέλλω, ἀπο-κτείνω, βάλλω, θνῄσκω, μένω, πίπτω, πορίζω, τείνω.

[1] St. Matthew, VII. 2.

308. Object Clauses. After a verb of *striving*, *caring for*, or *effecting*, ὅπως and the *future indicative* supply the object:[1]

βουλεύεται ὅπως αὐτοὺς πείσει *he is planning how to persuade them.*

The negative is μή.

309. VOCABULARY

ἀπο-κρῑ́νομαι, -οῦμαι[2]: *reply.*
ἀρετή, -ῆς, ἡ: *fitness, excellence, bravery, virtue.* Cf. **ἄριστος.** Cf. Lat. *virtus.*
γῆ,[3] **γῆς, ἡ**: *land, soil.* GEOLOGY.
κρῑ́νω, κρῐνῶ[2]: *pick out, judge, decide.* CRISIS, CRITIC.
σκέπτομαι, σκέψομαι, ἐσκεψάμην[4]: *look to see, inquire, consider.* SCEPTIC.
σκοπέω[5]: *look to see, inquire, consider.* MICROSCOPE, PERISCOPE.
φαίνω, φανῶ[2]: *shed light, show;* mid. and pass., *appear.* PHENOMENON.
φανερός, -ᾱ́, -όν: *visible, apparent.* PHANEROGAM.

310. EXERCISES

(*a*) Translate:

1. πρὸς ταῦτα ἀπο-κρῑνούμεθα, ἐπειδὰν ἥκῃ τις ἀγγελῶν τὰ περὶ τῆς μάχης. 2. ἀλλὰ τοῦτο δεῖ σκοπεῖν, ὅπως μὴ τὴν ἀρετὴν ἀπο-βαλεῖτε ἣν ἐλάβετε παρὰ τῶν πατέρων ὑμῶν. 3. παρα-σκευασόμεθα δ' ὅπως ταύτης τῆς γῆς φανούμεθα ἄξιοι εἶναι. 4. τῶν δὲ φίλων ἐπι-μελοῦμαι, ὅπως τὰ ἐμὰ μᾶλλον ἢ τὰ παρὰ βασιλεῖ ἕλωνται. 5. ὑμᾶς δὲ κρίνω πολλοῦ[6] ἀξίους εἶναι. 6. σκέψεται δ' ὅπως ἄνδρας ὅτι ἀρίστους λήψεται. 7. δεῖ δ' ἡμᾶς ἐπι-μελεῖσθαι ὅπως ἄξιοι εἶναι φανούμεθα ταύτης τῆς ἐλευθερίᾱς. 8. οὐ γὰρ

[1] This happens even after secondary tenses.
[2] For the aorist of this verb, see § 313.
[3] Contract noun: hence ῆ in all forms.
[4] Rare in present and imperfect, in which tenses σκοπέω is used.
[5] Present and imperfect only.
[6] Genitive of value.

τούς γ' ἐλευθέρους ἀπο κτενεῖτε, μὴ φανεροὶ γένησθε κακοὶ ὄντες.[1]

(*b*) Complete:

1. *ταῦτα μέλλει ἀγγελ— ἐπὰν πρὸς βασιλ— ἀφ-ικ—ται.* 2. *Κῦρον γὰρ χρὴ ἐπι-μελ—σθαι ὅπως τὰ δίκαια ἀπο-κρῖν—ται.* 3. *σκοπ—ντων ὅπως ἀμείνους φαν—νται ἢ πολλ— βαρβαρ—.*

(*c*) Write in Greek:

1. Let him remain in charge of the van. 2. Proceed along the mountain when you find those who are in difficulty. 3. Do not depart from (*ἀπ-αλλάττομαι*) that spot unless some faithful man is there present. 4. Let them be on their guard that the horsemen do not again get (*γίγνομαι*) in their rear.

311. **THE ALMIGHTY DOLLAR**

ὁ μὲν Ἐπίχαρμος τοὺς θεοὺς εἶναι λέγει
ἀνέμους (*winds*), *ὕδωρ, γῆν, ἥλιον* (*sun*), *πῦρ, ἀστέρας* (*stars*).
ἐγὼ δ' ὑπ-έλαβον (*supposed*) *χρησίμους* (*useful*) *εἶναι θεοὺς*
τἀργύριον[2] *ἡμῖν καὶ τὸ χρῡσίον.*
ἱδρῡσάμενος (*installing*) *τούτους γὰρ εἰς τὴν οἰκίᾱν*
εὖξαι (imperative)· *τί βούλει; πάντα σοι γενήσεται,*
ἀγρός (*land*), *οἰκίαι, θεράποντες* (*servants*), *ἀργυρώματα,*
φίλοι, δικασταί (*judges*), *μάρτυρες* (*witnesses*). *μόνον δίδου*
(*give*, imperative)·
αὐτοὺς γὰρ ἕξεις τοὺς θεοὺς ὑπ-ηρέτᾱς (*slaves*).

Menander, fragment.

Supply the nominative singular for as many of the nouns as you can. What English derivatives are suggested?

---

[1] § 214.

[2] An instance of crasis, similar to elision. Two words are *mixed*, i.e., *fused* into one: ὁ ἀνήρ often becomes ἁνήρ.

312. **PERSIAN TREACHERY**

ἐπεὶ δὲ ἦσαν ἐπὶ ταῖς θύραις ταῖς Τισσαφέρνους, οἱ μὲν στρατηγοὶ παρ-εκλήθησαν (*were summoned*) εἴσω. οἱ δὲ λοχαγοὶ ἐπὶ ταῖς θύραις ἔμενον. οὐ πολλῷ δὲ ὕστερον ἀπὸ τοῦ αὐτοῦ σημείου (*signal*, compare SEMAPHORE) οἵ τ' ἔνδον (*within*) συν-ελαμβάνοντο καὶ οἱ ἔξω (compare **ἐκ**) κατ-

Ewing Galloway.

ACROCORINTH

Behind these columns of Apollo's temple looms the rugged citadel from whose lofty summit the Corinthians often spied the approach of trader and pirate.

εκόπησαν (*were slain*). μετὰ δὲ ταῦτα τῶν βαρβάρων τινὲς ἱππέων διὰ τοῦ πεδίου ἐλαύνοντες ᾧ τινι ἐν-τυγχάνοιεν (*met*) Ἕλληνι πάντας ἔκτεινον. οἱ δὲ Ἕλληνες τὸ πρᾶγμα ἐθαύμαζον ἐκ τοῦ στρατοπέδου ὁρῶντες (*seeing*). ἐκ τούτου δὴ οἱ Ἕλληνες ἔθεον ἐπὶ τὰ ὅπλα πάντες ἐκ-πεπληγμένοι (*frightened*) καὶ νομίζοντες αὐτίκα (*immediately*) ἥξειν αὐτοὺς ἐπὶ τὸ στρατόπεδον.

Adapted from Xenophon, *Anabasis*, II. 5. 31–34.

LESSON LI

AORIST OF LIQUIDS

καιρὸς δ' ἐπὶ πᾶσιν ἄριστος. — *Everything in season.*[1]

313. The Aorist of Liquids. Verbs with stems ending in a liquid (§ 306) form the first aorist by lengthening their stem vowel and adding **α**. **α** lengthens to **η** (after **ι** or **ρ** to **ᾱ**), **ε** to **ει**, **ι** to **ῑ**, **υ** to **ῡ**:

φαίνω (stem φαν-), ἔφηνα; ἀγγέλλω (stem ἀγγελ-), ἤγγειλα.

In other respects these aorists resemble *ἔπαυσα.*

Inflect the aorist indicative, subjunctive, optative, imperative, infinitive, and participle active and middle of *φαίνω*. Compare with paradigm (§ 529).

314. Object Clauses after Verbs of Fearing. (*a*) After a verb of fearing in a *primary* tense *μή* *lest* and the *subjunctive* state the *object* of fear:

φοβεῖται μὴ κακὰ πάθῃ *he fears lest he may suffer harm.*

The negative form is *μὴ οὐ* *lest not.*

(*b*) After a *secondary* tense the *optative* may occur:

ἐφοβεῖτο μὴ κακὰ πάθοι *he was afraid that he might suffer harm.*

A subjunctive after a secondary tense emphasizes the object of fear.[2]

---

[1] Hesiod, *Works and Days*, 694. Literally: (*There is*) *a best moment for everything.*

[2] Compare § 192, *b* and note.

315. VOCABULARY

ἄκρος, -ᾱ, -ον: *top of;* τὸ ἄκρον: *the top.* ACROPOLIS, AKRON.

εἴθε, conj.: *O if, would that, if only.*

εἰρήνη, -ης, ἡ: *peace.* IRENIC.

καιρός, -οῦ, ὁ: *fitting moment, opportunity.*

μανθάνω, μαθήσομαι, ἔμαθον: *learn, understand.* POLYMATH.

μέλει, μελήσει, ἐμέλησε: *is a care, concerns.* Used impersonally.

ὀφείλω, ὀφειλήσω, ὠφείλησα: *owe.*

τέμνω, τεμῶ, ἔτεμον or ἔταμον: *cut.* ANATOMY.

τρέχω, δραμοῦμαι, ἔδραμον: *run,* TROCHAIC. Cf. **δρόμος**.

φοβέομαι, φοβήσομαι:[1] *fear.* Cf. **φόβος**.

χαλεπαίνω, -ανῶ, -ηνα: *be severe, angry.* Cf. **χαλεπός**.

316. EXERCISES

(*a*) Translate:

1. ἐμοὶ δὲ μελήσει ὅπως ἐν καιρῷ ἀφ-ιξόμεθα. 2. φοβεῖται μὴ οὐχ οἱ ἐκ τοῦ δεξιοῦ κέρᾱτος δράμωσιν ἐπὶ τὸ ἄκρον. 3. οὐκ ἔστι ῥᾴδιον τὴν σὴν βουλὴν μαθεῖν. 4. ἐφοβούμεθα μὴ ὁ λόχος χαλεπήνειεν ἡμῖν. 5. εἴθε ἐπ-αινοῖεν τὸν θῡμὸν τὸν τῆς βασιλείᾱς. 6. τοῦ δὲ Κύρου βασιλεὺς τήν τε κεφαλὴν καὶ τὰς χεῖρας ἀπ-έτεμεν. 7. τῆς νυκτὸς ἡμῖν ἦν φόβος μὴ μάθοιεν ὅπου ἐστὶ τὸ χρῡσίον. 8. ὥρᾱ ῡ̔μῖν σκοπεῖν πότερον ἐμοὶ ἕψεσθε ἢ οὔ. 9. καὶ ἔμελλον οἱ κράτιστοι δραμεῖσθαι κατὰ τῶν ὀρῶν.

(*b*) Complete:

1. φοβοῦμαι μὴ ὁ ἀνὴρ χαλεπην—, ἐπειδὰν αἰσθαν— τὴν οἰκίᾱν διαρπαζο—. 2. σκοπεῖσθε ὅπως τὸ πρᾶγμα μαθ—, πρὶν ἐκεῖ ἐλθ—. 3. ἡμ— ἦν φόβος μὴ οὐχ οἱ παῖδες τοὺς ἀπο-θαν— εὖ λεγ—.

(*c*) Write in Greek:

1. This orator appears (to be) inferior in wisdom. 2. Look to it that you are worthy of your freedom. 3. They reply

[1] Aorist follows.

at once, that they may not seem to lack bravery. 4. You must see to it that the men in the city decide this. 5. The commander is planning how he will turn their right wing.

"SERMONS IN STONES"

This bit of the Acropolis wall is a tribute to the energy of Themistocles. In his zeal to fortify Athens before the interference of other Greek states, he had column drums and any other available architectural pieces used.

317. POOR SERIPHOS!

The point of the following anecdote, one of many contained in Plutarch's *Life of Themistocles*, lies in the fact that Seriphos is an insignificant little island. All countries seem to have their joke-towns.

τοῦ δὲ Σερῑφίου πρὸς Θεμιστοκλέᾱ εἰπόντος, ὡς οὐ δι' αὑτὸν ἔχοι δόξαν (*fame*) ἀλλὰ διὰ τὴν πόλιν, 'Αληθῆ λέγεις, εἶπεν, ἀλλ' οὔτ' ἂν ἐγὼ Σερίφιος ὢν ἐγενόμην ἔν-δοξος οὔτε σὺ 'Αθηναῖος.

Plutarch, *Themistocles*, XVIII. 3.

318. SANG FROID

Hermes presents his bill to Charon.

ΧΑΡ. Νῦν μέν, ὦ Ἑρμῆ, ἀ-δύνατον[1] (*impossible*, that is, *to pay*), ἢν δὲ λοιμός (*pestilence*) τις ἢ πόλεμος κατα-πέμψῃ πολλούς, ἐν-έσται τότε ἀπο-κερδᾶναί τι (*make some profit*) ἀπὸ τῶν πορθμείων (*ferry charges*).

ΕΡΜ. Νῦν οὖν ἐγὼ καθ-εδοῦμαι (*will sit down*) τὰ κάκιστα εὐχόμενος γενέσθαι, ὡς ἀπὸ τούτων τὰ ὀφειλόμενα ἀπο-λάβοιμι.

ΧΑΡ. Οὐκ ἔστιν ἄλλως, ὦ Ἑρμῆ. νῦν δὲ ὀλίγοι, μανθάνεις, ἀφ-ικνοῦνται ἡμῖν· εἰρήνη γάρ.[1]

ΕΡΜ. Ἄμεινον[1] οὕτως, εἰ καὶ ἡμῖν παρα-τείνοιτο (*be extended*) ὑπὸ σοῦ τὸ ὄφλημα (compare **ὀφείλω**). ἀλλ' οἱ μὲν παλαιοί (compare PALÆONTOLOGY), ὦ Χάρων, ἧκον ἀνδρεῖοι ἅπαντες, αἵματος (compare HEMORRHAGE) μεστοὶ καὶ τραυματίαι ("*casualties*") οἱ πολλοί· νῦν δὲ ἢ φαρμάκῳ (compare PHARMACIST) τις ὑπὸ τοῦ παιδὸς ἀπο-θανὼν[2] ἢ ὑπὸ τῆς γυναικός, ὠχροὶ (*pale*, compare OCHER) ἅπαντες καὶ ἀ-γεννεῖς (*ignoble*), οὐχ ὅμοιοι (compare HOMOLOGOUS) ἐκείνοις. οἱ δὲ πλεῖστοι αὐτῶν διὰ χρήματα ἥκουσιν.

ΧΑΡ. Πάνυ γὰρ περι-μάχητά ἐστι ταῦτα.

ΕΡΜ. Δικαίως ἂν οὖν ἐγὼ ἀπ-αιτοίην τὰ ὀφειλόμενα παρὰ σοῦ.

Adapted from Lucian, *Dialogues of the Dead*, 4.

---

[1] Supply ἐστι.

[2] ἀπο-θνῄσκω is virtually a passive to ἀπο-κτείνω. Compare ποιέω and πάσχω.

LESSON LII

PERFECT ACTIVE[1]

εὕρηκα. — *I have it.*[2]

319. The Perfect Indicative. (*a*) The perfect denotes *completed* action with the effect of the action still continuing at the time of speaking or writing:

πέπαυκα *I have stopped* (*it*), that is, *I have* (*it*) *stopped* at the present time.

(*b*) The perfect often stresses the *lasting result* with little or no reference to the act of completion. It is then usually translated by a present:

τέθνηκε *he is dead* (*he has passed away*);
πέποιθα *I am confident, I trust.*

320. The pluperfect has a force which may be best explained by a mathematical formula:

pluperfect: perfect: : imperfect: present.

ἐπεπαύκη *I had stopped* (*it*), ἐπεποίθη *I was confident.*

Perfect Indicative of παύω

πέ-παυ-κα	πε-παύ-κα-μεν
πέ-παυ-κα-ς	πε-παύ-κα-τε
πέ-παυ-κε(ν)	πε-παύ-κᾱσι(ν)

Pluperfect Indicative of παύω

ἐ-πε-παύ-κη	ἐ-πε-παύ-κε-μεν
ἐ-πε-παύ-κη-ς	ἐ-πε-παύ-κε-τε
ἐ-πε-παύ-κει	ἐ-πε-παύ-κε-σαν

Perfect Infinitive	πε-παυ-κέ-ναι
Perfect Participle	πε-παυ-κώς, -κυῖα, -κός

[1] The perfect subjunctive, optative, and imperative occur infrequently and are, moreover, so easily recognized that detailed study is not asked for. If desired, they may be found in the *Grammatical Appendix* and learned.

[2] Archimedes. Motto of the state of California. Literally: *I have found.*

321. Reduplication is the sign of the perfect, whether active, middle, or passive, and is found in every perfect. It has different forms:

(*a*) Verbs beginning with a single consonant prefix this consonant and **ε** to the stem:

παύω, πέπαυκα.

φ is represented by **π**, **θ** by **τ**, **χ** by **κ** :

φαίνω, πέφηνα ; θνῄσκω, τέθνηκα.

(*b*) Verbs beginning with a mute and a liquid (Introduction I, *d*) usually reduplicate like those beginning with a single consonant.

γράφω, γέγραφα.

(*c*) Verbs beginning with a vowel, or with a double consonant, or with two or more consonants other than a mute and a liquid, have a reduplication identical with augment:

ἁρπάζω, ἥρπακα ; ζητέω, ἐζήτηκα ; στρατεύω, ἐστράτευκα.

322. The perfect active of most verbs is formed by adding **-κα** (**-κε**) to the reduplicated stem; of other verbs (especially those with mute or liquid stems) by adding **-α** (**-ε**). Perfects in **-κα** (**-κε**) are called first perfects; those in **-α** (**-ε**) second perfects. Second perfects may best be learned from the principal parts. Except for the **κ**, they have the same inflection as first perfects.[1]

323. The pluperfect prefixes a syllabic augment when the reduplicated perfect begins with a consonant. Otherwise it retains the reduplicated stem unchanged:

πέφηνα, ἐπεφήνη ; ἔσταλκα, ἐστάλκη.

Note the accents of the infinitive and participle. They are typical of these forms and often serve as clues.

---

[1] The second perfect usually shows the mute of the stem in its rough form: **π** and **β** become **φ** ; **κ** and **γ** become **χ** ; **τ** and **δ** become **θ**.

Inflect the perfect and pluperfect indicative active of *πέφηνα*; give the perfect infinitive active and the perfect participle active of the same.

324. The perfect participle active uses the endings of the consonant declension in the masculine and neuter, of the **α**-declension in the feminine. The stems should be noted: **ν** is absent before **τ** in the masculine and neuter; also **υι** and short **α** appear in the feminine nominative and accusative singular. The absence of **ν** or the presence of **υι** serve as clues.

Perfect Participle of **παύω**

πεπαυκώς	πεπαυκυῖα	πεπαυκός
πεπαυκότος	πεπαυκυίᾱς	πεπαυκότος
πεπαυκότι	πεπαυκυίᾳ	πεπαυκότι
πεπαυκότα	πεπαυκυῖαν	πεπαυκός
πεπαυκότες	πεπαυκυῖαι	πεπαυκότα
πεπαυκότων	πεπαυκυιῶν	πεπαυκότων
πεπαυκόσι(ν)	πεπαυκυίαις	πεπαυκόσι(ν)
πεπαυκότας	πεπαυκυίᾱς	πεπαυκότα

325. VOCABULARY

δέ-δοικα (δείδω) : *fear.*
εἴ-ληφα (λαμβάνω) : *have taken.*
ἔρ-ρῑφα (ῥί̄πτω) : *have thrown.*
ἐ-στράτευκα (στρατεύω) : *have made a campaign.*
εὕρηκα[1] (εὑρίσκω) : *have found.*
ᾕρηκα (αἱρέω) : *have seized, have captured.*
ἥρπακα (ἁρπάζω) :[2] *have seized, have plundered.*
λέ-λοιπα (λείπω) : *have left.*
πέ-πεικα (πείθω) : *have persuaded.*
πέ-ποιθα (πείθω) : *have been persuaded, am confident, trust.*
πέ-πομφα (πέμπω) : *have sent.*
πέ-πονθα (πάσχω) : *have experienced, have been treated.*
τέ-θνηκα (θνῄσκω) : *be dead.*

---

[1] Or ηὕρηκα. [2] Verbs in **-ζω** (stem **-δ**) drop the **δ** before the **κ** of the perfect as before the **σ** of the future and aorist.

326. **EXERCISES**

(*a*) What clues are afforded by the portions in heavy type?

λε λοίπαμεν	**ἐ** στρατευ **κότ** ι	**ἡ** ρπά **κε** σαν
ἐρρ ῑφ **έ** ναι	**ἐδε** δοί **κει**	ᾐρηκ **υῖ** αι

(*b*) Translate:

1. *ἐστρατεύκαμεν δὴ μετὰ τῶν βελτίστων.* 2. *τὴν σάλπιγγα εἰληφὼς πρὸς βασιλέᾱ θεῖ.* 3. *ἐδεδοίκετε δὲ μὴ οὐ πέμψαιμι ὑμῖν τὸν χρῡσόν;* 4. *τοῦ δὲ Κύρου τεθνηκότος οὐκέτι δεῖ ἡμᾶς ἐλαύνειν εἰς τὸ πρόσθεν.* 5. *ἐνομίζετε δὲ τοὺς βαρβάρους τὰ ἄκρα εἰληφέναι ἐν καιρῷ.* 6. *ἐκείνους ἐπεπείκει τὰ αὐτὰ πρᾱ́ττειν.* 7. *ἐπειδὴ δὲ ἥκομεν, οἱ φύλακες ἀπ-ελελοίπεσαν τὸ στρατόπεδον.* 8. *ἔστιν οὖν ὅ τι ὑπ' ἐμοῦ κακὸν πεπόνθατε;* 9. *πότε ὑπ-ώπτευσε τοὺς ἑτέρους τὸν οἶνον ᾐρηκέναι;* 10. *τὰ δὲ ὅπλα ἐρρῑφότες ἐν-έπεσον εἰς τὰς οἰκίᾱς.* 11. *ἡ δὲ βασίλεια ἄγγελον πεπομφυῖα ἐλαύνει πρὸς τὸ Ἑλληνικὸν στράτευμα.*

(*c*) Write in Greek:

1. He fears that they may show themselves (to be) more just than the king. 2. The boy did not become angry when he cut his hand. 3. We were afraid that the more cowardly might not be pleased. 4. They ran at full speed in order to arrive at the fitting moment.

327. **A CYNICAL THRUST**

Περικλεῖ δὲ βουλόμενος ἐν-τυχεῖν (*fall in with, meet*) *ἐπὶ θύρᾱς ἦλθεν αὐτοῦ. πυθόμενος δὲ οὐ σχολάζειν* (*be at leisure*) *ἀλλὰ σκοπεῖν καθ' ἑαυτὸν ὅπως λόγον ἀπο-δώσει* (*render account*) *Ἀθηναίοις, ἀπ-ερχόμενος ὁ Ἀλκιβιάδης, Εἶτα, ἔφη, βέλτῑον οὐκ ἦν αὐτὸν σκοπεῖν ὅπως οὐκ ἀπο-δώσει λόγον Ἀθηναίοις;*

Plutarch, *Alcibiades*, VII. 2.

LESSON LIII

PERFECT MIDDLE AND PASSIVE

Μνημοσύνη μήτηρ Μουσάων. — *Memory, mother of the Muses.*[1]

328. Perfect Middle and Passive. The perfect and pluperfect are formed by adding the proper endings directly to the reduplicated stem with no connecting vowel. The middle (and passive) endings of the present help form the perfect; those of the imperfect help form the pluperfect. The pluperfect, of course, has an augment. Accents are normal except in the infinitive and participle, where the penult is accented. This peculiarity of accent is a convenient clue to the infinitive and participle in the perfect middle (and passive).

Inflect the perfect and pluperfect indicative, the perfect infinitive and participle of παύω in the middle (and passive) voice. Compare with paradigm (§ 527).

329. Stem Changes. *Stems ending in a consonant* naturally undergo various changes through contact with the personal endings. Since it is easy to recognize these forms but a rather complicated matter to inflect them, detailed study is not asked for, but attention is called to the changes.

Note these significant facts:

1. A stem ending in π, β, or φ shows

μ	μαι	ψ	αι	π	ται	φ[2]	θε
	μην		ο		το		θαι
	μεθα						
	μενος						

[1] *Hymn to Hermes*, 429-430.

[2] The σ between consonants drops out.

2. A stem ending in **κ**, **γ**, or **χ** shows

	μαι						
γ	μην	ξ	αι	κ	ται	χ	θε
	μεθα		ο		το		θαι
	μενος						

3. A stem ending in **τ**, **δ**, **θ** shows

	μαι						
σ	μην	σ	αι	σ	ται	σ	θε
	μεθα		ο		το		θαι
	μενος						

4. A stem ending in **-ν** shows

	μαι						
σ	μην	ν	σαι	ν	ται	ν	θε
	μεθα		σο		το		θαι
	μενος						

5. A perfect participle and *εἰσί* or *ἦσαν* are used for the third person plural of the perfect or pluperfect indicative middle (and passive) respectively of such verbs.

330. Verbal Adjectives. Verbal adjectives in **-τέος**, **-τέᾱ**, **-τέον** denote *necessity* (like the Latin gerundive).

(*a*) They may be used personally:

διαβατέος ἐστὶν ὁ ποταμός *the river must be crossed.*

(*b*) They may be used impersonally:[1]

πρᾱκτέον ἐστίν *it must be done.*

331. Dative of Agent. The dative of reference, used with a perfect passive or a verbal in **-τέος**, denotes the *agent:*[2]

τοῦτο ἡμῖν πέπρᾱκται *this has been done by us;*
τοῦτο ἡμῖν πρᾱκτέον ἐστίν *this must be done by us.*

---

[1] The impersonal verbal may take an object:

διαβατέον ἐστὶ τὸν ποταμόν *the river must be crossed.*

[2] What uses of the dative have you now had?

332. VOCABULARY

ἀ-τῑμάζω, ἀτῑμάσω, ἠτίμακα, ἠτίμασμαι: *dishonor.*

ἕως, conj.: *while, until.*

θάπτω, θάψω, ἔθαψα, τέθαμμαι: *dig, bury.*

μιμνῄσκω, μνήσω, ἔμνησα: *remind;* μέμνημαι: *remember.* MNEMONIC.

οἰκέω, οἰκήσω, ᾤκησα, ᾤκηκα, ᾤκημαι: *dwell, inhabit.* ECUMENICAL. Cf. **οἰκίᾱ.**

παρασάγγης, -ου, ὁ: *parasang.* A Persian road measure = about 30 stades.

τάφος, -ου, ὁ: *burial, grave.* EPITAPH. Cf. **θάπτω.**

τάφρος, -ου, ἡ: *ditch, trench.* Cf. **θάπτω.**

τῑμή, -ῆς, ἡ: *honor, price.* TIMOCRACY.

333. EXERCISES

(*a*) Locate these forms, giving mood, tense, person, number, and present indicative of the verbs from which they come:

λελεῖφθαι, λελειμμένοι εἰσίν, πέπεμπται, ἐπέπειστο, ἥρπασται, ἐπέφαντο, ἡγμένοι ἦσαν, πέπρᾱξαι, ἐτέταχθε, πέπεισμαι, πεφάνθαι, πεπεμμένος,[1] ἐπέπρᾱκτο, τετάγμεθα, ἠθροῖσθαι, πεφάσμεθα.

(*b*) Translate:

1. ἐνταῦθα παρὰ τὸν ποταμὸν πόλις Ἑλληνικὴ ᾤκητο εὐδαίμων καὶ μεγάλη. 2. καὶ ἕως γε ἐκεῖ μένετε, σκεπτέον μοι δοκεῖ ὅπως ὡς ἀσφαλέστατα μενεῖτε. 3. ἐὰν δὲ εὖ γένηταί τι, οὐ μεμνήσεσθαί[2] σέ φᾱσιν. 4. τὸ δὲ σῶμα αὐτοῦ ἐνταῦθα τέθαπται ὅπου ἀπ-έθανε μαχόμενος. 5. οὐκέτι μέντοι διὰ τὸν χρόνον πολὺν ὄντα πάντα μέμνημαι. 6. οὗτος δὲ κακίων γενόμενος τῶν ἄλλων τῷ στρατηγῷ ἠ-τίμαστο. 7. πορευτέον δ' ἡμῖν πολλοὺς παρασάγγᾱς πρὶν εἰς τὴν τάφρον ἀφ-ικέσθαι. 8. οὗτος ὁ τάφος τῑμῆς[3] μεγάλης ἐπεποίητο. 9. σπεύσει ὁ λόχος ἕως ἂν φανερὰ γένηται ἡ τάφρος.

---

[1] Because three μ's are unpronounceable, one μ is dropped.

[2] Future perfect = future.

[3] Genitive of price.

(c) Write in Greek:

1. The pursuers have not found his body. 2. They are confident that the king has captured the largest cities. 3. The messenger has persuaded the Greeks that Cyrus is dead. 4. Your mother had sent some one to report his death.

334. CHRIST AND THE TEMPTER

Γέγραπται, Οὐκ ἐπ' ἄρτῳ (*bread*) μόνῳ ζήσεται (*live*) ὁ[1] ἄνθρωπος, ἀλλ' ἐπὶ παντὶ ῥήματι (*word*) ἐκ-πορευομένῳ διὰ στόματος θεοῦ.

St. Matthew, IV. 4.

335. A NARROW ESCAPE

τῇ δ' αὐτῇ ἡμέρᾳ Κλέαρχος ἐλθὼν ἐπὶ τὴν διά-βασιν (compare **δια-βαίνω**) τοῦ ποταμοῦ καὶ ἐκεῖ κατα-σκεψάμενος τὴν ἀγορὰν ἀφ-ιππεύει ἐπὶ τὴν ἑαυτοῦ σκηνὴν διὰ τοῦ Μένωνος στρατεύματος σὺν ὀλίγοις τοῖς περὶ αὐτόν· Κῦρος δὲ οὔπω ἧκεν, ἀλλ' ἔτι προσ-ήλαυνε· τῶν δὲ Μένωνος στρατιωτῶν ξύλα (compare XYLOPHONE) σχίζων (compare SCHISM) τις, ὡς ἐθεώρει Κλέαρχον δι-ελαύνοντα, ἔβαλε τὴν ἀξίνην (*ax*)· καὶ οὗτος μὲν αὐτοῦ[2] ἥμαρτεν (*missed*)· ἄλλος δὲ λίθον καὶ ἄλλος, εἶτα πολλοί, κραυγῆς γενομένης. ὁ δὲ κατα-φεύγει εἰς τὸ ἑαυτοῦ στράτευμα, καὶ εὐθὺς παρ-αγγέλλει εἰς τὰ ὅπλα· καὶ τοὺς μὲν ὁπλῑτᾱς αὐτοῦ (*there*) ἐκέλευσε μεῖναι τὰς ἀσπίδας πρὸς τὰ γόνατα (*knees*) ἔχοντας, αὐτὸς δὲ λαβὼν τοὺς Θρᾷκας ἤλαυνεν ἐπὶ τοὺς Μένωνος, ὥστε ἐκείνους ἐκ-πεπλῆχθαι καὶ αὐτὸν Μένωνα, καὶ τρέχειν ἐπὶ τὰ ὅπλα.

Xenophon, *Anabasis*, I. 5. 12–13.

(To be continued)

[1] The article is sometimes used in a generic sense and denotes one class as distinguished from other classes. Compare the French use of *le*: *l'homme est mortel.*

[2] A verb meaning *to miss* governs the genitive.

LESSON LIV

FUTURE AND AORIST PASSIVE[1]

τὸ νῑκᾶν αὐτὸν αὑτὸν πᾱσῶν νῑκῶν πρώτη τε καὶ ἀρίστη.
Self-mastery is the first and noblest victory of all.[2]

336. The first aorist passive forms its stem by adding **θη** (in indicative and infinitive) or **θε** (in subjunctive, optative, and participle) to the verb stem. To this are added the personal endings of the *active* voice. Contraction (**ε + ω, η, ῃ**) occurs throughout the subjunctive. The mood sign of the optative in the singular is **ιη**; in the plural **ι** and **ιε** (§ 187). These combine to form **ειη, ει, ειε**.

FIRST AORIST INDICATIVE PASSIVE OF **παύω**

ἐ-παύ-θη-ν	ἐ-παύ-θη-μεν
ἐ-παύ-θη-ς	ἐ-παύ-θη-τε
ἐ-παύ-θη	ἐ-παύ-θη-σαν

FIRST AORIST SUBJUNCTIVE PASSIVE

(παυ-θέ-ω)	παυ θῶ	(παυ-θέ-ωμεν)	παυ θῶμεν
(παυ-θέ-ῃς)	παυ θῇς	(παυ-θέ-ητε)	παυ θῆτε
(παυ-θέ-ῃ)	παυ θῇ	(παυ-θέ-ωσι)	παυ θῶσι

FIRST AORIST OPTATIVE PASSIVE

παυ θείην	παυ θεῖμεν or παυ θείημεν
παυ θείης	παυ θεῖτε or παυ θείητε
παυ θείη	παυ θεῖεν or παυ θείησαν

FIRST AORIST INFINITIVE PASSIVE παυ **θῆναι**

FIRST AORIST PARTICIPLE PASSIVE παυ **θείς, -εῖσα, -έν**

---

[1] The imperative is omitted because of its great rarity.

[2] Plato, *Laws*, 626 *E*.

337. All vowel stems have aorist passives like ἐπαύθην. Before **θ**, stems ending in **π** or **β** roughen to **φ**, those in **κ** or **γ** roughen to **χ**. Stems ending in **τ**, **δ**, **θ** change to **σ**:

πεμπ-, ἐπέμφθην; ἀγ-, ἤχθην; ἁρπαδ-, ἡρπάσθην.

338. The aorist participle passive has the endings of the consonant declension in the masculine and neuter, of the **α**-declension in the feminine. In the nominative masculine singular and the dative masculine and neuter plural **ντ** drops out and **ε** lengthens to **ει** (§ 107).

First Aorist Participle Passive of **παύω**

παυθείς	παυθεῖσα	παυθέν
παυθέντος	παυθείσης	παυθέντος
παυθέντι	παυθείσῃ	παυθέντι
παυθέντα	παυθεῖσαν	παυθέν
παυθέντες	παυθεῖσαι	παυθέντα
παυθέντων	παυθεισῶν	παυθέντων
παυθεῖσι(ν)	παυθείσαις	παυθεῖσι(ν)
παυθέντας	παυθείσᾱς	παυθέντα

339. A second aorist passive appears in some verbs. Such a form lacks **θ**. Otherwise, both as to form and meaning, a second aorist passive is the same as a first aorist passive.

Inflect the indicative, subjunctive, optative, infinitive, and participle of γράφω in the aorist passive (ἐγράφην). Compare with paradigm (§ 533).

340. The future passive forms its stem by adding **σο** (**σε**) to the stem of the aorist passive. It uses the personal endings of the present passive: first future passive, *παυ-θή-σο-μαι*; second future passive, *γραφ-ή-σο-μαι*.

Except for the difference in stem (the addition of θη), the future passive is inflected like the future middle.

Inflect the future indicative, optative, infinitive, and participle passive of *παύω* and *γράφω*. Compare with paradigms (§§ 528, 533).

341. VOCABULARY

ἀ-μελέω, ἀμελήσω, ἠμέλησα, ἠμέληκα, ἠμέλημαι: *be careless, neglect*, with G. Cf. **μέλει**.

δέομαι, δεήσομαι, δεδέημαι, ἐδεήθην: *lack, need, want, desire, request.* Freq. with G., or with G. of pers. and inf. Cf. **δεῖ**

δια-τρίβω, -τρίψω, -έτρῖψα, -τέτριφα, -τέτρῖμμαι, -ετρίβην: *rub through* or *away, spend, waste* (time), *delay*. DIATRIBE.

ὁπλίζω, ὥπλισα, ὥπλισμαι, ὡπλίσθην: *arm, equip.* Cf. **ὅπλα**.

παλτόν, -οῦ, τό: *javelin.*

φύσις, -εως, ἡ: *nature.* PHYSICS.

342. EXERCISES

(*a*) Translate:

1. οἱ Ἀθηναῖοι τῶν πολῑτῶν ἐδεήθησαν τριήρεις πέμψαι ὡς πλείστᾱς. 2. κατὰ φύσιν νόμος ἐστὶν ὁ πάντων βασιλεύς. 3. τῷ δὲ εὔρει τῷ τοῦ ποταμοῦ πολὺς χρόνος δι-ετρίβη ὑπὸ τῶν διωκόντων, ὥστε οἱ φυγάδες ἐξ-έφυγον. 4. ἐπιστολὴ δὲ γραφήσεται παρὰ βασιλέᾱ, ἐπὰν ᾖ καιρός. 5. λαβὼν τὰ παλτὰ εἰς τὰς χεῖρας ἐβοή-θησε τῷ ἥττονι. 6. ὦ ἄνδρες, ἐάν μοι πεισθῆτε, ἐν τῇ μεγίστῃ τῑμῇ ἔσεσθε. 7. ἐξ-οπλισθέντες οἱ κράτιστοι οὐ δεδοίκᾱσι μὴ κακὰ πάθωσιν. 8. ἀ-μελοῦντες κινδῡ́νου οὐκ ἤθελον εἰς φυγὴν τραπῆναι.

(*b*) Write in Greek:

1. While we remain, we must see to it that we remain safely. 2. We remembered that they had not stopped at the trench. 3. The large monument has been destroyed by the captain and his men. 4. Because of the breadth of the river, you must cross in a boat.

343. A NARROW ESCAPE — *Continued*

ὁ δὲ Πρόξενος (ὕστερος γὰρ προσ-ῆλθε καὶ τῶν ὁπλῑτῶν τινες αὐτῷ εἵποντο) εὐθὺς εἰς τὸ μέσον ἄγων ἐδεῖτο τοῦ

Κλεάρχου μὴ ποιεῖν ταῦτα. ὁ δ' ἐχαλέπαινεν ὅτι οὕτω πρᾴως (*mildly*) *λέγοι τὸ αὑτοῦ πάθος* (compare **πάσχω**), *ἐκέλευσέ τε αὐτὸν ἐκ τοῦ μέσου ἐξ-ίστασθαι* (*stand out*). *ἐν τούτῳ προσ-ῆλθε καὶ Κῦρος καὶ ἐπύθετο τὸ πρᾶγμα· εὐθὺς δ' ἔλαβε τὰ παλτὰ εἰς τὰς χεῖρας καὶ σὺν τοῖς παρ-οῦσι τῶν πιστῶν ἧκεν ἐλαύνων εἰς τὸ μέσον καὶ λέγει τάδε. Κλέαρχε καὶ Πρόξενε καὶ οἱ ἄλλοι οἱ παρ-όντες Ἕλληνες, τί ποιεῖτε; εἰ γὰρ ἀλλήλοις μαχεῖσθε, ἐν τῇδε τῇ ἡμέρᾳ ἐγὼ κατα-κεκόψομαι*[1] *καὶ ὑμεῖς οὐ πολὺ ἐμοῦ ὕστερον· κακῶς*[2] *γὰρ τῶν ἡμετέρων ἐχόντων πάντες οὗτοι οἱ βάρβαροι πολεμιώτεροι ἡμῖν ἔσονται τῶν παρὰ βασιλεῖ ὄντων. ἀκούσᾱς ταῦτα ὁ Κλέαρχος ἐν ἑαυτῷ ἐγένετο· καὶ ἐπαύσαντο ἀμφότεροι.*

THE VICTORY OF PÆONIUS

This memorial of a naval victory is one of Olympia's chief treasures. It represents Victory as a goddess about to alight on the prow of a ship.

Xenophon, *Anabasis*, I. 5. 14–17.

[1] Future perfect passive of *κατα-κόπτω*, a rare form easily recognized from the reduplication and **σ%ε**.

[2] An adverb with *ἔχω* is very common instead of the corresponding adjective with *εἰμί*.

LESSON LV

PRINCIPAL PARTS

ἐννέα τὰς Μούσᾱς φᾱσίν τινες· ὡς ὀλιγώρως·
ἠνίδε καὶ Σαπφὼ Λεσβόθεν ἡ δεκάτη.
Some say the Muses are nine. How careless!
Lo, Lesbian Sappho is the tenth.[1]

---

344. A normal verb has six principal parts: the first person singular indicative of the present, future, aorist, perfect, perfect middle, and aorist passive. These supply the stems for the various tenses (with all the moods of each) in the three voices (§ 548).

345. One or more parts are lacking in very many verbs, which therefore are not inflected or used in the tenses thus lacking. In many verbs one or more of the parts are irregular as to form.

346. Deponents that have an aorist middle are called *middle deponents:*

πυνθάνομαι, πεύσομαι, ἐπυθόμην.

Those that have an aorist passive but no aorist middle are called *passive deponents:*

βούλομαι, βουλήσομαι, ἐβουλήθην.

Middle deponents sometimes have an aorist passive with passive meaning:

κτάομαι *I acquire*, ἐκτησάμην *I acquired*, ἐκτήθη *it was acquired.*

---

[1] Greek Anthology.

347. PRINCIPAL PARTS OF VERBS ALREADY PRESENTED[1]

Pres. 1	*Fut.* 2	*Aor.* 3	*Perf.* 4	*Perf. Mid.* 5	*Aor. Pass.* 6
ἀγγέλλω	ἀγγελῶ	ἤγγειλα	ἤγγελκα	ἤγγελμαι	ἠγγέλθην
ἄγω	ἄξω	ἤγαγον	ἦχα	ἦγμαι	ἤχθην
αἱρέω	αἱρήσω	εἷλον	ᾕρηκα	ᾕρημαι	ᾑρέθην
αἰσθάνομαι	αἰσθήσομαι	ᾐσθόμην		ᾔσθημαι	
ἀκούω	ἀκούσομαι	ἤκουσα	ἀκήκοα		ἠκούσθην
ἁλίσκομαι	ἁλώσομαι	ἑάλων	ἑάλωκα		
ἀπο-θνῄσκω	ἀπο-θανοῦμαι	ἀπ-έθανον	τέθνηκα		
ἀπο-κτείνω	ἀπο-κτενῶ	ἀπ-έκτεινα	ἀπ-έκτονα		
ἀφ-ικνέομαι	ἀφ-ίξομαι	ἀφ-ῑκόμην		ἀφ-ῖγμαι	
βαίνω	βήσομαι	ἔβην	βέβηκα		
βάλλω	βαλῶ	ἔβαλον	βέβληκα	βέβλημαι	ἐβλήθην
βούλομαι	βουλήσομαι			βεβούλημαι	ἐβουλήθην
γίγνομαι	γενήσομαι	ἐγενόμην	γέγονα	γεγένημαι	
γιγνώσκω	γνώσομαι	ἔγνων	ἔγνωκα	ἔγνωσμαι	ἐγνώσθην
δέδοικα (perf. as pres.)		ἔδεισα			
δεῖ	δεήσει	ἐδέησε			
δέομαι	δεήσομαι			δεδέημαι	ἐδεήθην
δοκέω	δόξω	ἔδοξα		δέδογμαι	-εδόχθην[2]
ἐθέλω	ἐθελήσω	ἠθέλησα	ἠθέληκα		
εἰμί	ἔσομαι				
εἶπον (2d aor.)					
ἐλαύνω	ἐλῶ	ἤλασα	-ελήλακα[2]	ἐλήλαμαι	ἠλάθην
ἐπ-αινέω	ἐπ-αινέσω	ἐπ-ῄνεσα	ἐπ-ῄνεκα	ἐπ-ῄνημαι	ἐπ-ῃνέθην
ἐπι-μελέομαι	ἐπι-μελήσομαι			ἐπι-μεμέλημαι	ἐπ-εμελήθην
ἕπομαι	ἕψομαι	ἑσπόμην			
ἔρχομαι		ἦλθον	ἐλήλυθα		
εὑρίσκω	εὑρήσω	ηὗρον	ηὕρηκα	ηὕρημαι	ηὑρέθην
ἔχω	ἕξω or σχήσω	ἔσχον	ἔσχηκα	-έσχημαι[2]	
ἥδομαι	ἡσθήσομαι				ἥσθην
καλέω	καλῶ	ἐκάλεσα	κέκληκα	κέκλημαι	ἐκλήθην
κλέπτω	κλέψω	ἔκλεψα	κέκλοφα	κέκλεμμαι	ἐκλάπην
κρίνω	κρινῶ	ἔκρῑνα	κέκρικα	κέκριμαι	ἐκρίθην

[1] Verbs that conform to type have been omitted; also those that are not very common in tenses other than the present. [2] Only in compounds.

1	2	3	4	5	6
λαμβάνω	λήψομαι	ἔλαβον	εἴληφα	εἴλημμαι	ἐλήφθην
λείπω	λείψω	ἔλιπον	λέλοιπα	λέλειμμαι	ἐλείφθην
μανθάνω	μαθήσομαι	ἔμαθον	μεμάθηκα		
μάχομαι	μαχοῦμαι	ἐμαχεσάμην		μεμάχημαι	
μιμνῄσκω	-μνήσω [1]	-ἔμνησα [1]		μέμνημαι	ἐμνήσθην
νομίζω	νομιῶ	ἐνόμισα	νενόμικα	νενόμισμαι	ἐνομίσθην
πάσχω	πείσομαι	ἔπαθον	πέπονθα		
πείθω	πείσω	ἔπεισα	{ πέπεικα πέποιθα	πέπεισμαι	ἐπείσθην
πέμπω	πέμψω	ἔπεμψα	πέπομφα	πέπεμμαι	ἐπέμφθην
πίπτω	πεσοῦμαι	ἔπεσον	πέπτωκα		
πυνθάνομαι	πεύσομαι	ἐπυθόμην		πέπυσμαι	
[σκέπτομαι]	σκέψομαι	ἐσκεψάμην		ἔσκεμμαι	
σκοπέω (σκέπτομαι supplies the rest)					
σπεύδω	σπεύσω	ἔσπευσα			
τείνω	τενῶ	ἔτεινα	τέτακα	τέταμαι	ἐτάθην
τέμνω	τεμοῦμαι	ἔτεμον	τέτμηκα	τέτμημαι	ἐτμήθην
τρέπω	τρέψω	ἔτρεψα	τέτροφα	τέτραμμαι	ἐτράπην
τρέφω	θρέψω	ἔθρεψα	τέτροφα	τέθραμμαι	ἐτράφην
ὑπ-ισχνέομαι	ὑπο-σχήσο-μαι	ὑπ-εσχόμην		ὑπ-έσχημαι	
φαίνω	φανῶ	ἔφηνα	πέφηνα	πέφασμαι	ἐφάνην
φέρω	οἴσω	ἤνεγκα	ἐνήνοχα	ἐνήνεγμαι	ἠνέχθην
φεύγω	φεύξομαι	ἔφυγον	πέφευγα		
φημί	φήσω	ἔφησα			
χαλεπαίνω	χαλεπανῶ	ἐχαλέπηνα			

Learn the principal parts that are new and give the meaning of each present indicative.

348. **EXERCISE**

Write in Greek:

1. The javelins were found on the wagons before (any) time was wasted. 2. (Because) the city was (*being*) captured, we had to proceed to the mountain. 3. The messenger said that the letter would not be written. 4. The next day we learned that your money was stolen. 5. The boy is afraid that he may be chosen instead of his brother.

[1] Only in compounds.

349. SYNOPSIS OF **παύω**[1]

ACTIVE

	Pres.	*Imperf.*	*Fut.*	*Aor.*	*Perf.*	*Pluperf.*
	1	1	2	3	4	4
IND.	παύω	ἔπαυον	παύσω	ἔπαυσα	πέπαυκα	ἐπεπαύκη
SUBJV.	παύω			παύσω		
OPT.	παύοιμι		παύσοιμι	παύσαιμι		
IMV.	παῦε			παῦσον		
INF.	παύειν		παύσειν	παῦσαι	πεπαυκέναι	
PART.	παύων		παύσων	παύσᾱς	πεπαυκώς	

MIDDLE

	1	1	2	3	5	5
IND.	παύομαι	ἐπαυόμην	παύσομαι	ἐπαυσάμην	πέπαυμαι	ἐπεπαύμην
SUBJV.	παύωμαι			παύσωμαι		
OPT.	παυοίμην		παυσοίμην	παυσαίμην		
IMV.	παύου			παῦσαι		
INF.	παύεσθαι		παύσεσθαι	παύσασθαι	πεπαῦσθαι	
PART.	παυόμενος		παυσόμενος	παυσάμενος	πεπαυμένος	

PASSIVE

			6	6		
IND.	Like Mid.	Like Mid.	παυθήσομαι	ἐπαύθην	Like Mid.	Like Mid.
SUBJV.	" "			παυθῶ		
OPT.	" "		παυθησοίμην	παυθείην		
IMV.	" "			—		
INF.	" "		παυθήσεσθαι	παυθῆναι	" "	
PART.	" "		παυθησόμενος	παυθείς	" "	

350. *λείπω* has a second aorist active and middle where *παύω* has a first aorist. *γράφω* has a second aorist passive where *παύω* has a first aorist.

Give a complete synopsis of *λείπω* in the active and middle; of *γράφω* in the active and passive.

---

[1] The numerals that head the several columns denote the *principal part* on which the form is based.

351. **THE JEALOUS LOVER**

The following lines are the first stanza of a poem by Sappho, called by an early critic "a congress of passions harmonized into faultless phrase."

φαίνεταί μοι κῆνος (= *ἐκεῖνος*) *ἴσος θέοισιν*
ἔμμεν (= *εἶναι*) *ὤνηρ* (= *ὁ ἀνήρ*), *ὅστις ἐναντίος τοι* (= *σοι*)
ἰξάνει (*sits*) *καὶ πλᾱσίον* (*near*) *ἆδυ* (= *ἡδύ*) *φωνεύσᾱς* (compare TELEPHONE) *ὐπ-ακούει.*[1]

SAPPHO AND ALCÆUS

This painting by Alma Tadema shows the poet Alcæus singing to his own accompaniment before Sappho and her circle of Lesbian maidens.

J. A. Symonds has translated it into English Sapphics:

Peer of gods he seemeth to me, the blissful
Man who sits and gazes at thee before him,
Close beside thee sits, and in silence hears thee
Silverly speaking.

[1] This poem has been translated into Latin by Catullus (51) who apes the meter but cannot preserve the charm. The Æolic dialect in which Sappho wrote is characterized by smooth breathing and recessive accent.

LESSON LVI

NUMERALS

εἷς ἀνὴρ οὐδεὶς ἀνήρ. — *In union there is strength.*[1]

352. CARDINAL NUMBERS.

1. εἷς, μία, ἕν: *one.* HENDIADYS, HYPHEN.
   μη-δ-είς, μη-δε-μία, μη-δ-έν: *no one, no.*
   οὐ-δ-είς, οὐ-δε-μία, οὐ-δ-έν: *no one, no.*
2. δύο [δι- as prefix; DIMETER]. Lat. *duo.* DUET.
3. τρεῖς, τρία. TRIAD, TRIGONOMETRY.
4. τέτταρες, τέτταρα. TETRAHEDRON.
5. πέντε. PENTAGON.
6. ἕξ. HEXAMETER.
7. ἑπτά. HEPTAMETER.
8. ὀκτώ. OCTOPUS.
9. ἐννέα. ENNEAD.
10. δέκα. DECALOGUE.
11. ἕν-δεκα. HENDECASYLLABIC.
12. δώ-δεκα. DODECANESE.
13. τρεῖς καὶ δέκα.
14. τέτταρες καὶ δέκα.
15. πεντε-καί-δεκα.
16. ἑκ-καί-δεκα.
17. ἑπτα-καί-δεκα.
18. ὀκτω-καί-δεκα.
19. ἐννεα-καί-δεκα
20. εἴκοσι(ν).
21. εἷς καὶ εἴκοσι, εἴκοσι καὶ εἷς, εἴκοσιν εἷς.
30. τριάκοντα.
100. ἑκατόν. HECATOMB.
200. διακόσιοι.
1000. χίλιοι.
2000. δισ-χίλιοι.
10000. μύριοι. MYRIAD.

-κοντα indicates the tens (*-ty*) from *thirty* to *ninety.*
-κόσιοι indicates the hundreds from *200* to *900*, which are inflected.

[1] Greek maxim. Literally: *One man, no man.*

353. INFLECTION OF CARDINAL NUMBERS.

εἷς *one*

εἷς	μία	ἕν
ἑνός	μιᾶς	ἑνός
ἑνί	μιᾷ	ἑνί
ἕνα	μίαν	ἕν

οὐδείς (and μηδείς) are inflected like εἷς with οὐδ- (μηδ-) prefixed to the masculine and neuter, οὐδε- (μηδε-) to the feminine. The accent of the nominative masculine is acute. Inflect οὐδείς. Compare with paradigm (§ 517).

τρεῖς *three* / **τέτταρες** *four*

(m. and f.)	(n.)	(m. and f.)	(n.)
τρεῖς	τρία	τέτταρες	τέτταρα
τριῶν	τριῶν	τεττάρων	τεττάρων
τρισί(ν)	τρισί(ν)	τέτταρσι(ν)	τέτταρσι(ν)
τρεῖς	τρία	τέτταρας	τέτταρα

354. Genitive of Measure. The genitive denotes *measure of space, time,* or *value:*[1]

ἑπτὰ σταδίων τεῖχος *a wall seven stades long.*

355. EXERCISES

(*a*) Translate:

1. Ἀρίστιππος δὲ Κῦρον αἰτεῖ μισθὸν εἰς δισ-χῑλίους ξένους καὶ τριῶν μηνῶν. 2. ἐντεῦθεν ἐξ-ελαύνει διὰ τῆς Λυδίᾱς σταθμοὺς τέτταρας παρασάγγᾱς εἴκοσι καὶ δύο ἐπὶ τὸν Μαίανδρον ποταμόν. 3. ἐνταῦθα ἐπὶ τῇ τάφρῳ ἔμεινεν ἡμέρᾱς ἑπτά. 4. ἡ δὲ γυνὴ προτέρᾱ Κύρου ἓξ ἡμέραις ἀφῑκετο. 5. ἐντεῦθεν ἐξ-ελαύνει σταθμοὺς τρεῖς παρασάγγᾱς ὀκτω-καίδεκα ἐπὶ τὸν Εὐφράτην ποταμόν, ὄντα τὸ εὖρος[2] τεττάρων σταδίων. 6. ἔστι δὲ τριᾱ́-κοντα ἡμερῶν ὁδὸς ἀπὸ τῆς ἡμετέρᾱς πόλεως.

---

[1] What uses of the genitive have you now had?

[2] **Accusative of respect** (page 144, note 2).

(*b*) Complete:

1. *τρεῖς καὶ ἓξ εἰσι* ——. 2. *δέκα καὶ δέκα εἰσὶ* ——. 3. *ἕνδεκα καὶ δώδεκά εἰσι* ——. 4. *τὰ ἑξά-κις*[1] *πέντε ἐστὶ* ——. 5. *τὰ δεκά-κις ἑκατόν ἐστι* ——. 6. *τὰ πεντά-κις* —— *ἐστι τετταρά-κοντα.* 7. *ἔστι τὰ δώδεκα δὶς* —— *ἢ τρὶς* —— *ἢ τετρά-κις* —— *ἢ ἑξά-κις* ——.

356. GREEK VIEWS ON DEATH

(*a*) Socrates at the age of seventy was tried in Athens on a charge of impiety. The spirit that pervades his defense, as recorded by Plato in the *Apology*, is sufficient proof to modern minds that he was innocent; but he was condemned to death. Among other notable utterances addressed to friends and foes after the verdict, is the following characteristic statement of his creed.

SOCRATES

Ἀλλὰ καὶ ὑμᾶς χρή, ὦ ἄνδρες δικασταί, εὐ-έλπιδας εἶναι πρὸς τὸν θάνατον, καὶ ἕν τι τοῦτο ἡγεῖσθαι ἀληθές, ὅτι οὐκ ἔστιν ἀνδρὶ ἀγαθῷ κακὸν οὐδὲν οὔτε ζῶντι (*living*, compare ZOÖLOGY) *οὔτε τεθνηκότι, οὐδὲ ἀμελεῖται ὑπὸ θεῶν τὰ τούτου πρᾶγματα.*

Plato, *Apology*, 41 C, D.

(*b*) While few pagans of any age could approximate the sublime faith of such an utterance, in general the

[1] Numeral adverbs, except *ἅπαξ* *once*, *δίς* *twice*, *τρίς* *three times*, end in *-κις*.

sepulchral monuments and writings of the Greeks display a manly attitude toward death. The following verses are taken from a play written by Euripides :

ἔφυ (*lives*) μὲν οὐδεὶς ὅστις
οὐ πονεῖ (*has trouble*)
βροτῶν (*of mortals*),
θάπτει τε τέκνα (*children*)
χἄτερα (= καὶ ἕτερα)
κτᾶται (*obtains*) νέα,
αὐτός τε θνῄσκει, καὶ τάδ'
ἄχθονται βροτοὶ
εἰς γῆν φέροντες γῆν·
ἀναγκαίως δ' ἔχει
βίον θερίζειν (*harvest*)
ὥστε (*as*) κάρπιμον
(*ripe*) στάχυν (*grain*),
καὶ τὸν μὲν εἶναι, τὸν δὲ
μή· τί ταῦτα δεῖ
στένειν (*bemoan*), ἅ-περ
(stronger than ἅ) δεῖ
κατὰ φύσιν δι-εκ-περᾶν
(*go through*);
δεινὸν γὰρ οὐδὲν τῶν ἀναγκαίων βροτοῖς.

Euripides, fragment.

HEGESO

This tombstone is famous for its dignity and beauty and also for the simplicity of its inscription : ΗΓΗΣΩΠΡΟΞΕΝΟ, Hegeso (wife) of Proxenos.

LESSON LVII

REVIEW

Φιλοσοφίᾱ Βίου Κυβερνήτης. — *Philosophy the Guide of Life.*[1]

357. **ASSIGNMENTS**

(*a*) Review vocabulary, § 555, following the method indicated in § 27, *a*. Give principal parts of the verbs.

(*b*) Name and define the Greek words suggested by *heterogeneous*, *eleutheromania*, *criterion*, *diaphanous*, *Acropolis*, *dromedary*, *phanerogam*, *George*, *antistrophe*, *emblem*, *geometry*, *bema*, *enallage*, *mesolithic*, *telescope*, *mathematics*, *appendectomy*, *hexahedral*, *hendecagon*, *octastyle*, *pentathlon*, *heptad*, *eirenicon*.

(*c*) Add ten words to this list.

(*d*) Inflect *μηδείς*.

(*e*) Give complete synopsis of *κελεύω* in the third person singular active; *γίγνομαι* in the third person singular middle; *πλήττω* in the third person plural passive.

(*f*) What indications of mood and tense appear in heavy type?

ἥρπα **σται**   **πέ** *πομ* **φε**   **λε** *λει* **μμ** *ένος* **ᾖ**   **λυ θείη**
φαν **ῆναι**   *ἀγγε* **λεῖ σθαι**   **τε** *τά* **χθαι**   *τραπ* **ήσεται**
κρί **ναιεν**   **ἐ** *παύ* **σω**   **μαθ** *έ* **τω**   *ἠθροι* **σμένοι ἦσαν**

(*g*) What clues are given by the accents:[2]

κρίνοιεν, *κρῑνοῖεν*, *κώλῡσαι*, *κωλῦσαι*, *ἠθροικώς*, *φυγών*, *ἐστρατευμένον*, *γενέσθαι*, *φιλεῖ*, *φίλει*, *μαχεῖται*, *ἀγγέλλουσι*, *ἀγγελοῦσι*, *εἰλῆφθαι*, *ᾔσθου*, *αἰσθοῦ*.

[1] Motto of the Phi Beta Kappa Society.

[2] Of course, other clues are to be found in most of these verbs.

358. **EXERCISES**

(*a*) Complete:

1. εἴθε μηδε— τῶν γυναικῶν μαθ— τὸ τεῖχος λελυ— τ— πολεμι— (plural). 2. καὶ γὰρ φόβος ἐστὶ τοῖς ἡττ— γενομένοις μὴ δια-τριβόμενοι ἀ-τῑμασθ—. 3. μὴ Κῦρον αἰτ—τε —— (1000) ξένους. 4. —δενι μέλει ὅπως ὠφελ— τοὺς γέροντας. 5. μὴ νομισ—τε τοὺς —— (10,000) Ἕλληνας οὐ κακὰ πεπονθ— ὑπὸ πολλ— βαρβαρ—. 6. ὁ δὲ ἐλπίζει ἀμφοτέρους λόχους μάλα θαρρησ— πρὸς τ— ἀνα-βασ—.

(*b*) Write in Greek:

1. Judge not that you be not judged. 2. Now that the commander is dead[1] we must cross the trench. 3. Would that they may show themselves worthy of their freedom! 4. From there he marches three days' journey, twenty-one parasangs. 5. Did you report that five generals were chosen by the captains? 6. We were afraid that the tomb might be dishonored.

---

[1] Use genitive absolute.

Phi Beta Kappa Key

LESSON LVIII

READING

ζητῶ γὰρ τὴν ἀλήθειαν, ὑφ' ἧς οὐδεὶς πώποτε ἐβλάβη.
For I seek the truth, by which no man was ever harmed.[1]

359. VOCABULARY

ἐν-αντίος, -ᾱ, -ον: *facing, confronting*, with G. or D.; οἱ ἐν-αντίοι: *the opponents.*

ἔρημος, -η, -ον: *desert, deserted, lonely, deprived of.* HERMIT.

ἱερός, -ᾱ́, -όν: *sacred, holy*; τὸ ἱερόν: *the holy place*, i.e., *temple*; τὰ ἱερά: *sacrifices, sacrificial victims.* HIERARCHY.

πωλέω, πωλήσω, ἐπώλησα: *sell.* MONOPOLY.

360. THE ORIGINAL RESEARCH MAN

Οἱ δὲ Αἰγύπτιοι πρὶν μὲν Ψαμμήτιχον αὐτῶν βασιλεῦσαι, ἐνόμιζον ἑαυτοὺς πρώτους γενέσθαι πάντων ἀνθρώπων. ἐπειδὴ δὲ Ψαμμήτιχος βασιλεύσᾱς ἠθέλησε πυθέσθαι οἵτινες γένοιντο πρῶτοι, ἀπὸ τούτου νομίζουσι Φρύγας προτέρους γενέσθαι ἑαυτῶν, τῶν δὲ ἄλλων ἑαυτούς. Ψαμμήτιχος γάρ, ἵνα ταῦτα πύθοιτο, ἐποίει τάδε· παιδία (diminutive of παῖς) δύο νεο-γνὰ (*new born*) κελεύει ποιμένα (*herdsman*) οὕτω τρέφειν ὥστε μηδένα ἐν-αντίον αὐτῶν μηδὲν εἰπεῖν, ἀλλὰ τὰ μὲν παιδία καθ' αὐτὰ εἶναι ἐν οἰκίᾳ ἐρήμῃ, τὸν δὲ ποιμένα ἐν καιρῷ ἐπ-άγειν αὐτοῖς αἶγας (*goats*), ἵνα γάλα (compare GALACTIC) ἔχοι τὰ παιδία. ταῦτα δὲ ἐποίει τε καὶ ἐκέλευσεν

---

[1] Marcus Aurelius, *Meditations*, VI. 21.

MARCUS AURELIUS
This Roman emperor is famous for his writings in Greek.

ὁ Ψαμμήτιχος ἐθέλων ἀκοῦσαι τῶν παιδίων ἥντινα φωνὴν ῥήξουσι (*give forth*) πρώτην. μετὰ δ' οὖν χρόνον οὐκ ὀλίγον ἐπεὶ ὁ ποιμὴν εἰς ἐκείνην τὴν οἰκίᾱν εἰσ-ήρχετο, τὰ παιδία ἀμφότερα προσ-πίπτοντα "βεκὸς" εἶπον καὶ τὰ̄ς χεῖρας ἀνέτεινον. ἀκούσᾱς δὲ καὶ αὐτὸς ὁ Ψαμμήτιχος ἐπυνθάνετο οἵτινες ἀνθρώπων βεκός τι καλοῦσι, πυνθανόμενος δὲ εὕρισκε[1] Φρύγας καλοῦντας τὸν ἄρτον (*bread*). οὕτως οὖν ὡμολόγησαν οἱ Αἰγύπτιοι τοὺς Φρύγας πρεσβυτέρους εἶναι ἑαυτῶν.

Adapted from Herodotus, II. 2. 1–5.

361. BUSINESS AND RELIGION

καὶ εἰσ-ῆλθεν Ἰησοῦς εἰς τὸ ἱερὸν τοῦ θεοῦ καὶ ἐξ-έβαλε πάντας τοὺς πωλοῦντας καὶ ἀγοράζοντας ἐν τῷ ἱερῷ . . . . . καὶ λέγει αὐτοῖς, Γέγραπται, ὁ οἶκός μου οἶκος προσ-ευχῆς (compare **εὔχομαι**) κληθήσεται, ὑμεῖς δὲ αὐτὸν ποιεῖτε σπήλαιον (*cave*) λῃστῶν (*robbers*). καὶ προσ-ῆλθον αὐτῷ τυφλοὶ (*blind*) καὶ χωλοὶ (*lame*) ἐν τῷ ἱερῷ καὶ ἐθεράπευσεν αὐτούς. ἰδόντες (*having seen*) δὲ οἱ ἀρχιερεῖς καὶ οἱ γραμματεῖς τὰ θαυμάσια (compare **θαυμάζω**) ἃ ἐποίησεν . . . . . ἠγανάκτησαν (= ἐχαλέπηναν).

St. Matthew XXI. 12–16.

[1] Verbs beginning with a diphthong do not always have augment.

LESSON LIX

PRESENT OF ἵστημι

τῷ σοφῷ ξένον οὐδέν. — *To the wise nothing is foreign.*[1]

362. MI-Verbs. All verbs thus far studied, except εἰμί, have been **ω**-verbs and use the variable vowel **ο** or **ε** (**ω** or **η**) before the personal endings. Other verbs are called **μι**-verbs because they have **-μι** instead of **-ω** as the ending of the first person singular present indicative active. They also lack the variable vowel in the present system,[2] except in the subjunctive, where **ω** and **η** are retained. In other tense systems[3] than the present and second aorist, **μι**-verbs are inflected the same as **ω**-verbs.

363. ἵστημι in the Present. Learn the inflection of ἵστημι in the present system in all three voices (§ 535). Note that **α** occurs in all forms of the middle and passive and in all forms of the active, except in the singular of the present and imperfect indicative and in the second person singular of the imperative. In these forms **η** occurs. In the third person plural of the present indicative active **-άᾱσι** = **-ᾶσι**. In the subjunctive **α** + **ω** = **ω**, **α** + **η** = **η**, **α** + **ῃ** = **ῃ**.

364. The present participle, ἱστάς, is inflected like παύσᾱς except that it has an accent on the ultima. Write out its inflection. Compare with paradigm (§ 514, *f*).

365. δύναμαι is inflected like ἵσταμαι.[4] Inflect it.

---

[1] Antisthenes, as quoted by Diogenes Laertius, VI. 12.

[2] By *system* is meant a group of forms using a common stem.

[3] There are a few unimportant exceptions.

[4] But subjunctive and optative have recessive accent, and ἐδύνω is more usual than ἐδύνασο.

366. VOCABULARY

δύναμαι, δυνήσομαι, δεδύνημαι, ἐδυνήθην: *be able.* DYNAMIC.

δύναμις, -εως, ἡ: *power, force* (often in military usage).

δυνατός, -ή, -όν: *powerful, able, capable.*

ἐπίσταμαι, ἐπιστήσομαι, ἠπιστήθην: *know, understand, know how.* EPISTEMOLOGY.

ἵστημι, στήσω, ἔστησα or ἔστην, ἕστηκα, ἕσταμαι, ἐστάθην: *stand, halt, place.* Cf. **σταθμός.** STATIC.

κέρδος, -ους, τό: *gain, profit, pay.*

οἷος, -ᾱ, -ον: *of which (what) sort;* when followed by τε, *of the sort that, able to.*

υἱός, -οῦ, ὁ: *son.*

367. EXERCISE

Translate:

1. οὐδ' ἂν δυναίμην περὶ τῆς εἰρήνης θαρρεῖν. 2. ἀλλ' οὔπω ἐπίστασθε εἰς οἷον ἀγῶνα ἔρχεσθε. 3. οὐχ οἷόν τ' ἐστὶν ἡμῖν πᾶσαν τὴν δύναμιν ἐνταῦθα ἱστάναι. 4. ἔνθα δὴ φύλακες αὐτὸν ἵστασθαι ἐκέλευσαν. 5. ἐκεῖνος οὖν φοβεῖται μὴ ἄλλος εἰς τὴν ἀρχὴν καθ-ιστῆται σατράπης. 6. ἠπιστάμεθα δ' ἄρχειν[1] τε καὶ ἄρχεσθαι. 7. δύναμιν δ' ὡς οἷόν τε πλείστην ἤθροιζες. 8. ἐὰν δὲ τὴν φάλαγγα πρὸς τῷ ποταμῷ ἱστῇ, οὐκ ἔσται τοῖς πολεμίοις ὄπισθεν διώκειν. 9. ταῦτά γ' ἂν ἐπιστάμενος τούς τε φίλους ὠφελεῖν καὶ τοὺς πολεμίους κωλύειν δύναιτο.

368. FOND PARENTS

τὸν δὲ υἱὸν ἐν-τρυφῶντα (*making sport of*) τῇ μητρὶ καὶ δι' ἐκείνην αὐτῷ σκώπτων (*joking*) Θεμιστοκλῆς ἔφη αὐτὸν πλεῖστον τῶν Ἑλλήνων δύνασθαι· τοῖς μὲν γὰρ Ἕλλησιν ἐπι-τάττειν Ἀθηναίους, Ἀθηναίοις δὲ αὐτόν, αὐτῷ δὲ τὴν ἐκείνου μητέρα, τῇ μητρὶ δ' ἐκεῖνον.

Plutarch, *Themistocles*, XVIII. 4.

---

[1] The infinitive when dependent on certain verbs of *knowing*, but not in indirect discourse, means *how to* (*do*). Compare French *savoir faire*.

369. **A FISH IN THE HAND**

ἁλιεύς (*fisherman*) ποτε μῑκρὸν ἰχθὺν ἔλαβεν. ὁ δὲ ἰχθὺς ἔλεγεν· Ὦ ἄνθρωπε, πάνυ μῑκρός εἰμι. νῦν οὖν ἀπό-λῡσόν με, μείζω δὲ γενόμενον τότε δὴ ἄγρευε. τοῦτο γάρ σοι ποιοῦντι πολὺ κέρδος ἔσται. ὁ δὲ ἁλιεὺς ἀπ-εκρίνατο· Ἀλλ' ἔγωγε εὐηθέστατος (*very foolish*) ἂν εἴην, εἰ τὸ παρ-ὸν κέρδος μὴ λαβὼν ἄ-δηλον ἐλπίδα διώκοιμι.

ὁ λόγος δηλοῖ (*makes plain*) ὅτι βέλτῑόν ἐστι κέρδος τὸ παρ-όν, κἂν μῑκρὸν ᾖ, τοῦ μὴ παρ-όντος.

Adapted from Æsop.

370. The fish became a symbol for the early Christians because of the meaning that they attached to the letters of the word ἰχθύς :[1]

Ἰ(ησοῦς)	Jesus
Χ(ριστός)	Christ
Θ(εοῦ)	of God
Υ(ἱός)	Son
Σ(ωτήρ)	Saviour

However, the original thought may have been that Christ was the Great Fisher. In St. Matthew, IV. 19, He says to His disciples :

ποιήσω ὑμᾶς ἁλιεῖς ἀνθρώπων.

[1] The illustration shows an ancient signet. Note the mistake in spelling.

LESSON LX

SECOND AORIST ACTIVE OF ἵστημι[1]

δός μοι ποῦ στῶ, καὶ κῑνῶ τὴν γῆν.
Give me where I may stand and I will move the earth.[2]

371. ἵστημι in the Second Aorist. (*a*) Learn the inflection of *ἵστημι* in the second aorist active (§ 535). Note that **α** occurs in all forms of the optative and of the participle, and in the third person plural of the imperative. **η** occurs in all other forms except where **ω** is normal in the subjunctive.

Note the general similarity, apart from stem (**στα-**, not **ἱστα-**), between the second aorist and the present active (except in the indicative plural, the imperative, and the infinitive).

(*b*) Inflect *στάς* (like *ἱστάς*).

(*c*) In like manner inflect the aorist of *βαίνω* (*ἔβην*).

372. Meanings of ἵστημι. Besides the normal meanings appropriate to that voice, the middle of *ἵστημι* in the intransitive usage frequently means *to stand.* The second aorist, perfect, and pluperfect active of this verb are always intransitive.

373. **VOCABULARY**

ἔπ-ειτα, adv.: *thereupon, next.* Cf. **εἶτα**.

ἴσως, adv.: *perhaps.*

ὅμως, adv.: *all the same, however.*

στέλλω, στελῶ, ἔστειλα, ἔσταλκα, ἔσταλμαι, ἐστάλην: *send.* APOSTOLIC, PERISTALTIC.

τοίνυν, post-pos. adv.: *then, therefore.*

[1] *ἵστημι* has no second aorist middle.

[2] Archimedes.

374. **EXERCISES**

(*a*) Translate:

1. ὅμως οὐδὲν ὑπ' ἐμοῦ ἀ-δικούμενος, ἀπο-στὰς εἰς τοὺς πολεμίους κακῶς ἐποίεις τὴν ἐμὴν χώρᾱν ὅ τι ἐδύνω. 2. τὰ δὲ ἄλλα ῥίψᾱς εἰς τὸ πῦρ ἀν-έβη τε τὸν ἵππον καὶ ἀπ-ήλαυνεν. 3. ἐγὼ οὖν φημι χρῆναι ὑμᾶς δια-βῆναι τὸν Εὐφρᾱ́την ποταμὸν πρὶν φανερὸν εἶναι ὅ τι οἱ ἄλλοι Ἕλληνες ἀπο-κρῑνοῦνται. 4. ἔπειτα στρέψᾱς ἀπ-έστειλεν ἄνδρας οἳ ἀνὰ τὰ ὄρη ἔδραμον ῥᾳδίως. 5. ἐφοβούμην δὲ μὴ οὐ τὸ πεδίον δια-βαίησαν δρόμῳ. 6. ἀλλ' ὅμως στήσᾱς τὸ ἅρμα ἐπυνθάνετο ποῦ εἶεν οἱ ἱππεῖς. 7. ἀπο-θανόντος τοίνυν τοῦ Δᾱρείου ὁ μὲν πρεσβύτερος εἰς τὴν ἀρχὴν κατ-έστη. 8. ἐὰν δὲ ἀπο-στῶ πρὸς αὐτόν, δῶρά μοι ἴσως πολλοῦ ἄξια πέμψει.

(*b*) Write in Greek:

1. If you are able to sell the wine, the profit is yours. 2. Your son might know how to aid the most capable. 3. The boy's mother is standing at the door. 4. The captain halts his men at the monument.

375. **"O WAD SOME POWER"**

Κώνωψ (*mosquito*) ἐπι-στὰς κέρατι ταύρου (*bull*) καὶ πολὺν χρόνον δια-μείνᾱς, ἐπειδὴ ἀπ-αλλάττεσθαι ἔμελλεν, ἐπυνθάνετο τοῦ ταύρου, εἰ ἤδη βούλεται αὐτὸν ἀπ-ελθεῖν. ὁ δὲ ἀπ-εκρῖνατο· 'Αλλ' οὔθ' ὅτε ἦλθες ᾐσθόμην, οὔτ' ἐὰν ἀπ-έλθῃς γνώσομαι.

τούτῳ τῷ λόγῳ δύναιτο ἄν τις τὸν ἀ-δύνατον διδάσκειν ὅτι οὔτε παρ-ὼν οὔτ' ἀπ-ὼν οὔτ' ὠφέλιμός ἐστιν οὔτ' αὖ βλαβερός (*harmful*).

Adapted from Æsop, 235.

376. Word-formation. (*a*) Nouns in **-σιᾱ** express an *abstract* idea of *action*. Many such words have passed directly into English :

αἰσθάνομαι *perceive*, ἀναισθησίᾱ ANESTHESIA.

(*b*) Nouns in **-ιᾱ** express *quality*. Many such words have passed into English with **-ιᾱ** changed to *y* :

φιλάνθρωπος *fond of man*, φιλανθρωπίᾱ PHILANTHROPY;
πολύγαμος *much-married*, πολυγαμίᾱ POLYGAMY.

THE FOUNTAIN OF ARETHUSA

No relic of Syracusan splendor is better known than Arethusa, whose waters sparkle still as in the days of Archimedes.

LESSON LXI

φημί. INDIRECT DISCOURSE

αὐτὸς ἔφᾱ. — *Ipse dixit.*[1]

377. φημί in the Present. Learn the inflection of *φημί* in the present system (§ 536). Note the general similarity to *ἵστημι*; and, also, that like *εἰμί* (§ 93) the present indicative, with the exception of the second person singular, is enclitic. Instead of the participle *φάς*, Attic prose uses *φάσκων*.

378. Indirect Discourse. (*a*) Review the principles already studied for the various constructions that follow words of *saying*, *thinking*, *telling*, *knowing*, and *perceiving* (§§ 211–217).

(*b*) In complex sentences the main verbs undergo the same changes as in simple sentences. The subordinate verbs are either in the same mood and tense as in the original form, or, after secondary tenses, they may be changed to the same tense of the optative, *ἐάν* also changing to *εἰ*:

DIRECT	INDIRECT	
ἐὰν ἔλθῃ, μαχεῖται *if he comes, he will fight.*	λέγουσιν ὅτι ἐὰν ἔλθῃ, μαχεῖται.	φασὶν ἐὰν ἔλθῃ, αὐτὸν μαχεῖσθαι.
	ἔλεξαν ὅτι ἐὰν ἔλθῃ, μαχεῖται or εἰ ἔλθοι, μαχοῖτο.	ἔφασαν ἐὰν ἔλθῃ, αὐτὸν μαχεῖσθαι or, εἰ ἔλθοι, αὐτὸν μαχεῖσθαι.

[1] Said of the Great Master, Pythagoras, as quoted by Diogenes Laertius VIII. 46. ἔφᾱ is dialectic for ἔφη.

(*c*) Past tenses of the indicative, however, remain unchanged in subordinate clauses :

DIRECT	INDIRECT	
εἰ ἦλθεν, ἐμαχέσατο ἄν *if he had come, he would have fought.*	λέγουσιν (or ἔλεξαν) ὅτι εἰ ἦλθεν, ἐμαχέσατο ἄν.	φασίν (or ἔφασαν), εἰ ἦλθεν, αὐτὸν ἂν μαχέσασθαι.

379. **VOCABULARY**

βοῦς, βοός,[1] ὁ *or* ἡ : *ox, cow.*

ἐν-νοέω, -ήσω, -ησα : *have in mind, consider, conceive.*

νοῦς, νοῦ, ὁ : *mind* ; ἐν νῷ ἔχω : *intend* ; τὸν νοῦν προσ-έχω : *attend*, i.e., *pay heed.*

ὅλος, -η, -ον : *whole, all.* HOLOGRAPH, HOLOCAUST.

οὐκ-οῦν, adv. : *therefore.*

παίω, παίσω, ἔπαισα, πέπαικα : *strike.* ANAPÆST.

φημί, φήσω, ἔφησα : *say.*

ψευδής, -ές : *false.* PSEUDONYM, PSEUDOSCIENTIFIC.

ψεύδω, ψεύσω, ἔψευσα, ἔψευσμαι ἐψεύσθην : *deceive* ; mid., *lie.*

380. **EXERCISES**

(*a*) What clues are given by the portions in heavy type ?

φα **ίη**	φά **τω**	φά **ναι**	φα **μέν**
ἔ φαμεν	**ἔ** φη **σε**	φή **σει**	φ **ῶ** σι

(*b*) Translate :

1. τί ἐν νῷ ἔχετε περὶ τῆς εἰρήνης; 2. ταῦτ' οὖν ἐν-νοήσᾱς ὅλην τὴν νύκτα τὰς βοῦς ἐφύλαττον. 3. ὑπ-ισχνεῖτο δ' αὐτῷ, εἰ ἔλθοι, φίλον αὐτὸν Κύρῳ ποιήσειν, ὃν αὐτὸς ἔφη κρείττω ἑαυτῷ νομίζειν τῆς πατρίδος. 4. τὸν δὲ ψευδῆ ἀγγείλαντα ἐπαίσαμεν, ἵνα μηκέτι ψεύδοιτο. 5. οὐκ-οῦν ἀκούω τὰς τάφρους οὐ πλέον εἴκοσι σταδίων ἀπ-εχούσᾱς. 6. πότε ἔλεγον ὅτι οὐ δύναιτο τὰς ἑκατὸν βοῦς πωλεῖν ; 7. οὐ μέντοι γε θαυμάζουσιν εἰ ψευδὴς ἦν ὁ Θρᾷξ. 8. ποῦ ταύτην φασὶν ὑπὸ τῶν βαρβάρων ταφῆναι ; 9. τὸ ὅλον μεῖζον τοῦ μέρους ἐστίν.

---

[1] For inflection, see § 509, *g*.

(c) Write in Greek:

1. The women ran to the gate of the city (and) stood there. 2. Thereupon the heavy-armed soldiers crossed the plain on (the) run. 3. However, they did not yet know that the general was halting his men. 4. Do not halt unless you learn that we are safe.

381. Long before the traditional date of the founding of Rome, the Greeks were exploring and colonizing in the western Mediterranean. They secured so firm a grip upon southern Italy that that region came to be called *Magna Graecia.* The practical spirit of their Italian neighbors welcomed more readily the business methods and devices of the Greeks than their philosophy. But Greek gods found their way to Rome, and majestic Greek temples, like those still standing at Pæstum, gradually developed in Italy an appreciation of Greek art.

382. ATTIC SALT

εἰ δέ τις ὑμῶν ἀ-θῡμεῖ (compare **πρό-θῡμος**) ὅτι ἡμῖν μὲν οὐκ εἰσὶν ἱππεῖς, τοῖς δὲ πολεμίοις πολλοὶ πάρ-εισιν, ἐν-νοεῖτε ὅτι οἱ μύριοι ἱππεῖς οὐδὲν ἄλλο ἢ μύριοί εἰσιν ἄνθρωποι· ὑπὸ μὲν γὰρ ἵππου ἐν μάχῃ οὐδεὶς πώποτε οὔτε δηχθεὶς (*bitten*) οὔτε λακτισθεὶς (*kicked*) ἀπ-έθανεν, οἱ δὲ ἄνδρες εἰσὶν οἱ ποιοῦντες ὅ τι ἂν ἐν ταῖς μάχαις γίγνηται. οὐκοῦν τῶν ἱππέων πολὺ ἡμεῖς ἐπ' ἀσφαλεστέρου ὀχήματός (*support*) ἐσμεν· οἱ μὲν γὰρ ἐφ' ἵππων κρέμανται (*hang*) φοβούμενοι οὐκ ἡμᾶς μόνον ἀλλὰ καὶ τὸ κατα-πεσεῖν· ἡμεῖς δ' ἐπὶ γῆς βεβηκότες πολὺ μὲν ἰσχῡρότερον παίσομεν, ἐάν τις προσ-έλθῃ. ἑνὶ δὲ μόνῳ προ-έχουσιν οἱ ἱππεῖς ἡμᾶς· φεύγειν αὐτοῖς ἀσφαλέστερόν ἐστιν ἢ ἡμῖν.

Xenophon, *Anabasis*, III. 2. 18–19.

383. Word-formation. Nouns in -**μος** express some *abstract* idea of *action:* *διώκω* *pursue*, *διωγμός* *pursuit*. Added to stems of verbs in -*ιζω*, this ending gives nouns like Ἑλληνισμός HELLENISM (from ἑλληνίζω HELLENIZE). By analogy we have the many English words in -*ism* and -*ist* which have no other relation to Greek. To this type belong *Bolshevism*, *Bolshevist*; *Anglicism*; *purism*, *purist*; *rationalize*, *rationalism*, *rationalist*.

GREEK TEMPLES AT PÆSTUM

The Temple of Poseidon, in the left foreground, is one of the most impressive remains of Greek architecture in all Italy. It dates from the best period of Doric style. The town of Pæstum has vanished, but the temples attract visitors by the thousands.

LESSON LXII

PRESENT OF τίθημι AND ἵημι

μηδὲν ἄγαν. — *Nothing too much.*[1]

384. τίθημι in the Present. Learn the inflection of *τίθημι* in the present system of all three voices (§ 535). Note that **ε** occurs in all forms of the middle and passive voice and in all forms of the active, except in the singular of the present and imperfect indicative and in the second person singular of the imperative, where *ἵστημι* was likewise exceptional. The third person plural present indicative active **-έᾱσι** does not contract as in *ἵστημι*. In the subjunctive **ε** is absorbed (§ 127). The optative of the active voice has alternative forms that are like the forms of *φιλέω* (§ 584). In the active participle **ε** lengthens to **ει**.

385. ἵημι in the Present. (*a*) *ἵημι* in the present system is like *τίθημι*, except that it has an alternative form, *ἱεῖς*, in the second person singular present indicative active, contracts **-έᾱσι** to **-ᾶσι** in the third person plural of the same tense, and lacks the alternative forms in the optative of the active.

(*b*) Write the inflection of *ἵημι* in the present system. Compare with paradigm (§ 537).

386. The participles τιθείς and ἱείς are inflected like *παυθείς* (§ 514, *e*). Write out the inflection of *τιθείς*.

---

[1] Solon, as quoted by Diogenes Laertius, I. 63, and also said to have been inscribed on the temple of Apollo at Delphi.

387. VOCABULARY

ἅμα, adv.: *together with, at the same time as.* Cf. ἅμ-αξα. HAMADRYAD.

ἅ-παξ, adv.: *altogether, once for all.* Cf. ἅ-πᾶς.

εἶδον,[1] 2d. aor.: *saw.*

ἕνεκα, post-pos. prep. with G.: *on account of, for the sake of, for.*

ἵ-ημι, ἥσω, ἧκα, εἶκα, εἷμαι, εἵθην: *send, throw;* mid., *rush.*

ξύλον, -ου, τό: *wood.* XYLOPHONE.

τί-θημι, θήσω, ἔθηκα, τέθηκα, τέθειμαι, ἐτέθην: *put, place.* Frequently in compounds. ANTITHESIS.

τοιοῦτος, τοιαύτη, τοιοῦτο: *of such sort.*

τοσοῦτος, τοσαύτη, τοσοῦτο: *of such size* or *quantity.*

388. EXERCISES

(*a*) Translate:

1. ἤδη ἵεντο ὥσπερ ἂν δράμοι τις τοῦ σώματος ἕνεκα. 2. τῶν δὲ Μένωνος στρατιωτῶν τις ξύλα σχίζων (compare SCHISM) ὡς εἶδε Κλέαρχον δι-ελαύνοντα, ἵησι τῇ ἀξίνῃ[2] (*ax*). 3. ἀλλ' ἅμα ἰδὼν τὸν ἀδελφὸν ἵετο ἐπ' αὐτόν. 4. φοβούμεθα γὰρ μὴ ἅμα τῇ ἡμέρᾳ ἡμῖν ἐπι-τιθῶνται. 5. οὐδεὶς τῶν Ἀθηναίων τοιαύτην σοφίᾱν εἶχεν οἵᾱν Σωκράτης. 6. τὰ δὲ ὅπλα εἰς τὰ πλοῖα τιθέᾱσιν. 7. ἔφασαν τοίνυν αὐτοὺς τὰ ὅπλα εἰς τὰ πλοῖα τιθέναι. 8. τούτου ἕνεκα ἀφ-ῑᾶσι τοὺς ἵππους. 9. ἐπειδὰν δὲ ἅπαξ τοσαύτην πόλιν λάβωμεν, οὐ δεήσει ἀνδρῶν ἕνεκα δεδοικέναι.

(*b*) Write in Greek:

1. If they had said they desired peace, they would have lied. 2. He inquired what they intended to do with regard to the falsehoods. 3. The woman said that the man struck her son many (blows). 4. They promised him (that) if he should come they would make him king.

---

[1] Defective verb, other tenses being supplied by other verbs.

[2] Dative of means, instead of accusative. This is also commonly used with βάλλω.

389. **NOT ALL DEAD YET**

ὁ δὲ ἀδολέσχης (*garrulous*) τοιοῦτός ἐστιν οἷος,[1] ὃν μὴ γιγνώσκει, τούτῳ παρα-καθ-εζόμενος (*sit beside*) ἐγγὺς πρῶτον μὲν τῆς ἑαυτοῦ γυναικὸς εἰπεῖν ἐγκώμιον (what does the sound suggest?)· εἶτα ὃ τῆς νυκτὸς εἶδεν ἐν-ύπνιον (compare HYPNOTIC), τοῦτο δι-ηγήσασθαι (*narrate*)· εἶθ' ὧν εἶχεν ἐπὶ τῷ δείπνῳ (*dinner*) ἕκαστα δι-εξ-ελθεῖν· εἶτα δὲ προ-βαίνοντος τοῦ πράγματος λέγειν, ὡς πολὺ χείρονές εἰσιν οἱ νῦν ἄνθρωποι τῶν ἀρχαίων· καὶ ὡς ἄξιος (*good value*, that is, *cheap*) γέγονεν ὁ σῖτος ἐν τῇ ἀγορᾷ· καὶ ὡς πολλοὶ ἐπι-δημοῦσι (*be in town*) ξένοι· καὶ εἰ ποιήσειεν ὁ Ζεὺς ὕδωρ πλεῖον, τὰ ἐν τῇ γῇ βελτίω ἔσεσθαι· καὶ ὡς χαλεπόν ἐστι τὸ ζῆν (*life*)· καὶ ἐὰν ὑπομένῃ (*endures*) τις αὐτόν, οὐδέποτε ἀπο-στήσεται.

Ζεύς

Zeus was the supreme god of the universe.

Theophrastus, *Characters*, III.

390. Word-formation. Reference has already been made (§ 210) to certain ways in which Greek technical terms originated. Frequently the word as then used still applies. The Greeks would understand us if they heard us speak of *arithmetic*, *ethics*, *dialectics*, *oligarchy*.

Sometimes, however, the idea has changed, while the word has remained the same. Reference has been made to *scene* (§ 35) and *orchestra* (§ 163). *Economy* to the Greek was restricted to the house.

---

[1] οἷος here = ὥστε, hence εἰπεῖν, δι-ηγήσασθαι, κ.τ.λ.

Again, modern inventions have introduced ideas unknown before and terms with meanings previously impossible. *Hydrostatic* might have been intelligible to the ancient Greek, but *static* in the radio is a coinage of very recent date, whose meaning would be unintelligible to one unfamiliar with radio. At times these new adaptations of Greek words are in accord with the original meaning and an ancient Greek would have guessed what *telephone* or *photograph* meant without really understanding the things thus labeled. At other times the adaptations have done more or less violence to the original meaning and no Greek could have any idea of the modern meaning of his word *museum* (once a temple dedicated to the Muses). He would have shuddered to hear of such hybrids as watt*meter* or speedo*meter*, just as he would have required time to accustom himself to socio*logy* or *auto*mobile.

Even words that are now venerable and apparently good Greek may be of non-Greek origin. *Metaphysics* would have meant nothing to Aristotle. The Romans used the term to describe that part of Aristotle's works which came after (μετά) his "Physics." Later, it came to describe works of a similar nature and even a distinct phase of philosophy.

Boston Museum of Fine Arts.

COIN OF ELIS, ABOUT 400 B.C.; HEAD OF ZEUS, EAGLE OF ZEUS

LESSON LXIII

AORIST ACTIVE AND MIDDLE OF τίθημι AND ἵημι

τέκνον, ἢ ταύτᾱν ἢ ἐπὶ ταύτᾱς.
Son, come home with your shield or on it.[1]

391. τίθημι in the Aorist. (*a*) Learn the inflection of *τίθημι* in the aorist active and middle (§ 535). Note that first aorist forms occur in the singular of the indicative active. Note also the general similarity, apart from the stem (**θε-**, not **τιθε-**), between the second aorist and the present, except in the second person singular indicative middle, in the second person singular imperative active and middle, and in the infinitive active.

(*b*) Inflect *θείς* (like *τιθείς*).

392. ἵημι in the Aorist. Learn the inflection of *ἵημι* in the aorist active and middle (§ 537). Note the general similarity to the aorist of *τίθημι* as well as to the present of *ἵημι*.

393. Supplementary Participle. A participle often *supplements and completes* the idea expressed by the main verb. This is called the *supplementary participle.*[2]

(*a*) Such is the participle used *in indirect discourse* with verbs meaning *to see, hear, learn, know, show, appear,* and *ἀγγέλλω announce* (§ 214).

---

[1] Plutarch, *Moralia*, 241 F. Literally: *Son,* (*bring*) *this or* (*come*) *on this.* These were the words of a Spartan mother as she handed the shield to her son. It illustrates admirably both Laconic brevity and Laconic heroism. Dialectic; hence *ταύτᾱν* for *ταύτην*, *ταύτᾱς* for *ταύτης*.

[2] What other uses of the participle have you had?

(*b*) It is also used, but *not in indirect discourse*, with τυγχάνω *happen*, and words meaning *to begin, cease, continue, rejoice*:

οὗτος παρ-ὼν ἔτυχε *this man happened to be present;*
παύεται διώκων *he stops pursuing.*

394. **VOCABULARY**

ἔτος, -ους, τό: *year.*
ἐχθρός, -οῦ, ὁ: *personal enemy.*
κεῖμαι, κείσομαι: *lie, be placed.* Freq. instead of τέθειμαι.
νέμω, νεμῶ, ἔνειμα, νενέμηκα, νενέμημαι, ἐνεμήθην: *distribute, assign.*
σπουδαῖος, -ᾱ, -ον: *earnest, zealous, serious, weighty.*
σπουδή, -ῆς, ἡ: *haste, zeal.* Cf. **σπεύδω.**
στέφανος, -ου, ὁ: *crown, wreath.* STEPHEN.
τυγχάνω, τεύξομαι, ἔτυχον, τετύχηκα: *hit, attain,* with G.; *happen,* with suppl. part.

395. **EXERCISES**

(*a*) Translate:

1. *οὐκ ἔτη πολλὰ ἔτυχε στέφανον ἔχων.* 2. *ὥστε πᾶσαν τὴν ὁδὸν ἔσπευδε καὶ οὐ δι-έτρῖβεν εἰ μὴ σίτου ἕνεκα ἢ ἄλλου τινὸς σπουδαίου.* 3. *ἔπειτα οὐδενὸς ἀντι-λέγοντος οἱ ἄλλοι προσ-έθεντο ταύτῃ τῇ βουλῇ.* 4. *ἀφ-εὶς δὲ τοὺς ἐχθροὺς τούτῳ μόνῳ συμ-βουλεύσεται.* 5. *σπουδῇ τοίνυν πολλῇ τὰ ὅπλα εἰς τὰς ἁμάξᾱς ἔθεμεν.* 6. *καὶ γὰρ ἔργῳ δῆλον ἐποίει ὅτι οὐκ ἂν ποτε προ-εῖτο, ἐπεὶ ἅπαξ φίλος αὐτοῖς ἐγένετο.* 7. *ἐπαύσατο θύων, ἐπεὶ ὁ ἐχθρὸς ἀφ-ίκετο.* 8. *τὴν δίκην ἔφη βούλεσθαι ἐπι-θεῖναι τοῖς ἐχθροῖς.* 9. *ἡ δὲ γυνὴ ἀπ-ήγγειλε τοὺς ἄνδρας τὸν τάφον ἀ-τῑμάζοντας.* 10. *νείμᾱς οὖν τὰ ὅπλα ὁ λοχαγὸς ἐκέλευσε τοὺς ἄνδρας ἐπι-θέσθαι.*

(*b*) Write in Greek:

1. He makes an agreement (*συν-τίθεμαι*) with them that he will attack with all his force. 2. While they were

throwing (with) stones, he saw a man ride by. 3. The Greeks are letting the man go (ἀφ-ίημι) because they do not wish to put him to death. 4. So much farther (*longer*) was the boy able to throw than his father.

396. AB HOSTE DOCERI

ἀλλ' ἀπ' ἐχθρῶν δῆτα (*indeed*) πολλὰ μανθάνουσιν οἱ σοφοί.

Aristophanes, *Birds*, 375.

397. A PATRIOT

Οὗτος 'Αδειμάντου κείνου (ἐκείνου) τάφος, οὗ διὰ βουλὰς
'Ελλὰς ἐλευθερίᾱς ἀμφ-έθετο στέφανον.

Simonides.

398. UNDYING FAME

Εἰ τὸ καλῶς θνῄσκειν[1] ἀρετῆς μέρος ἐστὶ μέγιστον,
ἡμῖν ἐκ πάντων τοῦτ' ἀπ-ένειμε τύχη (*Fortune*).
'Ελλάδι γὰρ σπεύδοντες ἐλευθερίᾱν περι-θεῖναι
κείμεθ' ἀ-γηράντῳ (*ageless*) χρώμενοι (*enjoying*) εὐ-λογίᾳ.[2]

Simonides.

399. LIFE'S TRAGEDY

Δωδεκ-ετῆ τὸν παῖδα πατὴρ ἀπ-έθηκε Φίλιππος
ἐνθάδε (*here*), τὴν πολλὴν ἐλπίδα, Νῑκοτέλην.

Callimachus.

400. PLAY THE GAME

σκηνὴ πᾶς ὁ βίος καὶ παίγνιον (*game*)· ἢ μάθε παίζειν
τὴν σπουδὴν μετα-θείς, ἢ φέρε τὰς ὀδύνᾱς (compare AN-
ODYNE).

Greek Anthology.

---

[1] Infinitive as subject. See page 133, note 1. [2] χρώμενοι governs D

401. **THE SOBER SECOND THOUGHT**

οὔτ' ἐκ χερὸς μεθ-έντα καρτερὸν (mighty) λίθον
ῥᾷον[1] *κατα-σχεῖν, οὔτ' ἀπὸ γλώσσης (tongue) λόγον.*

Menander, fragment.

IN OLD STAMBOUL

The obelisk of Theodosius marks the site of the ancient Hippodrome, center of regal magnificence and of popular frenzy through the ages.

402. Word-formation. In passing down the ages, words often become corrupted in form but retain approximately their original meaning. *ἐπίσκοπος overseer* became the title of an officer of the church and through careless speech passed into *bishop*. *ἐλεημοσύνη* became Latin *eleemosyna*, then Anglo-Saxon *aelmesse*, finally *alms*. *σκίουρος shady-tailed* became the Latin *sciurus*, *sciurellus*, and today is *squirrel*. Byzantium was *the city* through a long period and people spoke of going *εἰς τὴν πόλιν* until finally it was called *Stamboul*. Stamboul is now the native section of *Constantinople*, Constantine's *πόλις*. *ἡ καλὴ πόλις* has become *Gallipoli* of Anzac glory.

[1] Comparative neuter nominative singular of *ῥᾴδιος*.

LESSON LXIV

PRESENT OF δίδωμι

λαμπάδια ἔχοντες διαδώσουσιν ἀλλήλοις.
Having torches, they will pass them to each other.[1]

403. δίδωμι in the Present. (*a*) Learn the inflection of *δίδωμι* in the present system in all three voices (§ 535). Note its great similarity to *τίθημι*, with **ο** replacing **ε**.

(*b*) The present participle, *διδούς*, is inflected like **λιπών** except for the nominative masculine singular. Write out its inflection. Compare with paradigm (§ 514, *f*).

404. Deliberative Subjunctive. The first person of the subjunctive may be used in *questions of appeal*, where some one asks himself or another *what he shall do* or *say:*[2]

τί πράξωμεν; *what are we to do?*

The negative is *μή*:

μὴ φύγωμεν; *are we not to flee?*

405. VOCABULARY

ἀπο-δίδωμι: *give back, pay what is due;* mid., *sell.* APODOSIS.

ἄρα, post-pos. partic.: *then* (inferential).

ἆρα, interrog. particle indicating an impatient question: *then.*

δί-δωμι, δώσω, ἔδωκα, δέδωκα, δέδομαι, ἐδόθην: *give.* Cf. **δῶρον.** DOSE.

ἕκαστος, -η, -ον: *each.*

εὔ-νους, εὔ-νουν: *well-intentioned, well-disposed.* Cf. **εὖ** and **νοῦς.**

καί-περ, concessive particle usually accomp. by a participle: *although.*

μή-ποτε, neg. adv.: *not ever, never.*

οὔ-ποτε, neg. adv.: *not ever, never.*

[1] Plato, *Republic*, I. 328 A.

[2] What other uses of the subjunctive have you had?

406. EXERCISES

(*a*) Translate:

1. τέλος δὲ Κῦρος δίδωσιν αὐτῷ εἰς ἑξα-κισ-χῑλίους στρατιώτᾱς καὶ ἓξ μηνῶν μισθόν. 2. τί φῶ τοῖς ἐχθροῖς; 3. ἀλλὰ ἐν τοιούτῳ καιρῷ φοβοίμην ἂν εἰς τὰ πλοῖα ἐμ-βαίνειν ἃ ἡμῖν διδοίη. 4. ὁ δὲ καίπερ ἐθέλων ἀπο-διδόναι οὐκ ἐδυνήθη. 5. ἆρα αἰτήσωμεν ἡγεμόνα, ἐὰν μὴ οὗτος πλοῖα διδῷ; 6. εὖνοι ἄρ' ὄντες τοῖς Ἕλλησι τὰ ἐπιτήδεια ἀπ-εδίδοσαν. 7. ὑπ-ισχνεῖται δὲ στέφανον κάλλιστον ἑκάστῳ δώσειν. 8. ὁπότε δέ τινα εὕροι χρήματα πολλὰ ἐκ τοῦ δικαίου λαμβάνοντα, οὔ-ποτε οὐδένα ἀφ-ῃρεῖτο, ἀλλ' ἀεὶ προσ-εδίδου. 9. ἀλλὰ τί πρᾱ́ξωμεν; δι' ἐρήμης γὰρ χώρᾱς ἐλαύνοντες οὔτ' ἀγορὰν ἕξομεν οὔτε τὸν ἡμῖν τὰ ἐπι-τήδεια διδόντα.

(*b*) Write in Greek:

1. I fear that he may take me (and) inflict punishment (on me). 2. The ruler happened to release (ἀφ-ῑ́ημι) your (plural) personal enemies. 3. Those men on the wall have not yet stopped throwing stones at the attackers. 4. We know that the man is (of) thirty years (old). 5. Whatever he happened to have he distributed among his friends.

407. OUT OF THE FRYING-PAN

ἄνθρωπόν τις ἀπο-κτείνᾱς ὑπὸ τῶν ἐκείνου συγ-γενῶν ἐδι-ώκετο. κατὰ δὲ τὸν Νεῖλον ποταμὸν γενομένῳ λύκος (*wolf*) αὐτῷ προσ-έρχεται. φοβηθεὶς οὖν ἀν-έβη ἐπὶ δένδρον παρὰ τὸν ποταμὸν καὶ ἐκρύπτετο (compare CRYPTIC) ἐκεῖ. οὕτω δὲ δια-κείμενος ἔχιν (*adder*) εἶδεν προσ-ερχόμενον, ὥστε εἰς τὸν ποταμὸν ἑαυτὸν καθ-ῆκε. ἐν δὲ τούτῳ ὑπο-δεξάμενος αὐτὸν κατ-έφαγε (*devoured*) κροκόδειλος.

Adapted from Æsop, 48

408. **THE PERSIAN COURIER POST**

τούτων δὲ τῶν ἀγγέλων ἔστιν οὐδὲν ὅ τι θᾶττον παραγίγνεται. λέγουσι γὰρ ὡς ὅσων ἂν ἡμερῶν ᾖ ἡ πᾶσα ὁδός, τοσοῦτοι ἵπποι τε καὶ ἄνδρες δι-εστᾶσι,[1] κατὰ τὴν ἑκάστης ἡμέρᾱς ὁδὸν ἵππος τε καὶ ἀνὴρ τεταγμένος, οὓς οὔτε νιφετός (*snow*), οὐκ ὄμβρος (*rain*), οὐ καῦμα (*heat*), οὐ νὺξ κωλύει μὴ[2] ποιῆσαι τὸν προ-κείμενον ἑαυτῷ δρόμον τὴν ταχίστην.[3]

THE "THESEUM"

The "Theseum," which lies northwest of the Acropolis, is the best preserved of the ancient Greek temples. It was probably the temple of Hephæstus, god of fire and forge, and not a shrine of Theseus.

ὁ μὲν δὴ πρῶτος δραμὼν παρα-δίδωσι τὴν ἀγγελίᾱν τῷ δευτέρῳ, ὁ δὲ δεύτερος τῷ τρίτῳ· τὸ[4] δ' ἐντεῦθεν ἤδη κατ' ἄλλον δι-εξ-έρχεται παρα-διδομένη, ὥσπερ Ἕλλησιν ἡ λαμπαδη-φορίᾱ (*torch-race*), ἣν τῷ Ἡφαίστῳ ἐπι-τελοῦσιν (*celebrate*).

Adapted from Herodotus, VIII. 98.

[1] Second perfect of δι-ίστημι.

[2] μή is redundant. Page 96, note 1.

[3] An English version of a portion of this sentence is inscribed on the front of the New York Post Office at 33rd Street and Eighth Avenue.

[4] Adverbial accusative (§ 270).

409. Word-formation. (*a*) Compound nouns and adjectives are formed by uniting to a substantive stem or to a verb stem with substantive suffix:

(1) A substantive or an adjective

φωσ-φόρος *bringing light*, PHOSPHORUS;
μητρό-πολις *mother-city*, METROPOLIS;
μόν-αρχος MONARCH.

(2) A verb stem

μῑσ-άνθρωπος *man-hating*, MISANTHROPE;
ἀρχι-τέκτων *chief artificer*, ARCHITECT.

(3) A numeral, a preposition, or an adverb

πέντ-αθλον PENTATHLON;
ἔξ-οδος EXODUS;
εὐ-λογίᾱ EULOGY.

(4) An inseparable prefix

ἀν-αρχίᾱ *lack of a leader*, ANARCHY;
ἡμι-σφαίριον HEMISPHERE.

(*b*) Compounding of similar words is constantly occurring in English, particularly in technical terms: *pro-ethnic*, *hyper*-acid, *anti*-saloon (a familiar hybrid), *dec-athlon*, Franco-*phile*. Greek prepositional prefixes are exceptionally common in English, largely usurping the functions of the native Anglo-Saxon prefixes (see Kent, *Language and Philology*, page 90).

LESSON LXV

AORIST ACTIVE AND MIDDLE OF δίδωμι

οὐ παντὸς ἀνδρὸς εἰς Κόρινθόν ἐσθ' ὁ πλοῦς.
Not every man may visit Corinth.[1]

410. δίδωμι in the Aorist. (*a*) Learn the inflection of *δίδωμι* in the aorist active and middle (§ 535). Note the general resemblance to the corresponding forms of *τίθημι*. Note also that, as *ἔθεμεν*, *κ.τ.λ.*, parallels *ἐτίθεμεν*, *κ.τ.λ.*, so *ἔδομεν*, *κ.τ.λ.*, parallels *ἐδίδομεν*, *κ.τ.λ.*

Note the similarity in form between *θές*, *ἕς*, *δός*, and between *θοῦ*, *οὗ*, *δοῦ*.

(*b*) Inflect *δούς* (like *διδούς*).

411. Unattainable Wishes.[2] (*a*) *εἴθε* or *εἰ γάρ* with the *imperfect indicative* expresses an *unattainable wish* in *present* time; with the *aorist indicative*, an *unattainable wish* in *past* time:

εἴθε ταῦτα ἔπρᾱττον *if only they were doing this;*
εἴθε ταῦτα ἔπρᾱξαν *if only they had done this.*

The negative is *μή*.

(*b*) *ὤφελον* (aorist of *ὀφείλω* *I owe*) with a *present* or *aorist infinitive* also expresses an *unattainable wish* in *present* or *past* time:

ὤφελε παρ-εῖναι *would that he were present;*
ὤφελες ταῦτα πρᾶξαι *would that you had done this.*

[1] Greek maxim.

[2] How do you express a possible wish in the future? See § 192, *a*.

412. **VOCABULARY**

δίς, adv.: *twice*. Cf. **δύο**. DISSYLLABIC.

μήν, post-pos. particle: *indeed, certainly*. Cf. **μέν**.

ὤφελον, sec. aor. of ὀφείλω, *owe*: most common as a device for expressing unattainable wishes in present or past time, with inf.

πλέω, πλεύσομαι, ἔπλευσα, πέπλευκα, πέπλευσμαι: *sail*.

πλοῦς, -οῦ, ὁ: *sailing, voyage*. Cf. **πλέω, πλοῖον**.

413. **EXERCISES**

(*a*) Translate:

1. ὤφελον μὴ ἐν-νοῆσαι ἡμᾶς ἀ-τῑμάζειν. 2. εἴθε κέρδος νομίζοι, ἐὰν ἅμα καὶ Σωκράτης παρ-ῇ. 3. εἰ γὰρ μὴ ἐσκέψατο ὅπως κρατήσει ἀντὶ τοῦ ἀδελφοῦ. 4. ὤφελε μὴ τὴν τοῦ ἐχθροῦ κεφαλὴν ἀπο-τεμεῖν. 5. ἀκούσαιεν ὑμᾶς εὔ-νους ὄντας τοῖς Ἕλλησιν. 6. εἰ γὰρ τοσαύτην δύναμιν εἶχον.

(*b*) Write in Greek:

1. Are we not to pay back what we owe? 2. If Cyrus should give him pay for six months, he would enlist the mercenaries. 3. All know that we are giving a crown to each soldier. 4. What am I to say to my opponents?

414. **A HARD CUSTOMER**

The scene of this lively dialogue of Lucian's, only a portion of which is here printed, is laid at the farther shore of the Stygian Lake. The speakers are Charon, ferryman of the dead, Menippus, famous Cynic philosopher, and Hermes, who numbered among his many and varied functions that of official escort to the departed. The wrangle that Lucian here reports is held to be typical of the Greeks, who have ever been passionately fond of argument. Incidentally,

Greek πορθμεῖς are still plying their trade and still enjoying many a lively encounter with their passengers.

Hermes Presenting a Woman to Charon

This picture is a Greek vase painting of the fifth century. Notice the winged souls of the dead flying around.

XAP. Ἀπό-δος, ὦ κατάρᾱτε (*scoundrel*), τὰ πορθμεῖα.

MEN. Βόᾱ (*bawl*), εἰ τοῦτό σοι, ὦ Χάρων, ἥδῑον.

XAP. Ἀπό-δος, φημί, ὅτι σε δι-επορθμεύσαμεν.

MEN. Οὐκ ἂν λάβοις παρὰ τοῦ μὴ ἔχοντος.

XAP. Ἔστι δέ τις ὀβολὸν (*thrippence*[1]) μὴ ἔχων;

MEN. Εἰ μὲν καὶ ἄλλος τις οὐ γιγνώσκω, ἐγὼ δ' οὐκ ἔχω.

XAP. Καὶ μὴν ἄγξω (*throttle*) σε νὴ τὸν Πλούτωνα[2] (*by Pluto*), ὦ μιαρέ (*loathsome*), ἢν μὴ ἀπο-δῷς.

MEN. Κἀγὼ (= καὶ ἐγὼ) τῷ ξύλῳ σου παίσᾱς δια-λῡ́σω τὴν κεφαλήν.

XAP. Μάτην (*in vain*) οὖν ἔσει πεπλευκὼς[3] τοσοῦτον πλοῦν.

---

[1] Not an exact translation, but convenient. [2] God of the underworld.

[3] The future perfect is not often found. This is one way of expressing the idea.

MEN. Ὁ Ἑρμῆς ὑπὲρ ἐμοῦ σοι ἀπο-δότω, ὅς με παρ-έδωκέ σοι.

XAP. Οὐδὲν ταῦτα[1] πρὸς τὰ πορθμεῖα· τὸν ὀβολὸν ἀπο-δοῦναί σε δεῖ· οὐ θέμις (*right*) ἄλλως γενέσθαι.

MEN. Οὐκοῦν ἄπ-αγέ με πάλιν εἰς τὸν βίον.

XAP. Χαρίεν (*jolly*) λέγεις, ἵνα καὶ πληγὰς (compare **πλήττω**) ἐπὶ τούτῳ παρὰ τοῦ Αἰακοῦ[2] προσ-λάβω.

MEN. Μὴ ἐν-όχλει (*bother*) οὖν.

XAP. Τί ἐν τῇ πήρᾳ (*wallet*) ἔχεις;

MEN. Θέρμους (*beans*), εἰ θέλεις, καὶ τῆς Ἑκάτης[3] τὸ δεῖπνον (*dinner*).

XAP. Πόθεν τοῦτον ἡμῖν, ὦ Ἑρμῆ, τὸν κύνα[4] (*dog*) ἤγαγες; οἷα δὲ καὶ ἐλάλει (*chattered*) παρὰ τὸν πλοῦν τοὺς ἐπι-βάτᾱς (compare **βαίνω**) ἐπι-σκώπτων (*mocking at*) καὶ μόνος ᾄδων (*singing*) οἰμωζόντων (*groaning*) ἐκείνων.

EPM. Ἀ-γνοεῖς (compare AGNOSTIC), ὦ Χάρων, ὁποῖον ἄνδρα δι-επόρθμευσας, πάνυ ἐλεύθερον; οὐδενὸς αὐτῷ μέλει. οὗτός ἐστιν ὁ Μένιππος.

XAP. Καὶ μὴν ἄν σε λάβω ποτέ ——

MEN. Ἂν λάβῃς, ὦ βέλτιστε· δὶς δὲ οὐκ ἂν λάβοις.

Lucian, *Dialogues of the Dead*, 22.

415. Word-formation. Verbals in **-τος** give rise to many English nouns:

ἀντι-δίδωμι *give for*, ἀντίδοτον ANTIDOTE;
ἐπι-τίθημι *place upon*, ἐπίθετον EPITHET;
κρύπτω *hide*, κρυπτός, κρυπτή CRYPT.

---

[1] As often, ἐστί has been omitted. The expression is stereotyped. Compare the English, *This has nothing to do with*.

[2] One of the judges of the underworld.

[3] Hecate, goddess of the crossroads. Tramps and irreligious scoundrels seem to have helped themselves to the viands offered at her wayside shrines.

[4] A punning reference to the Cynics.

LESSON LXVI

REVIEW

τέχνη δ' ἀνάγκης ἀσθενεστέρᾱ μακρῷ. — *Art is weaker far than need.*[1]

ASSIGNMENTS

416. (*a*) Review the words in § 556, following the method suggested in § 27, *a*. Give principal parts of the verbs.

(*b*) Name and define the Greek words from which are derived: *anathema*, *bucolic*, *xylograph*, *eremite*, *parenthesis*, *antidote*, *monopolist*, *apostasy*, *system*, *hierarchy*, *dynamite*, *aerodrome*, *Nemesis*, *catholic*, *pseudograph*, *dynamometer*, *diastole*, *dimorphous*.

(*c*) Add ten words to this list

(*d*) What do the endings of these words suggest: *anarchism*, *anecdote*, *euthanasia*, *polyandry?*

(*e*) Give synopses of the third person singular in present and aorist systems in active and middle voices (where both occur) of *ἵστημι*, *τίθημι*, *δίδωμι*. Inflect *στάς*, *ἱείς*, *δούς*.

417. EXERCISES

(*a*) Complete:

1. *εἴθε ἐμαθ— τοὺς Ἕλληνας τειν— ἄνω πρὸς τὸ ὄρος.* 2. *τί ποιήσωμεν, ἐὰν μὴ τοὺς ἑκατὸν ἄνδρας στειλ—σιν ἡμῖν βοηθησ— ;* 3. *οὐχ ὥρᾱν φᾶσὶν ἂν* —— (linking verb) *ὑμῖν ἀ-μελεῖν ὑμῶν αὐτῶν.* 4. *μέγα ἂν* —— (linking

[1] Æschylus, *Prometheus*, 514. Compare the English, *Necessity is the mother of invention.*

verb) *κέρδος, εἰ τύχοιεν αὐτῷ διδ— τοιοῦτον στέφανον.* 5. *εἰ γὰρ ἔτη πολλὰ δυν—το κρατεῖν τ— ἐναντι—* (plural). 6. *καίπερ δυν—μενος οὐ μέλλει ἀπο-διδ—.*

(*b*) Write in Greek:

1. The satrap thought that the Greek force might halt there. 2. I would that your son knew how to throw a javelin. 3. All-the-same we rushed at those standing on the wagon. 4. He says that Cyrus would have agreed to this, if no one had happened to deceive him. 5. May they cross (*use participle*) the trench (and) give something to each man.

THE HERÆUM AT OLYMPIA

This is probably the earliest extant temple of purely Greek workmanship. Its columns differ greatly in size, shape, and composition, and it is supposed that they were built one at a time to replace the original wooden ones as these decayed.

LESSON LXVII

τῑμάω. REVIEW OF THE GENITIVE

πάντα ῥεῖ. — *All is flux.*[1]

418. Rules for Contraction. (*a*) Review the principles of contraction in § 127.

(*b*) Rules for contraction of verbs in **-αω**:

α + an ο-sound (ο, ω, ου, οι) = ω (ῳ)
α + an ε-sound (ε, η, ει, ῃ) = ᾱ (ᾳ)

An ι in the uncontracted form becomes ι-subscript in the contracted form (note ῳ and ᾳ above).

(*c*) Write out the inflection of the present system of *τῑμάω*. Compare with paradigm (§ 534).

(*d*) In other systems than the present, **α** of the stem becomes **η**, except after **ε**, **ι**, or **ρ**, when it becomes **ᾱ**:

τῑμάω, τῑμήσω, ἐτί̄μησα, κ.τ.λ.;
πειράομαι, πειρᾱ́σομαι, κ.τ.λ.

419. Forms of the Genitive. Review all genitive endings (§ 544, *b*). What other endings resemble these of the genitive? Where the ending may suggest another case, modifying words and context usually prevent confusion.

420. Uses of the Genitive. Having clearly in mind the forms that indicate a genitive, review the possible uses of the genitive (§ 544, *b*). The Greek genitive has the functions of the Latin genitive and some functions of the

---

[1] Heraclitus. A curious and interesting foreshadowing of the modern theory of evolution.

Latin ablative. Genitives may *limit the meaning* of nouns, adjectives, adverbs, or verbs. The major functions, to which may be traced most of the uses, are *possessive*, *partitive*, *objective*, *separative*.

421. VOCABULARY

ἅπτω, ἅψω, ἧψα, ἧμμαι, ἥφθην: *lay hold of;* mid., *touch*, with G. Cf. Lat. *aptus*. APSE.

ἐρωτάω, ἐρωτήσω, ἠρώτησα, ἠρώτηκα, ἠρώτημαι, ἠρωτήθην: *ask, inquire.*

μέχρι, conj.: *until.* Sometimes used as a prep. with G.: *up to.*

μηχανάομαι, μηχανήσομαι, ἐμηχανησάμην: *contrive.*

μηχανή, -ῆς, ἡ: *contrivance, device, machine.* Cf. Lat. *māchina.* MECHANICAL.

ὁράω, ὄψομαι, εἶδον, ἑώρᾱκα or ἑόρᾱκα, ἑώρᾱμαι or ὦμμαι, ὤφθην: *see.* PANORAMA, OPTIC.

ῥέω, ῥυήσομαι, ἐρρύηκα, ἐρρύην: *flow.* RHEUMATIC.

τελευτάω, τελευτήσω, ἐτελεύτησα, τετελεύτηκα, τετελεύτημαι, ἐτελευτήθην; *end, finish, die.*

τῑμάω, τῑμήσω, ἐτῑ́μησα, τετῑ́μηκα, τετῑ́μημαι, ἐτῑμήθην: *honor, reward, pay.* Cf. τῑμή.

422. EXERCISES

(*a*) Translate:

1. ἀλλὰ μὴν ἠρώτησεν εἰ αὐτοῖς οὐ μέλει ἐκείνης τῆς μηχανῆς. 2. ἀκούσαντες τῆς σάλπιγγος ἵεντο ἄνω κατὰ τὴν φανερὰν ὁδόν. 3. καίπερ εὔνους οὐκ ἦρχε τοῦ λόγου, ὅπερ ἐβούλοντο. 4. τοῦ ἄρχοντος τελευτήσαντος μηχανῶνται ὅπως τεύξονται τῆς εἰρήνης. 5. ἐλθόντες αὖ ἐπὶ τᾱ̀ς θύρᾱς ἀπ-ῄτησαν μισθὸν τεττάρων μηνῶν. 6. δέονται δέ σου καὶ τοῦτο, ἑκάστῳ τῶν Ἑλλήνων τὰ ἄξια νεῖμαι. 7. τούτων οὖν ἕνεκα Κῦρος μᾶλλον ἐτῑμᾶτο ὑπὸ τῶν Περσῶν ἢ ὁ ἀδελφός.

(*b*) Write in Greek:

1. In five years he will pay back the greater part of the money. 2. Our hope of honor was destroyed by the

orators. 3. Although the danger was very great, the few Greeks were braver than many barbarians. 4. The water does not touch the wood of the gate. 5. The fugitives had provisions for six days.

423. THE EARLIEST EXPLORATION PARTY ON RECORD

ἀφ-ικόμενοι δὲ οἱ Νασαμῶνες καὶ ἐρωτώμενοι εἴ τι ἔχουσι πλέον λέγειν περὶ τῶν ἐρήμων τῆς Λιβύης, ἔφασαν παρὰ

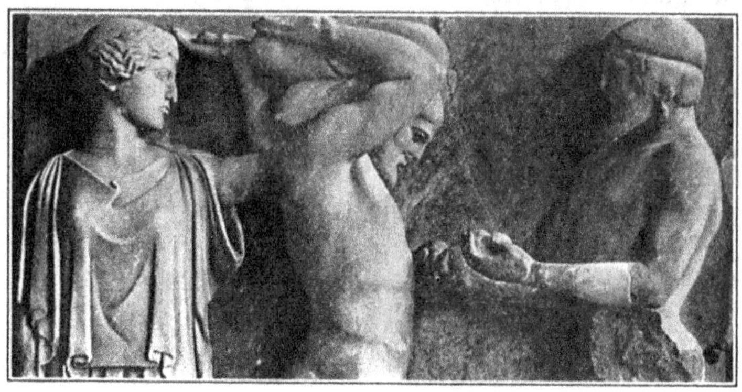

APPLES OF THE HESPERIDES

This metope from the Zeus temple at Olympia shows an episode in Hercules' famous eleventh labor. The hero (in the center) undertook to hold the heavens on his shoulders and sent Atlas to seek the golden apples. Here Atlas is seen returning with the apples while some goddess watches the scene.

ἑαυτοῖς γενέσθαι ἀνδρῶν δυναστῶν (compare DYNASTY) *παῖδας, οἳ ἄλλα τε ἐμηχανῶντο ἀνδρωθέντες* (compare **ἀνήρ**) *περισσὰ* (*unusual, odd*) *καὶ δὴ καὶ ἔπεμψαν πέντε ἑαυτῶν ὀψομένους τὰ ἔρημα τῆς Λιβύης, καὶ εἴ τι πλέον ἴδοιεν τῶν τὰ μακρότατα ἰδόντων. τῆς γὰρ Λιβύης τὰ μὲν κατὰ τὴν βορεία̅ν* (compare BOREAS) *θάλατταν ἀπ' Αἰγύπτου ἀρξάμενοι μέχρι Σολόεντος ἄκρα̅ς* (*Cape*), *ἢ τελευτᾷ τῆς Λιβύης, παρήκουσι παρὰ πα̂σαν Λίβυες, πλὴν ὅσον Ἕλληνες καὶ Φοίνικες ἔχουσι· τὰ δὲ ὑπὲρ θαλάττης τε καὶ τῶν ἐπὶ θάλατταν* *καθ-ηκόντων ἀνθρώπων, θηριώδης* (*savage, wild*) *ἐστὶν ἡ Λιβύη· τὰ δὲ ὑπὲρ τῆς θηριώδους ψάμμος* (*sand*) *τέ ἐστι καὶ ἄν-υδρος δεινῶς καὶ ἔρημος πάντων. ἐπεὶ οὖν οἱ παῖδες ἀπο-πεμπόμενοι ὑπὸ τῶν ἡλίκων* (*associates*) *ἦλθον πρῶτον μὲν διὰ τῆς οἰκουμένης, ταύτην δὲ δι-εξ-ελθόντες εἰς τὴν θηριώδη ἀφ-ίκοντο, ἐκ δὲ ταύτης τὴν ἔρημον δι-εξ-ῆλθον τὴν ὁδὸν ποιούμενοι πρὸς ζέφυρον ἄνεμον, δι-εξ-ελθόντες χώρᾱν πολλὴν ψαμμώδη μετὰ πολλὰς ἡμέρᾱς εἶδόν ποτε δένδρα ἐν πεδίῳ ὄντα. καὶ προσ-ελθόντες ἅπτονται τοῦ ἐπ-όντος ἐπὶ τῶν δένδρων καρποῦ* (*fruit*), *ἁπτομένοις δ' αὐτοῖς ἐπ-ῆλθον ἄνδρες μῑκροί, μετρίων* (*medium*) *ἐλάττους ἀνδρῶν, λαβόντες δὲ ἦγον αὐτούς· φωνῆς δὲ οὔτε τι τῆς ἐκείνων οἱ Νασαμῶνες ἐγίγνωσκον οὔτε οἱ ἄγοντες τῶν Νασαμώνων. ἦγον δ' αὐτοὺς εἰς πόλιν ἐν ᾗ πάντες ἦσαν τοῖς ἄγουσιν ἴσοι, χρῶμα* (*complexion*) *μέλανες. παρὰ δὲ τὴν πόλιν ἔρρει ποταμὸς μέγας, ἀφ' ἑσπέρᾱς* (compare HESPERIDES) *ῥέων πρὸς ἥλιον ἀνα-τέλλοντα* (*rising sun*), *ἐφαίνοντο δ' ἐν αὐτῷ κροκόδειλοι.*[1]

Adapted from Herodotus, II. 32.

424. Word-formation. (*a*) Verbs formed by adding **-αω** to noun (or adjective) stems denote action of a nature similar to that expressed by the noun (or adjective). They usually denote *to do*, *to be*, or *to have* what the stem expresses:

τόλμη *daring*, τολμάω *be daring, dare;*
νίκη *victory*, νῑκάω *have victory, conquer.*

(*b*) In like manner, form verbs from *βοή shout*, *σῑγή silence*, *ἄριστον breakfast*.

[1] For support to the history involved in this story, see How and Wells's *Commentary on Herodotus*, l. c.

LESSON LXVIII

οἶδα. REVIEW OF THE DATIVE

σκαιὸν τὸ πλουτεῖν κἄλλο μηδὲν εἰδέναι.
Wealth without knowledge makes a boor.[1]

---

425 Inflection of οἶδα. Learn the inflection of *οἶδα* (§ 542). *οἶδα* is second perfect with present meaning.

426. Forms of the Dative. Review all dative endings (§ 544, *c*). Note especially that ι is part of every dative ending.

427. Uses of the Dative. Having clearly in mind the forms that indicate a dative, review the possible uses of the dative (§ 544, *c*). The Greek dative has the functions of the Latin dative and some functions of the Latin ablative (instrumental and locative). The major functions, to which may be traced all of the uses, are *reference*, *instrument* or *means*, and *place*.

428. VOCABULARY

βίᾱ, -ᾱς, ἡ : *force, violence.* Cf. **δύναμις** : *force, power.*

δαπανάω, δαπανήσω, ἐδαπάνησα, δεδαπάνηκα, δεδαπάνημαι, ἐδαπανήθην : *spend, waste.*

ἔξω, adv. : *outside.* Cf. **ἐκ**, **ἐξ**. EXOTIC.

νῑκάω, νῑκήσω, ἐνίκησα, νενίκηκα, νενίκημαι, ἐνῑκήθην : *conquer, win.*

νίκη, -ης, ἡ : *victory.* EUNICE.

οἶδα, εἴσομαι : *know.*

ὅσος, -η, -ον : sing., *as large as, as much as* ; pl., *as many as.*

---

[1] Euripides, fragment. Literally: *It is a loutish thing to be wealthy and to know nothing else.*

429. **EXERCISES**

(*a*) Translate:

1. εἰ δὲ νῑκῴη, εἰδείη ἂν ὅσους χρὴ τῑμᾶν. 2. Τισσαφέρνει δ' ἐνόμιζε πολεμοῦντα Κῦρον ἀμφὶ τὰ στρατεύματα δαπανᾶν. 3. ἐν ταύτῃ τῇ κώμῃ παρ-αγγέλλει Κλεάρχῳ λαβόντι ἥκειν ὅσον ἦν αὐτῷ στράτευμα. 4. ἆρ' ἡμῖν νῑκήσᾱσιν ἀ-δύνατον ἔσται βίᾳ παρ-ελθεῖν; 5. ἀλλ' οἱ ἔξω οὐκ ἀπο-δεδράκᾱσιν· οἶδα γὰρ ὅπου φεύγουσιν. 6. ὥστε ἤχθοντο αὐτοῖς ὡς ταῦτα πάλαι εἰδόσιν. 7. μετὰ τὴν νίκην τοὺς ὠφελίμους γενομένους δώροις καλλίστοις ἐτῑ́μᾱ. 8. πάντων δὴ οὓς ἴσμεν πολλῷ βασιλικώτατος ἐγένετο.

THE VICTORY OF SAMOTHRACE

This noble statue commemorating a naval victory shows the goddess poised on a vessel's prow. In her right hand she once held a trumpet to her lips. Compare the Victory of Pæonius, page 184.

(*b*) Write in Greek:

1. They say that the satrap has[1] a much smaller force. 2. By this contrivance we must cross the trench. 3. That day they were fighting a great number of the enemy. 4. Because of their friendship the Greeks helped the exiles with great zeal. 5. The king was well-disposed to the people in the plain.

---

[1] Use the proper form of εἰμί.

430. THE PRAYER OF SOCRATES

ὦ φίλε Πάν τε καὶ ἄλλοι ὅσοι τῇδε (*here*) θεοί, δοίητέ μοι καλῷ γενέσθαι τὰ ἔνδοθεν (*inside*)· ἔξωθεν δ' ὅσα ἔχω τοῖς ἐντὸς (*inside*) εἶναί μοι φίλια. πλούσιον (*wealthy*) δὲ νομίζοιμι τὸν σοφόν. τὸ δὲ χρῡ́σου πλῆθος εἴη μοι ὅσον μήτε φέρειν μήτε ἄγειν δύναιτ' ἄλλος ἢ ὁ σώφρων (*sane*).

Plato, *Phædrus*, 279 B.C.

This, then, I ask, O thou beloved Pan
And all ye other gods: Help as ye can
That I may prosper in the inner man;

Grant ye that what I have or yet may win
Of those the outer things may be akin
And constantly at peace with those within.

May I regard the wise the rich, and care
Myself for no more gold as my earth share
Than he who's of an honest heart can bear.

John Finley.

431. THE RETORT COURTEOUS!

φιλόσοφός τις ἐρωτηθεὶς ὑπὸ Διονυσίου τοῦ τυράννου, διὰ τί οἱ μὲν φιλόσοφοι ἐπὶ τὰς τῶν πλουσίων θύρᾱς ἔρχονται, οἱ δὲ πλούσιοι ἐπὶ τὰς τῶν φιλοσόφων οὐκ-έτι, ἔφη, Ὅτι οἱ μὲν ἴσᾱσιν ὧν δέονται, οἱ δ' οὐκ ἴσᾱσιν.

Diogenes Laertius, II. 69.

432. IN PRAISE OF EROS

Ἔρωτα δ' ὅστις μὴ θεὸν κρῑ́νει μέγαν
καὶ τῶν ἁπάντων δαιμόνων ὑπέρ-τατον,
ἢ σκαιός ἐστιν ἢ καλῶν ἄ-πειρος (*inexperienced*) ὢν
οὐκ οἶδε τὸν μέγιστον ἀνθρώποις θεόν.

Euripides, fragment.

433. LOVELY WOMAN

φύσις κέρᾱτα ταύροις,
ὁπλὰς (*hoofs*) δ' ἔδωκεν ἵπποις,
ποδωκίην (*speed*) λαγωοῖς (*rabbits*),
λέουσι (*lions*) χάσμ' ὀδόντων (*teeth*),
. . . .
. . . .
τοῖς ἀνδράσιν φρόνημα (*brains*).
γυναιξὶν οὐκ ἔτ' εἶχεν.
τί οὖν; δίδωσι κάλλος
ἀντ' ἀσπίδων ἁπᾱσᾶν,[1]
ἀντ' ἐγχέων (*spears*) ἁπάντων.
νῑκᾷ δὲ καὶ σίδηρον (*steel*)
καὶ πῦρ καλή τις οὖσα.

Anacreontic.

434. Word-formation. (*a*) Numerous compounds in Greek and English derive their second part from the stem **ιδ** of εἶδον and οἶδα. **-ειδής** and English *-oid* both come from εἶδος *that which is seen, shape;* and from them come the many words like σφαιρο-ειδής *having the shape* (or *appearance*) *of a sphere*, SPHEROID; ἀστερο-ειδής ASTEROID; ἀνθρωπο-ειδής ANTHROPOID. It should be noted that this type of word suggests *approximate*, and not complete, *similarity* in appearance.

(*b*) What is the meaning of the English words *deltoid, hyoid, rhomboid, sigmoid, trapezoid?*

Metropolitan Museum of Art.

BOYS' HORSE RACE

One rider has been thrown from his horse and is being dragged along clinging to the rein.

---

[1] Dialectic genitive plural.

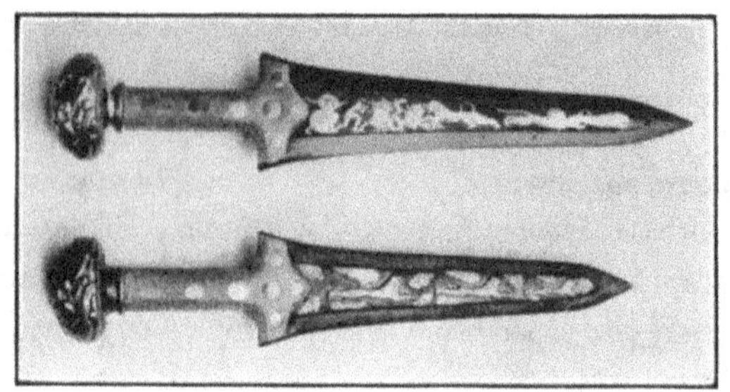

Metropolitan Museum of Art.

DAGGERS EXCAVATED AT MYCENÆ

LESSON LXIX

εἶμι. REVIEW OF THE ACCUSATIVE

ἀρχὴ ἄνδρα δείκνῡσιν. — *Power proves the man.*[1]

435. Inflection of εἶμι. Learn the inflection of *εἶμι* (§ 539). Note that the stem of *εἶμι* is **ι** (compare Latin *ī-re*).

436. Forms of the Accusative. Review all accusative endings (§ 544, *d*). Note that **-ν**, **-α**, or **-ς** is part of every accusative ending, except for neuter singulars, which have the same form as their respective nominatives. What other endings resemble these of the accusative? Where the ending may suggest another case, modifying words and context usually prevent confusion.

437. Uses of the Accusative. Having clearly in mind the forms that indicate an accusative, review the possible uses of the accusative (§ 544, *d*). The major function is that of the *direct object*. This direct object may be that of the person or thing *affected* (the usual direct object) or that of the thing *effected*.

[1] Bias, as quoted by Demosthenes, 1455, 15.

438. VOCABULARY

αἰτιάομαι, αἰτιάσομαι, ᾐτιᾱσάμην, ᾐτίᾱμαι, ᾐτιάθην: *blame, accuse, find fault.* Cf. **αἴτιος.**
ἐάω, ἐάσω, εἴᾱσα, εἴᾱκα, εἴᾱμαι, εἰάθην: *allow, let be.*
εἶμι, only pres., but freq. with fut. significance: *go.*
μάντις, -εως, ὁ: *seer, soothsayer, prophet.* MANTIC, NECROMANCY.
πειράομαι, πειρᾱ́σομαι, ἐπειρᾱσάμην, πεπείρᾱμαι, ἐπειρᾱ́θην: *try.* PIRATE, EMPIRIC.
τάξις, -εως, ἡ: *order, arrangement, position, division.* Cf. **τάττω.** TAXIDERMIST.
χράομαι,[1] χρήσομαι, ἐχρησάμην, κέχρημαι, ἐχρήσθην: *use,* with D. Cf. **χρῆμα.**

439. EXERCISES

(*a*) Translate:

1. *ἆρ᾽ οὐ ξύλοις ἐχρῶντο ταῖς ἀσπίσιν;* 2. *τοῦτο οὖν αἰτιῶμαί σε, ὅτι οὐκ εἴᾱς αὐτοὺς εἰς τὴν τάξιν ἰέναι.* 3. *καὶ πρὸς τᾱ̀ς θύρᾱς ἰόντες ἀπ-ῄτουν τὸν Κῦρον τὸν μισθόν.* 4. *καὶ μὴν τὴν τάφρον ἐπειρῶντο παρα-τείνειν ἄνω διὰ τοῦ πεδίου ἐπὶ δώδεκα παρασάγγᾱς.* 5. *ἀφ-ίκοντο δ᾽ εἰς πόλιν εὐδαίμονα Σόλους*[2] *τὸ ὄνομα.*[3] 6. *ὑπ-οπτεύσει δὲ τὸν μάντιν ἐλπίδας τινὰς ἔχειν.* 7. *τὸν δὲ κήρῡκα πρὸς βασιλέᾱ ἀπο-στέλλει τὴν ταχίστην ὁδόν.* 8. *καὶ ἅμα στρατηγοὶ πέντε ἀπο-τμηθέντες τᾱ̀ς κεφαλᾱ̀ς ἐτελεύτησαν.*

(*b*) Write in Greek:

1. All know the king is winning a fine victory. 2. From there he made a four days' march, (a distance of) twenty-six parasangs, to a city (that was) desolate. 3. The citizens honor him greatly by choosing him ruler. 4. What wrong did his opponents do the man? 5. The boys were trying to do it the quickest way.

---

[1] *χράομαι* contracts to **η** instead of **α**.
[2] Consult *Dictionary of Proper Names.*
[3] Page 144, note 2.

440. A GOOD LOSER

ἐνταῦθα Κῦρος Σῑλᾱνὸν καλέσᾱς τὸν Ἀμπρακιώτην μάντιν ἔδωκεν αὐτῷ δᾱρεικοὺς τρισ-χῑλίους, ὅτι τῇ ἐν-δεκάτῃ ἀπ' ἐκείνης ἡμέρᾳ πρότερον θῡόμενος εἶπεν αὐτῷ ὅτι βασιλεὺς οὐ μαχεῖται δέκα ἡμερῶν. Κῦρος δ' εἶπεν, Οὐκ ἄρα ἔτι μαχεῖται, εἰ ἐν ταύταις οὐ μαχεῖται ταῖς ἡμέραις· ἐὰν δ' ἀληθεύσῃς (compare **ἀληθής**) ὑπ-ισχνοῦμαί σοι δέκα τάλαντα. τοῦτο τὸ χρῡσίον τότε ἀπ-έδωκεν, ἐπεὶ παρ-ῆλθον αἱ δέκα ἡμέραι.

Xenophon, *Anabasis*, I. 7. 18.

441. ONE ADVENTURE AMONG MANY

In his so-called *True History*, Lucian takes the hero and his shipmates to a sea resembling the Sargasso Sea which we know today. Whether rumors of this sea had reached the ears of Lucian is not known, but in any event his imagination left reality far behind. He tells us that the voyagers hauled their ship to the tree tops and, spreading sail, skimmed along the branches as if on water. He goes on to say:

ἀφ-ῑκόμεθα εἰς τὸ ὕδωρ, καὶ πάλιν ὁμοίως κατα-θέντες τὴν ναῦν ἐπλέομεν μέχρι δὴ ἐπ-έστημεν χάσματι μεγάλῳ ἐκ τοῦ ὕδατος δι-εστῶτος γεγενημένῳ, ὥσπερ ἐν τῇ γῇ πολλάκις ὁρῶμεν ὑπὸ σεισμῶν (compare SEISMOGRAPH) γενόμενα δια-χωρίσματα (*fissures*). ἡ μὲν οὖν ναῦς καθ-ελόντων ἡμῶν τὰ ἱστία (*sails*) οὐ ῥᾳδίως ἔστη παρ' ὀλίγον ἐλθοῦσα κατ-ενεχθῆναι. ὑπερ-κύψαντες (*leaning over*) δὲ ἡμεῖς ὁρῶμεν βάθος (*depth*) ὅσον σταδίων χῑλίων μάλα φοβερόν. εἱστήκει γὰρ τὸ ὕδωρ ὥσπερ μεμερισμένον (compare **μέρος**)· περι-σκοποῦντες δὲ ὁρῶμεν κατὰ δεξιὰ γέφῡραν ἐκ τοῦ ὕδατος πεποιημένην, τὸ γὰρ ὕδωρ ἐκ τῆς ἑτέρᾱς θαλάττης εἰς τὴν ἑτέρᾱν δι-έρρει κατὰ τὴν ἐπι-φάνειαν (*surface*).

Adapted from Lucian, *True History*, II. 43.

East Front of the Propylæa

This monumental entrance to the Acropolis was built by Pericles at a cost of over $2,000,000. Earthquakes have played a large part in destroying it. Partial restoration has been accomplished by the use of its own fallen blocks.

LESSON LXX

SIMILARITIES IN FORM — εἰμί, εἶμι, ἵημι

Ἕλληνες ὄντες βαρβάροις δουλεύσομεν;
Shall Greeks be slaves to barbarians?[1]

442. Similarities in Form. Care must be taken to distinguish between certain forms of *εἰμί*, *εἶμι*, *ἵημι*. **ἱ-** and **εἱ-** (note the rough breathings) are distinguishing marks of *ἵημι*: **ἱ-** indicating the present system; **εἱ-** the second aorist. **ἰ-** (note the smooth breathing) is a distinguishing mark of *εἶμι*. **εἰ** (again a smooth breathing) is a mark of *εἰμί*.

Certain forms of *ἵστημι*, *οἶδα*, and a few other words, must also be carefully distinguished.

Review the inflection of *εἰμί*, *εἶμι*, and *ἵημι* (§§ 537–539).

443. **VOCABULARY**

δουλεύω, -σω, -σα: *be a slave* (**δοῦλος**), *serve*.
θνητός, -ή, -όν: *mortal*, *human*. Cf. **ἀπο-θνῄσκω**.
λιμήν, -ένος, ὁ: *haven*, *harbor*.
ὀρθός, -ή, -όν: *straight*, *erect*, *correct*. ORTHOGONAL, ORTHODOX.
πίνω, **πίομαι**, **ἔπιον**, **πέπωκα**, -**πέπομαι**, -**επόθην**: *drink*. Cf. Lat. *bibo*.
τέχνη, -ης, ἡ: *art*, *skill*, *craft*. Cf. TECHNIQUE.
τύχη, -ης, ἡ: *chance*, *lot*, *fate*. Cf. **τυ(γ)χάνω**.

444. **EXERCISES**

(*a*) Locate these forms:

εἴη, *εἴη*, *παρ-είη* (2),[2] *ἀπ-είην*, *ἀφ-είην*, *ἧμεν*, *ἦμεν*, *ἱῇ* (2), *ἴῃ*, *ἀφ-ιῇς*, *ἀπ-ίῃς*, *ᾗς*, *ᾖς*, *ᾖσαν* (2), *ᾖσαν*, *εἶσαν*, *ἵεσαν*,

[1] Euripides, fragment.

[2] The figures in parentheses show where two or more forms are identical.

ἀπ-ιέναι, ἀφ-ῑέναι, ἀφ-εῖναι, ἀπ-εῖναι, εἰδέναι, ἰδεῖν, ἕς, εἴς, εἶς, εἰς, ἴθι, ἴσθι (2), *ἔστω, ἴτω, ἕτω, ἴστω, ἱστῶ, ἱέτω, εἰδῇ, ἴδῃ, ἱστῇ, στῇ, ἵστη, ἴστη, παρ-εῖτε* (3), *εἶτε* (2), *εἶτε, ἔσεσθε, εἴσεσθαι, εἰδώς, ἰδών, εἰδῶ, ἱᾶσι, ἴᾱσι, ἱστῶσι, ἱστᾶσι.*

(*b*) Write in Greek:

1. They are, they go, they throw. 2. If the seer is wise, he will go at once. 3. The stranger did not know that you threw a second stone. 4. Were you in line (*formation*) when he went by (compound of **εἶμι**)?

EURIPIDES

445. POETRY PAYS

ἔνιοι δὲ τῶν ἐν Σικελίᾳ ἁλόντων Ἀθηναίων[1] *δι' Εὐρῑπίδην ἐσώθησαν. μάλιστα γὰρ οἱ περὶ Σικελίᾱν ἥδοντο αὐτῷ. ὅσοι μὲν οὖν ἐσώθησαν χάριν ᾖσαν τῷ Εὐρῑπίδῃ, ὅτι δουλεύοντες ἀφ-είθησαν, ἐκ-διδάξαντες ὅσα τῶν ἐκείνου ποιημάτων ἐμέμνηντο. τοὺς δὲ Καυνίους φασὶ διωκομένους ποτὲ οὐκ ἐᾶν τοὺς Συρᾱκοσίους εἰς τὸν λιμένα ἰέναι, ἐπεὶ δὲ ἐπύθοντο ὅτι γιγνώσκουσι ποιήματα τῶν Εὐρῑπίδου, οὕτω δὴ παρ-εῖναι καὶ κατ-αγαγεῖν τὸ πλοῖον.*

Adapted from Plutarch, *Nicias*, 29.

Upon this old tradition, Robert Browning founds his dramatic poem entitled *Balaustion's Adventure*, wherein

[1] Athenians who had been captured when the Sicilian expedition met with disaster.

Balaustion, a Greek girl, wins succor for her shipmates by reciting Euripides' *Alcestis*, a large part of which the English poet works in with splendid effect.

446. **οἶνος καὶ ἀλήθεια** [1]

In the following lines from that same play, the speaker is jovial Heracles, the heavy-drinker and heavy-hitter, who has come to visit king Admetus, not knowing that the king has just lost his devoted queen. Heracles is addressing a servant who has protested at his boisterous conduct.

δεῦρ' ἔλθ', ὅπως ἂν καὶ σοφώτερος γένῃ.
τὰ θνητὰ πρᾶγματ' οἶδας [2] ἣν ἔχει φύσιν ;
οἶμαι μὲν οὔ· πόθεν γάρ ; [3] ἀλλ' ἄκου' ἐμοῦ.
βροτοῖς (*mortals*) ἅπᾱσι κατ-θανεῖν ὀφείλεται,
κοὐκ ἔστι θνητῶν ὅστις ἐξ-επίσταται
τὴν αὔριον (*morrow*) μέλλουσαν εἰ βιώσεται·
τὸ τῆς τύχης [4] γὰρ ἀ-φανὲς (compare **φαίνω**) οἷ (*whither*) προ-βήσεται,
κἄστ' (κ α ὶ ἔ σ τ ι) οὐ διδακτὸν οὐδ' ἁλίσκεται τέχνῃ.
ταῦτ' οὖν ἀκούσᾱς καὶ μαθὼν ἐμοῦ πάρα (= π α ρ' ἐ μ ο ῦ),
εὔφραινε (*enjoy*) σαυτόν, πῖνε, τὸν καθ' ἡμέρᾱν
βίον λογίζου (*count*) σόν, τὰ δ' ἄλλα τῆς τύχης.
τίμᾱ δὲ καὶ τὴν πλεῖστον [5] ἡδίστην θεῶν
Κύπριν [6] βροτοῖσιν· εὐ-μενὴς (*kindly-minded*) γὰρ ἡ θεός,
τὰ δ' ἄλλ' ἔᾱσον ταῦτα καὶ πείθου λόγοις
ἐμοῖσιν, — εἴπερ ὀρθά σοι δοκῶ λέγειν.

Euripides, *Alcestis*, 779–793.

[1] Compare the Latin *in vino veritas*.

[2] Poetic form of οἶσθα.

[3] πόθεν = *whence*. The expression is elliptic and idiomatic = *How (could you)?*

[4] τὸ τῆς τύχης, a favorite periphrasis differing little from ἡ τύχη.

[5] Compare Shakespeare's "*most unkindest*."

[6] Κύπριν, the Cyprian goddess, *i.e.*, Aphrodite.

LESSON LXXI

INFLECTION OF δείκνῡμι

οὐκ ἀνδρὸς ὅρκοι πίστις, ἀλλ' ὅρκων ἀνήρ.
It is not the oath but the man that counts.[1]

447. Inflection of δείκνῡμι. (*a*) Learn the inflection of *δείκνῡμι* in the present system (§ 535).

Note the general similarity of the indicative, imperative, infinitive, and participle of *δείκνῡμι* to the same forms of *ἵστημι*. The subjunctive and optative are the same as for *παύω*.

(*b*) Write the inflection of *δεικνῡ́ς* (like *ἱστάς*). Compare with paradigm (§ 514, *f*).

(*c*) The aorist is regular, *ἔδειξα*. There is no second aorist.

448. VOCABULARY

ἀπο-δείκνῡμι: *prove, appoint.* APODEICTIC.

ἀπ-όλλῡμι, -ολῶ, -ώλεσα, -ωλόμην, -ολώλεκα, -όλωλα: *destroy, lose*; mid., *perish, be lost.* APOLLYON.

ἀριθμός, -οῦ, ὁ: *number.* LOGARITHM.

δείκνῡμι, δείξω, ἔδειξα, δέδειχα, δέδειγμαι, ἐδείχθην: *show, point out.* PARADIGM.

ἐπι-δείκνῡμι: *show off, display.* EPIDEICTIC.

ζεύγνῡμι, ζεύξω, ἔζευξα, ἔζευγμαι, ἐζεύχθην: *yoke, bind, unite.* ZEUGMA.

νεκρός, -οῦ, ὁ: *corpse.* NECROSIS.

ὄμνῡμι, ὀμοῦμαι, ὤμοσα, ὀμώμοκα, ὀμώμοσμαι, ὠμόσθην: *swear, take oath.*

ὅρκος, -ου, ὁ: *oath.*

ὀφθαλμός, -οῦ, ὁ: *eye.* Cf. **ὄψομαι.** OPHTHALMIA.

[1] Æschylus, fragment. Literally: *Oaths are not a guarantee of a man, but a man is a guarantee of oaths.*

449. **EXERCISES**

(*a*) Translate:

1. *στρατηγὸν δὲ ἀπο-δείκνῡσιν αὐτὸν πάντων ὅσοι εἰς Καστωλοῦ πεδίον ἀθροίζονται.* 2. *ἀλλ' ὅμως γέφῡρα ἐπ-ῆν ἐζευγμένη ἑκατὸν πλοίοις.* 3. *ἔφασαν δέ τινες τούτους τοὺς στρατιώτᾱς ὑπο-λειφθέντας ἀπ-ολέσθαι.* 4. *ὑπὲρ τὸν ὀφθαλμὸν πληγεὶς ἀπ-έθανεν.* 5. *καὶ ὅρκον μέγαν ὀμνύᾱσι τοὺς νεκροὺς ἀνα-λαβόντες θάψειν.* 6. *ἥδονται δὲ ἀπο-δεικνύντες ὅτι πολλῷ ἀμείνους εἰσὶ τῶν βαρβάρων.* 7. *ἆρ' οὐκ ἂν φοβοῖσθε μὴ ἀπ-ολλύῃ τὰς βοῦς;* 8. *κελεύω σε δεικνύναι ἡμῖν ὅπου εἰσὶν αἱ εἴκοσι νῆες.* 9. *ἐν-νοεῖτε δὲ καὶ τόδε· εἰ μή που ταῦτ' ὤμνυτε, οὐκ ἂν ὑμῖν ἐπιστεύομεν.*

(*b*) Write in Greek:

1. They appoint him leader because of his bravery. 2. The man swears a great oath that he will inflict punishment on his opponents. 3. Not being able to find the road, the captain perished. 4. By every art they are trying to bridge[1] the river.

450. **NO MATCH FOR SOCRATES**

ἀφ-ικόμενος γὰρ Ἱππίᾱς παρ-εγένετο Σωκράτει λέγοντι ὡς τοῦτο θαυμαστὸν (compare **θαυμάζω**) *εἴη, ὅτι εἰ μέν τις βούλοιτο τέχνην τινὰ διδάξασθαι, οὐκ ἀ-πορεῖ ὅποι ἂν ἰὼν ταύτην μάθοι, εἰ δὲ τὸ δίκαιον βούλοιτο διδάξασθαι, τότε ἀ-πορεῖ. καὶ ὁ μὲν Ἱππίᾱς ἀκούσᾱς ταῦτα ὥσπερ ἐπι-σκώπτων* (compare SCOFF) *αὐτόν, Ἔτι γὰρ σύ, ἔφη, ὦ Σώκρατες, ἐκεῖνα τὰ αὐτὰ λέγεις ἃ ἐγὼ πάλαι ποτέ σου ἤκουσα; καὶ ὁ Σωκράτης, Ὃ δέ γε τούτου δεινότερον, ἔφη, ὦ Ἱππίᾱ, οὐ μόνον ἀεὶ τὰ αὐτὰ λέγω ἀλλὰ καὶ περὶ τῶν αὐτῶν· σὺ δ' ἴσως πολυ-μαθὴς ὢν περὶ τῶν αὐτῶν οὐδέποτε*

[1] See sentence 2 in (*a*).

τὰ αὐτὰ λέγεις. Ἀμέλει (*certainly*), ἔφη, πειρῶμαι καινόν (*new*) τι λέγειν ἀεί. πότερον, ἔφη, καὶ περὶ ὧν ἐπίστασαι; οἷον περὶ γραμμάτων (*letters*), ἐάν τις ἐρωτᾷ σε πόσα καὶ ποῖα Σωκράτους (that is, *in the name Socrates*) ἐστίν, ἄλλα μὲν πρότερον ἄλλα δὲ νῦν πειρᾷ λέγειν; ἢ περὶ ἀριθμῶν τοῖς ἐρωτῶσιν, εἰ τὰ δὶς πέντε δέκα ἐστίν, οὐ τὰ αὐτὰ νῦν ἃ καὶ πρότερον ἀπο-κρίνει; περὶ μὲν τούτων, ἔφη, ὦ Σώκρατες.

Xenophon, *Memorabilia*, IV. 4. 5–7.

451. CARRY ON!

Ναυηγοῦ (*shipwrecked sailor*) τάφος εἰμί· σὺ δὲ πλέε· καὶ γὰρ ὅθ' (=ὅτε) ἡμεῖς
ὠλόμεθ', αἱ λοιπαὶ νῆες ἐποντοπόρουν (*were sailing the sea*).

Greek Anthology.

452. GREEK INFLUENCE

Under the plastic touch of conquered Greece, the Latin language was gradually moulded into an apter instrument, while the Roman intellect itself acquired, in some measure, a flexibility not native to it.

R. C. Jebb, *Essays and Addresses.*

Clearness of vision, cheerfulness of acceptance, easy grace of expression, are the qualities which delight us; and now when we affirm that we find all these in the genuine Grecian works, achieved in the noblest material, the best proportioned form, with certainty and completeness of execution, we shall be understood if we always refer to them as a basis and a standard. Let each be a Grecian in his own way, but let him be one.

Ibid. Quoted from Goethe.

LESSON LXXII

AORIST OF γιγνώσκω

γνῶθι σαυτόν. — *Know thyself.*[1]

453. γιγνώσκω in the Aorist. (*a*) Learn the inflection of ἔγνων (§ 543).

Although not a -μι verb, *γιγνώσκω* has an aorist much like that of *δίδωμι.* The difference lies chiefly in the indicative and imperative.

(*b*) In like manner inflect the second aorist of *ἁλίσκομαι* (imperative is lacking).

454. VOCABULARY

βλέπω, βλέψω, ἔβλεψα : *look, face, point.*

γυμνός, -ή, -όν : *bare, naked, lightly-clad.* GYMNAST.

δια-γιγνώσκω : *distinguish, decide between.* DIAGNOSIS.

ζάω, ζήσω : *live;* **τὸ ζῷον** : *living thing.* ZOÖLOGY.

πονέω, πονήσω, ἐπόνησα, πεπόνηκα, πεπόνημαι, ἐπονήθην : *toil, struggle.* Cf. **πόνος.**

σχολή, -ῆς, ἡ : *leisure, free time* for anything. SCHOLAR.

455. SOUND ADVICE

τὸ γνῶθι σαυτὸν [2] ἔστιν, ἂν τὰ πράγματα
εἰδῇς τὰ σαυτοῦ καὶ τί σοι ποιητέον.

Menander, fragment.

---

[1] Thales, as quoted by Diogenes Laertius, I. 40. Also said to have been inscribed on the temple of Apollo at Delphi.

[2] γνῶθι σαυτόν, being a set phrase, may receive an article (τό).

456. THE SIX-HOUR DAY

ἓξ ὧραι μόχθοις (*hard work*) ἱκανώταται· αἱ δὲ μετ' αὐτὰς γράμμασι (*letters*) δεικνύμεναι ζ ῆ θ ι[1] λέγουσι βροτοῖς (*mortals*). Greek Anthology.

457. AS A FLOWER OF THE FIELD

ΜΕΝΙΠΠΟΣ. ποῦ δὲ οἱ καλοί εἰσιν ἢ αἱ καλαί, Ἑρμῆ; ἐπί-δειξόν μοι αὐτούς.

ΕΡΜΗΣ. Οὐ σχολή μοι, ὦ Μένιππε· ἀλλὰ μὴν κατ' ἐκεῖνο ἀπό-βλεψον, ἐπὶ τὰ δεξιά, ἔνθα ὁ Ὑάκινθός τέ ἐστι

THE SKELETON AT THE FEAST

καὶ Νάρκισσος καὶ Ἀχιλλεὺς καὶ Τυρὼ καὶ Ἑλένη καὶ Λήδᾱ καὶ ὅλως πάντα τὰ ἀρχαῖα κάλλη.

ΜΕΝ. Ὀστᾶ (*bones*) μόνα ὁρῶ καὶ κρᾱνία (compare CRANIUM) τῶν σαρκῶν (compare SARCOPHAGUS) γυμνά, ὅμοια τὰ πολλά.

ΕΡΜ. Καὶ μὴν ἐκεῖνά ἐστιν ἃ πάντες οἱ ποιηταὶ θαυμάζουσιν, ἃ σὺ ὀλίγου ἄξια νομίζεις.

---

[1] Imperative of ζάω. The key is found in the fact that the Greeks used letters of the alphabet to represent numbers. 1 — 6 = α β γ δ ε ς and 7 — 10 = ζ η θ ι. Their day was from sunrise to sunset.

MEN. Ὅμως τὴν Ἑλένην μοι δεῖξον· οὐ γὰρ ἂν διαγνοίην ἔγω-γε.

ΕΡΜ. τοῦτο τὸ κρανίον ἡ Ἑλένη ἐστίν.

MEN. Εἶτα διὰ τοῦτο αἱ χίλιαι νῆες ἐπέμφθησαν ἐξ ἁπάσης τῆς Ἑλλάδος καὶ τοσοῦτοι ἔπεσον Ἕλληνές τε καὶ βάρβαροι καὶ τοσαῦται πόλεις ἀν-ετράπησαν;

ΕΡΜ. Ἀλλ' οὐκ εἶδες, ὦ Μένιππε, ζῶσαν τὴν γυναῖκα. ἔφης γὰρ ἂν καὶ σὺ ἀ-νεμέσητον[1] (*not surprising*) εἶναι
τοιῇδ'[2] ἀμφὶ γυναικὶ πολὺν χρόνον ἄλγεα[2] πάσχειν·

MEN. Οὐκοῦν τοῦτο, ὦ Ἑρμῆ, θαυμάζω, εἰ μὴ συν-ίεσαν (*understood*) οἱ Ἀχαιοὶ περὶ πράγματος οὕτως ὀλιγοχρονίου καὶ ῥᾳδίως ἀπ-ανθοῦντος (*fade*) πονοῦντες.

Lucian, *Dialogues of the Dead*, 18.

458. Which of the "beauties" above mentioned are familiar in English literature? Be prepared to state briefly the most important facts regarding each.

459. EXERCISE

Write in Greek:

1. Know thyself. 2. Knowing that, he would not have toiled to the limit of his strength (*as strongly as possible*). 3. The king then knew that the city was captured. 4. I do not have leisure to look at that.

460. Word-formation. *-εῖον, -ēum*, denotes *place where:*

Μουσεῖον MUSĒUM, haunt of the Muses (Μοῦσα *Muse*);

Μαυσωλεῖον MAUSOLĒUM, the tomb of Mausōlus (Μαύσωλος) in Halicarnassus;

Ὠιδεῖον ODĒUM, a building in Athens for musical performances (ᾠδή *song*), erected by Pericles.

---

[1] With ἀ-νεμέσητον associate NEMESIS (*resentment, retributive justice*).

[2] Quoted from Homer (note the dactylic hexameter); hence τοιῇδ' for τοιαύτῃ and ἄλγεα for ἄλγη.

LESSON LXXIII

INFLECTION OF δηλόω

οὔτοι τὰ χρήματ' ἴδια κέκτηνται βροτοί.
Man's wealth is but a loan from heaven.[1]

THE TEMPLE AT BASSÆ

The Greeks lavished their wealth on temples to the gods rather than on their own dwellings. This majestic shrine stands in a remote corner of mountainous Arcadia. It is said to have been built by the architect of the Parthenon.

461. Rules of Contraction. (*a*) Review the principles of contraction in § 127.

(*b*) Rules for contraction of verbs in **-οω**:

ο + **ε** or **ο** or **ου** = **ου**
ο + **η** or **ω** = **ω**
ο + **ι**-diphthong (**ει, οι, ῃ**) = **οι**

[1] Euripides, *Phœnissæ*, 555. Literally: *Mortals do not own their wealth as private property.*

462. Inflection of δηλόω. (*a*) Write out inflection of the present system of δηλόω. Compare with paradigm (§ 534).

(*b*) In other systems than the present, **ο** of the stem becomes **ω**: δηλόω, δηλώσω, ἐδήλωσα, κ.τ.λ.

463. VOCABULARY

ἀξιόω, ἀξιώσω, ἠξίωσα, ἠξίωκα, ἠξίωμαι, ἠξιώθην: *deem worthy, demand.* Cf. **ἄξιος**. AXIOM.

δηλόω, δηλώσω, ἐδήλωσα, δεδήλωκα, δεδήλωμαι, ἐδηλώθην: *make plain, show.* Cf. **δῆλος**.

ἑκών, -οῦσα, -όν: *willing, intentional.*

ἐξ-απατάω, -απατήσω, -ηπάτησα, -ηπάτηκα, -ηπάτημαι, -ηπατήθην: *deceive utterly.*

ἥλιος, -ου, ὁ: *sun.* HELIOGRAPH.

ἡττάομαι, ἡττήσομαι, ἥττημαι, ἡττήθην: *be worsted, defeated.* Cf. **ἥττων**.

κτάομαι, κτήσομαι, ἐκτησάμην, κέκτημαι, ἐκτήθην: *gain, get possession of.*

ὁρμάω, ὁρμήσω, ὥρμησα, ὥρμηκα, ὥρμημαι, ὡρμήθην: *set in motion, start* (trans.).

464. EXERCISES

(*a*) Translate:

1. *οὕτως αὖ ἐδήλου ὅτι οὐκ ἂν αὐτοὺς προ-δοίη, οὐδ' εἰ πολλῷ ἐλάττους τὸν ἀριθμὸν γένοιντο.* 2. *ἔδοξε δ' αὐτοῖς ἀξιοῦν πλείονα μισθόν.* 3. *ὥστε ἠξίουν αὐτὸν μὴ ἑκόντα ἐξ-απατᾶν.* 4. *κατὰ τὴν ὀρθὴν ὁδὸν ὁρμώμενος πάνθ' ὅσα ἐβούλετο ἐκτήσατο.* 5. *οὐ ῥᾳδίως ἂν ἡττήθησαν, εἰ μὴ ὁ ἥλιος ἐξ-έλιπεν.* 6. *εἰ δὲ δή ποτε πορεύοιτο καὶ πλεῖστοι μέλλοιεν εἰς αὐτὸν ἀπο-βλέψειν, προσ-καλῶν τοὺς εὔνους σπουδαίως δι-ελέγετο, ὡς δηλοίη οὓς τῑμᾷ.* 7. *καὶ δὴ ὅτου μάλιστα ὁρῴη ἕκαστον δεόμενον, δῆλος ἦν πειρώμενος παρ-έχεσθαι.* 8. *ἐὰν δὲ βασιλέᾱ ἐξ-απατᾷ, φοβοῦμαι μὴ ἀξιοῖ τοὺς Ἕλληνας ἀπο-κτεῖναι.*

(*b*) Write in Greek:

1. Willingly we started (*be careful of voice*) for the village. 2. Being defeated by a small force, they make it plain that

they are cowardly. 3. Demand whatever seems best, so that you may not perish on the march. 4. Although he was utterly deceived, he did not spend all his money.

465. "THE SEA! THE SEA!"

ἐντεῦθεν ἐπορεύθησαν διὰ Χαλύβων, οἳ ἦσαν ὧν δι-ῆλθον ἀλκιμώτατοι (*most warlike*)· ἐπεὶ δὲ παρ-έλθοιεν οἱ Ἕλληνες, οὗτοι εἵποντο ἀεὶ μαχόμενοι. ἐκ τούτου ἀφ-ίκοντο εἰς πόλιν

THE SHIP OF ODYSSEUS

According to legend, the ship which bore Odysseus home was turned by the angry gods into this island.

μεγάλην καὶ εὐδαίμονα, ἐξ ἧς ὁ ἄρχων τοῖς Ἕλλησιν ἡγεμόνα πέμπει· ἐλθὼν δ' ἐκεῖνος λέγει ὅτι ἄξει αὐτοὺς πέντε ἡμερῶν εἰς χωρίον ὅθεν (compare ἐντεῦ**θεν**) ὄψονται θάλατταν.

καὶ ἀφ-ικνοῦνται ἐπὶ τὸ ὄρος τῇ πέμπτῃ ἡμέρᾳ· ἐπεὶ δὲ οἱ πρῶτοι ἐγένοντο ἐπὶ τοῦ ὄρους, κραυγὴ πολλὴ ἐγένετο. ἀκούσᾱς δὲ ὁ Ξενοφῶν καὶ οἱ ὀπισθο-φύλακες ἐνόμισαν ἔμπροσθεν ἄλλους ἐπι-τίθεσθαι πολεμίους· ἐπειδὴ δ' ἡ βοὴ (*shouting*) πλείων τε ἐγίγνετο καὶ ἐγγύτερον καὶ οἱ ἀεὶ *ἐπ-ιόντες ἔθεον δρόμῳ ἐπὶ τοὺς ἀεὶ βοῶντας* (compare **βοή**) *καὶ πολλῷ μείζων ἐγίγνετο ἡ βοὴ ὅσῳ δὴ πλείους ἐγίγνοντο, ἐδόκει δὴ μεῖζόν τι εἶναι τῷ Ξενοφῶντι· καὶ ἀνα-βὰς ἐφ' ἵππον καὶ τοὺς ἱππέᾱς ἀνα-λαβὼν παρ-εβοήθει· καὶ τάχα δὴ ἀκούουσι βοώντων τῶν στρατιωτῶν Θ ά λ α τ τ α θ ά λ α τ τ α. ἔνθα δὴ ἔθεον πάντες καὶ οἱ ὀπισθο-φύλακες, καὶ τὰ ὑπο-ζύγια* (*pack animals*) *ἠλαύνετο καὶ οἱ ἵπποι.*

Adapted from Xenophon, *Anabasis*, IV. 7. 15–24.

466. SHADOW OR SUBSTANCE[1]

νεᾱνίᾱς (*youth*) *ὄνον* (*ass*) *μισθωσάμενος* (compare **μισθός**), *ἐπεὶ ὁ ἥλιος θερμὸς ἐγένετο, ἠξίωσεν ὑπὸ τῇ τοῦ ὄνου σκιᾷ* (*shade*) *κατα-κεῖσθαι. ὁ μὲν οὖν μισθώσᾱς ἐκώλῡεν αὐτόν, λέγων ὅτι τὸν μὲν ὄνον μισθώσειε, τὴν δὲ σκιὰν οὔ. ὁ δ' εἶπεν ὅτι τὸν ὄνον μισθωσάμενος μισθώσαιτο καὶ τὴν σκιάν. ἐν τούτῳ μαχομένους αὐτοὺς κατ-έλιπεν ὁ ὄνος.*

Adapted from Æsop, 339.

467. Word-formation. (*a*) Verbs formed by adding **-οω** to noun (or adjective) stems denote action of a nature similar to that expressed by the noun (or adjective). They are usually *causative:*

δοῦλος *slave*, δουλόω *enslave:*
δῆλος *clear*, δηλόω *make clear.*

In like manner, form verbs from ζῆλος *emulation*, μάστιξ, -ῑγος *whip*.

(*b*) From verbs in **-οω** come nouns in **-ωσις**:

νεκρός *dead body*, **νεκρόω** *make dead*, **νέκρωσις** *deadness*, NECROSIS;

From such nouns in turn have come the numerous medical terms in *osis*: *arterio-sclerosis*, *neurosis*, *psychosis*, etc. (§ 280).

[1] This fable is said to have been used by Demosthenes with telling effect upon an inattentive jury.

LESSON LXXIV

SUMMARY OF PARTICIPIAL FORMS AND USES

πρὸς κέντρα μὴ λάκτιζε. — *Kick not against the pricks.*[1]

---

468. Forms of Participles. Review all participial forms (§ 545, *f*). Note that the stem is that of the corresponding tense of the indicative, and that the clues to most participles and their tenses are:

-οντ-, **-ουσ-** (present, future, or second aorist active);
-αντ-, **-ᾱσ-** (first aorist active);[2]
-οτ-, **-υι-** (perfect active);
-ομεν- (present or future middle or passive, second aorist middle);
-αμεν- (first aorist middle);
-μεν- *without connecting vowel* (perfect middle or passive);
-εντ-, **-εισ-** (aorist passive).[3]

469. Uses of Participles. Having clearly in mind the clues that indicate a participle, review the possible uses of the participle (§ 545, *f*). Fix clearly the difference in meaning conveyed by the tenses, especially the present and aorist (§ 546, *a* and *c*).

---

[1] Æschylus, *Agamemnon*, 1624. Literally: *Kick not against the goads.* Compare The Acts of the Apostles, XXVI. 14.

[2] Also present of ἵστημι.

[3] Also present and aorist active of τίθημι and ἵημι.

470. VOCABULARY

ἁμαρτάνω, ἁμαρτήσομαι, ἥμαρτον, ἡμάρτηκα, ἡμάρτημαι, ἡμαρτήθην: *miss*, with G.; *err*.

θώρᾱξ, -ᾱκος, ὁ: *breastplate, corselet, cuirass*. THORAX, THORACIC.

λανθάνω, λήσω, ἔλαθον, λέληθα, λέλησμαι: *escape notice, elude; do secretly*, with suppl. part. LETHE.

πεζός, -ή, -όν: *afoot*; ὁ πεζός: *infantryman*.

τι-τρώσκω, τρώσω, ἔτρωσα, τέτρωμαι, ἐτρώθην: *wound*. TRAUMA.

φθάνω, φθήσομαι, ἔφθασα: *outstrip, beat, anticipate*. Usually with suppl. part.[1]

471. A GRUMBLER SHAMED

Καὶ ἐνταῦθα πολλὴ μὲν κραυγὴ ἦν τοῦ Ἑλληνικοῦ στρατεύματος δια-κελευομένων τοῖς ἑαυτῶν, πολλὴ δὲ κραυγὴ τῶν

ATALANTA'S RACE

Atalanta outran every youth with whom she raced. Finally she was vanquished by Hippomenes. He threw at her feet a golden apple, which she stopped to pick up.

ἀμφὶ Τισσαφέρνην τοῖς ἑαυτῶν δια-κελευομένων. Ξενοφῶν δὲ παρ-ελαύνων ἐπὶ τοῦ ἵππου παρ-εκελεύετο· Ἄνδρες, νῦν ἐπὶ τὴν Ἑλλάδα νομίζετε ἁμιλλᾶσθαι (*race*), νῦν πρὸς τοὺς παῖδας καὶ τὰς γυναῖκας, νῦν ὀλίγον πονήσαντες ἀ-μαχεὶ (adverb) τὴν λοιπὴν[2] πορευσόμεθα. Σωτηρίδᾱς δὲ ὁ Σικυώνιος εἶπεν· Οὐκ ἐξ ἴσου, ὦ Ξενοφῶν, ἐσμέν· σὺ μὲν γὰρ

---

[1] § 393, *b*. [2] Supply ὁδὸν

ἐφ' ἵππου ἐλαύνεις, ἐγὼ δὲ χαλεπῶς πονῶ τὴν ἀσπίδα φέρων. ὁ δὲ ἀκούσᾱς ταῦτα κατα-πηδήσᾱς ἀπὸ τοῦ ἵππου ὠθεῖται (*pushes*) αὐτὸν ἐκ τῆς τάξεως καὶ τὴν ἀσπίδα ἀφ-ελόμενος ὡς ἐδύνατο τάχιστα ἔχων ἐπορεύετο· ἐτύγχανε δὲ καὶ θώρᾱκα ἔχων τὸν ἱππικόν· ὥστε ἐπιέζετο (*was burdened*). καὶ τοῖς μὲν ἔμ-προσθεν (ἐν + πρόσθεν) σπεύδειν παρεκελεύετο, τοῖς δὲ ὄπισθεν παρ-ιέναι, μόλις (*with difficulty*) ἑπόμενος. οἱ δ' ἄλλοι στρατιῶται παίουσι καὶ βάλλουσι καὶ λοιδοροῦσι (*taunt*) Σωτηρίδᾱν μέχρι ἠνάγκασαν αὐτὸν λαβόντα τὴν ἀσπίδα πορεύεσθαι. ὁ δὲ ἀνα-βάς, ἕως μὲν οἷόν τ' ἦν, ἐπὶ τοῦ ἵππου ἦγεν, ἐπεὶ δὲ οὐκέτι οἷόν τ' ἦν, κατα-λιπὼν τὸν ἵππον ἔσπευδε πεζῇ. καὶ φθάνουσιν ἐπὶ τῷ ἄκρῳ γενόμενοι τοὺς πολεμίους.

Xenophon, *Anabasis*, III. 4. 45–49.

472. **EXERCISE**

Write in Greek:

1. A certain infantryman came away secretly. 2. While arming themselves they learned that their commander was wounded. 3. Although few had perished, the general was perplexed. 4. Already the wounded happen to be many. 5. He stopped drinking when his friends appeared.

LESSON LXXV

SUMMARY OF INFINITIVE FORMS AND USES

οὐκ ἔστι Πειθοῦς ἱερὸν ἄλλο πλὴν λόγος.
There is no shrine of Persuasion save only speech.[1]

---

473. Forms of the Infinitive. Review all infinitive forms (§ 545, *e*). Note that the stem is that of the corresponding tense of the indicative, and that the clues to most infinitives and their tenses are:

-ειν (present, future, or second aorist active);
-σαι or *stem liquid* + **αι** (first aorist active);
-έναι (perfect active);[2]
-εσθαι (present or future middle or passive, or second aorist middle);
-ασθαι (first aorist middle);
-σθαι *without connecting vowel* and *with accents on penult* (perfect middle or passive);
-ῆναι (aorist passive).

474. Uses of the Infinitive. Having clearly in mind the clues that indicate an infinitive, review the possible uses of the infinitive (§ 545, *e*). Note that in some of its uses the infinitive is a *noun*, in others a *verb*, in still others it *merges noun and verb* functions. Fix clearly the difference in meaning conveyed by the tenses, especially the present and aorist, both in indirect discourse and elsewhere (§ 546, *a* and *c*).

---

[1] Euripides, *Antigone*. Quoted by Aristophanes, *Frogs*, 1391.
[2] Also present active of τίθημι and ἵημι.

475. **VOCABULARY**

βασίλειος, -α, -ον: *royal*; τὰ βασίλεια: *palace*. BASILICA.

κύκλος, -ου, ὁ: *circle*. CYCLE.

λόγχη, -ης, ἡ: *spear point, spear*.

λόφος, -ου, ὁ: *hill, crest, plume*.

ὄρθιος, -ā, -ον: *straight up and down, steep*. Cf. **ὀρθός**.

πελταστής, -οῦ, ὁ: *peltast*, a light-armed soldier.

ὠνέομαι, ὠνήσομαι, ἐπριάμην: *buy*.

κύκλος Μυκηναῖος

This grave circle is on the acropolis of Mycenæ. Within it were discovered the graves of seventeen lords of the city and a sufficient wealth of treasure to justify the Homeric epithet "golden."

476. **EXERCISES**

(*a*) Translate:

1. τοὺς δὲ ἐναντίους ἐπειρῶντο φθάνειν τὰ ἅρματα ζεύξαντες. 2. καὶ ὑμεῖς αἴτιοι ἔσεσθε τοῦ τὰ βασίλεια διαρπάζειν. 3. ἀλλ' οὐκ ἔσται τὸν λόφον κτᾶσθαι, ἐὰν μὴ πελταστὰς περὶ τὸ ἄκρον κύκλῳ ἱστῆτε. 4. καὶ ὅσᾱς ἔλαβον κώμᾱς πάσᾱς ηὕρισκον μεστὰς οὔσᾱς σίτου καὶ οἴνου,

ὥστε μὴ δεῖν τὰ ἐπιτήδεια ὠνεῖσθαι. 5. *πρὶν μέντοι εἰς τὴν μάχην ἰέναι, πάντες οἱ Πέρσαι ὁπλίζονται θώρᾱξι καὶ ἀσπίσι καὶ λόγχαις.* 6. *ὁ δὲ λόφος κύκλῳ ἐστὶ πάνυ ὄρθιος, ὥστε οὐκ ἔστι τοῖς ἵπποις χρῆσθαι.* 7. *ἐκέλευσε γὰρ τοὺς Ἕλληνας θέσθαι τὰ ὅπλα.* 8. *τότε δὴ πρὶν πορευθῆναι πλέον ἢ τρεῖς παρασάγγᾱς, τοὺς ἱππέᾱς ἦν ὁρᾶν.* 9. *βέλτιστον εἶναι ἔφασαν τὰς λόγχᾱς ῥῖψαι εἰς τὸν λιμένα.*

(*b*) Write in Greek:

1. His opponents prevent him from reaching the palace. 2. The captain will order the peltasts to keep throwing their javelins. 3. The hill was full of men before the Greeks began to attack. 4. No one is so wise that he knows everything. 5. Would that the hill were not so steep.

477. "HEADS, I WIN; TAILS, YOU LOSE"

τί οὖν κελεύω ποιῆσαι; νῦν δεῖται Κῦρος ἕπεσθαι τοὺς Ἕλληνας ἐπὶ βασιλέᾱ· ἐγὼ οὖν φημι ὑμᾶς χρῆναι δια-βῆναι τὸν Εὐφράτην ποταμὸν πρὶν δῆλον εἶναι ὅ τι οἱ ἄλλοι Ἕλληνες ἀπο-κρῑνοῦνται Κύρῳ. ἢν μὲν γὰρ αὐτοῖς δόξῃ ἕπεσθαι, ὑμεῖς δόξετε αἴτιοι εἶναι ἄρξαντες τοῦ δια-βαίνειν, ἢν δὲ μὴ ταῦτα ἕλωνται οἱ ἄλλοι, ἄπ-ιμεν μὲν ἅπαντες πάλιν καὶ οὗτινος ἂν δέησθε οἶδα ὅτι ὡς φίλοι τεύξεσθε Κύρου.

Xenophon, *Anabasis*, I. 4. 14–15.

478. THE MARRIAGE MARKET

κατὰ κώμᾱς ἑκάστᾱς ἅπαξ τοῦ ἔτους ἑκάστου ἐποιεῖτο τάδε· ὅσαι παρθένοι (*maidens*) *γίγνοιντο γάμων* (compare POLYGAMY) *ὡραῖαι* (*ripe*), *ταύτᾱς πάσᾱς εἰς ἓν χωρίον εἰσ-ῆγον, πέριξ* (*around*) *δὲ αὐτὰς ἵσταντο πολλοὶ ἄνδρες. ἀν-ιστὰς δὲ κατὰ μίαν ἑκάστην κῆρυξ ἐπώλει, πρῶτα μὲν καλλίστην ἐκ πᾱσῶν, μετὰ* (adverb) *δέ, ὅτε αὕτη εὑροῦσα πολὺ χρῡσίον* πραθείη[1], ἄλλην ἀν-εκήρυσσε (compare **κῆρυξ**) ἣ μετ' ἐκείνην ἦν καλλίστη. ὅσοι μὲν δὴ ἦσαν εὐδαίμονες τῶν Βαβυλωνίων ἐπί-γαμοι (*marriageable*), οὗτοι ὑπερ-βάλλοντες ἀλλήλους ἐξ-ωνοῦντο τὰς καλλίστᾱς· ὅσοι δὲ τοῦ δήμου (*common people*) ἦσαν ἐπί-γαμοι, οὗτοι χρήματά τε καὶ αἰσχίονας παρθένους ἐλάμβανον. ὡς γὰρ δὴ δι-εξ-έλθοι ὁ κῆρυξ πωλῶν τὰς καλλίστᾱς τῶν παρθένων, ἀν-ίστη τὴν ἀ-μορφεστάτην (compare AMORPHOUS) ἢ ἔμπηρόν (*cripple*) τινα, καὶ ταύτην ἀν-εκήρυσσε· ὅσ-τις δ' ἐθέλοι ἐλάχιστον χρῡσίον λαβὼν συν-οικεῖν αὐτῇ, τούτῳ προσ-έκειτο ἡ παρθένος· τὸ δὲ χρῡσίον ἐγίγνετο ἀπὸ τῶν καλῶν παρθένων, καὶ οὕτω αἱ εὔ-μορφοι τὰς ἀ-μόρφους καὶ ἐμπήρους ἐξ-εδίδοσαν· ἐκ-δοῦναι δὲ τὴν ἑαυτοῦ θυγατέρα (*daughter*) ᾧ τινι βούλοιτο ἕκαστος οὐκ ἐξ-ῆν. Herodotus, I. 196.

THE PNYX

From the speaker's stand seen in this picture, Pericles, Demosthenes, and other great statesmen addressed the Athenians on matters of public policy.

[1] Used as aorist passive of πωλέω.

LESSON LXXVI

SUMMARY OF SUBJUNCTIVE FORMS AND USES

ἃ δ' ἂν μάθῃ παῖς, ταῦτα σῴζεσθαι φιλεῖ πρὸς γῆρας.
What you learn as a boy, you will likely keep to old age.[1]

479. Forms of the Subjunctive. Review all subjunctive forms. Note that the stem is that of the corresponding tense of the indicative and that **ω** or **η** occurs in all its forms (except in *-αω* and *-οω* verbs).

480. Uses of the Subjunctive. Having clearly in mind the clues that indicate a subjunctive, review the possible uses of the subjunctive (§ 545, *b*). The subjunctive is essentially *hortatory* or *jussive*, and from these ideas almost all its uses are derived. Note the implication of vividness suggested by the subjunctive in a purpose clause or a clause of fear after a past tense. Fix clearly the difference in meaning conveyed by the present and aorist tenses (§ 546, *a* and *c*).

481. VOCABULARY

ἀθρόος, -ᾱ, -ον: *together, in a body.* Cf. **ἀθροίζω.**

ἀπο-στερέω, -στερήσω, -εστέρησα, -εστέρηκα, -εστέρημαι, -εστερήθην: *deprive, withhold.*

θόρυβος, -ου, ὁ: *noise, din, outcry.*

κᾱ́ω (καίω), καύσω, ἔκαυσα, κέκαυκα, κέκαυμαι, ἐκαύθην: *burn.* CAUSTIC.

πολιορκέω, πολιορκήσω, ἐπολιόρκησα, πεπολιόρκηκα, πεπολιόρκημαι, ἐπολιορκήθην: *besiege.* Cf. **πόλις.**

τῑμωρέω, τῑμωρήσω, ἐτῑμώρησα, τετῑμώρηκα, τετῑμώρημαι, ἐτῑμωρήθην: *avenge;* mid., *exact vengeance, punish.*

[1] Euripides, *Supplices*, 916–917.

482. **EXERCISES**

(*a*) Translate:

1. *καύσωμεν οὖν τὰς ἁμάξᾱς καὶ τὰ ἐπιτήδεια, ὅσων ἂν μὴ δεώμεθα.* 2. *μὴ ἀπο-στερήσῃς ἡμᾶς φίλους ὄντας τὴν ἡμετέρᾱν ἐλευθερίᾱν.* 3. *ἀθρόοι ἴωμεν ὄρθιοι ἐπὶ τοὺς πελταστᾱ́ς;* 4. *φοβοῦνται ἄρα μὴ πολιορκηθῇ ἡ ἑαυτῶν πόλις.* 5. *ἐὰν δὲ θόρυβον ἱστῆτε, παρ-όντας ὑμᾶς πεύσονται.* 6. *ὅστις ἂν ἑκὼν* Κῦρον *κακῶς ποιῇ, τῑμωρεῖσθαι πειρᾶται.* 7. *ἐὰν δὲ πρὸς ὕδωρ ἢ σῖτον ἀφ-ικνεῖσθαι βούληται, ὡς τάχιστα πορεύεται.* 8. *ταῦτα τοίνυν λέγω, ἵνα μὴ ἀναγκασθῆτε τὸν ἄνδρα τὸ λοιπὸν φυλάττειν.* 9. *μὴ νομίσητε ἐμὲ στρατηγεῖν, ἐὰν μὴ ὑμεῖς* Κύρῳ *ἕπεσθαι ἐθέλητε.*

(*b*) Write in Greek:

1. Let us no longer besiege the city, if the commander does not give us our pay. 2. They (always) punish whoever speaks ill of Cyrus. 3. The women fear that there may be some noise. 4. The friends of the dead men will burn the village in order to exact vengeance. 5. What am I to say to the queen?

483. **A FRIEND IN NEED**

φίλη Πειθοῖ, *παρ-οῦσα σύμμαχος*
πόει (*ποίει*) *κατ-ορθοῦν* (*to prosper*) *τοὺς λόγους, οὓς ἂν λέγω.*

Menander, fragment.

484. **THE BEAM THAT IS IN THINE OWN EYE**

ὅταν τι μέλλῃς τὸν πέλας (*neighbor*) *κακ-ηγορεῖν* (*malign*),
αὐτὸς τὰ σαυτοῦ πρῶτον ἐπι-σκέπτου κακά.

Menander, fragment.

κατάλογος ἐφήβων

This monument records the athletic and literary victories of two ephebic companies or clubs for a single year. It gives the names of the members, their officers, and the events for which each was "crowned."

485. THE OATH OF THE EPHEBI[1]

οὐ κατ-αισχυνῶ (*disgrace*) *ὅπλα τὰ ἱερά, οὐδὲ ἐγ-κατα-λείψω τὸν παρα-στάτην* (compare **ἵστημι**), *ὅτῳ ἂν στοιχήσω* (*stand beside in battle*), *ἀμυνῶ* (*defend*) *δὲ καὶ ὑπὲρ ἱερῶν, καὶ ὑπὲρ ὁσίων* (*holy places*), *καὶ μόνος καὶ μετὰ πολλῶν, τὴν πατρίδα δὲ οὐκ ἐλάσσω παρα-δώσω, πλείω δὲ καὶ ἀρείω*[2] *ὅσην ἂν παρα-δέξωμαι. καὶ εὐ-ηκοήσω* (*obey*) *τῶν ἀεὶ κρῑ-νόντων καὶ τοῖς θεσμοῖς* (*laws*) *τοῖς ἱδρῡμένοις* (*established*) *πείσομαι καὶ οὕστινας ἂν ἄλλους τὸ πλῆθος*[3] *ἱδρῡ́σηται· καὶ ἐάν τις ἀν-αιρῇ* (*annul*) *τοὺς θεσμούς, ἢ μὴ πείθηται, οὐκ ἐπι-τρέψω* (*allow*), *ἀμυνῶ δὲ καὶ μόνος καὶ μετὰ πάντων· καὶ ἱερὰ τὰ πάτρια* (*the religion of my fathers*) *τῑμήσω· Ἵστορες* (*witnesses*) *θεοὶ τούτων.*

Stobæus, *Florilegium*, 43, 48.

486. THE FORGIVING SPIRIT

ἐὰν ἁμάρτῃ ὁ ἀδελφός σου, ἐπι-τίμησον (*rebuke*) *αὐτῷ. καὶ ἐὰν μετα-νοήσῃ* (*repent*), *ἄφ-ες αὐτῷ· καὶ ἐὰν ἑπτά-κις τῆς ἡμέρᾱς ἁμαρτήσῃ εἰς σὲ καὶ ἑπτά-κις ἐπι-στρέψῃ πρὸς σὲ λέγων, Μετα-νοῶ, ἀφ-ήσεις αὐτῷ.*

St. Luke, XVII. 3–4.

487. Word-formation. Prepare a list of Greek derivatives used in some special field of interest, such as botany, zoölogy, politics, philosophy, religion, literature. Consult standard works in the particular field to discover the words. Study their formation in an unabridged English dictionary.

---

[1] This oath was taken by every Athenian lad of eighteen years, probably at the close of his first year of military training, when the State presented him with shield and spear.

[2] Comparative of ἀγαθός.

[3] *Commons* or *commonwealth*.

LESSON LXXVII

SUMMARY OF OPTATIVE FORMS AND USES

δεινὸν δ' ἐστὶν ἡ μὴ 'μπειρίᾱ. — *A fearful thing is inexperience.*[1]

488. Forms of the Optative. Review all optative forms. Note that the stem is that of the corresponding tense of the indicative and that ι occurs in all its forms.

489. Uses of the Optative. Having clearly in mind the clues that indicate an optative, review the possible uses of the optative (§ 545, *c*). The optative is essentially a *mood of futurity*, expressing a *wish in the future* or a *contingent future action*, and from these ideas almost all its uses are derived. Fix clearly the difference in meaning conveyed by the present and aorist tenses, both in indirect discourse and not in indirect discourse (§ 546, *a* and *c*).

490. **VOCABULARY**

βλάπτω, βλάψω, ἔβλαψα, βέβλαφα, βέβλαμμαι, ἐβλάφθην, ἐβλάβην: *harm, hinder.*

ἔμ-πειρος, -ον: *acquainted with.* Cf. **πειράομαι.** EMPIRICISM.

ἐν-θῡμέομαι, -θῡμήσομαι, -τεθῡ́μημαι, -εθῡμήθην: *have in mind, consider, reflect.*

ἴδιος, -ᾱ, -ον: *private, peculiar.* IDIOM, IDIOSYNCRASY.

πλέθρον, -ου, τό: *plethron* (100 ft.).

σημαίνω, σημανῶ, ἐσήμηνα, σεσήμασμαι, ἐσημάνθην: *give a signal, signify, betoken.* SEMANTIC, SEMAPHORE.

491. **EXERCISES**

(*a*) Translate:

1. ἀλλ' εἴ τις αὐτὸν βλάπτοι, ἐτῑμωρεῖτο. 2. τότε δὴ ἠρώτησεν εἰ δέοι τοὺς ἐμπείρους φθάνειν ὠνουμένους τὰ ἐπι-

[1] Aristophanes, *Ecclesiazusæ*, 115.

τήδεια. 3. τίς ἂν ταῦτα ἐνθῡμούμενος ἔτι ἐκείνῳ ὀρθῶς πείθοιτο; 4. εἰ γὰρ ἡμῖν δοίη ἡγεμόνα πιστόν. 5. εἰ τὸ τοῦ ποταμοῦ εὖρος τριῶν ἢ τεττάρων πλέθρων εἴη, δέοι ἂν πλοίοις χρῆσθαι. 6. ὅστις δὲ τοῖς ἰδίοις μὴ καλῶς χρήσαιτο, πῶς ἂν οὗτος οὐ βλάψειε τὰ ἑτέρου; 7. ἐδεδοίκεμεν δὲ μὴ ἐκεῖνος περὶ τοῦ στρατεύματος βασιλεῖ σημήνειεν. 8. εἶπεν οὖν ὅτι οἱ φυγάδες εἰς τὸ ἴδιον κατα-θεῖντο αὑτοῖς τὰ χρήματα.

(*b*) Write in Greek:

1. May no one harm the children. 2. Clearchus said (εἶπε) that the sacrifices were favorable. 3. Who might deprive us of our freedom? 4. In order to stop the noise, he gave the signal to march. 5. If you should consider these things (well), you would not burn the city.

492. DURING THE TERROR

δια-λαβόντες δὲ τὰς οἰκίᾱς ἔβαινον. καὶ ἐμὲ μὲν ξένους ἑστιῶντα (*feasting*) κατ-έλαβον, οὓς ἐξ-ελάσαντες Πείσωνί με παρα-διδόᾱσιν· οἱ δ' ἄλλοι εἰς τὸ ἐργαστήριον (compare **ἔργον**) ἐλθόντες τὰ ἀνδράποδα (*slaves*) εἷλον. ἐγὼ δὲ Πείσωνα μὲν ἠρώτων εἰ βούλοιτό με σῶσαι χρήματα λαβών. ὁ δ' ἔφη, εἰ πολλὰ εἴη. εἶπον οὖν ὅτι τάλαντον ἀργυρίου ἐθέλοιμι δοῦναι. ὁ δ' ὡμολόγησε ταῦτα ποιήσειν. ἐγὼ δ' εἰσ-ελθὼν εἰς τὸ δωμάτιον (*bedroom*) τὴν κῑβωτὸν (*chest*) ἀν-οίγνῡμι (*open up*)· Πείσων δ' αἰσθόμενος εἰσ-έρχεται, καὶ ἰδὼν τὰ ἐν-όντα καλεῖ τῶν ὑπ-ηρετῶν (*servants*) δύο καὶ τὰ ἐν τῇ κῑβωτῷ λαβεῖν ἐκέλευσεν. ἐπεὶ δὲ τρία τάλαντα εἶχεν ἀργυρίου καὶ ἄλλα πολλά, ἐδεόμην αὐτοῦ ἐφ-όδιά (= τὰ ἐπὶ τὴν ὁδόν) μοι δοῦναι. ὁ δ' εὐ-τυχήσειν (compare **τυγχάνω**) μ' ἔφη, εἰ τὸ σῶμα σώσω. ἔμ-πειρος μὲν οὖν ὢν ἐτύγχανον τῆς οἰκίᾱς καὶ ᾔδη ὅτι ἀμφί-θυρος εἴη· ἐδόκει οὖν ταύτῃ πειρᾶσθαι σωθῆναι· ἐν-εθῡμούμην γὰρ ὅτι ἐὰν μὲν λάθω, σωθήσομαι, ἐὰν δὲ ληφθῶ, ὁμοίως ἀπο-θανοῦμαι. ὥστε ἔφευγον, ἐκείνων ἐπὶ τῇ αὐλείῳ (*courtyard*, that is, *street*) θύρᾳ τὴν φυλακὴν ποιουμένων· τριῶν δὲ θυρῶν οὐσῶν, ἃς ἔδει με δι-ελθεῖν, ἅπᾱσαι ἀν-εῳγμέναι ἔτυχον.

Adapted from Lysias, *Eratosthenes*, 8–16.

Βουλευτήριον

This attractive little Senate House recently unearthed at Messene reminds us that the ancient Greeks preferred sunshine to stuffy halls.

493. Word-formation. Nouns in **-τηριον** denote place: βουλή *senate*, βουλευτής *senator*, βουλευτήριον *senate house*; ἔργον *work*, ἐργαστής *workman*, ἐργαστήριον *workshop*: κοιμάω *put to sleep*, κοιμητήριον *sleeping place*, CEMETERY.

Ὅμηρος

LESSON LXXVIII

SUMMARY OF IMPERATIVE FORMS AND USES

θεῖος Ὅμηρος. — *Divine Homer.*[1]

494. Forms of the Imperative. Review all imperative forms. Note that the stem is that of the corresponding tense of the indicative, and that some of the clues are: **-ε** (stem being without augment), **-θι** (or **-τι**), **-τω**, **-σθω**, **-ντων**, **-σθων**.

495. Uses of the Imperative. Having clearly in mind the clues that indicate an imperative, review the possible uses of the imperative (§ 545, *d*). The imperative expresses a *command* or a *prohibition.* Note, however, that instead of an aorist imperative to express prohibition usually the aorist subjunctive is used. Fix clearly the difference in meaning conveyed by the present and aorist tenses (§ 546, *a* and *c*).

[1] Aristophanes, *Frogs*, 1034.

496. VOCABULARY

βασιλείᾱ, -ᾱς, ἡ: *kingdom.*[1] Cf. **βασίλειος.**

κοινός, -ή, -όν: *common.*

νόμος, -ου, ὁ: *usage, law.* Cf. **νομίζω.** DEUTERONOMY.

οἴομαι, οἰήσομαι, ᾠήθην: *think, suppose.*

παρα-βαίνω; *transgress.* Cf. Lat. *transgredior.*

πούς, ποδός, ὁ: *foot, leg.* OCTOPUS.

ὑπο-ζύγιον, -ου, τό: *beast of burden.* Cf. **ζεύγνῡμι.**

497. EXERCISES

(*a*) Translate:

1. ἀλλ' ὅστις ἂν τοὺς νόμους παρα-βαίνῃ, τὴν δίκην δότω. 2. τὰ ὑπο-ζύγια τοίνυν εἰς τὸ στρατόπεδον ἄγετε, μὴ χαλεπὸν γένηται αὐτὰ λαβεῖν. 3. μήδ' οἴου με στρατηγὸν ἂν γενέσθαι, εἰ μὴ πάντες ἄλλοι ἐτρώθησαν. 4. ὦ ἄνδρες στρατιῶται, τὰ ὅπλα λαβόντες περὶ τὴν ἐμὴν σκηνὴν κύκλῳ θέσθε. 5. μὴ αἰτιάσησθε τοὺς πελταστὰς ὅτι οὐκ ἐν τάξει μένοντες τοὺς πολεμίους ἐδέχοντο. 6. πάντα τὰ κοινὰ εἰς πλοῖα θῶμεν καὶ ἀπο-πλέωμεν. 7. τὸν αὐτὸν ὅρκον καὶ ὑμεῖς ὄμνυτε. 8. ὁπλίζου οὖν ὡς τάχιστα καὶ ἴθι εἰς τὸ πρόσθεν.

(*b*) Write in Greek:

1. Do not be supposing that he is going willingly. 2. Let us proceed in a circle until we see them signal. 3. Do not transgress the law. 4. Give them as many beasts of burden as they want. 5. Let them put their common belongings (*things*) into the ship.

498. THE LORD'S PRAYER

The New Testament was written in a dialect called the **κοινή** or "*vulgar*," that is, "*common.*" This dialect was the result of changes which Greek underwent after the

[1] Do not confuse with τὰ βασίλεια *palace*, or ἡ βασίλεια *queen.*

conquests of Alexander had made it the international language. When we reflect that four hundred years had elapsed between the close of the "classic" age and the writing of the New Testament, the wonder is that the changes were not more numerous.

The passage here printed is so familiar in English that to supply a translation seems unnecessary. See how much you can understand without turning to the general vocabulary.

Οὕτως οὖν προσ-εύχεσθε ὑμεῖς
Πάτερ ἡμῶν ὁ ἐν τοῖς οὐρανοῖς·
Ἁγιασθήτω τὸ ὄνομά σου,
ἐλθάτω ἡ βασιλείᾱ σου,
γενηθήτω τὸ θέλημά σου,
ὡς ἐν οὐρανῷ καὶ ἐπὶ γῆς·
Τὸν ἄρτον ἡμῶν τὸν ἐπιούσιον
δὸς ἡμῖν σήμερον.
καὶ ἄφ-ες ἡμῖν τὰ ὀφειλήματα ἡμῶν,
ὡς καὶ ἡμεῖς ἀφ-ήκαμεν τοῖς ὀφειλέταις ἡμῶν·
καὶ μὴ εἰσ-ενέγκῃς ἡμᾶς εἰς πειρασμόν,
ἀλλὰ ῥῦσαι ἡμᾶς ἀπὸ τοῦ πονηροῦ.

St. Matthew, VI. 9–12.

Identify all imperatives and imperatival expressions in this passage.

499. FATHER AND SON

Homer's Iliad is the world's first and greatest epic. It tells the events of a few days in the tenth year of a war waged by Greeks around the walls of Troy. But more than that, it is an epic of human life.

One of the unforgettable scenes, true to the life of all

ages, is the parting of Hector, chief warrior of the Trojans, from his wife and child. A detail of the scene follows.

At first the child shrinks back with a shriek, being frightened by his father's gorgeous helmet. With a laugh Hector removes the helmet and the child comes to him.

. . . ὅ γ' ὃν (= τὸν) φίλον υἱὸν ἐπεὶ κύσε (*kissed*) πῆλέ (*tossed*) τε χερσίν,
εἶπεν ἐπ-ευξάμενος Διί τ' ἄλλοισίν τε θεοῖσιν (θεοῖς)·
Ζεῦ ἄλλοι τε θεοί, δότε δὴ καὶ τόνδε γενέσθαι
παῖδ' ἐμόν, ὡς καὶ ἐγώ περ, ἀριπρεπέα (*eminent*) Τρώεσσιν,

THE PARTING OF HECTOR AND ANDROMACHE

ὧδε βίην (βίᾱν) τ' ἀγαθὸν καὶ Ἰλίου ἶφι (*mightily*) ἀνάσσειν.
καί ποτέ τις εἴποι, πατρός γ' ὅδε πολλὸν (πολὺ) ἀμείνων,
ἐκ πολέμου ἀν-ιόντα· φέροι δ' ἔναρα (*spoils*) βροτόεντα
κτείνᾱς δήιον (*foe-*) ἄνδρα, χαρείη (*be glad*) δὲ φρένα [1] (*heart*) μήτηρ.

Homer, *Iliad*, VI. 474–481.

[1] Page 144, note 2.

500. The Iliad has had an incalculable influence on the literature of the world. It has been read in the schools by boys of all nations from the earliest days of Greece to the present time. Greek poets quoted it, Latin poets borrowed from it, most modern poets have attempted to translate it. Keats bears eloquent testimony to his own feelings:

ON FIRST LOOKING INTO CHAPMAN'S HOMER

Much have I travell'd in the realms of gold,
And many goodly states and kingdoms seen;
Round many western islands have I been
Which bards in fealty to Apollo hold.
Oft of one wide expanse had I been told
That deep-brow'd Homer ruled as his demesne:
Yet did I never breathe its pure serene
Till I heard Chapman speak out loud and bold:
Then felt I like some watcher of the skies
When a new planet swims into his ken;
Or like stout Cortez when with eagle eyes
He star'd at the Pacific — and all his men
Look'd at each other with a wild surmise —
Silent, upon a peak in Darien.

LESSON LXXIX

SUMMARY OF INDICATIVE FORMS AND USES

Ζεῦς σωτὴρ καὶ νίκη. — *Zeus, saviour, and Victory.*[1]

501. Forms of the Indicative. Review all indicative forms. Unless an indication of some other mood occurs,

Ewing Galloway.

THE TEMPLE OF THE WINGLESS VICTORY

it is well to assume that the form is indicative. Context may suggest at once that the indicative is the only possible mood. Augment, except where used instead of reduplica-

[1] Xenophon, *Anabasis*, I. 8. 16. This was the watch-word of the Greeks at the battle of Cunaxa.

tion, suggests a past tense of the indicative. A simple **ο** or **ε** before the personal ending is usually (not always) another clue to an indicative.

502. Uses of the Indicative. Having clearly in mind the forms of the indicative, review its possible uses (§ 545, *a*). The indicative essentially *declares a fact*, asks a question that anticipates such a declaration, or conveys an exclamation. Variation of use in main and subordinate clauses must be learned. Note the implication of an indicative in indirect discourse after past tenses. Fix clearly the difference in meaning conveyed by the tenses, especially the present, imperfect, and aorist (§ 546).

503. VOCABULARY

κάθημαι, pres. and imperf.[1] only: *sit down, be seated.* CATHEDRAL.

ὅσ-περ, ἥ-περ, ὅ-περ, intensive form of ὅς, ἥ, ὅ. Cf. **ὥσ-περ.**

πίμπλημι, πλήσω, ἔπλησα, πέπληκα, πέπλημαι or πέπλησμαι, ἐπλήσθην: *fill,* with G. of the thing. Cf. **πλή-ρης, πλῆ-θος.**

πλευρᾱ́, -ᾶς, ἡ: *rib, side.* PLEURISY.

σπένδομαι, ἐσπεισάμην, ἔσπεισμαι: *pour libation for oneself, make a treaty.* Cf. **σπονδαί.**

504. EXERCISES

(*a*) Translate:

1. τότε δὴ ἀθρόοι ἐκαθήμεθα θαυμάζοντες ὅτι σίτου οὔπω ἔπλησαν τὸ πλοῖον. 2. κατα-στὰς εἰς τὴν βασιλείᾱν πρὸς τοὺς ἐναντίους ἐσπείσατο. 3. ἐπεὶ οὖν συν-εβουλεύετό μοι, τοῦ μάντεως ἠμέλησα. 4. ἀλλ' εἰ μὴ ἔπλησαν ὁπλῑτῶν πᾶσαν τὴν ὁδόν, οὐκ ἂν ἐσπεισάμεθα. 5. εἰ γὰρ οἱ Ἕλληνες μὴ ἐπίστευσαν τῷ βαρβάρῳ, ὅσπερ αὐτοὺς ἀπ-εστέρησε τῶν χρημάτων. 6. ἡ δὲ μήτηρ, ἥπερ καὶ ἀπ-έλῡσεν αὐτὸν ἀπὸ τῶν κινδῡ́νων, συν-έπρᾱττε ταῦτα.

---

[1] Imperfect, ἐκαθήμην or καθήμην.

7. ἀλλὰ ἐδεδαπάνητο τὰ χρήματα, ὥστε οὐκ ἐδύνατο ὠνεῖσθαι τὰ ὑποζύγια. 8. ἐπι-μελησόμεθα τοίνυν ὅπως ὡς ἄριστα ἀπο-θανούμεθα.

(*b*) Write in Greek:

1. Who is seeing to it that the citizens choose a good ruler? 2. If he had not given the signal to start, I should still be seated. 3. Cyrus paid (them) with the result that the Greeks were again willing to follow him. 4. He did not cease doing wrong until he himself had suffered many ills. 5. Would that the people of the village had filled the boat with food.

505. LEARNING IS BUT RECOLLECTION

One of Plato's most famous doctrines is that of ἀνά-μνησις *recollection*. The soul in its previous existence in the spirit world knows all things perfectly. At birth, it loses that perfect knowledge and only recovers it by dint of effort.

Καὶ μήν, ἔφη ὁ Κέβης, ὦ Σώκρατες, εἰ ἀληθής ἐστιν ὁ λόγος ὃν σὺ λέγεις, ὅτι ἡμῖν ἡ μάθησις οὐκ ἄλλο τι ἢ ἀνάμνησις τυγχάνει οὖσα, ἀνάγκη που ἡμᾶς ἐν προτέρῳ τινὶ χρόνῳ μεμαθηκέναι ἃ νῦν ἀνα-μιμνῃσκόμεθα. τοῦτο δὲ ἀδύνατον, εἰ μὴ ἦν που ἡμῶν ἡ ψῡχὴ πρὶν ἐν τῷδε τῷ ἀνθρωπίνῳ σώματι γενέσθαι· ὥστε οὕτως ἀθάνατόν τι δοκεῖ ἡ ψῡχὴ εἶναι. Ἀλλ', ὦ Κέβης, ἔφη ὁ Σιμμίᾱς, ποῖαι τούτων αἱ ἀπο-δείξεις (compare **ἀπο-δείκνῡμι**); ὑπό-μνησόν με· οὐ γὰρ πάνυ ἐν τῷ παρ-όντι μέμνημαι. Ἑνὶ μὲν λόγῳ, ἔφη ὁ Κέβης, καλλίστῳ, ὅτι ἐρωτώμενοι οἱ ἄνθρωποι, ἐᾱ́ν τις καλῶς ἐρωτᾷ, αὐτοὶ λέγουσι πάντα ὅπως ἔχει· καίτοι εἰ μὴ ἐτύγχανεν αὐτοῖς ἐπιστήμη (*knowledge*) ἐν-οῦσα καὶ ὀρθὸς λόγος, οὐκ ἂν οἷοί τ' ἦσαν τοῦτο ποιῆσαι.

Adapted from Plato, *Phædo*, XVIII. 72E–73A.

Compare these lines from Wordsworth's Ode, *Intimations of Immortality:*

> Our birth is but a sleep and a forgetting:
> The Soul that rises with us, our life's star,
> Hath had elsewhere its setting,
> And cometh from afar:
> Not in entire forgetfulness,
> And not in utter nakedness,
> But trailing clouds of glory do we come
> From God, who is our home.

506. **WHAT IS TRUTH?**

ἡ περὶ τῆς ἀληθείᾱς (compare **ἀληθής**) *θεωρίᾱ* (*inquiry*) *τῇ μὲν χαλεπὴ τῇ δὲ ῥᾳδίᾱ· σημεῖον* (compare **σημαίνω**) *δὲ τὸ μήτε ἀξίως μηδένα δύνασθαι τυχεῖν αὐτῆς μήτε πάντως ἀπο-τυγχάνειν ἀλλὰ ἕκαστον λέγειν τι περὶ τῆς φύσεως, ἐκ πάντων δὲ συν-αθροιζομένων γίγνεσθαί τι μέγεθος* (compare **μέγας**). Aristotle, *Metaphysics*, 993. A. 30. (Carved on the façade of the National Academy of Sciences, Washington, D. C.)

Courtesy National Academy of Sciences.

SEEKERS OF THE TRUTH

THE ENTRANCE TO THE STADIUM AT OLYMPIA.

GRAMMATICAL APPENDIX

NOUNS

507. A-Declension

(*a*) Feminines

S. N. V.	στρατιᾱ́	χώρᾱ	σκηνή	κώμη	μάχη	γέφῡρα	ἅμαξα
G.	στρατιᾶς	χώρᾱς	σκηνῆς	κώμης	μάχης	γεφῡ́ρᾱς	ἁμάξης
D.	στρατιᾷ	χώρᾳ	σκηνῇ	κώμῃ	μάχῃ	γεφῡ́ρᾳ	ἁμάξῃ
A.	στρατιᾱ́ν	χώρᾱν	σκηνήν	κώμην	μάχην	γέφῡραν	ἅμαξαν
D. N. A. V.	στρατιᾱ́	χώρᾱ	σκηνᾱ́	κώμᾱ	μάχᾱ	γεφῡ́ρᾱ	ἁμάξᾱ
G. D.[1]	στρατιαῖν	χώραιν	σκηναῖν	κώμαιν	μάχαιν	γεφῡ́ραιν	ἁμάξαιν
P. N. V.	στρατιαί	χῶραι	σκηναί	κῶμαι	μάχαι	γέφῡραι	ἅμαξαι
G.	στρατιῶν	χωρῶν	σκηνῶν	κωμῶν	μαχῶν	γεφῡρῶν	ἁμαξῶν
D.	στρατιαῖς	χώραις	σκηναῖς	κώμαις	μάχαις	γεφῡ́ραις	ἁμάξαις
A.	στρατιᾱ́ς	χώρᾱς	σκηνᾱ́ς	κώμᾱς	μάχᾱς	γεφῡ́ρᾱς	ἁμάξᾱς

(*b*) Masculines

S. N.	Ξενίᾱς	στρατιώτης	πελταστής
G.	Ξενίου	στρατιώτου	πελταστοῦ
D.	Ξενίᾳ	στρατιώτῃ	πελταστῇ
A.	Ξενίᾱν	στρατιώτην	πελταστήν
V.	Ξενίᾱ	στρατιῶτα	πελταστά
D. N. A. V.		στρατιώτᾱ	πελταστᾱ́
G. D.		στρατιώταιν	πελτασταῖν
P. N. V.		στρατιῶται	πελτασταί
G.		στρατιωτῶν	πελταστῶν
D.		στρατιώταις	πελτασταῖς
A.		στρατιώτᾱς	πελταστᾱ́ς

[1] In the *dual*, but two forms occur, the one serving as either nominative, accusative, or vocative, the other as either genitive or dative. The dual number is generally restricted in usage to two persons or things that form a natural pair. It is uncommon except in epic poetry.

(c) Contract Nouns

S. N.	(γέᾱ)	γῆ, ἡ	(Ἑρμέᾱς)	Ἑρμῆς, ὁ
G.	(γέᾱς)	γῆς	(Ἑρμέου)	Ἑρμοῦ
D.	(γέᾳ)	γῇ	(Ἑρμέᾳ)	Ἑρμῇ
A.	(γέᾱν)	γῆν	(Ἑρμέᾱν)	Ἑρμῆν
V.	(γέᾱ)	γῆ	(Ἑρμέᾱ)	Ἑρμῆ
D. N. A. V.			(Ἑρμέᾱ)	Ἑρμᾶ
G. D.			(Ἑρμέαιν)	Ἑρμαῖν
P. N. V.			(Ἑρμέαι)	Ἑρμαῖ
G.			(Ἑρμεῶν)	Ἑρμῶν
D.			(Ἑρμέαις)	Ἑρμαῖς
A.			(Ἑρμέᾱς)	Ἑρμᾶς

508. O-DECLENSION

(a) Masculines

S. N.	ποταμός	φίλος	ἄνθρωπος	οἶνος
G.	ποταμοῦ	φίλου	ἀνθρώπου	οἴνου
D.	ποταμῷ	φίλῳ	ἀνθρώπῳ	οἴνῳ
A.	ποταμόν	φίλον	ἄνθρωπον	οἶνον
V.	ποταμέ	φίλε	ἄνθρωπε	οἶνε
D. N. A. V.	ποταμώ	φίλω	ἀνθρώπω	οἴνω
G. D.	ποταμοῖν	φίλοιν	ἀνθρώποιν	οἴνοιν
P. N. V	ποταμοί	φίλοι	ἄνθρωποι	οἶνοι
G.	ποταμῶν	φίλων	ἀνθρώπων	οἴνων
D.	ποταμοῖς	φίλοις	ἀνθρώποις	οἴνοις
A.	ποταμούς	φίλους	ἀνθρώπους	οἴνους

(b) Neuters

(c) Contract Noun

S. N.	παλτόν	πεδίον	δῶρον	(νόος)	νοῦς, ὁ
G.	παλτοῦ	πεδίου	δώρου	(νόου)	νοῦ
D.	παλτῷ	πεδίῳ	δώρῳ	(νόῳ)	νῷ
A.	παλτόν	πεδίον	δῶρον	(νόον)	νοῦν
V.	παλτόν	πεδίον	δῶρον	(νόε)	νοῦ
D. N. A. V.	παλτώ	πεδίω	δώρω	(νόω)	νώ
G. D.	παλτοῖν	πεδίοιν	δώροιν	(νόοιν)	νοῖν
P. N. V.	παλτά	πεδία	δῶρα	(νόοι)	νοῖ
G.	παλτῶν	πεδίων	δώρων	(νόων)	νῶν
D.	παλτοῖς	πεδίοις	δώροις	(νόοις)	νοῖς
A.	παλτά	πεδία	δῶρα	(νόους)	νοῦς

509. Consonant Declension

(a) Π-mute and K-mute Stems

S. N. V.	κλώψ, ὁ	κῆρυξ, ὁ	φάλαγξ, ἡ	Θρᾷξ, ὁ
G.	κλωπός	κήρῡκος	φάλαγγος	Θρᾳκός
D.	κλωπί	κήρῡκι	φάλαγγι	Θρᾳκί
A.	κλῶπα	κήρῡκα	φάλαγγα	Θρᾷκα
D. N. A. V.	κλῶπε	κήρῡκε	φάλαγγε	Θρᾷκε
G. D.	κλωποῖν	κηρῡ́κοιν	φαλάγγοιν	Θρᾳκοῖν
P. N. V.	κλῶπες	κήρῡκες	φάλαγγες	Θρᾷκες
G.	κλωπῶν	κηρῡ́κων	φαλάγγων	Θρᾳκῶν
D.	κλωψί	κήρυξι	φάλαγξι	Θρᾳξί
A.	κλῶπας	κήρῡκας	φάλαγγας	Θρᾷκας

(b) T-mute Stems

S. N. V.	ἀσπίς, ἡ	χάρις, ἡ	πούς, ὁ	νύξ, ἡ	ἄρχων, ὁ	ἅρμα, τό
G.	ἀσπίδος	χάριτος	ποδός	νυκτός	ἄρχοντος	ἅρματος
D.	ἀσπίδι	χάριτι	ποδί	νυκτί	ἄρχοντι	ἅρματι
A.	ἀσπίδα	χάριν	πόδα	νύκτα	ἄρχοντα	ἅρμα
D. N. A. V.	ἀσπίδε	χάριτε	πόδε	νύκτε	ἄρχοντε	ἅρματε
G. D.	ἀσπίδοιν	χαρίτοιν	ποδοῖν	νυκτοῖν	ἀρχόντοιν	ἁρμάτοιν
P. N. V.	ἀσπίδες	χάριτες	πόδες	νύκτες	ἄρχοντες	ἅρματα
G.	ἀσπίδων	χαρίτων	ποδῶν	νυκτῶν	ἀρχόντων	ἁρμάτων
D.	ἀσπίσι	χάρισι	ποσί	νυξί	ἄρχουσι	ἅρμασι
A.	ἀσπίδας	χάριτας	πόδας	νύκτας	ἄρχοντας	ἅρματα

(c) Liquid Stems

S. N.	ἀγών, ὁ	ἡγεμών, ὁ	Ἕλλην, ὁ	ῥήτωρ, ὁ
G.	ἀγῶνος	ἡγεμόνος	Ἕλληνος	ῥήτορος
D.	ἀγῶνι	ἡγεμόνι	Ἕλληνι	ῥήτορι
A.	ἀγῶνα	ἡγεμόνα	Ἕλληνα	ῥήτορα
V.	ἀγών	ἡγεμών	Ἕλλην	ῥῆτορ
D. N. A. V.	ἀγῶνε	ἡγεμόνε	Ἕλληνε	ῥήτορε
G. D.	ἀγώνοιν	ἡγεμόνοιν	Ἑλλήνοιν	ῥητόροιν
P. N. V.	ἀγῶνες	ἡγεμόνες	Ἕλληνες	ῥήτορες
G.	ἀγώνων	ἡγεμόνων	Ἑλλήνων	ῥητόρων
D.	ἀγῶσι	ἡγεμόσι	Ἕλλησι	ῥήτορσι
A.	ἀγῶνας	ἡγεμόνας	Ἕλληνας	ῥήτορας

(*d*) Syncopated Liquid Stems

S. N.		πατήρ, ὁ		μήτηρ, ἡ		ἀνήρ, ὁ
G.	(πατέρ-ος)	πατρός	(μητέρ-ος)	μητρός	(ἀνέρ-ος)	ἀνδρός
D.	(πατέρ-ι)	πατρί	(μητέρ-ι)	μητρί	(ἀνέρ-ι)	ἀνδρί
A.		πατέρα		μητέρα	(ἀνέρ-α)	ἄνδρα
V.		πάτερ		μῆτερ		ἄνερ
D. N. A. V.		πατέρε		μητέρε	(ἀνέρ-ε)	ἄνδρε
G. D.		πατέροιν		μητέροιν	(ἀνέρ-οιν)	ἀνδροῖν
P. N. V.		πατέρες		μητέρες	(ἀνέρ-ες)	ἄνδρες
G.		πατέρων		μητέρων	(ἀνέρ-ων)	ἀνδρῶν
D.		πατράσι		μητράσι		ἀνδράσι
A.		πατέρας		μητέρας	(ἀνέρ-ας)	ἄνδρας

(*e*) Stems in σ

S. N.		γένος, τό		τριήρης, ἡ			κέρας, τό
G.	(γένεος)	γένους	(τριήρε-ος)	τριήρους	κέρᾱτος	(κέραος)	κέρως
D.	(γένεϊ)	γένει	(τριήρε-ϊ)	τριήρει	κέρᾱτι	(κέραϊ)	κέραι
A.		γένος	(τριήρε-α)	τριήρη			κέρας
V.		γένος		τριῆρες			κέρας
D. N. A. V.	(γένεε)	γένει	(τριήρε-ε)	τριήρει	κέρᾱτε	(κέραε)	κέρᾱ
G. D.	(γενέοιν)	γενοῖν	(τριηρέ-οιν)	τριήροιν	κερᾱ́τοιν	(κεράοιν)	κερῷν
P. N. V.	(γένεα)	γένη	(τριήρε-ες)	τριήρεις	κέρᾱτα	(κέραα)	κέρᾱ
G.	γενέων	γενῶν	(τριηρέ-ων)	τριήρων	κερᾱ́των	(κεράων)	κερῶν
D.		γένεσι		τριήρεσι			κέρᾱσι
A.	(γένεα)	γένη		τριήρεις	κέρᾱτα	(κέραα)	κέρᾱ

(*f*) Stems in ι and υ

S. N.		πόλις, ἡ		ἄστυ, τό	ἰχθῦς, ὁ
G.		πόλεως		ἄστεως	ἰχθύος
D.	(πόλε-ϊ)	πόλει	(ἄστε-ϊ)	ἄστει	ἰχθύϊ
A.		πόλιν		ἄστυ	ἰχθῦν
V.		πόλι		ἄστυ	ἰχθῦ
D. N. A. V.	(πόλε-ε)	πόλει	(ἄστε-ε)	ἄστει	ἰχθύε
G. D.		πολέοιν		ἀστέοιν	ἰχθύοιν
P. N. V.	(πόλε-ες)	πόλεις	(ἄστε-α)	ἄστη	ἰχθύες
G.		πόλεων		ἄστεων	ἰχθύων
D.		πόλεσι		ἄστεσι	ἰχθύσι
A.		πόλεις	(ἄστε-α)	ἄστη	ἰχθῦς

(*g*) Stems in a Diphthong

S. N.	βασιλεύς, ὁ	βοῦς, ὁ or ἡ	ναῦς, ἡ
G.	βασιλέως	βοός	νεώς
D.	βασιλεῖ	βοΐ	νηΐ
A.	βασιλέᾱ	βοῦν	ναῦν
V.	βασιλεῦ	βοῦ	ναῦ
D. N. A. V.	βασιλῆ	βόε	νῆε
G. D.	βασιλέοιν	βοοῖν	νεοῖν
P. N. V.	(βασιλέ-ες) βασιλεῖς	βόες	νῆες
G.	βασιλέων	βοῶν	νεῶν
D.	βασιλεῦσι	βουσί	ναυσί
A.	βασιλέᾱς	βοῦς	ναῦς

GODS FROM THE PARTHENON

This slab occupies a central place in the famous Parthenon frieze. The three deities, Poseidon, Apollo, and Artemis, seem to be watching the approach of the procession that is the motive of the frieze.

ADJECTIVES

510. A- and O-Declension

(a) Three Endings

	M.	F.	N.	M.	F.	N.
S. N.	ἀγαθός	ἀγαθή	ἀγαθόν	ἄξιος	ἀξίᾱ	ἄξιον
G.	ἀγαθοῦ	ἀγαθῆς	ἀγαθοῦ	ἀξίου	ἀξίᾱς	ἀξίου
D.	ἀγαθῷ	ἀγαθῇ	ἀγαθῷ	ἀξίῳ	ἀξίᾳ	ἀξίῳ
A.	ἀγαθόν	ἀγαθήν	ἀγαθόν	ἄξιον	ἀξίᾱν	ἄξιον
V.	ἀγαθέ	ἀγαθή	ἀγαθόν	ἄξιε	ἀξίᾱ	ἄξιον
D. N. A. V.	ἀγαθώ	ἀγαθᾱ́	ἀγαθώ	ἀξίω	ἀξίᾱ	ἀξίω
G. D.	ἀγαθοῖν	ἀγαθαῖν	ἀγαθοῖν	ἀξίοιν	ἀξίαιν	ἀξίοιν
P. N. V.	ἀγαθοί	ἀγαθαί	ἀγαθά	ἄξιοι	ἄξιαι	ἄξια
G.	ἀγαθῶν	ἀγαθῶν	ἀγαθῶν	ἀξίων	ἀξίων	ἀξίων
D.	ἀγαθοῖς	ἀγαθαῖς	ἀγαθοῖς	ἀξίοις	ἀξίαις	ἀξίοις
A.	ἀγαθούς	ἀγαθᾱ́ς	ἀγαθά	ἀξίους	ἀξίᾱς	ἄξια

	M.	F.	N.	M.	F.	N.
S. N.	μῑκρός	μῑκρᾱ́	μῑκρόν	δῆλος	δήλη	δῆλον
G.	μῑκροῦ	μῑκρᾶς	μῑκροῦ	δήλου	δήλης	δήλου
		κ.τ.λ.			κ.τ.λ.	
P. N. V.	μῑκροί	μῑκραί	μῑκρά	δῆλοι	δῆλαι	δῆλα
G.	μῑκρῶν	μῑκρῶν	μῑκρῶν	δήλων	δήλων	δήλων
		κ.τ.λ.			κ.τ.λ.	

(*b*) Two Endings

	M. AND F.	N.
S. N.	ἀδιάβατος	ἀδιάβατον
G.	ἀδιαβάτου	ἀδιαβάτου
D.	ἀδιαβάτῳ	ἀδιαβάτῳ
A.	ἀδιάβατον	ἀδιάβατον
V.	ἀδιάβατε	ἀδιάβατον
D. N. A. V.	ἀδιαβάτω	ἀδιαβάτω
G. D.	ἀδιαβάτοιν	ἀδιαβάτοιν
P. N. V.	ἀδιάβατοι	ἀδιάβατα
G.	ἀδιαβάτων	ἀδιαβάτων
D.	ἀδιαβάτοις	ἀδιαβάτοις
A.	ἀδιαβάτους	ἀδιάβατα

(*c*) Contract Adjectives

	M.		F.		N.	
S. N.	(χρύσεος)	χρῡσοῦς	(χρῡσέᾱ)	χρῡσῆ	(χρῡ́σεον)	χρῡσοῦν
G.	(χρῡσέου)	χρῡσοῦ	(χρῡσέᾱς)	χρῡσῆς	(χρῡσέου)	χρῡσοῦ
D.	(χρῡσέῳ)	χρῡσῷ	(χρῡσέᾳ)	χρῡσῇ	(χρῡσέῳ)	χρῡσῷ
A.	(χρῡ́σεον)	χρῡσοῦν	(χρῡσέᾱν)	χρῡσῆν	(χρῡ́σεον)	χρῡσοῦν
D. N. A.	(χρῡσέω)	χρῡσώ	(χρῡσέᾱ)	χρῡσᾶ	(χρῡσέω)	χρῡσώ
G. D.	(χρῡσέοιν)	χρῡσοῖν	(χρῡσέαιν)	χρῡσαῖν	(χρῡσέοιν)	χρῡσοῖν
P. N.	(χρῡ́σεοι)	χρῡσοῖ	(χρῡ́σεαι)	χρῡσαῖ	(χρῡ́σεα)	χρῡσᾶ
G.	(χρῡσέων)	χρῡσῶν	(χρῡσέων)	χρῡσῶν	(χρῡσέων)	χρῡσῶν
D.	(χρῡσέοις)	χρῡσοῖς	(χρῡσέαις)	χρῡσαῖς	(χρῡσέοις)	χρῡσοῖς
A.	(χρῡσέους)	χρῡσοῦς	(χρῡσέᾱς)	χρῡσᾶς	(χρῡ́σεα)	χρῡσᾶ

511. CONSONANT AND A-DECLENSION

	M.	F.	N.	M.	F.	N.
S. N.	χαρίεις	χαρίεσσα	χαρίεν	πᾶς	πᾶσα	πᾶν
G.	χαρίεντος	χαριέσσης	χαρίεντος	παντός	πάσης	παντός
D.	χαρίεντι	χαριέσσῃ	χαρίεντι	παντί	πάσῃ	παντί
A.	χαρίεντα	χαρίεσσαν	χαρίεν	πάντα	πᾶσαν	πᾶν
V.	χαρίεν	χαρίεσσα	χαρίεν	πᾶν	πᾶσα	πᾶν
D. N. A. V.	χαρίεντε	χαριέσσᾱ	χαρίεντε			
G. D.	χαριέντοιν	χαριέσσαιν	χαριέντοιν			
P. N. V.	χαρίεντες	χαρίεσσαι	χαρίεντα	πάντες	πᾶσαι	πάντα
G.	χαριέντων	χαριεσσῶν	χαριέντων	πάντων	πᾱσῶν	πάντων
D.	χαρίεσι	χαριέσσαις	χαρίεσι	πᾶσι	πάσαις	πᾶσι
A.	χαρίεντας	χαριέσσᾱς	χαρίεντα	πάντας	πάσᾱς	πάντα

	M.	F.	N.	M.	F.	N.
S. N.	ἑκών	ἑκοῦσα	ἑκόν	μέλᾱς	μέλαινα	μέλαν
G.	ἑκόντος	ἑκούσης	ἑκόντος	μέλανος	μελαίνης	μέλανος
D.	ἑκόντι	ἑκούσῃ	ἑκόντι	μέλανι	μελαίνῃ	μέλανι
A.	ἑκόντα	ἑκοῦσαν	ἑκόν	μέλανα	μέλαιναν	μέλαν
V.	ἑκών	ἑκοῦσα	ἑκόν	μέλαν	μέλαινα	μέλαν
D. N. A. V.	ἑκόντε	ἑκούσᾱ	ἑκόντε	μέλανε	μελαίνᾱ	μέλανε
G. D.	ἑκόντοιν	ἑκούσαιν	ἑκόντοιν	μελάνοιν	μελαίναιν	μελάνοιν
P. N. V.	ἑκόντες	ἑκοῦσαι	ἑκόντα	μέλανες	μέλαιναι	μέλανα
G.	ἑκόντων	ἑκουσῶν	ἑκόντων	μελάνων	μελαινῶν	μελάνων
D.	ἑκοῦσι	ἑκούσαις	ἑκοῦσι	μέλασι	μελαίναις	μέλασι
A.	ἑκόντας	ἑκούσᾱς	ἑκόντα	μέλανας	μελαίνᾱς	μέλανα

	M.	F.	N.
S. N.	ταχύς	ταχεῖα	ταχύ
G.	ταχέος	ταχείᾱς	ταχέος
D.	ταχεῖ	ταχείᾳ	ταχεῖ
A.	ταχύν	ταχεῖαν	ταχύ
V.	ταχύ	ταχεῖα	ταχύ
D. N. A. V.	ταχέε	ταχείᾱ	ταχέε
G. D.	ταχέοιν	ταχείαιν	ταχέοιν
P. N. V.	ταχεῖς	ταχεῖαι	ταχέα
G.	ταχέων	ταχειῶν	ταχέων
D.	ταχέσι	ταχείαις	ταχέσι
A.	ταχεῖς	ταχείᾱς	ταχέα

512. CONSONANT DECLENSION

	M. AND F.	N.
S. N.	εὐδαίμων	εὔδαιμον
G.	εὐδαίμονος	εὐδαίμονος
D.	εὐδαίμονι	εὐδαίμονι
A.	εὐδαίμονα	εὔδαιμον
V.	εὔδαιμον	εὔδαιμον
D. N. A. V.	εὐδαίμονε	εὐδαίμονε
G. D.	εὐδαιμόνοιν	εὐδαιμόνοιν
P. N. V.	εὐδαίμονες	εὐδαίμονα
G.	εὐδαιμόνων	εὐδαιμόνων
D.	εὐδαίμοσι	εὐδαίμοσι
A.	εὐδαίμονας	εὐδαίμονα

		M. AND F.		N.
S. N.		ἀληθής		ἀληθές
G.	(ἀληθέ-ος)	ἀληθοῦς	(ἀληθέ-ος)	ἀληθοῦς
D.	(ἀληθέ-ϊ)	ἀληθεῖ	(ἀληθέ-ϊ)	ἀληθεῖ
A.	(ἀληθέ-α)	ἀληθῆ		ἀληθές
V.		ἀληθές		ἀληθές
D. N. A. V.	(ἀληθέ-ε)	ἀληθεῖ	(ἀληθέ-ε)	ἀληθεῖ
G. D.	(ἀληθέ-οιν)	ἀληθοῖν	(ἀληθέ-οιν)	ἀληθοῖν
P. N. V.	(ἀληθέ-ες)	ἀληθεῖς	(ἀληθέ-α)	ἀληθῆ
G.	(ἀληθέ-ων)	ἀληθῶν	(ἀληθέ-ων)	ἀληθῶν
D.		ἀληθέσι		ἀληθέσι
A.		ἀληθεῖς	(ἀληθέ-α)	ἀληθῆ

	M. AND F.	N.
S. N. V.	ἡδίων	ἥδῖον
G.	ἡδίονος	ἡδίονος
D.	ἡδίονι	ἡδίονι
A.	ἡδίονα, ἡδίω	ἥδῖον
D. N. A. V.	ἡδίονε	ἡδίονε
G. D.	ἡδῖόνοιν	ἡδῖόνοιν
P. N. V.	ἡδίονες, ἡδίους	ἡδίονα, ἡδίω
G.	ἡδῖόνων	ἡδῖόνων
D.	ἡδίοσι	ἡδίοσι
A.	ἡδίονας, ἡδίους	ἡδίονα, ἡδίω

513. IRREGULAR DECLENSION

	M.	F.	N.	M.	F.	N.
S. N.	μέγας	μεγάλη	μέγα	πολύς	πολλή	πολύ
G.	μεγάλου	μεγάλης	μεγάλου	πολλοῦ	πολλῆς	πολλοῦ
D.	μεγάλῳ	μεγάλῃ	μεγάλῳ	πολλῷ	πολλῇ	πολλῷ
A.	μέγαν	μεγάλην	μέγα	πολύν	πολλήν	πολύ
V.	μεγάλε	μεγάλη	μέγα			
D. N. A. V.	μεγάλω	μεγάλᾱ	μεγάλω			
G. D.	μεγάλοιν	μεγάλαιν	μεγάλοιν			
P. N. V.	μεγάλοι	μεγάλαι	μεγάλα	πολλοί	πολλαί	πολλά
G.	μεγάλων	μεγάλων	μεγάλων	πολλῶν	πολλῶν	πολλῶν
D.	μεγάλοις	μεγάλαις	μεγάλοις	πολλοῖς	πολλαῖς	πολλοῖς
A.	μεγάλους	μεγάλᾱς	μεγάλα	πολλούς	πολλᾱ́ς	πολλά

THE WALLS OF TIRYNS

The great size of the stones with which Tiryns and Mycenae were fortified may explain the story that it was the work of the Cyclopes, a race of giants.

514. PARTICIPLES

(*a*) PRESENT OF εἰμί AND 2 AORIST OF λείπω

	M.	F.	N.
S. N. V.	ὤν	οὖσα	ὄν
G.	ὄντος	οὔσης	ὄντος
D.	ὄντι	οὔσῃ	ὄντι
A.	ὄντα	οὖσαν	ὄν
D. N. A. V.	ὄντε	οὔσᾱ	ὄντε
G. D.	ὄντοιν	οὔσαιν	ὄντοιν
P. N. V.	ὄντες	οὖσαι	ὄντα
G.	ὄντων	οὐσῶν	ὄντων
D.	οὖσι	οὔσαις	οὖσι
A.	ὄντας	οὔσᾱς	ὄντα

Second aorist active participles are declined like ὤν:

S. N. V.	λιπών	λιποῦσα	λιπόν
G.	λιπόντος	λιπούσης	λιπόντος
		κ.τ.λ.	

(*b*) PRESENT AND FUTURE OF παύω

S. N. V.	παύων	παύουσα	παῦον
G.	παύοντος	παυούσης	παύοντος
D.	παύοντι	παυούσῃ	παύοντι
A.	παύοντα	παύουσαν	παῦον
D. N. A. V.	παύοντε	παυούσᾱ	παύοντε
G. D.	παυόντοιν	παυούσαιν	παυόντοιν
P. N. V.	παύοντες	παύουσαι	παύοντα
G.	παυόντων	παυουσῶν	παυόντων
D.	παύουσι	παυούσαις	παύουσι
A.	παύοντας	παυούσᾱς	παύοντα

Future active participles are declined like παύων:

S. N. V.	παύσων	παύσουσα	παῦσον
G.	παύσοντος	παυσούσης	παύσοντος
		κ.τ.λ.	

Participles (*continued*)

(*c*) Aorist Active of *παύω*

	M.	F.	N.
S. N. V.	παύσᾱς	παύσᾱσα	παῦσαν
G.	παύσαντος	παυσᾱ́σης	παύσαντος
D.	παύσαντι	παυσᾱ́σῃ	παύσαντι
A.	παύσαντα	παύσᾱσαν	παῦσαν
D. N. A. V.	παύσαντε	παυσᾱ́σᾱ	παύσαντε
G. D.	παυσάντοιν	παυσᾱ́σαιν	παυσάντοιν
P. N. V.	παύσαντες	παύσᾱσαι	παύσαντα
G.	παυσάντων	παυσᾱσῶν	παυσάντων
D.	παύσᾱσι	παυσᾱ́σαις	παύσᾱσι
A.	παύσαντας	παυσᾱ́σᾱς	παύσαντα

(*d*) Perfect Active of *παύω*

	M.	F.	N.
S. N. V.	πεπαυκώς	πεπαυκυῖα	πεπαυκός
G.	πεπαυκότος	πεπαυκυίᾱς	πεπαυκότος
D.	πεπαυκότι	πεπαυκυίᾳ	πεπαυκότι
A.	πεπαυκότα	πεπαυκυῖαν	πεπαυκός
D. N. A. V.	πεπαυκότε	πεπαυκυίᾱ	πεπαυκότε
G. D.	πεπαυκότοιν	πεπαυκυίαιν	πεπαυκότοιν
P. N. V.	πεπαυκότες	πεπαυκυῖαι	πεπαυκότα
G.	πεπαυκότων	πεπαυκυιῶν	πεπαυκότων
D.	πεπαυκόσι	πεπαυκυίαις	πεπαυκόσι
A.	πεπαυκότας	πεπαυκυίᾱς	πεπαυκότα

(*e*) Aorist Passive of *παύω*

	M.	F.	N.
S. N. V.	παυθείς [1]	παυθεῖσα	παυθέν
G.	παυθέντος	παυθείσης	παυθέντος
D.	παυθέντι	παυθείσῃ	παυθέντι
A.	παυθέντα	παυθεῖσαν	παυθέν
D. N. A. V.	παυθέντε	παυθείσᾱ	παυθέντε
G. D.	παυθέντοιν	παυθείσαιν	παυθέντοιν
P. N. V.	παυθέντες	παυθεῖσαι	παυθέντα
G.	παυθέντων	παυθεισῶν	παυθέντων
D.	παυθεῖσι	παυθείσαις	παυθεῖσι
A.	παυθέντας	παυθείσᾱς	παυθέντα

[1] *τιθείς* is declined like *παυθείς*.

PARTICIPLES (*continued*)

(*f*) PRESENT ACTIVE OF MI-VERBS

ἵστημι

	M.	F.	N.
S. N. V.	ἱστᾱ́ς	ἱστᾶσα	ἱστάν
G.	ἱστάντος	ἱστᾱ́σης	ἱστάντος
D.	ἱστάντι	ἱστᾱ́σῃ	ἱστάντι
A.	ἱστάντα	ἱστᾶσαν	ἱστάν
D. N. A. V.	ἱστάντε	ἱστᾱ́σᾱ	ἱστάντε
G. D.	ἱστάντοιν	ἱστᾱ́σαιν	ἱστάντοιν
P. N. V.	ἱστάντες	ἱστᾶσαι	ἱστάντα
G.	ἱστάντων	ἱστᾱσῶν	ἱστάντων
D.	ἱστᾶσι	ἱστᾱ́σαις	ἱστᾶσι
A.	ἱστάντας	ἱστᾱ́σᾱς	ἱστάντα

δείκνῡμι

	M.	F.	N.
S. N. V.	δεικνῡ́ς	δεικνῦσα	δεικνύν
G.	δεικνύντος	δεικνῡ́σης	δεικνύντος
D.	δεικνύντι	δεικνῡ́σῃ	δεικνύντι
A.	δεικνύντα	δεικνῦσαν	δεικνύν
D. N. A. V.	δεικνύντε	δεικνῡ́σᾱ	δεικνύντε
G. D.	δεικνύντοιν	δεικνῡ́σαιν	δεικνύντοιν
P. N. V.	δεικνύντες	δεικνῦσαι	δεικνύντα
G.	δεικνύντων	δεικνῡσῶν	δεικνύντων
D.	δεικνῦσι	δεικνῡ́σαις	δεικνῦσι
A.	δεικνύντας	δεικνῡ́σᾱς	δεικνύντα

δίδωμι

	M.	F.	N.
S. N. V.	διδούς	διδοῦσα	διδόν
G.	διδόντος	διδούσης	διδόντος
D.	διδόντι	διδούσῃ	διδόντι
A.	διδόντα	διδοῦσαν	διδόν
D. N. A. V.	διδόντε	διδούσᾱ	διδόντε
G. D.	διδόντοιν	διδούσαιν	διδόντοιν
P. N. V.	διδόντες	διδοῦσαι	διδόντα
G.	διδόντων	διδουσῶν	διδόντων
D.	διδοῦσι	διδούσαις	διδοῦσι
A.	διδόντας	διδούσᾱς	διδόντα

Participles (*continued*)

(*g*) Present Active of Contract Verbs

τῑμάω

	M.	F.	N.
S. N. V.	**τῑμῶν** (τῑμάων)	**τῑμῶσα** (τῑμάουσα)	**τῑμῶν** (τῑμάον)
G.	**τῑμῶντος** (τῑμάοντος)	**τῑμώσης** (τῑμαούσης)	**τῑμῶντος** (τῑμάοντος)
D.	**τῑμῶντι** (τῑμάοντι)	**τῑμώσῃ** (τῑμαούσῃ)	**τῑμῶντι** (τῑμάοντι)
A.	**τῑμῶντα** (τῑμάοντα)	**τῑμῶσαν** (τῑμάουσαν)	**τῑμῶν** (τῑμάον)
D. N. A. V.	**τῑμῶντε** (τῑμάοντε)	**τῑμώσᾱ** (τῑμαούσᾱ)	**τῑμῶντε** (τῑμάοντε)
G. D.	**τῑμώντοιν** (τῑμαόντοιν)	**τῑμώσαιν** (τῑμαούσαιν)	**τῑμώντοιν** (τιμαόντοιν)
P. N. V.	**τῑμῶντες** (τῑμάοντες)	**τῑμῶσαι** (τῑμάουσαι)	**τῑμῶντα** (τῑμάοντα)
G.	**τῑμώντων** (τῑμαόντων)	**τῑμωσῶν** (τῑμαουσῶν)	**τῑμώντων** (τῑμαόντων)
D.	**τῑμῶσι** (τῑμάουσι)	**τῑμώσαις** (τῑμαούσαις)	**τῑμῶσι** (τῑμάουσι)
A.	**τῑμῶντας** (τῑμάοντας)	**τῑμώσᾱς** (τῑμαούσᾱς)	**τῑμῶντα** (τῑμάοντα)

φιλέω

	M.	F.	N.
S. N. V.	**φιλῶν** (φιλέων)	**φιλοῦσα** (φιλέουσα)	**φιλοῦν** (φιλέον)
G.	**φιλοῦντος** (φιλέοντος)	**φιλούσης** (φιλεούσης)	**φιλοῦντος** (φιλέοντος)
D.	**φιλοῦντι** (φιλέοντι)	**φιλούσῃ** (φιλεούσῃ)	**φιλοῦντι** (φιλέοντι)
A.	**φιλοῦντα** (φιλέοντα)	**φιλοῦσαν** (φιλέουσαν)	**φιλοῦν** (φιλέον)
D. N. A. V.	**φιλοῦντε** (φιλέοντε)	**φιλούσᾱ** (φιλεούσᾱ)	**φιλοῦντε** (φιλέοντε)
G. D.	**φιλούντοιν** (φιλεόντοιν)	**φιλούσαιν** (φιλεούσαιν)	**φιλούντοιν** (φιλεόντοιν)

φιλέω (*continued*)

	M.	F.	N.
P. N. V.	**φιλοῦντες**	**φιλοῦσαι**	**φιλοῦντα**
	(φιλέοντες)	(φιλέουσαι)	(φιλέοντα)
G.	**φιλούντων**	**φιλουσῶν**	**φιλούντων**
	(φιλεόντων)	(φιλεουσῶν)	(φιλεόντων)
D.	**φιλοῦσι**	**φιλούσαις**	**φιλοῦσι**
	(φιλέουσι)	(φιλεούσαις)	(φιλέουσι)
A.	**φιλοῦντας**	**φιλούσᾱς**	**φιλοῦντα**
	(φιλέοντας)	(φιλεούσᾱς)	(φιλέοντα)

Present participles of verbs in -όω are declined like **φιλῶν**:

S. N. V.	**δηλῶν**	**δηλοῦσα**	**δηλοῦν**
G.	**δηλοῦντος**	**δηλούσης**	**δηλοῦντος**
		κ.τ λ.	

THE GENNADEION

This library, belonging to the American School of Classical Studies at Athens, shows marked influence of classic Greek architecture.

515. NUMERALS

	Cardinal	Ordinal	Adverb
1	εἷς, μία, ἕν *one*	πρῶτος, -η, -ον *first*	ἅπαξ *once*
2	δύο *two*	δεύτερος, -ᾱ, -ον *second*	δίς *twice*
3	τρεῖς, τρία	τρίτος	τρίς
4	τέτταρες, τέτταρα	τέταρτος	τετράκις
5	πέντε	πέμπτος	πεντάκις
6	ἕξ	ἕκτος	ἑξάκις
7	ἑπτά	ἕβδομος	ἑπτάκις
8	ὀκτώ	ὄγδοος	ὀκτάκις
9	ἐννέα	ἔνατος	ἐνάκις
10	δέκα	δέκατος	δεκάκις
11	ἕνδεκα	ἑνδέκατος	ἑνδεκάκις
12	δώδεκα	δωδέκατος	δωδεκάκις
13	τρεῖς καὶ δέκα	τρίτος καὶ δέκατος	
14	τέτταρες καὶ δέκα	τέταρτος καὶ δέκατος	
15	πεντεκαίδεκα	πέμπτος καὶ δέκατος	
16	ἑκκαίδεκα	ἕκτος καὶ δέκατος	
17	ἑπτακαίδεκα	ἕβδομος καὶ δέκατος	
18	ὀκτωκαίδεκα	ὄγδοος καὶ δέκατος	
19	ἐννεακαίδεκα	ἔνατος καὶ δέκατος	
20	εἴκοσι	εἰκοστός	εἰκοσάκις
21	εἷς καὶ εἴκοσι, εἴκοσι καὶ εἷς or εἴκοσιν εἷς		
30	τριᾱ́κοντα	τριᾱκοστός	τριᾱκοντάκις
40	τετταράκοντα	τετταρακοστός	τετταρακοντάκις
50	πεντήκοντα	πεντηκοστός	πεντηκοντάκις
60	ἑξήκοντα	ἑξηκοστός	ἑξηκοντάκις
70	ἑβδομήκοντα	ἑβδομηκοστός	ἑβδομηκοντάκις
80	ὀγδοήκοντα	ὀγδοηκοστός	ὀγδοηκοντάκις
90	ἐνενήκοντα	ἐνενηκοστός	ἐνενηκοντάκις
100	ἑκατόν	ἑκατοστός	ἑκατοντάκις

NUMERALS (*continued*)

	CARDINAL	ORDINAL	ADVERB
200	διᾱκόσιοι, -αι, -α	διᾱκοσιοστός	διᾱκοσιάκις
300	τριᾱκόσιοι, -αι, -α	τριᾱκοσιοστός	
400	τετρακόσιοι, -αι, -α	τετρακοσιοστός	
500	πεντακόσιοι, -αι, -α	πεντακοσιοστός	
600	ἑξακόσιοι, -αι, -α	ἑξακοσιοστός	
700	ἑπτακόσιοι, -αι, -α	ἑπτακοσιοστός	
800	ὀκτακόσιοι, -αι, -α	ὀκτακοσιοστός	
900	ἐνακόσιοι, -αι, -α	ἐνακοσιοστός	
1,000	χίλιοι, -αι, -α	χῑλιοστός	χῑλιάκις
2,000	δισχίλιοι, -αι, -α	δισχῑλιοστός	
3,000	τρισχίλιοι, -αι, -α	τρισχῑλιοστός	
10,000	μῡ́ριοι, -αι, -α	μῡριοστός	μῡριάκις
20,000	δισμῡ́ριοι, -αι, -α		
100,000	δεκακισμῡ́ριοι, -αι, -α		

516. DECLENSION OF THE FIRST FOUR CARDINALS

SINGULAR				DUAL		PLURAL			PLURAL	
N.	εἷς	μία	ἕν	N. A.	δύο	N.	τρεῖς	τρία	τέτταρες	τέτταρα
G.	ἑνός	μιᾶς	ἑνός	G. D.	δυοῖν	G.	τριῶν	τριῶν	τεττάρων	τεττάρων
D.	ἑνί	μιᾷ	ἑνί			D.	τρισί	τρισί	τέτταρσι	τέτταρσι
A.	ἕνα	μίαν	ἕν			A.	τρεῖς	τρία	τέτταρας	τέτταρα

517.

	M.	F.	N.
S. N.	οὐδείς	οὐδεμία	οὐδέν
G.	οὐδενός	οὐδεμιᾶς	οὐδενός
D.	οὐδενί	οὐδεμιᾷ	οὐδενί
A.	οὐδένα	οὐδεμίαν	οὐδέν

Masc. pl.: N. οὐδένες, G. οὐδένων, D. οὐδέσι, A. οὐδένας

518. THE DEFINITE ARTICLE

	M.	F.	N.
S. N.	ὁ	ἡ	τό
G.	τοῦ	τῆς	τοῦ
D.	τῷ	τῇ	τῷ
A.	τόν	τήν	τό
D. N. A.	τώ	τώ	τώ
G. D.	τοῖν	τοῖν	τοῖν
P. N.	οἱ	αἱ	τά
G.	τῶν	τῶν	τῶν
D.	τοῖς	ταῖς	τοῖς
A.	τούς	τᾱ́ς	τά

PRONOUNS

519. Personal and Intensive

			M.	F.	N.
S. N.	ἐγώ	σύ	αὐτός	αὐτή	αὐτό
G.	ἐμοῦ, μου	σοῦ	αὐτοῦ	αὐτῆς	αὐτοῦ
D.	ἐμοί, μοι	σοί	αὐτῷ	αὐτῇ	αὐτῷ
A.	ἐμέ, με	σέ	αὐτόν	αὐτήν	αὐτό
D. N. A.	νώ	σφώ	αὐτώ	αὐτᾱ́	αὐτώ
G. D.	νῷν	σφῷν	αὐτοῖν	αὐταῖν	αὐτοῖν
P. N.	ἡμεῖς	ὑμεῖς	αὐτοί	αὐταί	αὐτά
G.	ἡμῶν	ὑμῶν	αὐτῶν	αὐτῶν	αὐτῶν
D.	ἡμῖν	ὑμῖν	αὐτοῖς	αὐταῖς	αὐτοῖς
A.	ἡμᾶς	ὑμᾶς	αὐτούς	αὐτᾱ́ς	αὐτά

520. ἄλλος is inflected like *αὐτός*:

	M.	F.	N.
S. N.	ἄλλος	ἄλλη	ἄλλο
G.	ἄλλου	ἄλλης	ἄλλου
		κ.τ.λ.	
P. N.	ἄλλοι	ἄλλαι	ἄλλα
G.	ἄλλων	ἄλλων	ἄλλων
		κ.τ.λ.	

PRONOUNS (*continued*)

521. REFLEXIVE

		M.	F.
1. S.	G.	ἐμαυτοῦ	ἐμαυτῆς
	D.	ἐμαυτῷ	ἐμαυτῇ
	A.	ἐμαυτόν	ἐμαυτήν
P.	G.	ἡμῶν αὐτῶν	ἡμῶν αὐτῶν
	D.	ἡμῖν αὐτοῖς	ἡμῖν αὐταῖς
	A.	ἡμᾶς αὐτούς	ἡμᾶς αὐτάς
2. S.	G.	σεαυτοῦ [1]	σεαυτῆς
	D.	σεαυτῷ	σεαυτῇ
	A.	σεαυτόν	σεαυτήν
P.	G.	ὑμῶν αὐτῶν	ὑμῶν αὐτῶν
	D.	ὑμῖν αὐτοῖς	ὑμῖν αὐταῖς
	A.	ὑμᾶς αὐτούς	ὑμᾶς αὐτᾱ́ς

		M.	F.	N.
3. S.	G.	ἑαυτοῦ [2]	ἑαυτῆς	ἑαυτοῦ
	D.	ἑαυτῷ	ἑαυτῇ	ἑαυτῷ
	A.	ἑαυτὸν	ἑαυτήν	ἑαυτό
P.	G.	ἑαυτῶν [2]	ἑαυτῶν	ἑαυτῶν
	D.	ἑαυτοῖς	ἑαυταῖς	ἑαυτοῖς
	A.	ἑαυτούς	ἑαυτᾱ́ς	ἑαυτά
		or	or	
P.	G.	σφῶν αὐτῶν	σφῶν αὐτῶν	
	D.	σφίσιν αὐτοῖς	σφίσιν αὐταῖς	
	A.	σφᾶς αὐτούς	σφᾶς αὐτᾱ́ς	

522. RECIPROCAL

		M.	F.	N.
D.	G. D.	ἀλλήλοιν	ἀλλήλαιν	ἀλλήλοιν
	A.	ἀλλήλω	ἀλλήλᾱ	ἀλλήλω
P.	G.	ἀλλήλων	ἀλλήλων	ἀλλήλων
	D.	ἀλλήλοις	ἀλλήλαις	ἀλλήλοις
	A.	ἀλλήλους	ἀλλήλᾱς	ἄλληλα

[1] Or, contracted, σαυτοῦ, σαυτῆς, *etc.*
[2] Or, contracted, αὑτοῦ, αὑτῆς, αὑτοῦ, *etc.*

Pronouns (*continued*)

523. Demonstrative

	M.	F.	N.	M.	F.	N.
S. N.	ὅδε	ἥδε	τόδε	οὗτος	αὕτη	τοῦτο
G.	τοῦδε	τῆσδε	τοῦδε	τούτου	ταύτης	τούτου
D.	τῷδε	τῇδε	τῷδε	τούτῳ	ταύτῃ	τούτῳ
A.	τόνδε	τήνδε	τόδε	τοῦτον	ταύτην	τοῦτο
D. N. A.	τώδε	τώδε	τώδε	τούτω	τούτω	τούτω
G. D.	τοῖνδε	τοῖνδε	τοῖνδε	τούτοιν	τούτοιν	τούτοιν
P. N.	οἵδε	αἵδε	τάδε	οὗτοι	αὗται	ταῦτα
G.	τῶνδε	τῶνδε	τῶνδε	τούτων	τούτων	τούτων
D.	τοῖσδε	ταῖσδε	τοῖσδε	τούτοις	ταύταις	τούτοις
A.	τούσδε	τᾱ́σδε	τάδε	τούτους	ταύτᾱς	ταῦτα

	M.	F.	N.
S. N.	ἐκεῖνος	ἐκείνη	ἐκεῖνο
G.	ἐκείνου	ἐκείνης	ἐκείνου
D.	ἐκείνῳ	ἐκείνῃ	ἐκείνῳ
A.	ἐκεῖνον	ἐκείνην	ἐκεῖνο
D. N. A.	ἐκείνω	ἐκείνω	ἐκείνω
G. D.	ἐκείνοιν	ἐκείνοιν	ἐκείνοιν
P. N.	ἐκεῖνοι	ἐκεῖναι	ἐκεῖνα
G.	ἐκείνων	ἐκείνων	ἐκείνων
D.	ἐκείνοις	ἐκείναις	ἐκείνοις
A.	ἐκείνους	ἐκείνᾱς	ἐκεῖνα

524. Interrogative — Indefinite

	Interrogative M. and F.	N.	Indefinite M. and F.	N.
S. N.	τίς	τί	τις	τι
G.	τίνος, τοῦ	τίνος, τοῦ	τινός, του	τινός, του
D.	τίνι, τῷ	τίνι, τῷ	τινί, τῳ	τινί, τῳ
A.	τίνα	τί	τινά	τι
D. N. A.	τίνε	τίνε	τινέ	τινέ
G. D	τίνοιν	τίνοιν	τινοῖν	τινοῖν
P. N.	τίνες	τίνα	τινές	τινά
G.	τίνων	τίνων	τινῶν	τινῶν
D.	τίσι	τίσι	τισί	τισί
A.	τίνας	τίνα	τινάς	τινά

Pronouns (*continued*)

525. Relative

	M.	F.	N.	M.	F.	N.
S. N.	ὅς	ἥ	ὅ	ὅστις	ἥτις	ὅ τι
G.	οὗ	ἧς	οὗ	οὗτινος, ὅτου	ἧστινος	οὗτινος, ὅτου
D.	ᾧ	ᾗ	ᾧ	ᾧτινι, ὅτῳ	ᾗτινι	ᾧτινι, ὅτῳ
A.	ὅν	ἥν	ὅ	ὅντινα	ἥντινα	ὅ τι
D. N. A.	ὥ	ὥ	ὥ	ὥτινε	ὥτινε	ὥτινε
G. D.	οἷν	οἷν	οἷν	οἷντινοιν	οἷντινοιν	οἷντινοιν
P. N.	οἵ	αἵ	ἅ	οἵτινες	αἵτινες	ἅτινα, ἅττα
G.	ὧν	ὧν	ὧν	ὧντινων, ὅτων	ὧντινων	ὧντινων, ὅτων
D.	οἷς	αἷς	οἷς	οἷστισι, ὅτοις	αἷστισι	οἷστισι, ὅτοις
A.	οὕς	ἅς	ἅ	οὕστινας	ἅστινας	ἅτινα, ἅττα

The Delphic Gymnasium

In the central foreground may be seen the plunge pool shown on page xxviii.

VERBS

Ω-Verbs

526. Active Voice of παύω

		Present	Imperfect	Future
INDICATIVE	S. 1.	παύω	ἔπαυον	παύσω
	2.	παύεις	ἔπαυες	παύσεις
	3.	παύει	ἔπαυε	παύσει
	D. 2.	παύετον	ἐπαύετον	παύσετον
	3.	παύετον	ἐπαυέτην	παύσετον
	P. 1.	παύομεν	ἐπαύομεν	παύσομεν
	2.	παύετε	ἐπαύετε	παύσετε
	3.	παύουσι	ἔπαυον	παύσουσι
SUBJUNCTIVE	S. 1.	παύω		
	2.	παύῃς		
	3.	παύῃ		
	D. 2.	παύητον		
	3.	παύητον		
	P. 1.	παύωμεν		
	2.	παύητε		
	3.	παύωσι		
OPTATIVE	S. 1.	παύοιμι		παύσοιμι
	2.	παύοις		παύσοις
	3.	παύοι		παύσοι
	D. 2.	παύοιτον		παύσοιτον
	3.	παυοίτην		παυσοίτην
	P. 1.	παύοιμεν		παύσοιμεν
	2.	παύοιτε		παύσοιτε
	3.	παύοιεν		παύσοιεν
IMPERATIVE	S. 2.	παῦε		
	3.	παυέτω		
	D. 2.	παύετον		
	3.	παυέτων		
	P. 2.	παύετε		
	3.	παυόντων		
INFINITIVE		παύειν		παύσειν
PARTICIPLE		παύων, παύουσα, παῦον		παύσων, παύσουσα, παῦσον

Active Voice of παύω (continued)

		1 Aorist	*1 Perfect*	*1 Pluperfect*
INDICATIVE	S. 1.	ἔπαυσα	πέπαυκα	ἐπεπαύκη
	2.	ἔπαυσας	πέπαυκας	ἐπεπαύκης
	3.	ἔπαυσε	πέπαυκε	ἐπεπαύκει(ν)
	D. 2.	ἐπαύσατον	πεπαύκατον	ἐπεπαύκετον
	3.	ἐπαυσάτην	πεπαύκατον	ἐπεπαυκέτην
	P. 1.	ἐπαύσαμεν	πεπαύκαμεν	ἐπεπαύκεμεν
	2.	ἐπαύσατε	πεπαύκατε	ἐπεπαύκετε
	3.	ἔπαυσαν	πεπαύκᾱσι	ἐπεπαύκεσαν
SUBJUNCTIVE	S. 1.	παύσω	πεπαύκω	
	2.	παύσῃς	πεπαύκῃς	
	3.	παύσῃ	πεπαύκῃ	
	D. 2.	παύσητον	πεπαύκητον	
	3.	παύσητον	πεπαύκητον	
	P. 1.	παύσωμεν	πεπαύκωμεν	
	2.	παύσητε	πεπαύκητε	
	3.	παύσωσι	πεπαύκωσι	
OPTATIVE	S. 1.	παύσαιμι	πεπαύκοιμι	
	2.	παύσαις, παύσειας	πεπαύκοις	
	3.	παύσαι, παύσειε	πεπαύκοι	
	D. 2.	παύσαιτον	πεπαύκοιτον	
	3.	παυσαίτην	πεπαυκοίτην	
	P. 1.	παύσαιμεν	πεπαύκοιμεν	
	2.	παύσαιτε	πεπαύκοιτε	
	3.	παύσαιεν, παύσειαν	πεπαύκοιεν	
IMPERATIVE	S. 2.	παῦσον		
	3.	παυσάτω		
	D. 2.	παύσατον		
	3.	παυσάτων		
	P. 2.	παύσατε		
	3.	παυσάντων		
INFINITIVE		παῦσαι	πεπαυκέναι	
PARTICIPLE		παύσᾱς, παύσᾱσα, παῦσαν	πεπαυκώς, πεπαυκυῖα, πεπαυκός	

527. Middle Voice of παύω

		Present	*Imperfect*	*Future*
INDICATIVE	S. 1.	παύομαι	ἐπαυόμην	παύσομαι
	2.	παύῃ, παύει	ἐπαύου	παύσῃ, παύσει
	3.	παύεται	ἐπαύετο	παύσεται
	D. 2.	παύεσθον	ἐπαύεσθον	παύσεσθον
	3.	παύεσθον	ἐπαυέσθην	παύσεσθον
	P. 1.	παυόμεθα	ἐπαυόμεθα	παυσόμεθα
	2.	παύεσθε	ἐπαύεσθε	παύσεσθε
	3.	παύονται	ἐπαύοντο	παύσονται
SUBJUNCTIVE	S. 1.	παύωμαι		
	2.	παύῃ		
	3.	παύηται		
	D. 2.	παύησθον		
	3.	παύησθον		
	P. 1.	παυώμεθα		
	2.	παύησθε		
	3.	παύωνται		
OPTATIVE	S. 1.	παυοίμην		παυσοίμην
	2.	παύοιο		παύσοιο
	3.	παύοιτο		παύσοιτο
	D. 2.	παύοισθον		παύσοισθον
	3.	παυοίσθην		παυσοίσθην
	P. 1.	παυοίμεθα		παυσοίμεθα
	2.	παύοισθε		παύσοισθε
	3.	παύοιντο		παύσοιντο
IMPERATIVE	S. 2.	παύου		
	3.	παυέσθω		
	D. 2.	παύεσθον		
	3.	παυέσθων		
	P. 2.	παύεσθε		
	3.	παυέσθων		
INFINITIVE		παύεσθαι		παύσεσθαι
PARTICIPLE		παυόμενος, -η, -ον		παυσόμενος, -η, -ον

Middle Voice of *παύω* (*continued*)

		1 Aorist	Perfect		Pluperfect
INDICATIVE	S. 1.	ἐπαυσάμην	πέπαυμαι		ἐπεπαύμην
	2.	ἐπαύσω	πέπαυσαι		ἐπέπαυσο
	3.	ἐπαύσατο	πέπαυται		ἐπέπαυτο
	D. 2.	ἐπαύσασθον	πέπαυσθον		ἐπέπαυσθον
	3.	ἐπαυσάσθην	πέπαυσθον		ἐπεπαύσθην
	P. 1.	ἐπαυσάμεθα	πεπαύμεθα		ἐπεπαύμεθα
	2.	ἐπαύσασθε	πέπαυσθε		ἐπέπαυσθε
	3.	ἐπαύσαντο	πέπαυνται		ἐπέπαυντο
SUBJUNCTIVE	S. 1.	παύσωμαι	πεπαυμένος	ὦ	
	2.	παύσῃ	"	ᾖς	
	3.	παύσηται	"	ᾖ	
	D. 2.	παύσησθον	πεπαυμένω	ἦτον	
	3.	παύσησθον	"	ἦτον	
	P. 1.	παυσώμεθα	πεπαυμένοι	ὦμεν	
	2.	παύσησθε	"	ἦτε	
	3.	παύσωνται	"	ὦσι	
OPTATIVE	S. 1.	παυσαίμην	πεπαυμένος	εἴην	
	2.	παύσαιο	"	εἴης	
	3.	παύσαιτο	"	εἴη	
	D. 2.	παύσαισθον	πεπαυμένω	εἴητον or εἶτον	
	3.	παυσαίσθην	"	εἰήτην " εἴτην	
	P. 1.	παυσαίμεθα	πεπαυμένοι	εἴημεν " εἶμεν	
	2.	παύσαισθε	"	εἴητε " εἶτε	
	3.	παύσαιντο	"	εἴησαν " εἶεν	
IMPERATIVE	S. 2.	παῦσαι	πέπαυσο		
	3.	παυσάσθω	πεπαύσθω		
	D. 2.	παύσασθον	πέπαυσθον		
	3.	παυσάσθων	πεπαύσθων		
	P. 2.	παύσασθε	πέπαυσθε		
	3.	παυσάσθων	πεπαύσθων		
INFINITIVE		παύσασθαι	πεπαῦσθαι		
PARTICIPLE		παυσάμενος, -η, -ον	πεπαυμένος, -η, -ον		

528. **Passive Voice of παύω**[1]

		Future Perfect	Aorist	Future
INDICATIVE	S. 1.	πεπαύσομαι	ἐπαύθην	παυθήσομαι
	2.	πεπαύσῃ, πεπαύσει	ἐπαύθης	παυθήσῃ, παυθήσει
	3.	πεπαύσεται	ἐπαύθη	παυθήσεται
	D. 2.	πεπαύσεσθον	ἐπαύθητον	παυθήσεσθον
	3.	πεπαύσεσθον	ἐπαυθήτην	παυθήσεσθον
	P. 1.	πεπαυσόμεθα	ἐπαύθημεν	παυθησόμεθα
	2.	πεπαύσεσθε	ἐπαύθητε	παυθήσεσθε
	3.	πεπαύσονται	ἐπαύθησαν	παυθήσονται
SUBJUNCTIVE	S. 1.		παυθῶ	
	2.		παυθῇς	
	3.		παυθῇ	
	D. 2.		παυθῆτον	
	3.		παυθῆτον	
	P. 1.		παυθῶμεν	
	2.		παυθῆτε	
	3.		παυθῶσι	
OPTATIVE	S. 1.	πεπαυσοίμην	παυθείην	παυθησοίμην
	2.	πεπαύσοιο	παυθείης	παυθήσοιο
	3.	πεπαύσοιτο	παυθείη	παυθήσοιτο
	D. 2.	πεπαύσεσθον	παυθείητον or παυθεῖτον	παυθήσοισθον
	3.	πεπαύσεσθον	παυθειήτην " παυθείτην	παυθησοίσθην
	P. 1.	πεπαυσόμεθα	παυθείημεν " παυθεῖμεν	παυθησοίμεθα
	2.	πεπαύσεσθε	παυθείητε " παυθεῖτε	παυθήσοισθε
	3.	πεπαύσονται	παυθείησαν " παυθεῖεν	παυθήσοιντο
IMPERATIVE	S. 2.		παύθητι	
	3.		παυθήτω	
	D. 2.		παύθητον	
	3.		παυθήτων	
	P. 2.		παύθητε	
	3.		παυθέντων	
INFINITIVE		πεπαύσεσθαι	παυθῆναι	παυθήσεσθαι
PARTICIPLE		πεπαυσόμενος, -η, -ον	παυθείς, παυθεῖσα, παυθέν	παυθησόμενος -η, -ον

[1] The forms of *παύω* for the passive voice are the same as for the middle voice in the present, imperfect, perfect, and pluperfect tenses.

529.

		Future System of Liquid Verbs: φαίνω		First Aorist System of Liquid Verbs: φαίνω	
		Active	Middle	Active	Middle
Indicative	s. 1.	φανῶ	φανοῦμαι	ἔφηνα	ἐφηνάμην
	2.	φανεῖς	φανεῖ	ἔφηνας	ἐφήνω
	3.	φανεῖ	φανεῖται	ἔφηνε	ἐφήνατο
	d. 2.	φανεῖτον	φανεῖσθον	ἐφήνατον	ἐφήνασθον
	3.	φανεῖτον	φανεῖσθον	ἐφηνάτην	ἐφηνάσθην
	p. 1.	φανοῦμεν	φανούμεθα	ἐφήναμεν	ἐφηνάμεθα
	2.	φανεῖτε	φανεῖσθε	ἐφήνατε	ἐφήνασθε
	3.	φανοῦσι	φανοῦνται	ἔφηναν	ἐφήναντο
Subjunctive	s. 1.			φήνω	φήνωμαι
	2.			φήνῃς	φήνῃ
	3.			φήνῃ	φήνηται
	d. 2.			φήνητον	φήνησθον
	3.			φήνητον	φήνησθον
	p. 1.			φήνωμεν	φηνώμεθα
	2.			φήνητε	φήνησθε
	3.			φήνωσι	φήνωνται
Optative	s. 1.	φανοίην or φανοῖμι	φανοίμην	φήναιμι	φηναίμην
	2.	φανοίης " φανοῖς	φανοῖο	φήνειας, φήναις	φήναιο
	3.	φανοίη " φανοῖ	φανοῖτο	φήνειε, φήναι	φήναιτο
	d. 2.	φανοῖτον	φανοῖσθον	φήναιτον	φήναισθον
	3.	φανοίτην	φανοίσθην	φηναίτην	φηναίσθην
	p. 1.	φανοῖμεν	φανοίμεθα	φήναιμεν	φηναίμεθα
	2.	φανοῖτε	φανοῖσθε	φήναιτε	φήναισθε
	3.	φανοῖεν	φανοῖντο	φήνειαν, φήναιεν	φήναιντο
Imperative	s. 2.			φῆνον	φῆναι
	3.			φηνάτω	φηνάσθω
	d. 2.			φήνατον	φήνασθον
	3.			φηνάτων	φηνάσθων
	p. 2.			φήνατε	φήνασθε
	3.			φηνάντων	φηνάσθων
Infinitive		φανεῖν	φανεῖσθαι	φῆναι	φήνασθαι
Participle		φανῶν, -οῦσα, -οῦν	φανούμενος, -η, -ον	φήνᾱς, -ᾱσα, -αν	φηνάμενος, -η, -ον

530.

		Second Aorist System of λείπω		Second Perfect System of λείπω	
		Active	Middle	Active	
				2 Perfect	*2 Pluperfect*
Indicative	s. 1.	ἔλιπον	ἐλιπόμην	λέλοιπα	ἐλελοίπη
	2.	ἔλιπες	ἐλίπου	λέλοιπας	ἐλελοίπης
	3.	ἔλιπε	ἐλίπετο	λέλοιπε	ἐλελοίπει
	d. 2.	ἐλίπετον	ἐλίπεσθον	λελοίπατον	ἐλελοίπετον
	3.	ἐλιπέτην	ἐλιπέσθην	λελοίπατον	ἐλελοιπέτην
	p. 1.	ἐλίπομεν	ἐλιπόμεθα	λελοίπαμεν	ἐλελοίπεμεν
	2.	ἐλίπετε	ἐλίπεσθε	λελοίπατε	ἐλελοίπετε
	3.	ἔλιπον	ἐλίποντο	λελοίπᾱσι	ἐλελοίπεσαν
Subjunctive	s. 1.	λίπω	λίπωμαι	λελοίπω	
	2.	λίπῃς	λίπῃ	λελοίπῃς	
	3.	λίπῃ	λίπηται	λελοίπῃ	
	d. 2.	λίπητον	λίπησθον	λελοίπητον	
	3.	λίπητον	λίπησθον	λελοίπητον	
	p. 1.	λίπωμεν	λιπώμεθα	λελοίπωμεν	
	2.	λίπητε	λίπησθε	λελοίπητε	
	3.	λίπωσι	λίπωνται	λελοίπωσι	
Optative	s. 1.	λίποιμι	λιποίμην	λελοίποιμι	
	2.	λίποις	λίποιο	λελοίποις	
	3.	λίποι	λίποιτο	λελοίποι	
	d. 2.	λίποιτον	λίποισθον	λελοίποιτον	
	3.	λιποίτην	λιποίσθην	λελοιποίτην	
	p. 1.	λίποιμεν	λιποίμεθα	λελοίποιμεν	
	2.	λίποιτε	λίποισθε	λελοίποιτε	
	3.	λίποιεν	λίποιντο	λελοίποιεν	
Imperative	s. 2.	λίπε	λιποῦ	[λέλοιπε	
	3.	λιπέτω	λιπέσθω	λελοιπέτω	
	d. 2.	λίπετον	λίπεσθον	λελοίπετον	
	3.	λιπέτων	λιπέσθων	λελοιπέτων	
	p. 2.	λίπετε	λίπεσθε	λελοίπετε	
	3.	λιπόντων	λιπέσθων	λελοιπόντων]	
Infinitive		λιπεῖν	λιπέσθαι	λελοιπέναι	
Participle		λιπών, -οῦσα, -όν	λιπόμενος, -η, -ον	λελοιπώς, -υῖα, -ός	

531. Perfect Middle and Passive System of Mute Verbs

(*a*) Π-mutes: λείπω

Middle and Passive

		Perfect		*Pluperfect*	
INDICATIVE	S. 1.	(λελειπ-μαι)	λέλειμμαι	(ἐ-λελειπ-μην)	ἐλελείμμην
	2.	(λελειπ-σαι)	λέλειψαι	(ἐ-λελειπ-σο)	ἐλέλειψο
	3.	(λελειπ-ται)	λέλειπται	(ἐ-λελειπ-το)	ἐλέλειπτο
	D. 2.	(λελειπ-σθον)	λέλειφθον	(ἐ-λελειπ-σθον)	ἐλέλειφθον
	3.	(λελειπ-σθον)	λέλειφθον	(ἐ-λελειπ-σθην)	ἐλελείφθην
	P. 1.	(λελειπ-μεθα)	λελείμμεθα	(ἐ-λελειπ-μεθα)	ἐλελείμμεθα
	2.	(λελειπ-σθε)	λέλειφθε	(ἐ-λελειπ-σθε)	ἐλέλειφθε
	3.	(λελειπ-μενοι)	λελειμμένοι εἰσί	(λελειπ-μενοι)	λελειμμένοι ἦσαν

			Perfect
SUBJUNCTIVE	S.	(λελειπ-μενος)	λελειμμένος ὦ, *etc.*
	D.	(λελειπ-μενω)	λελειμμένω ἦτον, *etc.*
	P.	(λελειπ-μενοι)	λελειμμένοι ὦμεν, *etc.*
OPTATIVE	S.	(λελειπ-μενος)	λελειμμένος εἴην, *etc.*
	D.	(λελειπ-μενω)	λελειμμένω εἶτον, *etc.*
	P.	(λελειπ-μενοι)	λελειμμένοι εἶμεν, *etc.*
IMPERATIVE	S. 2.	(λελειπ-σο)	λέλειψο
	3.	(λελειπ-σθω)	λελείφθω
	D. 2.	(λελειπ-σθον)	λέλειφθον
	3.	(λελειπ-σθων)	λελείφθων
	P. 2.	(λελειπ-σθε)	λέλειφθε
	3.	(λελειπ-σθων)	λελείφθων
INFINITIVE		(λελειπ-σθαι)	λελεῖφθαι
PARTICIPLE		(λελειπ-μενος)	λελειμμένος, -η, -ον

		Future Perfect
INDICATIVE	(λελειπ-σο-μαι)	λελείψομαι, *etc.*
OPTATIVE	(λελειπ-σοι-μην)	λελειψοίμην, *etc.*
INFINITIVE	(λελειπ-σε-σθαι)	λελείψεσθαι
PARTICIPLE	(λελειπ-σο-μενος)	λελειψόμενος, -η, -ον

		(*b*) **K-mutes: ἄγω**		(*c*) **T-mutes: πείθω**	
		MIDDLE AND PASSIVE		MIDDLE AND PASSIVE	
		Perfect		*Perfect*	
INDICATIVE	S. 1.	(ἠγ-μαι)	**ἦγμαι**	(πεπειθ-μαι)	**πέπεισμαι**
	2.	(ἠγ-σαι)	**ἦξαι**	(πεπειθ-σαι)	**πέπεισαι**
	3.	(ἠγ-ται)	**ἦκται**	(πεπειθ-ται)	**πέπεισται**
	D. 2.	(ἠγ-σθον)	**ἦχθον**	(πεπειθ-σθον)	**πέπεισθον**
	3.	(ἠγ-σθον)	**ἦχθον**	(πεπειθ-σθον)	**πέπεισθον**
	P. 1.	(ἠγ-μεθα)	**ἤγμεθα**	(πεπειθ-μεθα)	**πεπείσμεθα**
	2.	(ἠγ-σθε)	**ἦχθε**	(πεπειθ-σθε)	**πέπεισθε**
	3.	(ἠγ-μενοι)	**ἠγμένοι εἰσί**	(πεπειθ-μενοι)	**πεπεισμένοι εἰσί**
		Pluperfect		*Pluperfect*	
	S. 1.	(ἠγ-μην)	**ἤγμην**	(ἐ-πεπειθ-μην)	**ἐπεπείσμην**
	2.	(ἠγ-σο)	**ἦξο**	(ἐ-πεπειθ-σο)	**ἐπέπεισο**
	3.	(ἠγ-το)	**ἦκτο**	(ἐ-πεπειθ-το)	**ἐπέπειστο**
	D. 2.	(ἠγ-σθον)	**ἦχθον**	(ἐ-πεπειθ-σθον)	**ἐπέπεισθον**
	3.	(ἠγ-σθην)	**ἤχθην**	(ἐ-πεπειθ-σθην)	**ἐπεπείσθην**
	P. 1.	(ἠγ-μεθα)	**ἤγμεθα**	(ἐ-πεπειθ-μεθα)	**ἐπεπείσμεθα**
	2.	(ἠγ-σθε)	**ἦχθε**	(ἐ-πεπειθ-σθε)	**ἐπέπεισθε**
	3.	(ἠγ-μενοι)	**ἠγμένοι ἦσαν**	(ἐ-πεπειθ-μενοι)	**πεπεισμένοι ἦσαν**
		Perfect		*Perfect*	
SUBJUNCTIVE		(ἠγ-μενος)	**ἠγμένος ὦ**, *etc.*	(πεπειθ-μενος)	**πεπεισμένος ὦ**, *etc.*
OPTATIVE		(ἠγ-μενος)	**ἠγμένος εἴην**, *etc.*	(πεπειθ-μενος)	**πεπεισμένος εἴην**, *etc.*
IMPERATIVE	S. 2.	(ἠγ-σο)	**ἦξο**	(πεπειθ-σο)	**πέπεισο**
	3.	(ἠγ-σθω)	**ἤχθω**	(πεπειθ-σθω)	**πεπείσθω**
	D. 2.	(ἠγ-σθον)	**ἦχθον**	(πεπειθ-σθον)	**πέπεισθον**
	3.	(ἠγ-σθων)	**ἤχθων**	(πεπειθ-σθων)	**πεπείσθων**
	P. 2.	(ἠγ-σθε)	**ἦχθε**	(πεπειθ-σθε)	**πέπεισθε**
	3.	(ἠγ-σθων)	**ἤχθων**	(πεπειθ-σθων)	**πεπείσθων**
INFINITIVE		(ἠγ-σθαι)	**ἦχθαι**	(πεπειθ-σθαι)	**πεπεῖσθαι**
PARTICIPLE		(ἠγ-μενος)	**ἠγμένος, -η, -ον**	(πεπειθ-μενος)	**πεπεισμένος, -η, -ον**
		NO FUTURE PERFECT		NO FUTURE PERFECT	

532. PERFECT MIDDLE AND PASSIVE SYSTEM OF LIQUID VERBS: **φαίνω, στέλλω**

MIDDLE AND PASSIVE

		φαίνω *Perfect*	**φαίνω** *Pluperfect*	**στέλλω** *Perfect*	**στέλλω** *Pluperfect*
INDICATIVE	S. 1.	**πέφασμαι**	**ἐπεφάσμην**	**ἔσταλμαι**	**ἐστάλμην**
	2.	**(πέφανσαι)**	**(ἐπέφανσο)**	**ἔσταλσαι**	**ἔσταλσο**
	3.	**πέφανται**	**ἐπέφαντο**	**ἔσταλται**	**ἔσταλτο**
	D. 2.	**πέφανθον**	**ἐπέφανθον**	**ἔσταλθον**	**ἔσταλθον**
	3.	**πέφανθον**	**ἐπεφάνθην**	**ἔσταλθον**	**ἐστάλθην**
	P. 1.	**πεφάσμεθα**	**ἐπεφάσμεθα**	**ἐστάλμεθα**	**ἐστάλμεθα**
	2.	**πέφανθε**	**ἐπέφανθε**	**ἔσταλθε**	**ἔσταλθε**
	3.	**πεφασμένοι εἰσί**	**πεφασμένοι ἦσαν**	**ἐσταλμένοι εἰσί**	**ἐσταλμένοι ἦσαν**
SUBJUNCTIVE		**πεφασμένος ὦ,** *etc.*			**ἐσταλμένος ὦ,** *etc.*
OPTATIVE		**πεφασμένος εἴην,** *etc.*			**ἐσταλμένος εἴην,** *etc.*
IMPERATIVE	S. 2.	**(πέφανσο)**			**ἔσταλσο**
	3.	**πεφάνθω**			**ἐστάλθω**
	D. 2.	**πέφανθον**			**ἔσταλθον**
	3.	**πεφάνθων**			**ἐστάλθων**
	P. 2.	**πέφανθε**			**ἔσταλθε**
	3.	**πεφάνθων**			**ἐστάλθων**
INFINITIVE		**πεφάνθαι**			**ἐστάλθαι**
PARTICIPLE		**πεφασμένος, -η, -ον**			**ἐσταλμένος, -η, -ον**

NO FUTURE PERFECT — NO FUTURE PERFECT

533. Second Aorist Passive System of γράφω

		2 Aorist	*2 Future*
INDICATIVE	S. 1.	ἐγράφην	γραφήσομαι
	2.	ἐγράφης	γραφήσῃ, γραφήσει
	3.	ἐγράφη	γραφήσεται
	D. 2.	ἐγράφητον	γραφήσεσθον
	3.	ἐγραφήτην	γραφήσεσθον
	P. 1.	ἐγράφημεν	γραφησόμεθα
	2.	ἐγράφητε	γραφήσεσθε
	3.	ἐγράφησαν	γραφήσονται
SUBJUNCTIVE	S. 1.	γραφῶ	
	2.	γραφῇς	
	3.	γραφῇ	
	D. 2.	γραφῆτον	
	3.	γραφῆτον	
	P. 1.	γραφῶμεν	
	2.	γραφῆτε	
	3.	γραφῶσι	
OPTATIVE	S. 1.	γραφείην	γραφησοίμην
	2.	γραφείης	γραφήσοιο
	3.	γραφείη	γραφήσοιτο
	D. 2.	γραφείητον or γραφεῖτον	γραφήσοισθον
	3.	γραφειήτην " γραφείτην	γραφησοίσθην
	P. 1.	γραφείημεν " γραφεῖμεν	γραφησοίμεθα
	2.	γραφείητε " γραφεῖτε	γραφήσοισθε
	3.	γραφείησαν " γραφεῖεν	γραφήσοιντο
IMPERATIVE	S. 2.	γράφηθι	
	3.	γραφήτω	
	D. 2.	γράφητον	
	3.	γραφήτων	
	P. 2.	γράφητε	
	3.	γραφέντων	
INFINITIVE		γραφῆναι	γραφήσεσθαι
PARTICIPLE		γραφείς, γραφεῖσα, γραφέν	γραφησόμενος, -η, -ον

534. CONTRACT VERBS

Active

Present Indicative

S. 1.	**τῑμῶ**	**φιλῶ**	**δηλῶ**
	(τῑμάω)	(φιλέω)	(δηλόω)
2.	**τῑμᾷς**	**φιλεῖς**	**δηλοῖς**
	(τῑμάεις)	(φιλέεις)	(δηλόεις)
3.	**τῑμᾷ**	**φιλεῖ**	**δηλοῖ**
	(τῑμάει)	(φιλέει)	(δηλόει)
D. 2.	**τῑμᾶτον**	**φιλεῖτον**	**δηλοῦτον**
	(τῑμάετον)	(φιλέετον)	(δηλόετον)
3.	**τῑμᾶτον**	**φιλεῖτον**	**δηλοῦτον**
	(τῑμάετον)	(φιλέετον)	(δηλόετον)
P. 1.	**τῑμῶμεν**	**φιλοῦμεν**	**δηλοῦμεν**
	(τῑμάομεν)	(φιλέομεν)	(δηλόομεν)
2.	**τῑμᾶτε**	**φιλεῖτε**	**δηλοῦτε**
	(τῑμάετε)	(φιλέετε)	(δηλόετε)
3.	**τῑμῶσι**	**φιλοῦσι**	**δηλοῦσι**
	(τῑμάουσι)	(φιλέουσι)	(δηλόουσι)

Imperfect Indicative

S. 1.	**ἐτίμων**	**ἐφίλουν**	**ἐδήλουν**
	(ἐτίμαον)	(ἐφίλεον)	(ἐδήλοον)
2.	**ἐτίμᾱς**	**ἐφίλεις**	**ἐδήλους**
	(ἐτίμαες)	(ἐφίλεες)	(ἐδήλοες)
3.	**ἐτίμᾱ**	**ἐφίλει**	**ἐδήλου**
	(ἐτίμαε)	(ἐφίλεε)	(ἐδήλοε)
D. 2.	**ἐτῑμᾶτον**	**ἐφιλεῖτον**	**ἐδηλοῦτον**
	(ἐτῑμάετον)	(ἐφιλέετον)	(ἐδηλόετον)
3.	**ἐτῑμᾱ́την**	**ἐφιλείτην**	**ἐδηλούτην**
	(ἐτῑμαέτην)	(ἐφιλεέτην)	(ἐδηλοέτην)
P. 1.	**ἐτῑμῶμεν**	**ἐφιλοῦμεν**	**ἐδηλοῦμεν**
	(ἐτῑμάομεν)	(ἐφιλέομεν)	(ἐδηλόομεν)
2.	**ἐτῑμᾶτε**	**ἐφιλεῖτε**	**ἐδηλοῦτε**
	(ἐτῑμάετε)	(ἐφιλέετε)	(ἐδηλόετε)
3.	**ἐτίμων**	**ἐφίλουν**	**ἐδήλουν**
	(ἐτίμαον)	(ἐφίλεον)	(ἐδήλοον)

Contract Verbs, Active (*continued*)

Present Subjunctive

S.	1. **τῑμῶ** (τῑμάω)	**φιλῶ** (φιλέω)	**δηλῶ** (δηλόω)
	2. **τῑμᾷς** (τῑμάῃς)	**φιλῇς** (φιλέῃς)	**δηλοῖς** (δηλόῃς)
	3. **τῑμᾷ** (τῑμάῃ)	**φιλῇ** (φιλέῃ)	**δηλοῖ** (δηλόῃ)
D.	2. **τῑμᾶτον** (τῑμάητον)	**φιλῆτον** (φιλέητον)	**δηλῶτον** (δηλόητον)
	3. **τῑμᾶτον** (τῑμάητον)	**φιλῆτον** (φιλέητον)	**δηλῶτον** (δηλόητον)
P.	1. **τῑμῶμεν** (τῑμάωμεν)	**φιλῶμεν** (φιλέωμεν)	**δηλῶμεν** (δηλόωμεν)
	2. **τῑμᾶτε** (τῑμάητε)	**φιλῆτε** (φιλέητε)	**δηλῶτε** (δηλόητε)
	3. **τῑμῶσι** (τῑμάωσι)	**φιλῶσι** (φιλέωσι)	**δηλῶσι** (δηλόωσι)

Present Optative

S.	1. [**τῑμῷμι** (τῑμάοιμι)	[**φιλοῖμι** (φιλέοιμι)	[**δηλοῖμι** (δηλόοιμι)
	2. **τῑμῷς** (τῑμάοις)	**φιλοῖς** (φιλέοις)	**δηλοῖς** (δηλόοις)
	3. **τῑμῷ**] (τῑμάοι)	**φιλοῖ**] (φιλέοι)	**δηλοῖ**] (δηλόοι)
D.	2. **τῑμῷτον** (τῑμάοιτον)	**φιλοῖτον** (φιλέοιτον)	**δηλοῖτον** (δηλόοιτον)
	3. **τῑμῴτην** (τῑμαοίτην)	**φιλοίτην** (φιλεοίτην)	**δηλοίτην** (δηλοοίτην)
P.	1. **τῑμῷμεν** (τῑμάοιμεν)	**φιλοῖμεν** (φιλέοιμεν)	**δηλοῖμεν** (δηλόοιμεν)
	2. **τῑμῷτε** (τῑμάοιτε)	**φιλοῖτε** (φιλέοιτε)	**δηλοῖτε** (δηλόοιτε)
	3. **τῑμῷεν** (τῑμάοιεν)	**φιλοῖεν** (φιλέοιεν)	**δηλοῖεν** (δηλόοιεν)

Contract Verbs, Active (*continued*)

Present Optative (alternative form)

S. 1.	**τῑμῴην** (τῑμαοίην)	**φιλοίην** (φιλεοίην)	**δηλοίην** (δηλοοίην)
2.	**τῑμῴης** (τῑμαοίης)	**φιλοίης** (φιλεοίης)	**δηλοίης** (δηλοοίης)
3.	**τῑμῴη** (τῑμαοίη)	**φιλοίη** (φιλεοίη)	**δηλοίη** (δηλοοίη)
D. 2.	[**τῑμῴητον** (τῑμαοίητον)	[**φιλοίητον** (φιλεοίητον)	[**δηλοίητον** (δηλοοίητον)
3.	**τῑμῳήτην**] (τῑμαοιήτην)	**φιλοιήτην**] (φιλεοιήτην)	**δηλοιήτην**] (δηλοοιήτην)
P. 1.	[**τῑμῴημεν** (τῑμαοίημεν)	[**φιλοίημεν** (φιλεοίημεν)	[**δηλοίημεν** (δηλοοίημεν)
2.	**τῑμῴητε** (τῑμαοίητε)	**φιλοίητε** (φιλεοίητε)	**δηλοίητε** (δηλοοίητε)
3.	**τῑμῴησαν**] (τῑμαοίησαν)	**φιλοίησαν**] (φιλεοίησαν)	**δηλοίησαν**] (δηλοοίησαν)

Present Imperative

S. 2.	**τίμᾱ** (τίμαε)	**φίλει** (φίλεε)	**δήλου** (δήλοε)
3.	**τῑμᾱ́τω** (τῑμαέτω)	**φιλείτω** (φιλεέτω)	**δηλούτω** (δηλοέτω)
D. 2.	**τῑμᾶτον** (τῑμάετον)	**φιλεῖτον** (φιλέετον)	**δηλοῦτον** (δηλόετον)
3.	**τῑμᾱ́των** (τῑμαέτων)	**φιλείτων** (φιλεέτων)	**δηλούτων** (δηλοέτων)
P. 2.	**τῑμᾶτε** (τῑμάετε)	**φιλεῖτε** (φιλέετε)	**δηλοῦτε** (δηλόετε)
3.	**τῑμώντων** (τῑμαόντων)	**φιλούντων** (φιλεόντων)	**δηλούντων** (δηλοόντων)

Present Infinitive

τῑμᾶν (τῑμάειν)	**φιλεῖν** (φιλέειν)	**δηλοῦν** (δηλόειν)

Present Participle

τῑμῶν, τῑμῶσα, τῑμῶν (τῑμάων)	**φιλῶν, φιλοῦσα, φιλοῦν** (φιλέων)	**δηλῶν, δηλοῦσα, δηλοῦν** (δηλόων)

Contract Verbs (*continued*)

Middle and Passive

Present Indicative

S. 1.	**τῑμῶμαι**	**φιλοῦμαι**	**δηλοῦμαι**
	(τῑμάομαι)	(φιλέομαι)	(δηλόομαι)
2.	**τῑμᾷ**	**φιλεῖ, φιλῇ**	**δηλοῖ**
	(τῑμάει, τῑμάῃ)	(φιλέει, φιλέῃ)	(δηλόει, δηλόῃ)
3.	**τῑμᾶται**	**φιλεῖται**	**δηλοῦται**
	(τῑμάεται)	(φιλέεται)	(δηλόεται)
D. 2.	**τῑμᾶσθον**	**φιλεῖσθον**	**δηλοῦσθον**
	(τῑμάεσθον)	(φιλέεσθον)	(δηλόεσθον)
3.	**τῑμᾶσθον**	**φιλεῖσθον**	**δηλοῦσθον**
	(τῑμάεσθον)	(φιλέεσθον)	(δηλόεσθον)
P. 1.	**τῑμώμεθα**	**φιλούμεθα**	**δηλούμεθα**
	(τῑμαόμεθα)	(φιλεόμεθα)	(δηλοόμεθα)
2.	**τῑμᾶσθε**	**φιλεῖσθε**	**δηλοῦσθε**
	(τῑμάεσθε)	(φιλέεσθε)	(δηλόεσθε)
3.	**τῑμῶνται**	**φιλοῦνται**	**δηλοῦνται**
	(τῑμάονται)	(φιλέονται)	(δηλόονται)

Imperfect Indicative

S. 1.	**ἐτῑμώμην**	**ἐφιλούμην**	**ἐδηλούμην**
	(ἐτῑμαόμην)	(ἐφιλεόμην)	(ἐδηλοόμην)
2.	**ἐτῑμῶ**	**ἐφιλοῦ**	**ἐδηλοῦ**
	(ἐτῑμάου)	(ἐφιλέου)	(ἐδηλόου)
3.	**ἐτῑμᾶτο**	**ἐφιλεῖτο**	**ἐδηλοῦτο**
	(ἐτῑμάετο)	(ἐφιλέετο)	(ἐδηλόετο)
D. 2.	**ἐτῑμᾶσθον**	**ἐφιλεῖσθον**	**ἐδηλοῦσθον**
	(ἐτῑμάεσθον)	(ἐφιλέεσθον)	(ἐδηλόεσθον)
3.	**ἐτῑμάσθην**	**ἐφιλείσθην**	**ἐδηλούσθην**
	(ἐτῑμαέσθην)	(ἐφιλεέσθην)	(ἐδηλοέσθην)
P. 1.	**ἐτῑμώμεθα**	**ἐφιλούμεθα**	**ἐδηλούμεθα**
	(ἐτῑμαόμεθα)	(ἐφιλεόμεθα)	(ἐδηλοόμεθα)
2.	**ἐτῑμᾶσθε**	**ἐφιλεῖσθε**	**ἐδηλοῦσθε**
	(ἐτῑμάεσθε)	(ἐφιλέεσθε)	(ἐδηλόεσθε)
3.	**ἐτῑμῶντο**	**ἐφιλοῦντο**	**ἐδηλοῦντο**
	(ἐτῑμάοντο)	(ἐφιλέοντο)	(ἐδηλόοντο)

Contract Verbs, Middle and Passive (*continued*)

Present Subjunctive

S. 1.	**τῑμῶμαι**	**φιλῶμαι**	**δηλῶμαι**
	(τῑμάωμαι)	(φιλέωμαι)	(δηλόωμαι)
2.	**τῑμᾷ**	**φιλῇ**	**δηλοῖ**
	(τῑμάῃ)	(φιλέῃ)	(δηλόῃ)
3.	**τῑμᾶται**	**φιλῆται**	**δηλῶται**
	(τῑμάηται)	(φιλέηται)	(δηλόηται)
D. 2.	**τῑμᾶσθον**	**φιλῆσθον**	**δηλῶσθον**
	(τῑμάησθον)	(φιλέησθον)	(δηλόησθον)
3.	**τῑμᾶσθον**	**φιλῆσθον**	**δηλῶσθον**
	(τῑμάησθον)	(φιλέησθον)	(δηλόησθον)
P. 1.	**τῑμώμεθα**	**φιλώμεθα**	**δηλώμεθα**
	(τῑμαώμεθα)	(φιλεώμεθα)	(δηλοώμεθα)
2.	**τῑμᾶσθε**	**φιλῆσθε**	**δηλῶσθε**
	(τῑμάησθε)	(φιλέησθε)	(δηλόησθε)
3.	**τῑμῶνται**	**φιλῶνται**	**δηλῶνται**
	(τῑμάωνται)	(φιλέωνται)	(δηλόωνται)

Present Optative

S. 1.	**τῑμῴμην**	**φιλοίμην**	**δηλοίμην**
	(τῑμαοίμην)	(φιλεοίμην)	(δηλοοίμην)
2.	**τῑμῷο**	**φιλοῖο**	**δηλοῖο**
	(τῑμάοιο)	(φιλέοιο)	(δηλόοιο)
3.	**τῑμῷτο**	**φιλοῖτο**	**δηλοῖτο**
	(τῑμάοιτο)	(φιλέοιτο)	(δηλόοιτο)
D. 2.	**τῑμῷσθον**	**φιλοῖσθον**	**δηλοῖσθον**
	(τῑμάοισθον)	(φιλέοισθον)	(δηλόοισθον)
3.	**τῑμῴσθην**	**φιλοίσθην**	**δηλοίσθην**
	(τῑμαοίσθην)	(φιλεοίσθην)	(δηλοοίσθην)
P. 1.	**τῑμῴμεθα**	**φιλοίμεθα**	**δηλοίμεθα**
	(τῑμαοίμεθα)	(φιλεοίμεθα)	(δηλοοίμεθα)
2.	**τῑμῷσθε**	**φιλοῖσθε**	**δηλοῖσθε**
	(τῑμάοισθε)	(φιλέοισθε)	(δηλόοισθε)
3.	**τῑμῷντο**	**φιλοῖντο**	**δηλοῖντο**
	(τῑμάοιντο)	(φιλέοιντο)	(δηλόοιντο)

Contract Verbs, Middle and Passive (*continued*)

Present Imperative

S.	2. **τῑμῶ** (τῑμάου)	**φιλοῦ** (φιλέου)	**δηλοῦ** (δηλόου)
	3. **τῑμᾱ́σθω** (τῑμαέσθω)	**φιλείσθω** (φιλεέσθω)	**δηλούσθω** (δηλοέσθω)
D.	2. **τῑμᾶσθον** (τῑμάεσθον)	**φιλεῖσθον** (φιλέεσθον)	**δηλοῦσθον** (δηλόεσθον)
	3. **τῑμᾱ́σθων** (τῑμαέσθων)	**φιλείσθων** (φιλεέσθων)	**δηλούσθων** (δηλοέσθων)
P.	2. **τῑμᾶσθε** (τῑμάεσθε)	**φιλεῖσθε** (φιλέεσθε)	**δηλοῦσθε** (δηλόεσθε)
	3. **τῑμᾱ́σθων** (τῑμαέσθων)	**φιλείσθων** (φιλεέσθων)	**δηλούσθων** (δηλοέσθων)

Present Infinitive

τῑμᾶσθαι (τῑμάεσθαι)	**φιλεῖσθαι** (φιλέεσθαι)	**δηλοῦσθαι** (δηλόεσθαι)

Present Participle

τῑμώμενος, -η, -ον (τῑμαόμενος)	**φιλούμενος, -η, -ον** (φιλεόμενος)	**δηλούμενος, -η, -ον** (δηλοόμενος)

Orchestra Seats in the Theater of Dionysus, Athens.

535. **MI-Verbs**

Active

Present Indicative

S. 1.	ἵστημι	τίθημι	δίδωμι	δείκνῡμι
2.	ἵστης	τίθης	δίδως	δείκνῡς
3.	ἵστησι	τίθησι	δίδωσι	δείκνῡσι
D. 2.	ἵστατον	τίθετον	δίδοτον	δείκνυτον
3.	ἵστατον	τίθετον	δίδοτον	δείκνυτον
P. 1.	ἵσταμεν	τίθεμεν	δίδομεν	δείκνυμεν
2.	ἵστατε	τίθετε	δίδοτε	δείκνυτε
3.	ἱστᾶσι	τιθέᾱσι	διδόᾱσι	δεικνύᾱσι

Imperfect Indicative

S. 1.	ἵστην	ἐτίθην	ἐδίδουν	ἐδείκνῡν
2.	ἵστης	ἐτίθεις	ἐδίδους	ἐδείκνῡς
3.	ἵστη	ἐτίθει	ἐδίδου	ἐδείκνῡ
D. 2.	ἵστατον	ἐτίθετον	ἐδίδοτον	ἐδείκνυτον
3.	ἱστάτην	ἐτιθέτην	ἐδιδότην	ἐδεικνύτην
P. 1.	ἵσταμεν	ἐτίθεμεν	ἐδίδομεν	ἐδείκνυμεν
2.	ἵστατε	ἐτίθετε	ἐδίδοτε	ἐδείκνυτε
3.	ἵστασαν	ἐτίθεσαν	ἐδίδοσαν	ἐδείκνυσαν

Present Subjunctive

S. 1.	ἱστῶ	τιθῶ	διδῶ	δεικνύω
2.	ἱστῇς	τιθῇς	διδῷς	δεικνύῃς
3.	ἱστῇ	τιθῇ	διδῷ	δεικνύῃ
D. 2.	ἱστῆτον	τιθῆτον	διδῶτον	δεικνύητον
3.	ἱστῆτον	τιθῆτον	διδῶτον	δεικνύητον
P. 1.	ἱστῶμεν	τιθῶμεν	διδῶμεν	δεικνύωμεν
2.	ἱστῆτε	τιθῆτε	διδῶτε	δεικνύητε
3.	ἱστῶσι	τιθῶσι	διδῶσι	δεικνύωσι

MI-Verbs, Active (*continued*)

Present Optative

s. 1.	ἱσταίην	τιθείην	διδοίην	δεικνύοιμι
2.	ἱσταίης	τιθείης	διδοίης	δεικνύοις
3.	ἱσταίη	τιθείη	διδοίη	δεικνύοι
d. 2.	ἱσταίητον	τιθείητον	διδοίητον	δεικνύοιτον
3.	ἱσταιήτην	τιθειήτην	διδοιήτην	δεικνυοίτην
p. 1.	ἱσταίημεν	τιθείημεν	διδοίημεν	δεικνύοιμεν
2.	ἱσταίητε	τιθείητε	διδοίητε	δεικνύοιτε
3.	ἱσταίησαν	τιθείησαν	διδοίησαν	δεικνύοιεν

but usually contracted into: —

d. 2.	ἱσταῖτον	τιθεῖτον	διδοῖτον	[δεικνύοιτον, etc. *does not contract.*]
3.	ἱσταίτην	τιθείτην	διδοίτην	
p. 1.	ἱσταῖμεν	τιθεῖμεν	διδοῖμεν	
2.	ἱσταῖτε	τιθεῖτε	διδοῖτε	
3.	ἱσταῖεν	τιθεῖεν	διδοῖεν	

Present Imperative

s. 2.	ἵστη	τίθει	δίδου	δείκνῡ
3.	ἱστάτω	τιθέτω	διδότω	δεικνύτω
d. 2.	ἵστατον	τίθετον	δίδοτον	δείκνυτον
3.	ἱστάτων	τιθέτων	διδότων	δεικνύτων
p. 2.	ἵστατε	τίθετε	δίδοτε	δείκνυτε
3.	ἱστάντων	τιθέντων	διδόντων	δεικνύντων

Present Infinitive

ἱστάναι	τιθέναι	διδόναι	δεικνύναι

Present Participle

ἱστάς, ἱστᾶσα, ἱστάν	τιθείς, τιθεῖσα, τιθέν	διδούς, διδοῦσα, διδόν	δεικνῡ́ς, δεικνῦσα, δεικνύν

MI-Verbs, Active (*continued*)

Second Aorist Indicative

S. 1.	ἔστην	(ἔθηκα)	(ἔδωκα)
2.	ἔστης	(ἔθηκας)	(ἔδωκας)
3.	ἔστη	(ἔθηκε)	(ἔδωκε)
D. 2.	ἔστητον	ἔθετον	ἔδοτον
3.	ἐστήτην	ἐθέτην	ἐδότην
P. 1.	ἔστημεν	ἔθεμεν	ἔδομεν
2.	ἔστητε	ἔθετε	ἔδοτε
3.	ἔστησαν	ἔθεσαν	ἔδοσαν

Second Aorist Subjunctive

S. 1.	στῶ	θῶ	δῶ
2.	στῇς	θῇς	δῷς
3.	στῇ	θῇ	δῷ
D. 2.	στῆτον	θῆτον	δῶτον
3.	στῆτον	θῆτον	δῶτον
P. 1.	στῶμεν	θῶμεν	δῶμεν
2.	στῆτε	θῆτε	δῶτε
3.	στῶσι	θῶσι	δῶσι

Second Aorist Optative

S. 1.	σταίην	θείην	δοίην
2.	σταίης	θείης	δοίης
3.	σταίη	θείη	δοίη
D. 2.	σταίητον	θείητον	δοίητον
3.	σταιήτην	θειήτην	δοιήτην
P. 1.	σταίημεν	θείημεν	δοίημεν
2.	σταίητε	θείητε	δοίητε
3.	σταίησαν	θείησαν	δοίησαν

but usually contracted into:—

D. 2.	σταῖτον	θεῖτον	δοῖτον
3.	σταίτην	θείτην	δοίτην
P. 1.	σταῖμεν	θεῖμεν	δοῖμεν
2.	σταῖτε	θεῖτε	δοῖτε
3.	σταῖεν	θεῖεν	δοῖεν

MI-Verbs, Active (*continued*)

Second Aorist Imperative

S.	2. στῆθι	θές	δός
	3. στήτω	θέτω	δότω
D.	2. στῆτον	θέτον	δότον
	3. στήτων	θέτων	δότων
P.	2. στῆτε	θέτε	δότε
	3. στάντων	θέντων	δόντων

Second Aorist Infinitive

στῆναι	θεῖναι	δοῦναι

Second Aorist Participle

στάς, στᾶσα, στάν	θείς, θεῖσα, θέν	δούς, δοῦσα, δόν

Second Perfect

	Ind.	*Subj.*	*Opt.* (poetic)	*Imp.* (poetic)
S. 1.	(ἕστηκα)	ἑστῶ	ἑσταίην	
2.	(ἕστηκας)	ἑστῇς	ἑσταίης	ἕσταθι
3.	(ἕστηκε)	ἑστῇ	ἑσταίη	ἑστάτω
D. 2.	ἕστατον	ἑστῆτον	ἑσταίητον or -αῖτον	ἕστατον
3.	ἕστατον	ἑστῆτον	ἑσταιήτην " -αίτην	ἑστάτων
P. 1.	ἕσταμεν	ἑστῶμεν	ἑσταίημεν " -αῖμεν	
2.	ἕστατε	ἑστῆτε	ἑσταίητε " -αῖτε	ἕστατε
3.	ἑστᾶσι	ἑστῶσι	ἑσταίησαν " -αῖεν	ἑστάντων

Infinitive ἑστάναι *Participle* ἑστώς, ἑστῶσα, ἑστός

Second Pluperfect

S. 1.	(εἱστήκη)	D. 2.	ἕστατον	P. 1.	ἕσταμεν
2.	(εἱστήκης)	3.	ἑστάτην	2.	ἕστατε
3.	(εἱστήκει)			3.	ἕστασαν

Middle and Passive

Present Indicative

S. 1.	ἵσταμαι	τίθεμαι	δίδομαι	δείκνυμαι
2.	ἵστασαι	τίθεσαι	δίδοσαι	δείκνυσαι
3.	ἵσταται	τίθεται	δίδοται	δείκνυται
D. 2.	ἵστασθον	τίθεσθον	δίδοσθον	δείκνυσθον
3.	ἵστασθον	τίθεσθον	δίδοσθον	δείκνυσθον
P. 1.	ἱστάμεθα	τιθέμεθα	διδόμεθα	δεικνύμεθα
2.	ἵστασθε	τίθεσθε	δίδοσθε	δείκνυσθε
3.	ἵστανται	τίθενται	δίδονται	δείκνυνται

Imperfect Indicative

S. 1.	ἱστάμην	ἐτιθέμην	ἐδιδόμην	ἐδεικνύμην
2.	ἵστασο	ἐτίθεσο	ἐδίδοσο	ἐδείκνυσο
3.	ἵστατο	ἐτίθετο	ἐδίδοτο	ἐδείκνυτο
D. 2.	ἵστασθον	ἐτίθεσθον	ἐδίδοσθον	ἐδείκνυσθον
3.	ἱστάσθην	ἐτιθέσθην	ἐδιδόσθην	ἐδεικνύσθην
P. 1.	ἱστάμεθα	ἐτιθέμεθα	ἐδιδόμεθα	ἐδεικνύμεθα
2.	ἵστασθε	ἐτίθεσθε	ἐδίδοσθε	ἐδείκνυσθε
3.	ἵσταντο	ἐτίθεντο	ἐδίδοντο	ἐδείκνυντο

Present Subjunctive

S. 1.	ἱστῶμαι	τιθῶμαι	διδῶμαι	δεικνύωμαι
2.	ἱστῇ	τιθῇ	διδῷ	δεικνύῃ
3.	ἱστῆται	τιθῆται	διδῶται	δεικνύηται
D. 2.	ἱστῆσθον	τιθῆσθον	διδῶσθον	δεικνύησθον
3.	ἱστῆσθον	τιθῆσθον	διδῶσθον	δεικνύησθον
P. 1.	ἱστώμεθα	τιθώμεθα	διδώμεθα	δεικνυώμεθα
2.	ἱστῆσθε	τιθῆσθε	διδῶσθε	δεικνύησθε
3.	ἱστῶνται	τιθῶνται	διδῶνται	δεικνύωνται

Present Optative

S. 1.	ἱσταίμην	τιθείμην	διδοίμην	δεικνυοίμην
2.	ἱσταῖο	τιθεῖο	διδοῖο	δεικνύοιο
3.	ἱσταῖτο	τιθεῖτο	διδοῖτο	δεικνύοιτο
D. 2.	ἱσταῖσθον	τιθεῖσθον	διδοῖσθον	δεικνύοισθον
3.	ἱσταίσθην	τιθείσθην	διδοίσθην	δεικνυοίσθην
P. 1.	ἱσταίμεθα	τιθείμεθα	διδοίμεθα	δεικνυοίμεθα
2.	ἱσταῖσθε	τιθεῖσθε	διδοῖσθε	δεικνύοισθε
3.	ἱσταῖντο	τιθεῖντο	διδοῖντο	δεικνύοιντο

MI-Verbs, Middle and Passive (*continued*)

Present Imperative

s. 2.	ἵστασο	τίθεσο	δίδοσο	δείκνυσο
3.	ἱστάσθω	τιθέσθω	διδόσθω	δεικνύσθω
d. 2.	ἵστασθον	τίθεσθον	δίδοσθον	δείκνυσθον
3.	ἱστάσθων	τιθέσθων	διδόσθων	δεικνύσθων
p. 2.	ἵστασθε	τίθεσθε	δίδοσθε	δείκνυσθε
3.	ἱστάσθων	τιθέσθων	διδόσθων	δεικνύσθων

Present Infinitive

ἵστασθαι	τίθεσθαι	δίδοσθαι	δείκνυσθαι

Present Participle

ἱστάμενος, -η, -ον	τιθέμενος, -η, -ον	διδόμενος, -η, -ον	δεικνύμενος, -η, -ον

Second Aorist Middle

Indicative

s. 1.	ἐθέμην	ἐδόμην
2.	ἔθου	ἔδου
3.	ἔθετο	ἔδοτο
d. 2.	ἔθεσθον	ἔδοσθον
3.	ἐθέσθην	ἐδόσθην
p. 1.	ἐθέμεθα	ἐδόμεθα
2.	ἔθεσθε	ἔδοσθε
3.	ἔθεντο	ἔδοντο

Subjunctive

s. 1.	θῶμαι	δῶμαι
2.	θῇ	δῷ
3.	θῆται	δῶται
d. 2.	θῆσθον	δῶσθον
3.	θῆσθον	δῶσθον
p. 1.	θώμεθα	δώμεθα
2.	θῆσθε	δῶσθε
3.	θῶνται	δῶνται

Optative

s. 1.	θείμην	δοίμην
2.	θεῖο	δοῖο
3.	θεῖτο	δοῖτο
d. 2.	θεῖσθον	δοῖσθον
3.	θείσθην	δοίσθην
p. 1.	θείμεθα	δοίμεθα
2.	θεῖσθε	δοῖσθε
3.	θεῖντο	δοῖντο

Imperative

s. 2.	θοῦ	δοῦ
3.	θέσθω	δόσθω
d. 2.	θέσθον	δόσθον
3.	θέσθων	δόσθων
p. 2.	θέσθε	δόσθε
3.	θέσθων	δόσθων

Infinitive θέσθαι δόσθαι

Participle θέμενος, -η, -ον δόμενος, -η, -ον

536. PRESENT SYSTEM OF φημί

ACTIVE

		Present	Imperfect
INDICATIVE	S. 1.	φημί	ἔφην
	2.	φῄς or φής	ἔφησθα or ἔφης
	3.	φησί	ἔφη
	D. 2.	φατόν	ἔφατον
	3.	φατόν	ἐφάτην
	P. 1.	φαμέν	ἔφαμεν
	2.	φατέ	ἔφατε
	3.	φᾱσί	ἔφασαν
SUBJUNCTIVE	S. 1.	φῶ	
	2.	φῇς	
	3.	φῇ	
	D. 2.	φῆτον	
	3.	φῆτον	
	P. 1.	φῶμεν	
	2.	φῆτε	
	3.	φῶσι	
OPTATIVE	S. 1.	φαίην	
	2.	φαίης	
	3.	φαίη	
	D. 2.	φαίητον or φαῖτον	
	3.	φαιήτην " φαίτην	
	P. 1.	φαίημεν " φαῖμεν	
	2.	φαίητε " φαῖτε	
	3.	φαίησαν " φαῖεν	
IMPERATIVE	S. 2.	φαθί or φάθι	
	3.	φάτω	
	D. 2.	φάτον	
	3.	φάτων	
	P. 2.	φάτε	
	3.	φάντων	
INFINITIVE		φάναι	
PARTICIPLE		φάσκων, φάσκουσα, φάσκον	

537. PRESENT AND AORIST SYSTEMS OF ἵημι

			Active			Middle (Passive)		Middle
			Pres.	*Impf.*	*2 Aor.*	*Pres.*	*Impf.*	*2 Aor.*
INDICATIVE	S.	1.	ἵημι	ἵην	(ἧκα)	ἵεμαι	ἱέμην	εἵμην
		2.	ἵης, ἱεῖς	ἵεις	(ἧκας)	ἵεσαι	ἵεσο	εἷσο
		3.	ἵησι	ἵει	(ἧκε)	ἵεται	ἵετο	εἷτο
	D.	2.	ἵετον	ἵετον	εἷτον	ἵεσθον	ἵεσθον	εἷσθον
		3.	ἵετον	ἱέτην	εἵτην	ἵεσθον	ἱέσθην	εἵσθην
	P.	1.	ἵεμεν	ἵεμεν	εἷμεν	ἱέμεθα	ἱέμεθα	εἵμεθα
		2.	ἵετε	ἵετε	εἷτε	ἵεσθε	ἵεσθε	εἷσθε
		3.	ἱᾶσι	ἵεσαν	εἷσαν	ἵενται	ἵεντο	εἷντο
			Pres.		*2 Aor.*	*Pres.*		*2 Aor.*
SUBJUNCTIVE	S.	1.	ἱῶ		ὧ	ἱῶμαι		ὧμαι
		2.	ἱῇς		ᾗς	ἱῇ		ᾗ
		3.	ἱῇ		ᾗ	ἱῆται		ἧται
	D.	2.	ἱῆτον		ἧτον	ἱῆσθον		ἧσθον
		3.	ἱῆτον		ἧτον	ἱῆσθον		ἧσθον
	P.	1.	ἱῶμεν		ὧμεν	ἱώμεθα		ὥμεθα
		2.	ἱῆτε		ἧτε	ἱῆσθε		ἧσθε
		3.	ἱῶσι		ὧσι	ἱῶνται		ὧνται
OPTATIVE	S.	1.	ἱείην		εἵην	ἱείμην		εἵμην
		2.	ἱείης		εἵης	ἱεῖο		εἷο
		3.	ἱείη		εἵη	ἱεῖτο		εἷτο
	D.	2.	ἱεῖτον or ἱείητον		εἷτον or εἵητον	ἱεῖσθον		εἷσθον
		3.	ἱείτην or ἱειήτην		εἵτην or εἱήτην	ἱείσθην		εἵσθην
	P.	1.	ἱεῖμεν or ἱείημεν		εἷμεν or εἵημεν	ἱείμεθα		εἵμεθα
		2.	ἱεῖτε or ἱείητε		εἷτε or εἵητε	ἱεῖσθε		εἷσθε
		3.	ἱεῖεν or ἱείησαν		εἷεν or εἵησαν	ἱεῖντο		εἷντο
IMPERATIVE	S.	2.	ἵει		ἕς	ἵεσο		οὗ
		3.	ἱέτω		ἕτω	ἱέσθω		ἕσθω
	D.	2.	ἵετον		ἕτον	ἵεσθον		ἕσθον
		3.	ἱέτων		ἕτων	ἱέσθων		ἕσθων
	P.	2.	ἵετε		ἕτε	ἵεσθε		ἕσθε
		3.	ἱέντων		ἕντων	ἱέσθων		ἕσθων
INFINITIVE			ἱέναι		εἷναι	ἵεσθαι		ἕσθαι
PARTICIPLE			ἱείς, ἱεῖσα, ἱέν		εἵς, εἷσα, ἕν	ἱέμενος, -η, -ον		ἕμενος, -η, -ον

538. Present and Future Systems of εἰμί — **539.** Present System of εἶμι

		538. Active: *Present*	*Imperfect*	*Future*	539. Active: *Present*	*Imperfect*
INDICATIVE	S. 1.	εἰμί	ἦ or ἦν	ἔσομαι	εἶμι	ᾖα or ᾔειν
	2.	εἶ	ἦσθα	ἔσῃ or ἔσει	εἶ	ᾔεις " ᾔεισθα
	3.	ἐστί	ἦν	ἔσται	εἶσι	ᾔει " ᾔειν
	D. 2.	ἐστόν	ἦστον or ἦτον	ἔσεσθον	ἴτον	ᾖτον
	3.	ἐστόν	ἤστην or ἤτην	ἔσεσθον	ἴτον	ᾔτην
	P. 1.	ἐσμέν	ἦμεν	ἐσόμεθα	ἴμεν	ᾖμεν
	2.	ἐστέ	ἦστε or ἦτε	ἔσεσθε	ἴτε	ᾖτε
	3.	εἰσί	ἦσαν	ἔσονται	ἴᾱσι	ᾖσαν or ᾔεσαν
SUBJUNCTIVE	S. 1.	ὦ			ἴω	
	2.	ᾖς			ἴῃς	
	3.	ᾖ			ἴῃ	
	D. 2.	ἦτον			ἴητον	
	3.	ἦτον			ἴητον	
	P. 1.	ὦμεν			ἴωμεν	
	2.	ἦτε			ἴητε	
	3.	ὦσι			ἴωσι	
OPTATIVE	S. 1.	εἴην		ἐσοίμην	ἴοιμι or ἰοίην	
	2.	εἴης		ἔσοιο	ἴοις	
	3.	εἴη		ἔσοιτο	ἴοι	
	D. 2	εἶτον or εἴητον		ἔσοισθον	ἴοιτον	
	3.	εἴτην " εἰήτην		ἐσοίσθην	ἰοίτην	
	P. 1.	εἶμεν " εἴημεν		ἐσοίμεθα	ἴοιμεν	
	2.	εἶτε " εἴητε		ἔσοισθε	ἴοιτε	
	3.	εἶεν " εἴησαν		ἔσοιντο	ἴοιεν	
IMPERATIVE	S. 2.	ἴσθι			ἴθι	
	3.	ἔστω			ἴτω	
	D. 2.	ἔστον			ἴτον	
	3.	ἔστων			ἴτων	
	P. 2.	ἔστε			ἴτε	
	3.	ἔστων			ἰόντων	
INFINITIVE		εἶναι		ἔσεσθαι	ἰέναι	
PARTICIPLE		ὤν, οὖσα, ὄν		ἐσόμενος, -η, -ον	ἰών, ἰοῦσα, ἰόν	

540. Present System of κεῖμαι

541. Present System of κάθημαι

		540. Present	540. Imperfect	541. Present	541. Imperfect	
INDICATIVE	S. 1.	κεῖμαι	ἐκείμην	κάθημαι	ἐκαθήμην	or καθήμην
	2.	κεῖσαι	ἔκεισο	κάθησαι	ἐκάθησο	" καθῆσο
	3.	κεῖται	ἔκειτο	κάθηται	ἐκάθητο	" καθῆστο
	D. 2.	κεῖσθον	ἔκεισθον	κάθησθον	ἐκάθησθον	" καθῆσθον
	3.	κεῖσθον	ἐκείσθην	κάθησθον	ἐκαθήσθην	" καθήσθην
	P. 1.	κείμεθα	ἐκείμεθα	καθήμεθα	ἐκαθήμεθα	" καθήμεθα
	2.	κεῖσθε	ἔκεισθε	κάθησθε	ἐκάθησθε	" καθῆσθε
	3.	κεῖνται	ἔκειντο	κάθηνται	ἐκάθηντο	" καθῆντο
SUBJUNCTIVE	S. 1.	κέωμαι		καθῶμαι		
	2.	κέῃ		καθῇ		
	3.	κέηται		καθῆται		
	D. 2.	κέησθον		καθῆσθον		
	3.	κέησθον		καθῆσθον		
	P. 1.	κεώμεθα		καθώμεθα		
	2.	κέησθε		καθῆσθε		
	3.	κέωνται		καθῶνται		
OPTATIVE	S. 1.	κεοίμην		καθοίμην		
	2.	κέοιο		καθοῖο		
	3.	κέοιτο		καθοῖτο		
	D. 2.	κέοισθον		καθοῖσθον		
	3.	κεοίσθην		καθοίσθην		
	P. 1.	κεοίμεθα		καθοίμεθα		
	2.	κέοισθε		καθοῖσθε		
	3.	κέοιντο		καθοῖντο		
IMPERATIVE	S. 2.	κεῖσο		κάθησο		
	3.	κείσθω		καθήσθω		
	D. 2.	κεῖσθον		κάθησθον		
	3.	κείσθων		καθήσθων		
	P. 2.	κεῖσθε		κάθησθε		
	3.	κείσθων		καθήσθων		
INFINITIVE		κεῖσθαι		καθῆσθαι		
PARTICIPLE		κείμενος, -η, -ον		καθήμενος, -η, -ον		

542. SECOND PERFECT SYSTEM OF **οἶδα**

543. SECOND AORIST SYSTEM OF **γιγνώσκω**

		ACTIVE		ACTIVE
		2 Perfect	*2 Pluperfect*	*2 Aorist*
INDICATIVE	S. 1.	οἶδα	ᾔδη or ᾔδειν	ἔγνων
	2.	οἶσθα	ᾔδησθα or ᾔδεισθα	ἔγνως
	3.	οἶδε	ᾔδει or ᾔδειν	ἔγνω
	D. 2.	ἴστον	ᾖστον	ἔγνωτον
	3.	ἴστον	ᾔστην	ἐγνώτην
	P. 1.	ἴσμεν	ᾖσμεν	ἔγνωμεν
	2.	ἴστε	ᾖστε	ἔγνωτε
	3.	ἴσᾱσι	ᾖσαν or ᾔδεσαν	ἔγνωσαν
SUBJUNCTIVE	S. 1	εἰδῶ		γνῶ (γ ν ό - ω)
	2.	εἰδῇς		γνῷς
	3.	εἰδῇ		γνῷ
	D. 2.	εἰδῆτον		γνῶτον
	3.	εἰδῆτον		γνῶτον
	P. 1.	εἰδῶμεν		γνῶμεν
	2.	εἰδῆτε		γνῶτε
	3.	εἰδῶσι		γνῶσι
OPTATIVE	S. 1.	εἰδείην		γνοίην
	2.	εἰδείης		γνοίης
	3.	εἰδείη		γνοίη
	D. 2.	εἰδεῖτον		γνοῖτον
	3.	εἰδείτην		γνοίτην
	P. 1.	εἰδεῖμεν or εἰδείημεν		γνοῖμεν
	2.	εἰδεῖτε " εἰδείητε		γνοῖτε
	3.	εἰδεῖεν " εἰδείησαν		γνοῖεν
IMPERATIVE	S. 2.	ἴσθι		γνῶθι
	3.	ἴστω		γνώτω
	D. 2.	ἴστον		γνῶτον
	3.	ἴστων		γνώτων
	P. 2.	ἴστε		γνῶτε
	3.	ἴστων		γνόντων
INFINITIVE		εἰδέναι		γνῶναι
PARTICIPLE		εἰδώς, εἰδυῖα, εἰδός		γνούς, γνοῦσα, γνόν

544. A Conspectus of the Most Common Case Uses[1]

(*a*) **Nominative** — used as
Subject (§ 4 *a*).
Predicate nominative (p. 37, note 4).

(*b*) **Genitive** (-ᾱς, -ης, -ου, -ος, -ους; ων)[2] — may indicate
Possession (§ 4 *b* and p. 138, note 2).
The whole, of which a part is mentioned — Partitive (§ 275).
The object of an action or feeling expressed by a noun or adjective — Objective (p. 70, note 1).
Material (p. 127, note 2).
Measure (§ 354).
Price or value (p. 12, note 2).
Time within which (§ 103).
Place from which — Separation (§ 9).
Source (p. 115, note 4).
Comparison (§ 254).
Agency (§ 139).
It may also be used absolutely (§ 128).

(*c*) **Dative** (-ᾳ, -ῃ, -ῳ, -ι; -αις, -οις, -σι(ν))[2] — may indicate
Indirect object (§ 4 *c*).
Reference (§ 331).
Possession (§ 32).
Agency (§ 331).
Association (§ 236).
Means (§ 77).
Cause (p. 127, note 3).
Manner (§ 44).
Degree of difference (§ 261).
Place where (§ 23).
Time when (§ 228).
It may also be used with adjectives (§ 16).

---

[1] The references are to text discussions of the uses.
[2] Significant endings and clues to the case.

(*d*) **Accusative** (-ᾱν, -ην, -αν, -ον, -α, -ν, -ᾱ; -ᾱς, -ους, -ας, -εις, -α, -η)[1] may indicate
Direct object (§ 4 *d*).
Cognate object (§ 269).
Adverbial modifier (§ 270).
Respect (p. 144, note 2).
Place to which (§ 24).
Extent of time or space (§ 37).
Subject of an infinitive (§ 50 *c*).
Some verbs take two accusatives (§ 245).

(*e*) **Vocative** — indicates
Person addressed (p. 90, note 1).

545. A Conspectus of the Most Common Mood Uses

(*a*) **Indicative** — may be used in
Main Clauses — to convey
Direct statements, including
Conclusions to conditions
Particular (§ 83), Present general (§ 183),
Past general (§ 199 *a*), Future more vivid (§ 183).
(With ἄν) Present or past statements qualified by some circumstance or condition (§ 97).
(With εἴθε or εἰ γάρ) Unattainable wishes in present or past time (§ 411 *a*).
Subordinate clauses — with
Ordinary relatives
Temporal conjunctions (ἐπεί, ἐπειδή, ὅτε, ἕως, ἔστε, μέχρι, πρίν) (§ 144 *a* and *c*).
Causal conjunctions (ἐπεί, ἐπειδή, ὡς, ὅτι) (§ 144 *b*).
ὥστε — Actual result (§ 108).
εἰ — Particular or contrary to fact conditions, to be determined by the presence or absence of ἄν in the conclusion (§§ 83, 97).
ὅτι — If the main verb is in the past tense, the presence of the indicative shows the vivid nature of the account (§ 211).
ὅπως and future tense — Object clause with a verb of effort, etc. (§ 308).

---

[1] Significant endings and clues to the case.

(*b*) **Subjunctive** (mood sign ω or η) — may be used in
Main clauses — to convey
Exhortation (§ 176 *a*).
(With μή and in aorist) Prohibition (§ 294 *b*).
Deliberative question (§ 404).
Subordinate clauses — with
ἵνα, ὡς, ὅπως — Purpose — If the main verb is in a past tense, the presence of the subjunctive shows that the purpose is vivid (§ 176 *b* and 192 *b*).
μή or μὴ οὐ after verbs of fearing — Effect after a past tense as above (§ 314).
ἐάν — Present general or future more vivid condition, to be determined by the present or the future time of the conclusion (§ 183).
Relative pronoun or adverb + ἄν — The same conditional force as above (§ 206).

(*c*) **Optative** (mood sign ι combined with stem vowel) — may be used in
Main clauses — to convey
(With ἄν) a future statement qualified by some circumstance or condition — Future less vivid condition (§ 199 *b*).
(With or without εἴθε or εἰ γάρ) Attainable wishes (§ 192 *a*).
Subordinate clauses — with
ἵνα, ὡς, ὅπως — Purpose (§ 192 *b*).
μή or μὴ οὐ after verbs of fearing (§ 314 *b*).
εἰ — Past general or future less vivid conditions, to be determined by the presence of the indicative or the optative in the conclusion (§ 199 *a*).
Relative pronouns or adverbs (the same conditional force as above) (§ 206).
ὅτι — Indirect discourse (§ 211).
Interrogatives — Indirect questions (§ 217)

(*d*) **Imperative** — may be used to convey a
Command (§ 294 *a*).
(With μή and in the present tense) Prohibition (§ 294 *b*).

(*e*) **Infinitive** (mood signs -ειν, -αι, -ναι, -σθαι) — may be used as
Subject of a verb (§ 262 *a*).
Complementary object (p. 8, note 2).
Object of certain verbs of *saying* and *thinking* (§ 213).
It may be used with
ὥστε — Probable result (§ 108).
πρίν, which in this instance means *before* (§ 144 *d*).
ὤφελον — Unattainable wishes: (pres. inf.) in present time; or (aor. inf.) in past time (§ 411 *b*).

(*f*) **Participle** (mood signs -οντ-, -ουσ-; -αντ-, -ασ-; -οτ-, -υι-; -μενο-, -μενη-; -εντ-, -εισ-).
Attributive adjective or noun (§ 116 *a*).
Circumstantial modifier of a noun or pronoun
Equivalent to a clause of *time*, *manner*, *means*, *cause*, *concession*, *condition*, or *purpose* (§§ 116 *b* and 154).
Occurs absolutely in the genitive (§ 128).
Supplementary to
ἄρχω, παύω, τυγχάνω, λανθάνω, κ.τ.λ., being not in indirect discourse (§ 393 *b*).
ἀκούω, πυνθάνομαι, ὁράω, οἶδα, κ τ.λ., being in indirect discourse (§§ 214, 393 *a*).

546. A Conspectus of Some Important Tense Uses

(*a*) **Present**
Indicative
Continuance, *repetition*, or *occurrence at the time of*
Speaking or writing — *absolute time* (§ 13).
Main verb — *relative time* (§ 212).
Subjunctive and Imperative
Continuance or *repetition*, any time implication being due to the mood (§§ 176 *a*, 294 *a*).
Optative, Infinitive, and Participle (if in indirect discourse)
Continuance, *repetition*, or *occurrence*, at the time of the main verb (§§ 212–214).
Optative and Infinitive (if not in indirect discourse)
Continuance or *repetition*, any time implication being due to the mood (§ 192 *a*).
But the participle not in indirect discourse is usually as in indirect discourse (§ 117).

(*b*) **Imperfect**

Continuance or *repetition, before the time of*
Speaking or writing – *absolute time* (§ 41).
Main verb — *relative time.*
With ἄν *continuance* or *repetition at the time of*
Speaking or writing (§ 97).

(*c*) **Aorist**

Indicative
Mere occurrence, before the time of
Speaking or writing — *absolute time* (§ 54).
Main verb — *relative time* (§ 212).
With ἄν *mere occurrence, before the time of*
Speaking or writing (§ 97).
Subjunctive and Imperative
Mere occurrence, time implication due to mood (§§ 176 *a*, 294 *a*).
Optative, Infinitive, and Participle (if in indirect discourse)
Mere occurrence, before the time of the main verb (§ 212).
Optative and Infinitive (if not in indirect discourse)
Mere occurrence, time implication due to mood (§ 192 *a*).
The Participle is usually as in indirect discourse (§ 117).

547. TABLE OF CONDITIONAL SENTENCES

(*a*) **Simple Particular** (§ 83)

	Protasis	Apodosis
Present	— εἰ with pres. ind.	ind. or any appropriate form
Past	— εἰ with past ind.	ind. or any appropriate form

(*b*) **Contrary to Fact** (§ 97)

Present	— εἰ with imperf. ind.	imperf. ind. with ἄν.
Past	— εἰ with aor. ind.	aor. ind. with ἄν.

(*c*) **General** (§§ 183 and 199 *a*)

Present	— ἐάν (ἤν, ἄν) with subjv.	pres. ind.
Past	— εἰ with opt.	imperf. ind.

(*d*) **Future** (§§ 183 *b* and 199 *a*)

Most Vivid	— εἰ with fut. ind.	fut. ind. or equivalent
More Vivid	— ἐάν (ἤν, ἄν) with subjv.	fut. ind. or equivalent
Less Vivid	— εἰ with opt.	opt. with ἄν.

548. A CONSPECTUS OF THE FUNCTION OF PRINCIPAL PARTS

	ACT.	MID.	PASS.
PRES.	1	1	1
IMPERF.	1	1	1
FUT.	2	2	6
AOR.	3	3	6
PERF.	4	5	5
PLUPERF.	4	5	5

<table>
<tr><th>ACT.</th><th>MID.</th><th>PASS.</th></tr>
<tr><td colspan="3">1</td></tr>
<tr><td colspan="2">2</td><td rowspan="2">6</td></tr>
<tr><td colspan="2">3</td></tr>
<tr><td>4</td><td colspan="2">5</td></tr>
</table>

The above diagrams show the relative importance of the principal parts that supply the stems for the various tenses (with all the moods of each) in the three voices. The numerals employed correspond to those used in the following tables.

Many verbs lack one or more of the principal parts. The subjoined list gives examples of such. It also furnishes examples of many important and common variations in the formation of the various parts:

1 *Pres.*	2 *Fut.*	3 *Aor.*	4 *Perf.*	5 *Perf. Mid.*	6 *Aor. Pass.*
παύω	παύσω	ἔπαυσα	πέπαυκα	πέπαυμαι	ἐπαύθην
λείπω	λείψω	ἔλιπον	λέλοιπα	λέλειμμαι	ἐλείφθην
ἄγω	ἄξω	ἤγαγον	ἦχα	ἦγμαι	ἤχθην
πείθω	πείσω	ἔπεισα	πέπεικα πέποιθα	πέπεισμαι	ἐπείσθην
φαίνω	φανῶ	ἔφηνα	πέφηνα	πέφασμαι	ἐφάνθην ἐφάνην
θνῄσκω	-θανοῦμαι	-έθανον	τέθνηκα		
ἵστημι	στήσω	ἔστησα ἔστην	ἕστηκα	ἕσταμαι	ἐστάθην
τίθημι	θήσω	ἔθηκα ἔθετον	τέθηκα	τέθειμαι	ἐτέθην
δέχομαι	δέξομαι	ἐδεξάμην		δέδεγμαι	
πυνθάνομαι	πεύσομαι	ἐπυθόμην		πέπυσμαι	
βούλομαι	βουλήσομαι			βεβούλημαι	ἐβουλήθην
γίγνομαι	γενήσομαι	ἐγενόμην	γέγονα	γεγένημαι	
ἥδομαι					ἥσθην

549. Review Vocabulary I (Lessons I–IV)

ἀγαθός
ἄγγελος
ἄγω
ἀδελφός
ἄνθρωπος
ἄξιος
ἀπό
γράφω
δέ
δένδρον
δῆλος
δίκαιος
δῶρον
ἐθέλω
εἰς
ἐκ, ἐξ
Ἑλλήσποντος
ἐν
ἔχω
ἦν, ἦσαν
ἵππος
καί
καλός
κίνδῡνος
λίθος
λῡ́ω
μακρός
μῑκρός
ὁ, [ἡ], τό
παρά
παύω
πεδίον
πέμπω
πολέμιος
πόλεμος
ποταμός
στάδιον
στρατηγός
φίλος

550. Review Vocabulary II (Lessons VI–X)

ἀγορᾱ́
ἀθροίζω
ἀλλά
ἁρπάζω
ἀρχαῖος
ἀρχή
ἄρχω
βάρβαρος
γάρ
δέκα
διά
διώκω
ἐνταῦθα
ἐντεῦθεν
ἐπιστολή
ἐπιτήδειος
ἔργον
ἡμέρᾱ
θύρᾱ
ἰσχῡρός
κραυγή
κώμη
λείπω
λόγος
λοιπός
μάχη
μέλλω
μέν
νομίζω
ὁδός
οἰκίᾱ
οὐ, οὐκ, οὐχ
πείθω
πύλη
σῑγή
σκηνή
σπονδή
στρατιᾱ́
ὑποπτεύω
φεύγω
φιλίᾱ
φίλιος
φυγή
φυλακή
φυλάττω
χώρᾱ

551. Review Vocabulary III (Lessons XII–XIX)

ἀδιάβατος
Ἀθῆναι
Ἀθηναῖος
ἀλλήλων
ἄλλος
ἅμαξα
ἄν
ἀπέχω
ἅρμα
ἄρχων
ἀσπίς
αὐτός
βασίλεια
βουλεύω
βουλή
γέφῡρα
γυνή
διαβαίνω
διαβατός
διαρπάζω
δόρυ
δρόμος
ἑαυτοῦ
ἐγώ
εἰ
εἰμί
ἐκεῖνος
Ἑλλάς
ἐμαυτοῦ
ἐξελαύνω
ἔξεστι
ἐπί
ἐπιβουλεύω
ἐπιβουλή
ἑπτά
ἥκω
θάλαττα
Θρᾷξ
ἴσος
κακός
κατά
κελεύω
κῆρυξ
μένω

μεστός
μή
νύξ
Ξενίᾱς
ὅδε
ὀκτώ
ὁπλίτης
ὅπλον
ὅς
οὖν
οὔπω
οὗτος
παῖς
πέντε
πλοῖον
πολίτης
πρᾶγμα
πρός
σάλπιγξ
σατράπης
σεαυτοῦ
σῖτος
σπεύδω
σταθμός
στρατιώτης
στρατόπεδον
σύ
συμβουλεύω
σύν
τόπος
τότε
ὕδωρ
φάλαγξ
φησί, φᾱσί
φύλαξ
χάρις
χρῆμα
ὥρᾱ
ὥστε

552. Review Vocabulary IV (Lessons XXI–XXVI)

ἀδικέω
αἱρέω
αἰτέω
ἁλίσκομαι
ἀνά
ἀφικνέομαι
ἄχθομαι
βούλομαι
γίγνομαι
δεσπότης
δεξιός
δέχομαι
δή
δοκέω
εἶτα
ἐλπίς
ἐπεί
ἐπειδή
ἐπιμελέομαι
ἕπομαι
ἔρχομαι
ἡγέομαι
ἥδομαι
θῡμός
ἱκανός
καλέω
κωλῡ́ω
λαμβάνω
μάχομαι
μετά
μεταπέμπομαι
μόνος
νέος
ὀλίγος
ὁμολογέω
ὄνομα
οὕτω(s)
παρασκευάζω
παρέχω
πᾶς
περί
πιστεύω
ποιέω
πολεμέω
πορείᾱ
πορεύομαι
πρίν
πρόθῡμος
πρῶτος(πρῶτον)
τρέπω
τρόπος
ὑπισχνέομαι
ὑπό
φιλέω
φόβος
φυγάς
χαλεπός
ὧδε
ὡς

553. Review Vocabulary V (Lessons XXVIII–XXXV)

ἀγγέλλω
ἄδικος
ἀεί
αἰσθάνομαι
ἀκούω
ἀναγκαῖος
ἀναγκάζω
ἀποθνῄσκω
ἀνάγκη
ἀργύριον
βίος
γε
γιγνώσκω
δεύτερος
δεῖ
διδάσκω
δίκη
ἐάν
εἶπον
ἐπᾱ́ν
ἐπειδάν
ἐπήν
ἐπιθῡμέω
ἔτι
εὑρίσκω
ἤ
ἦν
θάνατος
θαυμάζω
θεός
ἵνα
καλῶς
κεφαλή
κλέπτω
λέγω
μᾶλλον

μηδέ
μηκέτι
μήποτε
μήτε
μισθός
νῦν
ξένος
οἶνος
ὁπόσος
ὁπότε
ὅπου
ὅπως
ὅστις
ὅταν
ὅτε
ὅτι
οὐδέ
οὐκέτι
οὔποτε
οὔτε
πάλαι
πάλιν
πάσχω
πόνος
πορίζω
πόσος
πότε
ποτέ
ποῦ
που
πρᾱ́ττω
πυνθάνομαι
πῶς
πως
σοφίᾱ
σοφός
στρατεύω
σῴζω
σωτηρίᾱ
τάττω
τε
τίς
τις
τράπεζα
τρέφω
τρίτος
φέρω
χρόνος
χρῡσίον
χρῡσός
ὦ
ὡς
ὥσπερ
ὠφελέω
ὠφέλιμος

554. Review Vocabulary VI (Lessons XXXVII–XLV)

ἀγών
αἰσχρός
αἴτιος
ἀληθής
ἀμείνων
ἀνάβασις
ἀνήρ
ἀπορέω
ἀπορίᾱ
ἄπορος
ἄριστος
ἀσφαλής
βασιλεύς
βασιλεύω
βέλτιστος
βελτίων
βοηθέω
γένος
γέρων
δεινός
ἐγγύς
ἔδεισα
ἐλᾱ́ττων
ἐλάχιστος
Ἕλλην
Ἑλληνικός
ἐμός
ἐπαινέω
εὖ
εὐδαίμων
εὐθύς
εὖρος
εὔχομαι
ἡγεμών
ἡδύς
ἡμέτερος
ἥττων
Θεμιστοκλῆς
θᾱ́ττων
θέω
θῡ́ω
ἱππεύς
κάκιστος
κακίων
κάλλιστος
καλλίων
κέρας
κρατέω
κράτιστος
κράτος
κρείττων
λοχᾱγός
λόχος
μάλα
μάλιστα
μέγας
μέγιστος
μείζων
μείων
μέντοι
μέρος
μήν (noun)
μήτηρ
ναῦς
Ξενοφῶν
ὄπισθεν
ὄρος
ὅτι
πάνυ
πατήρ
πατρίς
πίπτω
πιστός
πλεῖστος
πλείων
πλῆθος
πλήν
πλήττω
πόλις
πολύς
πότερος
πρό
πρόσθεν
πρότερος
πῦρ
ῥᾴδιος
ῥήτωρ
ῥίπτω
σός
στενός
στόμα
Σωκράτης

σῶμα
ταχύς
τεῖχος
τέλος
τριήρης
ὑμέτερος
ὑπέρ
ὕστερος
φοβερός
χείρ
χείρων
ὡς

555. Review Vocabulary VII (Lessons XLVII–LVI)

ἄκρος
ἀλλάττω
ἀμελέω
ἀμφότερος
ἀντί
ἄνω
ἀποκρῖνομαι
ἀποκτείνω
ἀρετή
ἀτῑμάζω
αὖ
βαίνω
βάλλω
γῆ
δέδοικα
δέομαι
διατρίβω
δύο
εἴθε
εἴκοσι
εἰρήνη
εἷς
ἑκατόν
ἐκεῖ
ἐλευθερίᾱ
ἐλεύθερος
ἐλπίζω
ἔνθα
ἕξ
ἕτερος
ἕως
Ζεύς
ἤδη
θάπτω
θαρρέω
καιρός
κρίνω
μανθάνω
μέλει
μέσος
μηδείς
μιμνῄσκω
μνῆμα
μῡ́ριοι
οἰκέω
ὁπλίζω
οὐδείς
ὀφείλω
παλτόν
παρασάγγης
σκέπτομαι
σκοπέω
στράτευμα
στρέφω
τάφος
τάφρος
τείνω
τέμνω
τέτταρες
τῑμή
τρεῖς
τρέχω
ὑστεραῖος
φαίνω
φοβέομαι
φανερός
φύσις
χαλεπαίνω
χῑ́λιοι
χρή
χωρίον

556. Review Vocabulary VIII (Lessons LVIII–LXV)

ἅμα
ἅπαξ
ἀποδίδωμι
ἄρα
ἆρα
βοῦς
δίδωμι
δίς
δύναμαι
δύναμις
δυνατός
εἶδον
ἕκαστος
ἐναντίος
ἕνεκα
ἐννοέω
ἔπειτα
ἐπίσταμαι
ἔρημος
ἔτος
εὔνους
ἐχθρός
ἱερός
ἵημι
ἵστημι
ἴσως
καίπερ
κεῖμαι
κέρδος
μήν (adv.)
μήποτε
νέμω
νοῦς
ξύλον
οἷος
ὅλος
ὅμως
οὐκοῦν
οὔποτε
παίω
πλέω
πλοῦς
πωλέω
σπουδαῖος
σπουδή
στέλλω
στέφανος
τίθημι
τοίνυν
τοιοῦτος
τοσοῦτος
τυγχάνω
υἱός
φημί
ψευδής
ψεύδω

557. Review Vocabulary IX (Lessons LXVII–LXXIX)

ἀθρόος
αἰτιάομαι
ἁμαρτάνω
ἀξιόω
ἀποδείκνῡμι
ἀπόλλῡμι
ἀποστερέω
ἅπτω
ἀριθμός
βασιλείᾱ
βασίλειος
βίᾱ
βλάπτω
βλέπω
γυμνός
δαπανάω
δείκνῡμι
δηλόω
διαγιγνώσκω
δουλεύω
ἐάω
εἶμι
ἑκών
ἔμπειρος
ἐνθῡμέομαι
ἐξαπατάω
ἔξω
ἐπιδείκνῡμι
ἐρωτάω
ζάω
ζεύγνῡμι
ἥλιος
ἡττάομαι
θνητός
θόρυβος
θώρᾱξ
ἴδιος
κάθημαι
κᾱ́ω
κοινός
κτάομαι
κύκλος
λανθάνω
λιμήν
λόγχη
λόφος
μάντις
μεστός
μέχρι
μηχανάομαι
μηχανή
νεκρός
νῑκάω
νίκη
νόμος
οἶδα
οἴομαι
ὄμνῡμι
ὁράω
ὄρθιος
ὀρθός
ὅρκος
ὁρμάω
ὅσος
ὅσπερ
ὀφθαλμός
παραβαίνω
πεζός
πειράομαι
πελταστής
πίμπλημι
πίνω
πλέθρον
πλευρᾱ́
πολιορκέω
πονέω
πούς
ῥέω
σημαίνω
σπένδομαι
σχολή
τάξις
τελευτάω
τέχνη
τῑμάω
τῑμωρέω
τιτρώσκω
τύχη
ὑποζύγιον
φθάνω
χράομαι
ὠνέομαι

The West View of the Erechtheum

DICTIONARY OF PROPER NAMES

'Αδείμαντος, *Adiman'tus,* leader of the Corinthian troops against Xerxes in 480 B.C.

"Αδμητος, *Admē'tus,* Thessalian king of the heroic period, whose wife Alcestis, as narrated by Euripides in his play of that name, saved him from death through her vicarious self-sacrifice.

'Αθῆναι, *Athens,* the chief city of Attica.

> "Athens, the eye of Greece, mother of arts
> And eloquence." [1]

'Αθηναῖος, -ᾱ, -ον, *Athenian,* pertaining to Athens.

'Αθήνη, *Athēna,* patron deity of Athens, Latin Minerva. Like her Roman counterpart, she was goddess of war and of handicraft. In these spheres she typified the activities of her people. A favorite epithet was Pallas, whence comes *palladium,* referring to an ancient wooden statue of the deity supposed to have fallen from the skies. Christianized Athens readily substituted the Virgin Mary for the virgin Athena.

Αἴακος, *Æ'acus,* son of Zeus and grandfather of Achilles. Famed for wisdom and justice, he became a judge of the underworld.

Αἰσχύλος, *Æs'chylus* (525–456 B.C.), earliest of the three great tragic poets of Athens. He composed about ninety plays, of which seven are extant. Of these, the *Prometheus* has been a favorite with many poets. His young manhood fell in the time of the Persian Wars and he justly prided himself on having borne his share in the defense of Greece.

Αἴσωπος, *Æsop,* the reputed author of a collection of brief beast fables which have been the vehicle for much homely wisdom. Little is known about his date or career. The fables that bear his name were very popular in antiquity and still live because of their charm and truth.

"Αλκηστις, *Alces'tis.* See "Αδμητος.

---

[1] Milton, *Paradise Regained,* IV. 240.

Ἀλκιβιάδης, *Alcibi′ades* (about 450–404 B.C.), an Athenian, brilliant and wealthy, but viewed with suspicion by many of his fellow citizens because of his extravagant habits. He was unfortunate in his political activities and died in exile. Plutarch gave him a place in his collection of *Lives.*

Ἀμπρακιῶτης, *Ambra′ciot,* native of Ambracia, a district near the west coast of Greece.

Ἀνακρέων, *Anac′reon* (about 563–478 B.C.), famous Greek lyric poet. Born on the island of Tēos, he spent most of his life at the courts of tyrants. His poetry is devoted largely to the praise of "wine, women, and song." Such was the popularity of his verse that many compositions were falsely attributed to him. These are now called *Anacreontics.*

Ἀνδρομάχη, *Androm′ache,* wife of Hector, chief Trojan warrior of the *Iliad.* Andromache is one of Homer's noblest creations.

Ἀνθολογίᾱ, *Anthology,* i.e., "Collection of Flowers," a name given to a collection of short poems. The well-known *Greek Anthology* is the result of gradual additions to a collection that was compiled about 60 B.C. by Meleager of Gadara.

Ἀντισθένης, *Antis′thenes* (about 444–365 B.C.), a very intimate friend of Socrates and the founder of the Cynic school of philosophy. See Κυνικοί.

Ἀπόλλων, *Apollo,* god of light, of healing, of music, and of prophecy. Born on the island of Delos, he migrated to Delphi, where he set up the most celebrated oracle of ancient times.

Ἄρειος πάγος, *Areop′agus,* believed by the Greeks to signify *Hill of Ares* (Latin Mars), a rugged rock west of the Acropolis at Athens. It was the home of the Furies, avenging spirits that pursued murderers, and also the seat of the old aristocratic council of Athens. St. Paul probably addressed the Athenians from this vantage ground.

Ἀρίστιππος, *Aristip′pus,* a pupil of Socrates and the founder of the system of hedonism (ἡδονή *pleasure*). Because he came from Cyrē′ne in Africa, his school of philosophy was known as the Cyrenā′ic School.

Ἀριστοτέλης, *Aristotle* (384–322 B.C.), the most distinguished pupil of Plato and founder at Athens of the Peripatet′ic School of philosophy.

His prodigious scientific interest led him into many fields of research, and the results of his studies have been the basis of scientific thought down to modern times. He was tutor to Alexander the Great, who later supplied his former master with funds and material for the conduct of his investigations.

Ἀριστοφάνης, *Aristoph'anes* (about 450–386 B.C.), the most famous comic poet of his period. The eleven plays that survive form a priceless record of both the private and the political life of the Athens of his day.

Ἄρτεμις, *Ar'temis,* Latin Diana, sister of Apollo, virgin goddess of the hunt. As her brother was associated with the phenomena of the sun, so she was associated with the moon.

Ἀρχιμήδης, *Archimē'des* (287–212 B.C.), a remarkable mathematician and engineer of Syracuse. Although credited with wonderful inventions of practical importance, he was a true scientist in aiming primarily to enlarge the bounds of knowledge.

Ἀσίᾱ, *Asia,* a term much more limited in meaning among the ancients than at the present time. In the fifth century B.C. it embraced roughly what later came to be called Asia Minor.

Ἀτρεῖδαι, *Atrei'dæ,* sons of Atreus: (1) Agamem'non, leader of the expedition against Troy, whose seat of government was at Mycēnæ, and (2) Menelāus, King of Sparta and husband of Helen whose abduction by Paris of Troy was the occasion of the Trojan War.

Ἀττικός, -ή, -όν, *Attic,* pertaining to Attica, that part of Greece whose capital was Athens.

Ἀφροδῑ́τη, *Aphrodī'tē,* Latin Venus, goddess of love, wife of Hephæstus and mother of Eros. Her most familiar epithet is Cypris, alluding to her birth near the island of Cyprus, which she made her favorite haunt.

Ἀχαιοί, *Achæ'ans,* the name most commonly employed by Homer to designate the Greeks who fought at Troy. They seem to have been pretty widely scattered over the Greek peninsula and the Ægean islands at that time (12th century B.C.). In classic times the name was confined to the inhabitants of a narrow strip of land south of the Corinthian Gulf.

Ἀχιλλεύς, *Achil'les*, hero of Homer's *Iliad*. His wrath against Agamemnon, leader of the Greek forces, forms the main theme of the poem. Bravest of the Greek heroes, Achilles at last slays Hector, the champion of the Trojans.

Balaus'tion, the heroine of Robert Browning's poem, *Balaustion's Adventure*. A maiden from the island of Rhodes, she wins safe entry into Syracuse for herself and shipmates by the recital of Euripides' *Alcestis*. Balaustion herself is the poetic creation of Browning, but the incident is briefly told by Plutarch in his *Life of Nicias*.

Βίας, *Bi'as* (born about 570 B.C.), one of the so-called Seven Wise Men of Greece. He was not a formal philosopher but a student of the laws of his native Ionia, where he won fame and wealth by aiding his fellow-citizens in legal disputes.

Γέλα, *Ge'la*, a town in Sicily whose chief claim to glory consists in the fact that Æschylus died there.

Γοργίας, *Gor'gias*, a famous orator and sophist from Sicily. Going to Athens on an official mission in 427 B.C., he enthralled the young Athenians by his art as a public speaker. Plato used his name as the title of one of his dialogues.

Δᾱρεῖος, *Darī'us*, a name borne by a number of Persian kings. *Darius Hystaspis* was the greatest of them all. It was he who launched the first Persian invasion against Greece. *Darius Nothus* was king of Persia toward the close of the fifth century, B.C., and was the father of Artaxerxes II and Cyrus the Younger, under whom Xenophon and the Ten Thousand served.

Δελφοί, *Del'phī*, celebrated seat of Apollo's oracle, situated on the slopes of Mt. Parnassus, above the beautiful Crisæan plain. Recent excavations have disclosed the foundations of Apollo's temple and other ancient structures, including the stadium, scene of the Pythian Games. Delphi was regarded by the Greeks as the mid-point of the earth. The priests of the shrine for many centuries exerted a powerful influence throughout the world.

Δημοσθένης, *Demosthenes* (384–322 B.C.). Handicapped by nature and by fortune, through indomitable will, he forced his way to the foremost place among Greek orators and set the standard of eloquence for all time. His fame is most closely connected with his unremitting but unavailing struggle against Philip of Macedon and his son, Alexander the Great.

Διογένης, *Diogenes* (about 412–323 B.C.), a famous Cynic philosopher. See Κυνικοί. A native of Sinōpē, he spent most of his life in Athens and Corinth. He early gave up all thought of personal ambition and sought to make himself conspicuous for his contempt of riches and honors, and by his attacks on luxury. The stories of his residence in a tub and his search with a lantern in broad daylight for an honest man are but two of many anecdotes about this unique personality.

Ἑκάτη, *Hec'atē*, goddess of the crossroads and of the sorcery associated with darkness and the world of spirits. Propitiatory offerings of food at her wayside shrines appear to have been a godsend to irreligious vagabonds.

Ἕκτωρ, *Hector*, the most valiant of the many sons of Priam, King of Troy. Homer's *Iliad* closes with an account of the funeral rites in his honor after his death in single combat with Achilles. Though himself a Greek, the poet makes Trojan Hector one of the most attractive figures in all literature.

Ἑλένη, *Helen*, "fairest among women," wife of Menelāus. Her abduction by Paris of Troy was the occasion for the Trojan War.

Ἑλλάς, *Hellas*, the name the Greeks gave their own country. It was also applied to all lands which they occupied.

Ἕλληνες, *Hel'lēnes*, the Greeks.

Ἑλληνικός, -ή, -όν, *Hellen'ic, Greek*.

Ἐπίδαυρος, *Epidau'rus*, the most celebrated center of the worship of Asclepius, Latin Æsculapius, god of healing. It was situated near the east coast of Argolis in southern Greece. While not really a town, Epidaurus possessed a temple, dormitories, a gymnasium, a stadium, a large theater — perhaps the most beautiful now extant — and other equipment testifying to the popularity of that health resort.

Ἐπίχαρμος, *Epichar'mus*, the first great Greek comic poet. He lived in Sicily through the first half of the 5th century B.C.

Ἐρεχθεῖον, *Erechthē'um*, one of the most beautiful architectural achievements of fifth century Athens. Imposing remains are still to be seen on the Acropolis. Here were enshrined the sacred olive tree of Athena and the salt spring of Poseidon, mute witnesses to the famous contest of those deities for the honor of being patron of the city.

Ἑρμῆς, *Hermes,* Latin Mercury, a god of many functions — messenger of the gods, conductor of souls, god of trade, of thieves, of lucky chance.

Ἔρως, *Ēros,* Latin Cupid, son of Aphrodite and himself god of love, whose symbols were the bow and quiver.

Εὐκλείδης, *Euclid,* whose career fell in the third century B.C., was a distinguished mathematician of Alexandria. His chief contribution was the *Elements of Geometry,* in thirteen books. He was by no means the first to work in that field, but he wrote a treatise which has been studied by schoolboys ever since.

Εὐρῑπίδης, *Euripides* (480–406 B.C.), the youngest of the three great tragic poets of Athens. Of the ninety-two plays that were ascribed to him, we have nineteen. While not so popular in his lifetime as his rivals, he exerted a tremendous influence upon later literature. He employed the same myths as they did but humanized the action. His sententious style made him as quotable as Shakespeare.

Εὐφορίων, *Euphor'ion,* known only as the father of Æschylus.

Εὐφρᾱ́της, *Euphrā'tes,* the well-known river that forms the western boundary of Mesopotamia.

Ἐφιάλτης, *Ephial'tes,* the Greek traitor who revealed to the Persians the mountain trail that enabled them to outflank and massacre the defenders of Thermopylæ.

Ζεύς, *Zeus,* "father of gods and of men," the supreme deity in the Homeric pantheon.

Ἡράκλειτος, *Heraclī'tus* (born about 550 B.C.), one of the group of Ionian philosophers whose chief purpose was to explain the universe in which we live. His best known doctrine maintains that all things are really one and that apparent differences are due to the fact that there is always in progress a flow from one state of being to another. He was so gloomy in his view of life as to be called "The Weeping Philosopher," and so careless and profound in his writing that he was called "The Obscure."

Ἡρακλῆς, *Her'acles,* Latin Hercules, one of the most famous of the Greek heroes or demigods, noted for his great strength and hearty appetite.

Ἡρόδοτος, *Herod'otus* (484–about 425 B.C.), native of Halicarnassus in Asia Minor. His story of the Persian War, in nine books, is the earliest extant history. He traveled widely in search of material, took keen interest in all he heard and saw, and recorded his reflections and observations with a freshness that time can never dim. He recorded many false tales, but many of his stories have historical fact at their center. Above all, at a very early time he sensed the truth, that Greece was a beacon of civilization.

Ἡσίοδος, *Hē'siod,* of unknown date but commonly believed to belong to the period subsequent to Homer. His home was in Bœotia, a part of Greece that was more noted for the fertility of its soil than for the splendor of its intellectual attainments. Hesiod used the dialect of epic poetry and its metrical form but did not often rise to the level of its grandeur. His writings convey homely wisdom on practical affairs and preserve for us much that is of interest in the popular lore of his day.

Ἥφαιστος, *Hephæs'tus*, Latin Vulcan, god of the forge.

Θαλῆς, *Thales* (about 636–546 B.C.), foremost of the so-called Seven Wise Men of Greece. He lived in Ionia, was contemporary with Solon and Crœsus, and is regarded as the founder of Greek philosophy.

Θεμιστοκλῆς, *Themis'tocles* (about 525–460 B.C.), famous statesman and general of Athens, largely responsible for her maritime development.

Θέογνις, *Theog'nis* (sixth century B.C.), one of the few literary figures of Athens' neighbor, Megara, that were fated to escape oblivion. His verse is didactic in form and not of the highest order, but it contains much that is quotable.

Θεόφραστος, *Theophras'tus* (about 372–287 B.C.). Born on the island of Lesbos, he became the most distinguished pupil of Aristotle and succeeded him in charge of the Lycēum at Athens.

Θερμοπύλαι, *Thermop'ylæ,* the famous pass from Thessaly into Locris, where in 480 B.C. Leonidas and his three hundred held in check for a time the Persian horde of Xerxes. To-day the sea has receded some distance, so that it is now difficult to visualize the ancient setting. See **Λεωνίδας**.

Θουκυδίδης, *Thucyd'ides*, an Athenian (born about 471 B.C.). He took part in the wars and politics of his country, but was finally exiled from home. He spent some of his time traveling. He also wrote a history of Greece beginning where Herodotus left off. In this he narrates many events in which he himself had a part. Yet he does not glorify himself or condone his failures. Nor does he hold any grudge against the country which exiled him. His attitude toward the writing of history is very scientific. Throughout, his work shows impartiality and accuracy, as well as a keen analytical and critical power. His style is intensely vivid.

Θρᾷξ, *Thracian,* one of an ancient people occupying the territory northeast of Macedonia as far as the mouth of the Danube.

Ἴλιος, *Ilius,* the scene of Homer's *Iliad.* Once thought to have been but a dream city, it is now known to have been a city of importance in history. So strategic a position did it occupy in the trade route between East and West that, although repeatedly destroyed, it was as often resettled. At least nine cities succeeded one another on the same site from 3000 B.C. to the days of Imperial Rome. Homer's Ilium was the sixth from the bottom.

Ἱππίας, *Hip'pias,* son of Peisistratus, from whom he inherited the post of tyrant of Athens. Expelled in 510 B.C., he accompanied the Persians on their fruitless invasion of Greece.

Ἱπποκλείδης, *Hippoclī'des,* a wealthy Athenian noble of the early part of the sixth century B.C.

Κάδμος, *Cadmus,* mythical founder of Thebes and credited with having brought with him from Phœnicia a knowledge of the alphabet.

Καλλίμαχος, *Callim'achus* (about 310–240 B.C.). Born at Cȳrēnē in north Africa, he spent most of his days at Alexandria, where he may have been in charge of the great Library. A learned man, he became also a most famous elegiac poet.

Καστωλός, *Castō'lus,* a Lydian town of Asia Minor.

Καύνιοι, *Caunians,* inhabitants of Caunus in Asia Minor, opposite Rhodes.

Κεῖος, -ᾱ, -ον, *Cēan, i.e.,* from Cēos, one of the islands of the Cyclades.

Κίλισσα (ἡ), *Cilician woman.* Xenophon uses this term in speaking of the Cilician queen who visited Cyrus on his march inland to fight his brother, Artaxerxes.

Κλέαρχος, *Clear'chus*, a Spartan exile. He proved an able general under Cyrus the Younger, as depicted by Xenophon in the *Anabasis*.

Κλεισθένης, *Clīs'thenes*, tyrant of Sicyon.

Κνωσσός, *Cnossus*, ancient seat of the Cretan king, Minos. The excavations of Sir Arthur Evans prove that the people of Cnossus as early as 2500 B.C. enjoyed a high degree of civilization and possessed a powerful empire. His discoveries go far to revive belief in the essential truth of the Minos legend, the famous labyrinth being probably the elaborate palace of that king.

Κρήτη, *Crēte*, one of the largest of the Greek islands and the earliest center of culture in the Mediterranean because of its contact with Egypt and the Orient.

Κυνικοί, *Cynics*, name given to a school of philosophers that developed in Athens during the early part of the fourth century B.C. They defined virtue as extreme simplicity in living and in fact themselves lived so simply and with such utter disregard for the ordinary conventions and decencies of life that they were said to be *dog-like* (κυνικοί, from κύων, κυνός *dog*).

Κύπρις, *Cypris*, a favorite epithet of Aphrodite, due to her association with the island of Cyprus.

Κῦρος, *Cyrus*. There were two famous Persians of that name: (1) *Cyrus the Great* (about 550 B.C.), founder of the Persian empire, about whose youth Xenophon has given us a romantic account in his *Cyropædia*; (2) *Cyrus the Younger*, son of Darius Nothus, slain in the battle of Cunaxa (401 B.C.) while heading an expedition against his brother Artaxerxes, who held the Persian throne. The account of that ill-fated expedition is contained in Xenophon's *Anabasis*.

Λακεδαιμόνιοι, *Lac'edemo'nians*, inhabitants of Lacedēmon, often synonymous with Spartans.

Λακεδαίμων, *Lac'edē'mon*, a fertile valley of southern Greece, whose capital was Sparta.

Λακωνικός, -ή, -όν, *Laco'nian*, a synonym for Spartan. (Compare English LACONIC.)

Λεωνίδᾱς, *Leon'idas*, king of Sparta, who won undying fame through the voluntary sacrifice of himself and three hundred of his fellow countrymen in the heroic endeavor to check the Persians at Thermopylæ.

Λήδα, *Lēda,* mother of Clytemnestra, Agamemnon's haughty queen, of Helen, the wife of Menelaus, and of Castor and Polydeuces, Latin Pollux, patrons of horsemanship and boxing.

Λῆμνος, *Lemnos,* an island in the Ægean not far from the coast of Asia Minor.

Λιβύη, *Lib'ya,* the ancient Greek name for Africa.

Λουκιανός, *Lucian* (about 120–200 A.D.), born of humble parents in the frontier town of Samosata on the headwaters of the Euphrates. He called himself a Syrian, but although his career fell nearly half a millennium after the bloom of Greek literature, his copious writings in that language, delightfully phrased, testify not only to his excellent schooling and genius but also to the spread of Greek culture and the remarkable vitality of Greek letters.

Λυσίας, *Lys'ias,* son of a wealthy and cultured foreign resident at Athens. Because of the political and economic troubles that followed the Peloponnesian War, he became a professional speechwriter and one of the most famous of the Attic orators.

Μαραθών, *Marathon,* a swampy meadow northeast of Athens, where the Athenians in 490 B.C. administered a severe defeat to the invading Persians. As a result, further attacks were postponed ten years, during which time the Greeks had opportunity to prepare for the glorious victories of Salamis and Platæa. The Athenians never tired of referring to the day of the battle.

Μαρδόνιος, *Mardonius,* son-in-law of Darius, king of Persia, and prominent in the Persian struggle against the Greeks. He lost his life in the rout at Platæa.

Μάρκος Αὐρήλιος, *Marcus Aurēlius* (121–180 A.D.), best known as author of the famous *Meditations.* Although a Roman and for nineteen years an emperor of the Romans, he chose Greek as the medium for recording his intimate reflections.

Μένανδρος, *Menan'der* (about 342–292 B.C.), the most celebrated representative of the New Comedy. Early in the twentieth century considerable fragments of four of his plays were recovered from the sands of Egypt. He shares with Euripides, to whom he was much indebted, the honor of having been quoted more than most of the other Greek men of letters.

Μένιππος, *Menippus*, a Cynic philosopher of the third century B.C. famed for the sting of his satire.

Μένων, *Menon*, one of the Greek generals of the *Anabasis*.

Μῆδοι, *Mēdes*, the name most commonly used by Greeks to denote the Persians. Properly speaking it belonged rather to the people whose overthrow was the first step in the creation of the Persian empire.

Μηλιεύς, *Mēlian* or *Malian*, an inhabitant of Melis or Malis, a district in southern Thessaly.

Μίμνερμος, *Mimner'mus*, an elegiac poet of Asia Minor who lived in the seventh century B.C.

Μίνως, *Mīnos*, semi-mythical ruler and lawgiver of Crete and judge in the lower world.

Μοῦσαι, *Muses*, originally nymphs of springs that gave inspiration, such as Castalia at Delphi. Later, they were the goddesses of song in general. Still later, they became the representatives of the various kinds of poetry, arts, and sciences. Usually they are referred to as nine in number.

Μύρων, *Myron*, celebrated Athenian sculptor of the fifth century B.C. He had a leaning toward statues of athletes and he did much to free art from its rigid pose.

Νάρκισσος, *Narcissus*, a beautiful youth who fell in love with his own reflection in the water and pined away because his love was not returned.

Νασαμῶνες, *Nasamo'nians*, a people of north Africa, dwelling near the Mediterranean, west of Egypt.

Ξενοφῶν, *Xen'ophon* (about 430–357 B.C.). Athenian historian and essayist, pupil of Socrates, whose advice he sought before joining the expedition of Cyrus, the fortunes of which he described from personal experience in the celebrated *Anabasis*.

Ξέρξης, *Xerxes* (about 519–465 B.C.), king of Persia and leader of the expedition for the conquest of Greece (480 B.C.).

Ὀδυσσεύς, *Odysseus*, Latin Ulysses, king of Ithaca, famed for his resourcefulness. His ten years of adventure in the effort to regain his native land after the fall of Troy and his exciting struggle against his faithful wife's suitors constitute the fabric of Homer's *Odyssey*.

Ὅμηρος, *Homer*, greatest epic poet in the world's history. Having no reliable evidence regarding the poet other than his poems, critics once doubted his existence. For a long time, because of the magnitude of his work and because of certain small inconsistencies of detail, this doubt continued. Modern scholarship, however, is tending to revive a belief in his personality and in his right to be regarded as creator of both *Iliad* and *Odyssey*. The most recent investigations place him not long after the Trojan War (1184 B.C.) of which he sang.

Ὀρόντᾱς, *Oron'tas*, a Persian courtier whose treachery toward Cyrus the Younger and subsequent conviction are dramatically related by Xenophon in the *Anabasis*.

Πάν, *Pan*, an uncouth deity of field and woodland, with the legs and tail of a goat.

Παρύσατις, *Parys'atis*, wife of Darius Nothus and mother of Artaxerxes and Cyrus.

Πειθώ, *Persuasion*, as a goddess.

Πείσων, *Piso*, one of the Thirty Tyrants, who for a brief period at the close of the Peloponnesian War terrorized Athens.

Περίανδρος, *Periander*, ruler of Corinth (625–585 B.C.). Like other Greek sovereigns he was a patron of literature and philosophy. By many he was considered one of the so-called Seven Wise Men of Greece.

Περικλῆς, *Pericles* (about 495–429 B.C.), great Athenian statesman and orator. In spite of being aristocratic in his tastes and associating with intellectuals, he is noted for his democratic reforms. Under his leadership Athens reached her greatest brilliance in art and letters.

Πίνδαρος, *Pindar* (518–438 B.C.), the most famous Greek lyric poet. Although a citizen of Bœotian Thebes, his interest was national in its scope. His poetry is known now principally through his epinician odes, songs of almost barbaric splendor composed in honor of victors in the great athletic festivals of Greece.

Πλάτων, *Plato* (427–347 B.C.), the most illustrious pupil of Socrates, founder of the Academy, and author of numerous dialogues wherein he expounded and developed the philosophic doctrines of his great master.

Πλούταρχος, *Plutarch* (about 46–120 A.D.), one of the few literary figures of Bœotia. Best known for his *Parallel Lives*, a collection of fascinating biographies, whose title reveals the author's purpose to pit against each other Greek and Roman. He deals with lawgivers, statesmen, soldiers, orators, and other types of men in public life.

Πλούτων, *Pluto,* god of the underworld.

Ποσειδῶν, *Posei'don,* Latin Neptune, god of the sea.

Πραξιτέλης, *Praxit'eles* (about 400–336 B.C.), a most brilliant Athenian sculptor, famed for the grace of his compositions. His Hermes (at Olympia) is especially celebrated to-day both for its rare charm and also because it is the only extant Greek original from a great sculptor whose identity is undisputed. The ancients rated much higher his Satyr, a Roman copy of which figures in Hawthorne's *Marble Faun.*

Πρόξενος, *Prox'enus,* a Bœotian general in the army of Cyrus the Younger and friend of Xenophon, who joined the celebrated expedition at his invitation.

Πρωταγόρᾱς, *Protag'oras* (about 481–411 B.C.), a famous Sophist from Abdēra. He visited Athens and other Greek cities and was highly valued for his teaching, one pupil paying as much as 100 minæ for his course.

Πῡθαγόρᾱς, *Pythag'oras* (latter half of the sixth century B.C.), founder of the influential school of philosophy at Croton, Italy. He left no writings, so that it is difficult to know what to ascribe to master and what to pupils who rendered him unusual homage. He was deeply interested in mathematics and is thought to have attached mystic value to certain mathematical phenomena. Metempsychosis, or reincarnation, has been listed among his doctrines.

Πυθίᾱ, *Pythia,* the priestess of Apollo at Delphi, who, when under the spell of the god, gave forth frenzied utterances which the priests interpreted as oracles of Apollo.

Σαλαμίς, *Sal'amis,* an island belonging to Athens and lying opposite its port of Piræus. Its chief claim to glory rests upon the naval battle off its shores in 480 B.C. in which the Greeks crushed the Persians, who outnumbered them.

Σαπφώ, *Sappho,* born on the island of Lesbos in the second half of the seventh century B.C., the most brilliant poetess of all antiquity. She seems to have gathered about her a circle of girls and women who admired and emulated her. Additional fragments of her verse have in recent years been recovered in Egypt.

Σέρῑφος, *Serī'phos*, an obscure islet southeast of Attica.

Σικελιώτης, *a Sicilian Greek.*

Σικυών, *Sic'yon*, a city on the south shore of the Corinthian Gulf.

Σικυώνιος, -ᾱ, -ον, *Sicyo'nian*, pertaining to Sicyon.

Σῑλᾱνός, *Silānus*, a Greek soothsayer in the army of Cyrus.

Σιμωνίδης, *Simon'ides* (556–468 B.C.), a famous lyric poet, born on the island of Cēos, and known as Simonides of Cēos.

Σόλοι, *Soli*, a city on the coast of Cilicia. It had been colonized by Greeks from Rhodes, but in time its inhabitants came to speak such bad Greek that their name became, and still is, a by-word for incorrectness in the use of language: σολοικισμός, *solecism.*

Σόλων, *Solon* (about 640–558 B.C.), Athenian statesman and lawgiver, to whose genius his fellow-countrymen of later days were inclined to attribute most that was worthwhile in the constitution of Athens. His reflections on society and politics he committed to verse of no mean merit. Some fragments of his verse survive.

Σοφοκλῆς, *Sophocles* (495–406 B.C.), one of the three great tragic poets of Athens. A most prolific writer, he retained his mental vigor and his popularity till his death. Seven of his plays are extant.

Σπάρτη, *Sparta*, capital of Laconia in southern Greece, famed for its brave and hardy warriors but sterile in intellectual achievement.

Σπαρτιᾱ́της, *Spartan.*

Συρᾱκοῦσαι, *Syracuse*, most famous Greek settlement in Sicily, possessing an excellent harbor and a prosperous trade. Its rulers were patrons of arts and letters.

Σωκράτης, *Socrates* (470–399 B.C.), most famous Athenian of all time. Not claiming to have any special wisdom, he was devoted to the pursuit of truth and in his search he developed the art of dialectic (question and answer). He had no regular school and left no writings. His most distinguished pupil was Plato, but his influence is to be found in most later philosophy.

Σωτηρίδᾱς, *Soter'idas*, an obscure Sicyonian in the Greek contingent that followed Cyrus.

Τίσανδρος, *Tisander*, father of Hippoclides.

Τισσαφέρνης, *Tissapher'nes*, a Persian provincial governor under Artaxerxes, brother of Cyrus the Younger, and intensely hostile to the latter.

Τρῶες, *Trojans.*

Τυρταῖος, *Tyrtæ'us* (about 650 B.C.), writer of Spartan hymns and warsongs. Only a few specimens of his verses are extant.

Τυρώ, *Tyro*, a princess beloved of Poseidon.

Ὑάκινθος, *Hyacin'thus*, a beautiful youth beloved of Apollo, and accidentally slain by his discus. From the blood sprang up the hyacinth flower bearing the letters AI, AI, "woe, woe," upon its petals to signify Apollo's deep sorrow.

Φειδίας, *Phidias*, universally regarded as one of the world's greatest sculptors. He is said to have been chosen by Pericles to oversee the entire work connected with the erection of the Parthenon about the middle of the fifth century B.C. He deserves credit for its general excellence and may have done with his own hand much of the sculptural work. His colossal gold and ivory statue of Athena was greatly admired. A similar statue of Zeus, executed by him for the god's temple at Olympia, fixed the Greek conception of the king of gods and of men.

Φιλήμων, *Philēmon* (361–about 260 B.C.), a prolific writer of the New Comedy, which was a comedy of manners. Roman writers paid him the compliment of borrowing freely from his plays.

Φίλιππος, *Philip* (382–336 B.C.), king of Macedonia. He developed the Macedonian phalanx, by means of which, as well as by his genius for diplomacy, he became the overlord of Greece and paved the way for the conquests of his illustrious son, Alexander.

Φρύγες, *Phrygians*, a non-Greek people dwelling in Asia Minor.

Χάρων, *Charon*, an uncouth, gray-bearded boatman who ferried to Hades the souls of the dead. Lucian with his sardonic humor and skepticism delights to caricature Charon and his calling.

Ψαμμήτιχος, *Psamme'tichus*, ruler of Egypt (666–610 B.C.) and friendly to the Greeks, by whose aid he was enabled to establish his throne.

THE PORCH OF THE MAIDENS

For different views of this porch of the Erechtheum, see pages 74 and 334.

GREEK-ENGLISH VOCABULARY

The complete list of principal parts is given only when a verb is irregular. For regular verbs only the present and future tenses are given, followed by *etc.* For proper names, consult pages 335–349.

A

ἀ-, a negativing prefix ; **ἀν-** before vowels.

ἁ, dialectic for ἡ.

ἅ, see ὅς.

ἀγαγεῖν, ἀγάγω, etc., see ἄγω.

ἀγαθός, -ή, -όν : *good*, in general ; hence good in special fields, *e.g.*, *brave*, *useful.*

ἄγαν, adv.: *too much.*

ἀγανακτάω, ἀγανακτήσω, etc.: *be angry.*

ἀγαπάω, ἀγαπήσω, etc.: *love*, *be thankful.*

ἀγγελίᾱ, -ᾱς, ἡ : *message*, *tidings.*

ἀγγέλλω (ἀγγελ-), ἀγγελῶ, ἤγγειλα, ἤγγελκα, ἤγγελμαι, ἠγγέλθην : *bring word*, *announce*, *report.*

ἄγγελος, -ου, ὁ : *messenger.*

ἀ-γεννής, -ές : *illborn*, *base.*

ἀ-γήραντος, -ον : *unaging*, *ageless*, *undying*, *immortal.*

ἁγιάζω, ἁγιάσω, etc. : *make holy*, *sanctify.*

ἀ-γνοέω, ἀγνοήσω, etc. [γι-γνώ-σκω] : *fail to know*, *be ignorant of.*

ἄ-γνωστος, -ον : *unknown.*

ἀγορᾱ́, -ᾶς, ἡ : *assembly*, *market*, *market-place.*

ἀγοράζω (ἀγοραδ-), ἀγοράσω, etc.: *do marketing*, *visit market*, *buy.*

ἀγρεύω, ἀγρεύσω, etc.: *hunt.*

ἄγροικος, -ου, ὁ : *of the country*, *rustic.*

ἀγρός, -οῦ, ὁ : *field*, *farm*, *country.*

ἄγχω, ἄγξω, etc.: *throttle*, *choke.*

ἄγω, ἄξω, ἤγαγον, ἦχα, ἦγμαι, ἤχθην : *drive*, *lead*, *bring*, *march* (drive an army). εἰρήνην ἄγειν : *maintain peace.*

ἀγών, -ῶνος, ὁ : *a bringing together*, *contest* (cf. "meet"), *struggle.*

ἀγωνίζομαι (ἀγωνιδ-), ἀγωνιοῦμαι, etc.: *contend*, *struggle.*

ἀδελφός, -οῦ, ὁ : *brother.*

ἄ-δηλος, -ον : *not clear*, *obscure.*

ἀ-διάβατος, -ον [βαίνω]: *uncrossable*, *impassable.*

ἀ-δικέω, ἀδικήσω, etc. : *be unjust*, *mistreat*, *injure*, *do wrong.*

ἄ-δικος, -ον [δίκη]: *unjust*, *wicked*, *wrong.*

ἀδο-λέσχης, -ου, ὁ: *talkative person*, *garrulous man.*

ἁδυ, dialectic for ἡδύ, see ἡδύς.

ἀ-δύνατος, -ον [δύναμαι]: *unable*, *impossible*, *impotent.*

ᾄδω, ᾄσω or ᾄσομαι : *sing*, *chant.*

ἀεί, adv.: *always*, *ever*, *at any given time.*

ἀ-εργίη, -ης, ἡ [ἔργον]: *idleness*, *laziness.*

ἆθλον, -ου, τό: *prize.*

ἀθροίζω (ἀθροιδ-), ἀθροίσω, etc.: *collect.*

ἀθρόος, -ā, -ον: *collected, together, in a body.*

ἀ-θῡμέω, ἀθῡμήσω, etc. [θῡμός]: *be disheartened* or *discouraged.*

αἱ, see ὁ.

αἵ, see ὅς.

αἰδήμων, -ον: *modest, respectful.*

αἷμα, -ατος, τό: *blood.*

αἶξ, αἰγός, ὁ or ἡ: *goat.*

αἱρέω (αἱρε-, ἑλ-), αἱρήσω, εἷλον, ᾕρηκα, ᾕρημαι, ᾑρέθην: *take, seize, capture;* mid., *choose, elect.*

αἷς, see ὅς.

αἰσθάνομαι (αἰσθ-), αἰσθήσομαι, ᾐσθόμην, ᾔσθημαι: *perceive* (in any way).

αἰσχρός, -ά, -όν: *ugly, disgraceful, shameful.*

αἰσχῡ́νω, αἰσχυνῶ, ᾔσχῡνα, ᾐσχύνθην: *dishonor, shame;* mid. as pass. depon., *be* or *feel ashamed, stand in awe of.*

αἰτέω, αἰτήσω, etc.: *ask for, demand.*

αἰτίᾱ, -ᾱς, ἡ: *cause, blame.*

αἰτιάομαι, αἰτιάσομαι, etc., mid. depon.: *accuse, blame, charge, find fault with.*

αἴτιος, -ā, -ον: *responsible, blameworthy;* with G., *responsible for, the cause of.*

αἰχμητής, -οῦ, ὁ: *spearman, warrior.* Poetic.

αἰών, -ῶνος, ὁ: *age, time, period.*

ἀκούω, ἀκούσομαι, ἤκουσα, ἀκήκοα, ἠκούσθην [ACOUSTIC]: *hear, listen to.*

ἄκρᾱ, -ᾱς, ἡ [ἄκρος]: *point* (of land), *promontory, cape.*

ἀκρό-πολις, -εως, ἡ: *upper city, citadel.*

ἄκρος, -ā, -ον: *at the point* or *peak,* hence *topmost, top;* τὸ ἄκρον: *summit, top.*

ἄλγος, -ους, τό: *pain.*

ἀ-λήθεια, -ᾱς, ἡ [λανθάνω]: *truth, truthfulness.*

ἀ-ληθεύω, ἀληθεύσω, etc.: *speak truly, prove correct.*

ἀ-ληθής, -ές: *true;* τὸ ἀληθές: *the truth.*

ἁλιεύς, -έως, ὁ: *fisherman.*

ἁλίσκομαι (ἁλ-, ἁλο-), ἁλώσομαι, ἑάλων, ἑάλωκα, used as pass. of αἱρέω: *be taken, be captured.*

ἀλκή, -ῆς, ἡ: *strength.*

ἄλκιμος, -η, -ον: *strong, valiant.*

ἀλλά, adversative conj. [ἄλλος]: *but, however, yet;* exclamatory: *well, why.*

ἀλλάττω (ἀλλαγ-), ἀλλάξω, ἤλλαξα, ἤλλαχα, ἤλλαγμαι, ἠλλάχθην or ἠλλάγην: *alter, change.*

ἀλλήλων, reciprocal pron.: *of each other, of one another.*

ἄλλος, -η, -ο: *other, another;* with the article, *the other, the rest of;* when repeated, *some one, others another, e.g.*, ἄλλοι ἄλλην ὁδὸν ἀπῆλθον.

ἄλλως, adv.: *otherwise.*

ἄλσος, -ους, τό: *grove.*

ἁλώσομαι, see ἁλίσκομαι.

ἅμα, adv.: *at the same time as, together with;* with D., ἅμα τῇ ἡμέρᾳ: *at daybreak.*

ἅμαξα, -ης, ἡ: *cart, wagon.*

ἁμαρτάνω (ἁμαρτ-), ἁμαρτήσομαι, ἥμαρτον, ἡμάρτηκα, ἡμάρτημαι, ἡμαρτήθην: *miss one's aim,* with G.; *fail, err, do wrong.*

ἀ-μαχεί, adv. [μάχη]: *without a fight.*

ἀμείβω, ἀμείψω, ἤμειψα, ἠμείφθην: *change, exchange, interchange.*

ἀμείνων, -ον, comp. of ἀγαθός: *better, braver, stronger.*

ἀ-μελέω, ἀμελήσω, etc. [μέλει]: *not care, disregard, neglect, be careless*, with G.; ἀμέλει, imperative, as interjection: *never mind, of course.*

ἁμιλλάομαι, ἁμιλλήσομαι, etc.: *race.*

ἄ-μορφος, -ον: *misshapen, unshapely, shapeless, ugly.*

ἀμῡ́νω, ἀμυνῶ, ἤμῡνα: *ward off;* mid., *ward off from oneself, defend oneself against.*

ἀμφί, prep. with G. and A.: *on both sides of, about;* with G., *about, concerning;* with A., *about, around, near* (of numbers); in compounds, *around, about.*

ἀμφί-θυρος, -ον: *with doors on both sides.*

ἀμφι-τίθημι, see τίθημι: *place about, surround.*

ἀμφότερος, -ᾱ, -ον: *both.*

ἄν, post-positive particle belonging to certain types of conditional clauses but lacking an exact English equivalent.

ἄν, contracted form of ἐάν.

ἀνά, prep. with A.: *up;* of place, *up, upon, up along;* with numerals, denoting distribution, *by;* of manner, ἀνὰ κράτος, *at full speed.* In compounds, *up, back, again* (with intensive force, often with a reversing force.)

ἀνα-βαίνω, see βαίνω: *go up, mount, march inland, i.e.*, up from the coast.

ἀνα-βάλλω, see βάλλω: *throw up, throw back, postpone.*

ἀνά-βασις, -εως, ἡ [ἀναβαίνω]: *inland march.*

ἀνα-γιγνώσκω, see γιγνώσκω: *recognize, read.*

ἀναγκάζω (ἀναγκαδ-), ἀναγκάσω, etc.: *compel.*

ἀναγκαῖος, -ᾱ, -ον; *necessary.*

ἀνάγκη, -ης, ἡ: *necessity;* frequently used as verb, ἐστί being omitted.

ἀνα-γνούς, see ἀναγιγνώσκω.

ἀνα-θεωρέω, see θεωρέω: *observe anew* or *again.*

ἀν-αιδείᾱ, -ᾱς, ἡ: *shamelessness, effrontery.*

ἀν-αιρέω, see αἱρέω: *take up, take away, abolish, annul.*

ἀνα-κηρύττω, see κηρύττω: *proclaim, put up* (for sale).

ἀνα-κρούω, ἀνακρούσω, etc.: *push back, back water, strike up* (a song).

ἀνα-μιμνῄσκω, see μιμνῄσκω: *remind, recall to mind.*

ἀνά-μνησις, -εως, ἡ: *recollection, reminding.*

ἀνάσσω, ἀνάξω, ἄναξα: *be king, rule.*

ἀνα-τείνω, see τείνω: *stretch up, hold up.*

ἀνα-τέλλω, ἀνέτειλα: *rise* (especially of sun and moon).

ἀνα-τρέπω, see τρέπω: *upturn, turn upside down, overturn.*

ἄναυρος, -ου, ὁ: *stream, river.* Poetic.

ἀνδράποδον, -ου, τό: *slave, captive in war.*

ἀνδρεῖος, -ᾱ, -ον [ἀνήρ]: *manly, brave, bold.*

ἀνδρόω, ἀνδρώσω, etc.: *become a man, come of age.*

ἀ-νεμέσητος, -ον: *blameless, free of reproach.*

ἄνεμος, -ου, ὁ: *wind.*

ἄνευ, improper prep. with G.: *without.*

ἀνήρ, ἀνδρός, ὁ: *man* (as differentiated from woman or child), *husband.*

ἀνθέω, ἀνθήσω, etc.: *flower, bloom, flourish.*

ἀνθρώπινος, -η, -ον: *human.*

ἄνθρωπος, -ου, ὁ: *human being, person, man;* often contemptuous.

ἄν-ισος, -ον: *unequal, uneven.*

ἀν-οίγνῡμι, ἀνοίξω, ἀνέῳξα, ἀνέῳγα or ἀνέῳχα, ἀνέῳγμαι, ἀνεῴχθην: *open up.*

ἀ-νόμημος, -ον: *illegal, lawless.*

ἀντ-έχω, see ἔχω: *hold (out) against, withstand.*

ἀντί, prep. with G.: *against, instead of, in return for.* In compounds, *in opposition* and all of above meanings.

ἀντίος, -ᾱ, -ον: *opposed to, facing, hostile.*

ἄν-υδρος, -ον: *unwatered, arid.*

ἀν-υπόπτως [ὑπ-οπτεύω], adv.: *without suspicion.*

ἄνω, adv. [ἀνά]: *up, upwards, above.*

ἀξίνη, -ης, ἡ: *ax.*

ἄξιος, -ᾱ, -ον: *worthy, worth* (with G.), *valuable.*

ἀξιόω, ἀξιώσω, etc.: *think worthy* or *fit,* hence *ask as one's right, demand, expect.*

ἀξίως, adv.: *worthily, fittingly.*

ἀοίδιμος, -ον [ᾄδω]: *renowned in song, celebrated.*

ἀπ-αιτέω, see αἰτέω: *ask back, ask what is due.*

ἀπ-αλλάττω, see ἀλλάττω: *change from, depart from;* pass., *be relieved from.*

ἀπ-ανθέω, see ἀνθέω: *lose one's bloom, fade, wither.*

ἅπαξ, adv.: *altogether, once, once for all.*

ἅ-πᾱς, see πᾶς: *altogether, all, entire.*

ἄπ-ειμι, see εἰμί: *be away, be absent.*

ἄπ-ειμι, see εἶμι: *go away.*

ἀ-πειρίᾱ, -ᾱς, ἡ: *inexperience, unacquaintance.*

ἄ-πειρος, -ον: *inexperienced, unacquainted.*

ἅπερ, see ὅσπερ.

ἀπ-έχω, see ἔχω: *hold off, be distant, be away;* mid., *hold oneself off, refrain.*

ἀπ-ιέναι, see ἄπειμι.

ἀπό, prep. with G.: *from;* of place, *away from;* of time, *starting from, after;* of source, *from, because of.* In compounds, generally *away from, back, in return, completely.* In elision, before rough breathing, ἀφ'.

ἀπο-βάλλω, see βάλλω: *throw away.*

ἀπο-βλέπω, see βλέπω: *look away at,* hence *look at intently.*

ἀπο-δείκνῡμι, see δείκνῡμι: *point out, appoint, prove.*

ἀπό-δειξις, -εως, ἡ: *demonstration, proof.*

ἀπο-δίδωμι, see δίδωμι: *give back, repay, pay what is due;* mid., *sell.*

ἀπο-θνῄσκω, ἀποθανοῦμαι, ἀπέθανον, τέθνηκα: *die, be killed.*

ἀπο-κερδαίνω, ἀποκερδήσω or ἀποκερδανῶ, ἀπεκέρδησα or ἀπεκέρδᾱνα: *make profit from.*

ἀπο-κρίνομαι, ἀποκρινοῦμαι, etc.: *give answer, answer. reply.*

ἀπο-κρύπτω, see κρύπτω: *hide away.*

ἀπο-κτείνω, ἀποκτενῶ, ἀπέκτεινα, ἀπέκτονα: *kill off.*

ἀπ-όλλῡμι, see ὄλλῡμι: *destroy, lose;* mid., *perish, be lost.*

ἀπο-λῡ́ω, see λύω: *set free from, release.*

ἀπ-ολώλεκα, see ἀπόλλῡμι.

ἀπο-νέμω, see νέμω: *apportion, divide.*

ἀ-πορέω, ἀπορήσω, etc. [πόρος]: *be without a way, be at a loss, be in distress, be troubled, be helpless.*

ἀ-πορίᾱ, -ᾱς, ἡ: *helplessness, lack, distress, difficulty.*

ἄ-πορος, -ον: *without means, helpless; impassable.*

ἀπ-ορχέομαι, ἀπορχήσομαι, etc.: *dance away, lose by dancing.*

ἀπο-στερέω, ἀποστερήσω, etc.: *deprive, defraud, rob, withhold.*

ἀπο-τίθημι, see τίθημι: *put away, put aside.*

ἀπο-τυγχάνω, see τυγχάνω: *fail to hit, miss, lose.*

ἀπο-φεύγω, see φεύγω: *flee away, escape, be acquitted* (legal).

ἄρα, post-pos. particle: *therefore, then.*

ἆρα, interr. particle indicating an impatient question: *then, surely.* Most often untranslated.

ἀργύριον, -ου, τό: *silver, money.* Compare French *argent.*

ἀργύρωμα, -ατος, τό: *silver work.*

ἀρετή, -ῆς, ἡ: *goodness* (in whatever sense), *fitness, excellence, bravery.*

ἀριθμός, -οῦ, ὁ: *number, numbering.*

ἀρι-πρεπής, -ές: *very prominent, distinguished.*

ἄριστος, -η, -ον, superlative of ἀγαθός: *best* (in whatever sense).

ἅρμα, -ατος, τό: *chariot.*

ἁρμ-άμαξα, -ης, ἡ: *covered carriage.*

ἁρπάζω (ἁρπαδ-), ἁρπάσω, etc.: *seize, carry off, plunder.*

ἄρτος, -ου, ὁ: *bread.*

ἀρχαῖος, -ᾱ, -ον: *original, ancient, primitive.*

ἀρχή, -ῆς, ἡ: *beginning, leadership, rule, government; principle* (philosophy).

ἀρχ-ιερεύς, -έως, ὁ: *chief priest.*

ἄρχω, ἄρξω, ἦρξα, ἦργμαι, ἤρχθην: *begin, take the lead, command, rule,* with G.

ἄρχων, -οντος, ὁ: *archon, ruler, commander, leader.*

ἀ-σθενέω, ἠσθένησα: *be* or *become weak, be ill.*

ᾆσμα, -ατος, τό [ᾄδω]: *song.*

ἀσπίς, -ίδος, ἡ: *shield.*

ἀστράγαλος, -ου, ὁ: *knucklebones* used as *dice.*

ἀ-σφαλής, -ές: *not slipping, safe, certain, sure.*

ἄ-σχημος, -ον: *illformed, ungainly, awkward.*

ἄτερ, improper prep. with G.: *without.*

ἀ-τῑμάζω, ἀτῑμάσω, etc. [τῑμή]: *dishonor, disgrace, disfranchize.*

ἀτραπός, -οῦ, ἡ: *path, side path.*

ἀτύζομαι, ἠτύχθην: *be amazed* or *crazed.*

αὖ, adv.: *again, on the other hand.*

αὖθις, adv.: *again.*

αὐλεῖος, -ᾱ,-ον: *of the courtyard.*

αὐλέω, αὐλήσω, etc.: *play the pipe.*

αὐλητής, -οῦ, ὁ: *piper.*

αὔριον, adv.: *to-morrow.*

αὐτίκα, adv.: *at this very moment, immediately.*

αὐτό-ματος, -ον : *self-acting, of one's own accord, voluntarily.*

αὐτός, -ή, -ό, intensive pronoun : *self, same;* also *him, her, it,* though never in the nominative.

αὐτοῦ, adv. : *here, there.*

αὑτοῦ, see ἑαυτοῦ.

ἀφ', see ἀπό.

ἀφ-αιρέω, see αἱρέω : *take away.*

ἀ-φανής, -ές [φαίνω] : *invisible, obscure, out of sight.*

ἀφ-ίημι, see ἵημι : *send away, let go, dismiss.*

ἀφ-ικνέομαι, ἀφίξομαι, ἀφῑκόμην, ἀφῖγμαι : *come from, arrive, reach.*

ἀφ-ιππεύω, ἀφιππεύσω, etc. [ἵππος] : *ride away.*

ἀφ-ίστημι, see ἵστημι : *cause to stand aside;* mid. and 2d aor. act., *stand aside, revolt.*

ἄχθομαι, ἤχθημαι, ἠχθέσθην : *be annoyed, be burdened, be vexed.*

ἄψ, adv. : *back.*

B

βάθος, -ους, τό : *depth.*

βαθυ-χαιτήεις, -εσσα, -εν : *long-haired.*

βαίνω, βήσομαι, ἔβην, βέβηκα, βέβαμαι, ἐβάθην : *go, walk.*

βάλλω, βαλῶ, ἔβαλον, βέβληκα, βέβλημαι, ἐβλήθην : *throw, hurl.*

βάρβαρος, -ου, ὁ : *foreigner, barbarian.*

βάρβιτος, -ου, ὁ or ἡ : *lyre.*

βασίλεια, -ᾱς, ἡ : *queen.*

βασιλείᾱ, -ᾱς, ἡ : *kingdom.*

βασίλειος, -ᾱ, -ον : *royal;* in the neuter, generally pl., with the article, *palace.*

βασιλεύς, -έως, ὁ : *king.*

βασιλεύω, βασιλεύσω, etc. : *be king;* aor., *became king.*

βασιλικός, -ή, -όν : *royal, kingly, of the king.*

βεκός, -οῦς, τό : *bread.*

βέλτιστος, -η, -ον, superlative of ἀγαθός : *best, most desirable.*

βελτίων, -ον, comparative of ἀγαθός : *better, more desirable.*

βίᾱ, -ᾱς, ἡ : *force, violence.*

βιβλίον, -ου, τό : *book.*

βίος, -ου, ὁ : *life, living.*

βλαβερός, -ά, -όν : *harmful.*

βλάπτω, βλάψω, ἔβλαψα, βέβλαφα, βέβλαμμαι, ἐβλάφθην or ἐβλάβην : *harm.*

βλέπω, βλέψω, ἔβλεψα : *look, face, point.*

βοάω, βοήσομαι, ἐβόησα : *shout, call out.*

βοή, -ῆς, ἡ : *shout, cry.*

βοη-θέω, βοηθήσω, etc. : with D., *run to a cry* (for help), *help, succor, assist.*

βολή, -ῆς, ἡ [βάλλω] : *cast, throw.*

βόρειος, -ᾱ, -ον : *of the north wind, northern.*

βου-κόλος, -ου, ὁ [βοῦς] : *cowherd, herdsman.*

βουλεύω, βουλεύσω, etc. : *plan;* mid., *deliberate, determine.*

βουλή, -ῆς, ἡ : *plan, council.*

βούλομαι, βουλήσομαι, βεβούλημαι, ἐβουλήθην : *will, wish, desire, be willing.*

βοῦς, βοός, ὁ, ἡ : *ox, cow.*

βραδέως, adv. : *slowly.*

βραχύς, -εῖα, -ύ : *short, brief.*

βροτόεις, -εσσα, -εν ; *bloody, murderous.*

βροτός, -οῦ, ὁ : *a mortal.*

βωμός, -οῦ, ὁ : *altar.*

Γ

γάλα, -ακτος, τό : *milk.*

γαμβρός, -οῦ, ὁ : *son-in-law.*

γαμέω, γαμῶ, etc. : *marry.*

γάμος, -ου, ὁ : *marriage*; pl., *marriage feast.*

γάρ, post-pos. conj. : *for, indeed,* etc. ; ἀλλὰ γάρ : *but indeed;* καὶ γάρ : *and indeed.*

γε, enclit. and post-pos. intensive particle : *at least, indeed, to be sure.*

γελάω, γελάσω, etc.: *laugh.*

γέλως, -ωτος, ὁ : *laugh, laughter.*

γένος, -ους, τό [γί-γν-ομαι] : *birth, family, race, kind.*

γέρων, -οντος, ὁ : *old man.*

γεύω, γεύσω, ἔγευσα, γέγευμαι : *give a taste*; mid., *take a taste.*

γέφῡρα, -ᾱς, ἡ : *bridge.*

γεωργός, -οῦ, ὁ [γῆ] : *tiller of soil, farmer.*

γῆ, -ῆς, ἡ : *earth, land, soil.*

γῆρας, -ως, τό : *old age.*

γηράσκω, γηράσομαι : *grow old.*

γίγνομαι (γεν, γενη), γενήσομαι, ἐγενόμην, γέγονα, γεγένημαι : *become, be born, be, be made, happen,* "*get,*" etc.

γιγνώσκω, γνώσομαι, ἔγνων, ἔγνωκα, ἔγνωσμαι, ἐγνώσθην : *perceive, know, determine, decide, have opinion.*

γλυκύς, -εῖα, -ύ : *sweet, pleasant.*

γνώμη, -ης, ἡ : *opinion, decision.*

γνωρίζω, γνωριῶ, etc.: *make known.*

γόνυ, γόνατος, τό : *knee.*

γράμμα, (for γραφ-μα), -ατος, τό : *writing.*

γραμματεύς, -έως, ὁ : *scribe, secretary.*

γραμμή, -ῆς, ἡ: *line, mark,* "*scratch.*"

γράφω, γράψω, ἔγραψα, γέγραφα, γέγραμμαι, ἐγράφην : *mark, write, draw, depict.*

γυμνάζω, γυμνάσω, etc.: *train naked, exercise.*

γυμνός, -ή, -όν : *bare, naked, not fully dressed, lightly-clad.*

γυνή, γυναικός, ἡ : *woman, wife.*

Δ

δαίμων, -ονος, ὁ : *deity,* usually of inferior rank.

δάκνω, δήξομαι, ἔδακον, δέδηγμαι, ἐδήχθην : *bite.*

δαπανάω, δαπανήσω, etc. : *spend, consume, waste.*

δαρεικός, -οῦ, ὁ : *daric,* a Persian coin equal to 20 Attic drachmæ, worth about $5.40.

δέ, post-pos. conj. : *but* or *and.*

δείκνῡμι (δεικ), δείξω, etc. : *point out, show.*

δειλός, -ή, -όν : *cowardly.*

δεινός, -ή, -όν [δεί-σομαι] : *dreadful, to be dreaded,* hence *clever.*

δεινῶς, adv. : *dreadfully, very* (Eng. *awfully good*).

δεῖπνον, -ου, τό : *chief meal, dinner.*

δεισι-δαίμων, -ον : *god-fearing, superstitious.*

δείσομαι, ἔδεισα, δέδοικα (used in Attic instead of δείδω) : *fear.*

δέκα, indeclinable : *ten.*

δέκατος, -η, -ον : *tenth.*

δένδρον, -ου, τό : *tree, shrub.*

δεξιός, -ά, -όν : *right, right-hand, clever* (*i.e.*, right-handed.)

δέσποινα, -ης, ἡ : *female master, mistress.*

δεσπότης, -ου, ὁ : *master, lord, despot.*

δεῦρο, adv. : *hither, here.*

δεύτερος, -ᾱ, -ον : *second.*

δέχομαι, δέξομαι, etc. : *accept, await, receive.*

δέω, δεήσω, etc. : *lack, want, need;* mid., *need, desire, want, beg, request;* δεῖ : *it is necessary.*

δή, post-pos. intensive particle : *indeed, so, then.*

δήϊος, -α, -ον : *hostile.*

δῆλος, -η, -ον : *clear, plain, evident.*

δηλόω, δηλώσω, etc. : *make plain, show.*

δῆμος, -ου, ὁ : *a district, the people* (of a district), *the democracy.*

δῆτα, post-pos. particle : *then, therefore.*

διά, prep. with G. or A. : *through;* with G., *through, throughout, by means of;* with A., *through, on account of, for the sake of.* In compounds, *through, across, over, apart, asunder, thoroughly.*

δια-βαίνω, see βαίνω : *go through, cross, ford.*

διά-βασις, -εως, ἡ : *a crossing, ford.*

δια-βατός, -ή, -όν : *crossable, fordable.*

δια-γιγνώσκω, see γιγνώσκω : *distinguish, decide between.*

δια-δίδωμι, see δίδωμι : *give in different directions, distribute.*

διά-κειμαι, see κεῖμαι : *be disposed, be situated.*

δια-κελεύω, see κελεύω : *give orders in different directions.*

διᾱ-κόσιοι, -αι, -α (δια = δύο) : *two hundred.*

δια-λαμβάνω, see λαμβάνω : *take apart, separate, allot.*

δια-λύω, see λύω : *break in pieces, separate.*

δια-μένω, see μένω : *stay through.*

δια-πορθμεύω, διαπορθμεύσω, etc. : *ferry across.*

δι-αρπάζω, see ἁρπάζω : *tear to pieces, ravage, sack, pillage.*

δια-ρρέω, see ῥέω : *flow through.*

δια-τρίβω, διατρίψω, etc. : *rub through* or *away, wear out, waste* or *spend* (time), *delay.*

δια-φθείρω, see φθείρω : *destroy thoroughly, ruin.*

δια-χώρισμα, -ατος, τό : *separation, split, cleft, fissure.*

διδακτός, -ή, -όν : *teachable.*

διδάσκω, διδάξω, etc. : *teach.*

δίδωμι, δώσω, ἔδωκα, δέδωκα, δέδομαι, ἐδόθην : *give, grant.*

δι-εκ-περάω, διεκπεράσω : *pass out through.*

δι-ελαύνω, see ἐλαύνω : *drive through, march through.*

δι-εξ-έρχομαι, see ἔρχομαι : *go through completely.*

δι-έρχομαι, see ἔρχομαι : *go through.*

δι-ηγέομαι, see ἡγέομαι : *lead through* (a narrative), *expound, narrate, relate.*

δι-ίστημι, see ἵστημι : *cause to stand apart;* mid. and 2d aor. act., *stand apart, separate, open ranks.*

δίκαιος, -ᾱ, -ον : *just, upright, righteous.*

δικαστής, -οῦ, ὁ : *dispenser of justice, judge, juryman.*

δίκη, -ης, ἡ : *justice, punishment, trial, law-suit.*

δί-οδος, -ου, ἡ : *a way through, passage.*

δι-ότι, conj. [διά + ὅτι] : *because, why.*

δι-πλάσιος, -ον : *two-fold, double.*

δίς, numeral adv. : *twice.*

δισ-χίλιοι, -αι, -α : *two thousand.*

διώκω, διώξω, etc. : *pursue, chase.*

δοκέω (δοκ), δόξω, etc. : *seem, seem best, think.* Often impersonal.

δόξα, -ης, ἡ : *what is thought* or *believed, opinion, fame.*

δόρυ, δόρατος, τό : *spearshaft, spear.*

δουλεύω, δουλεύσω, etc. : *be a slave, serve.*

δοῦναι, see δίδωμι.

δραμεῖν, etc., see τρέχω.

δρόμος, -ου, ὁ : *a running, run, race; δρόμῳ : on the run.*

δύναμαι, δυνήσομαι, δεδύνημαι, ἐδυνήθην : *be able, can, equal.*

δύναμις, -εως, ἡ : *force, power, resources, troops* (cf. Elizabethan *power*).

δυναστής, -οῦ, ὁ : *man of power, prince, king.*

δυνατός, -ή, -όν : *powerful, able, capable.*

δύο, δυοῖν : *two.*

δυσ-, inseparable prefix : *difficult, disagreeable, hard.*

δώ-δεκα, indeclinable [δύο + δέκα] : *twelve.*

δωδεκ-έτης, -ου, ὁ : *a twelve-year-old* (boy).

δωμάτιον, -ου, τό : *dwelling place, room, bedroom.*

δῶρον, -ου, τό [δί-δω-μι] : *gift.*

E

ἑάλων, etc., see ἁλίσκομαι.

ἐάν, conditional conj. with subj. : *if.* Sometimes contracted to ἄν or ἤν.

ἑ-αυτοῦ, -ῆς, -οῦ, reflexive pron. : *of himself, herself, itself.*

ἐάω, ἐάσω, εἴᾱσα, εἴᾱκα, εἴᾱμαι, εἰάθην : *allow, permit, let be.*

ἐγγύς, adv., prep. with G. : *near.*

ἐγ-κατα-λείπω, see λείπω : *leave behind, leave out.*

ἐγκώμιον, -ου, τό : *eulogy, praise.*

ἔγχος, -ους, τό : *spear.*

ἐγώ, ἐμοῦ or μου, pron. of the 1st pers. : *I.*

ἔγω-γε, emphatic form of ἐγώ.

ἕδος, ἕδεος, τό : *seat, habitation.*

ἐθέλω (often θέλω), ἐθελήσω, ἠθέλησα, ἠθέληκα : *wish, be willing, consent.*

εἰ, conj.: *if,* (1) in conditional clauses with ind. or opt.; (2) in indirect questions.

εἴᾱ, etc., see ἐάω.

εἶδον, see ὁράω.

εἴθε, particle frequent in wishes : *O if, would that, if only.*

εἴκοσι, indeclinable numeral: *twenty.*

εἴκω, εἴξω, εἶξα : *yield, give way, retire.*

εἴληφα, etc., see λαμβάνω.

εἷλον, etc., see αἱρέω.

εἰμί, ἔσομαι : *be, exist.*

εἶμι, ᾖα or ᾔειν : *go.*

εἶπον (2d aor.), ἐρῶ, εἴρηκα, εἴρημαι, ἐρρήθην : *say, tell, command.*

εἰρήνη, -ης, ἡ : *peace.*

εἰς, prep. with A.: *into, to, for, against.* In compounds, *into, in, to.*

εἷς, μία, ἕν : *one.*

εἰσ-βάλλω, see βάλλω : *throw into; empty* (of rivers); *invade* (of armies).

εἴσ-ειμι, see εἶμι : *go into, enter.*

εἰσ-έρχομαι, see ἔρχομαι : *come* or *go into.*

εἰσ-πίπτω, see πίπτω : *tumble in, rush in* or *into.*

εἴσω, adv. [εἰς]: *inside, within.*

εἶτα, adv.: *next, then, thereupon.*

ἐκ (before vowels ἐξ), prep. with G.: *out of, from, from out.* In compounds, *out, from, off, away,* frequently *out and out, utterly.*

ἕκαστος, -η, -ον; *each, every.*

ἑκατόν, indeclinable numeral: *hundred.*

ἐκ-βάλλω, see βάλλω: *throw out, exile, expel.*

ἐκ-διδάσκω, see διδάσκω: *teach thoroughly.*

ἐκ-δίδωμι, see δίδωμι: *give out, give in marriage.*

ἐκεῖ, adv.: *there.*

ἐκεῖνος, -η, -ο, demonstrative pron.: *that there, that* in contrast with οὗτος, *the former.*

ἐκ-λέγω, ἐξέλεξα, ἐξείλοχα, ἐξείλεγμαι, ἐξελέγην or ἐξελέχθην: *pick out, choose, select.*

ἐκ-πλήττω, see πλήττω: *strike out of one's senses, thoroughly frighten.*

ἐκ-πορεύομαι, see πορεύομαι: *make one's way out, march out.*

ἐκ-φεύγω, see φεύγω: *flee out.*

ἑκών, -οῦσα, -όν: *willing, voluntary, intentional.* Often as adv.: *willingly,* etc.

ἐλάττων, -ον, comparative of ὀλίγος: *smaller, less, fewer.*

ἐλαύνω, ἐλῶ, ἤλασα, ἐλήλακα, ἐλήλαμαι, ἠλάθην: *drive, march, ride.*

ἐλάχιστος, -η, -ον, superlative of ὀλίγος: *least, fewest.*

ἑλεῖν, etc., see αἱρέω.

ἐλευθερίᾱ, -ᾱς, ἡ: *freedom, liberty.*

ἐλεύθερος, -ᾱ, -ον: *free.*

ἐλευθερόω, ἐλευθερώσω, etc.: *set free.*

ἐλθεῖν, etc., see ἔρχομαι.

ἐλπίζω (ἐλπιδ-), ἐλπιῶ, etc.: *hope, expect.*

ἐλπίς, -ίδος, ἡ: *hope, expectation.*

ἐμ-, for ἐν, before μ, π, β, φ.

ἐμ-αυτοῦ, -ῆς, reflexive pron. of the 1st person: *of myself.*

ἐμ-μέλεια, -ᾱς, ἡ: *harmony.*

ἔμμεν, dialectic for εἶναι.

ἐμός, -ή, -όν, possessive adj.: *my, mine.*

ἐμ-πειρίᾱ, -ᾱς, ἡ: *experience, acquaintance.*

ἔμ-πειρος, -ον: *experienced, acquainted with.*

ἔμ-πηρος, -ον: *crippled, maimed.*

ἔμ-προσθεν, adv.: *in front.*

ἐν, prep. with D.: *in, among, at, on, during.* In compounds, *in, at, on, among.*

ἕν, see εἷς.

ἐν-αντίος, -ᾱ, -ον: *in opposition to, facing, confronting;* **οἱ ἐν-αντίοι**: *opponents.*

ἔναρα, -ων, τά, only in pl.: *armor.*

ἐν-αρμόττω: *fit, adapt, attune.*

ἐν-δέκατος, -η, -ον: *eleventh.*

ἔνδοθεν, adv.: *from within.*

ἔνδον, adv.: *inside, within.*

ἔν-δοξος, -ον: *in repute, esteemed.*

ἔν-ειμι, see εἰμί: *be in, be possible.*

ἕνεκα, improper prep. with G., postpos.: *on account of, for the sake of, for.*

ἐνενήκοντα, indeclinable numeral: *ninety.*

ἔνθα, adv.: (1) of place, *here, there, where;* (2) of time, *then, thereupon.*

ἐνθάδε, adv.: *there.*

ἐν-θῡμέομαι, ἐνθυμήσομαι, etc. [θῡμός]: *have in mind, consider, reflect.*

ἔνιοι, -αι, -α: *some.*

ἐννέα, indeclinable numeral: *nine,*

ἐν-νοέω, ἐννοήσω, etc. [νοῦς]: *have*

in mind, consider, conceive, observe.

ἐν-οικέω, see οἰκέω: *live in, inhabit.*

ἑνός, etc., see εἷς.

ἐν-οχλέω, ἐνοχλήσω, etc.: *annoy, disturb.*

ἐνταῦθα, adv.: *there, thereupon; here, hereupon.*

ἐντεῦθεν, adv.: *from there, from here, next.*

ἐντός, adv.: *inside, within.*

ἐν-τρυφάω, ἐντρυφήσω, etc.: *revel in*, with D.; *be luxurious; mock at*, with D.

ἐν-τυγχάνω, see τυγχάνω: *happen upon, meet with, find.*

ἐν-ύπνιον, -ου, τό: *vision, dream.*

ἐξ, see ἐκ.

ἕξ, indeclinable numeral: *six.*

ἐξ-άγω, see ἄγω: *lead* or *drive out, export.*

ἑξακισ-χίλιοι, -αι, -α: *six thousand.*

ἑξακόσιοι, -αι, -α: *six hundred.*

ἐξ-αμαρτάνω, see ἁμαρτάνω: *miss out and out, be thoroughly mistaken.*

ἐξ-απατάω, ἐξαπατήσω, etc.: *deceive utterly.*

ἔξ-ειμι, found only in the 3d pers. sing., ἔξεστι: *it is permitted, possible.*

ἐξ-ελαύνω, see ἐλαύνω: *march out, march on, drive out, expel.*

ἐξ-επίσταμαι, see ἐπίσταμαι: *know thoroughly.*

ἔξ-εστι, etc., see ἔξειμι.

ἐξ-ίστημι, see ἵστημι: *put out of position;* intrans., *stand aside, retire*, etc.

ἔξω, adv.: *outside.*

ἔξωθεν, adv.: *from outside.*

ἐπ-άγω, see ἄγω: *lead against.*

ἐπ-αινέω, ἐπαινέσω, etc.: *praise.*

ἐπάν, temporal conj., with subjv. [ἐπεί + ἄν]: *when, whenever.*

ἐπεί, temporal and causal conj.: *when, since, because.*

ἐπειδάν, temporal conj. with subjv.: *when, as soon as.*

ἐπειδή, temporal and causal conj.: *when, since, because.*

ἔπ-ειτα, adv. [εἶτα]: *thereupon, next.*

ἐπ-έρομαι, see ἔρομαι: *put a question to, inquire of.*

ἐπ-έρχομαι, see ἔρχομαι: *approach.*

ἐπ-εύχομαι, see εὔχομαι: *vow to* (a god).

ἐπ-έχω, see ἔχω: *hold upon, restrain, delay, hesitate.*

ἐπήν, temporal conj. with subjv., see ἐπάν.

ἐπί (ἐφ' in elision, before rough breathing), prep. with G., D., and A.: (1) with G., *on, upon;* (2) with D., of place, *on, at, near, by;* of time, *upon;* of cause or purpose, *on the basis of, in command of;* (3) with A., of place, *on, upon, to, against;* of time, *for;* of purpose, *for.* In compounds, it frequently means *upon, against, besides.*

ἐπι-βάτης, -ου, ὁ [βαίνω]: *passenger on board ship, marine.*

ἐπι-βουλεύω, see βουλεύω: *plot against.*

ἐπι-βουλή, -ῆς, ἡ: *plot.*

ἐπί-γαμος, -ον [γάμος]: *marriageable.*

ἐπί-γραμμα, -ατος, τό: *writing* (on stone), *inscription.*

ἐπι-γράφω, see γράφω: *inscribe.*

ἐπι-δείκνῡμι, see δείκνῡμι: *show to, display, show off.*

ἐπι-δημέω, ἐπιδημήσω, etc.: *visit* (a people — δῆμος), *be in town.*

ἐπι-θῡμέω, ἐπιθῡμήσω, etc. [θῡμός]: *set one's heart upon, desire*, with G.

ἐπι-μελέομαι, ἐπιμελήσομαι, etc., opposite of ἀ-μελέω: *care for, take care of*, with G. or obj. clause.

ἐπ-ιούσιος, -ον [ἐπ + εἶμι]: *sufficient for the day, daily.*

ἐπι-πίπτω, see πίπτω: *fall upon, attack.*

ἐπι-σκέπτομαι, see σκέπτομαι: *look at* or *to.*

ἐπι-σκώπτω, see σκώπτω: *make fun of, mock at.*

ἐπίσταμαι, ἐπιστήσομαι, ἠπιστήθην: *understand, know, know how.*

ἐπιστήμη, -ης, ἡ [ἐπίσταμαι]: *knowledge, understanding, science.*

ἐπι-στολή, -ῆς, ἡ: *message, letter.*

ἐπι-στρέφω, see στρέφω: *turn toward.*

ἐπι-τάττω, see τάττω: *array against, give orders to.*

ἐπι-τελέω, see τελέω: *complete.*

ἐπιτήδειος, -ā, -ον: *fit, suitable;* τὰ ἐπιτήδεια: *provisions, supplies.*

ἐπι-τίθημι, see τίθημι: *put upon, inflict;* mid., *attack.*

ἐπι-τῑμάω, see τῑμάω: *set a price upon, assess a penalty, censure.*

ἐπι-τρέπω, see τρέπω: *turn to, turn over to, give up, yield.*

ἐπι-φάνεια, -ᾱς, ἡ: *appearance, surface appearance, surface.*

ἐπι-χωρέω, ἐπιχωρήσω, etc.: *move to* or *against, approach.*

ἐπι-ψαύω, ἐπιψαύσω, etc.: *touch.*

ἕπομαι, ἕψομαι, ἑσπόμην: *follow*, with D.

ἑπτά, indeclinable numeral: *seven.*

ἑπτάκις, adv.: *seven times.*

ἑπτακόσιοι, -αι, -α: *seven hundred.*

ἐργαστήριον, -ου, τό: *work shop, factory.*

ἔργον, -ου, τό: *work, deed, action;* frequently opposed to λόγος.

ἐρείδω, ἐρείσω, etc.: *lean on, prop, press upon.*

ἔρεισμα, -ατος, τό: *prop, support.*

ἔρημος, -η, -ον: *deserted, barren; in the desert, lonely; deprived of*, with G.

ἐρίζω, ἤρισα: *contend, strive, rival.*

ἔρομαι, ἐρήσομαι, ἠρόμην: *ask, question, inquire.*

ἔρρῑφα, see ῥίπτω.

ἔρχομαι, ἦλθον, ἐλήλυθα: *come, go.* Future, ἐλεύσομαι, poetic.

ἐρῶ, see εἶπον.

ἐρωτάω, ἐρωτήσω, etc.: *ask, question, inquire.*

ἐσθλός, -ή, -όν: *noble, of noble birth.*

ἕσπερα, -ᾱς, ἡ: *evening.*

ἔσται, etc., see εἰμί.

ἑστιάω, ἑστιάσω, etc.: *feast, entertain at table.*

ἑταῖρος, -ου, ὁ: *comrade, mate.*

ἕτερος, -ā, -ον: *other* (of two); θάτερον: *the other* (of two).

ἔτι, adv.: *again, still, yet.*

ἔτος, -ους, τό: *year.*

εὖ, adv.: *well.*

εὐ-ανδρίᾱ, -ᾱς, ἡ: *noble manhood, manliness.*

εὔ-ανδρος, -ον: *of brave* or *noble men.*

εὐ-δαίμων, -ον: *possessing a good genius, fortunate, lucky, prosperous.*

εὐ-δόκιμος, -ον [δοκέω]: *of fair fame, well thought of, famous.*

εὔ-ελπις, -πι: *of good hope, hopeful.*

εὔ-ζωνος, -ον: *fair-girdled.*

εὐ-ηθής, -ές: *good natured; foolish.*

εὐ-ηκοέω, εὐηκοήσω, etc.: *listen and obey willingly.*

εὐθύς, -εῖα, -ύ: *straight, direct.*

εὐθύς, adv.: *directly, at once, immediately.*

εὐ-κλεῖᾱ, -ᾱς, ἡ: *fair fame, renown.*

εὐκτός, -ή, -όν [εὔχομαι]: *to be prayed for, suitable for prayer.*

εὐ-λογίᾱ, -ᾱς, ἡ [λόγος]: *eulogy, praise.*

εὐ-μαρής, -ές: *easy.*

εὐ-μενής, -ές: *fair-minded, kindly, propitious.*

εὔ-μορφος, -ον: *fair of form, comely, handsome.*

εὔ-νοος, -ον [νοῦς]: *well-intentioned, well-disposed, friendly, favorable.*

εὑρετός, -ή, -όν: *to be found, capable of being found.*

εὑρίσκω, εὑρήσω, ηὗρον, ηὕρηκα, ηὕρημαι, ηὑρέθην: *discover, find, obtain.*

εὖρος, -ους, τό: *breadth.*

εὐ-σεβέω: *be pious* or *reverent.*

εὐ-τόλμως, adv.: *with good courage, bravely.*

εὐ-τυχέω, εὐτυχήσω, etc. [τύχη]: *prosper.*

εὐ-φραίνω, εὐφρανῶ, etc.: *cheer, make glad* or *merry.*

εὔχομαι, εὔξομαι, ηὐξάμην: *pray, vow.*

ἐφ', see ἐπί.

ἐφάνην, see φαίνω.

ἔφασαν, see φημί.

ἔφ-ηβος, -ου, ὁ: *a youth of eighteen to twenty years.*

ἐφ-ίστημι, see ἵστημι: *cause to stop;* mid. and 2d aor. and perf. act., *stop.*

ἐφ-όδια, -ων, τά, rare in sing. [ὁδός]: *traveling supplies* or *money.*

ἔφῡ, see φύω.

ἐχθρός, -ά, -όν: *hostile;* ὁ ἐχθρός: *personal enemy.*

ἔχις, -εως, ὁ: *adder, viper.*

ἔχω, ἕξω or σχήσω, ἔσχον, ἔσχηκα, ἔσχημαι: *have, hold,* (aor., *got*); with an adv., *be.*

ἑώρᾱ, etc., see ὁράω.

ἕως, conj.: *as long as, while, until.*

Z

ζάω, ζήσω: *live.*

ζεύγνῡμι, ζεύξω, etc.: *unite, harness, yoke, bind.*

ζέφυρος, -ου, ὁ: *west wind.*

ζῆν, see ζάω.

ζητέω, ζητήσω, etc.: *seek.*

H

ἡ, see ὁ.

ἥ, see ὅς.

ἤ, conj.: *or;* ἤ . . . ἤ, *either . . . or.*

ἤ, conj., *than.*

ἤγγειλα, etc., see ἀγγέλλω.

ἡγεμών, -όνος, ὁ: *leader, guide.*

ἡγέομαι, ἡγήσομαι, etc.: *lead, command,* with G. or D.; *believe,* with inf. Compare Lat. *duco.*

ᾔδειν, etc., see οἶδα.

ἡδέως, adv.: *gladly.*

ἤδη, adv.: *already, at last, now.*

ἥδομαι, ἡσθήσομαι, ἥσθην: *be glad, be pleased, rejoice.*

ἡδονή, -ῆς, ἡ: *pleasure, enjoyment.*

ἡδύς, -εῖα, -ύ: *sweet, pleasing, pleasant.*

ἦθος, -ους, τό: *custom, habit; accustomed haunt.*

ἥκιστα, adv.: *least, by no means.*

ἥκω, ἥξω: *come, have come.*

ἤλασα, etc., see ἐλαύνω.

ἦλθον, see ἔρχομαι.

ἥλιος, -ου, ὁ : *sun.*

ἧλιξ, -ικος, ὁ : *fellow, companion, associate of like age.*

ἡμεῖς, etc., see ἐγώ.

ἡμέρᾱ, -ᾱς, ἡ : *day.*

ἡμέτερος, -ᾱ, -ον [ἡμεῖς] : *our, ours.*

ἥμισυς, -εια, -υ : *half.* Compare Latin *semi.*

ἤν, see ἐάν.

ἦν, see εἰμί.

ἠνίδε, interjection : *behold, lo.*

ἥρως, ἥρωος : *hero, demi-god.*

ἥσθην, see ἥδομαι.

ἡσυχίᾱ, -ᾱς, ἡ : *leisure, quiet.*

ἡττάομαι, ἡττήσομαι, etc. : *be inferior, be defeated, be worsted.*

ἥττων, -ον : *inferior, weaker, less.*

ἠχέω, ἠχήσω : *sound, ring, resound.*

Θ

θάλαττα, -ης, ἡ : *sea.*

θάνατος, -ου, ὁ : *death.*

θάπτω, θάψω, ἔθαψα, τέθαμμαι, ἐτάφην [τάφος] : *dig, bury.*

θαρρέω, θαρρήσω, etc. : *be courageous, have courage.*

θᾶτερον = τὸ ἕτερον.

θᾶττων, -ον, comparative of ταχύς : *swifter.*

θαυμάζω, θαυμάσομαι, ἐθαύμασα, etc. : *admire, wonder at, be surprised.*

θαυμάσιος, -ᾱ, -ον : *wonderful, surprising.*

θαυμαστός, -ή, -όν : *wonderful, surprising.*

θεῖος, -ᾱ, -ον [θεός] : *divine, supernatural.*

θέλημα, -ατος, τό : *will, desire.*

θέλω, see ἐθέλω.

θέμις, ἡ (other forms rare or lacking): *ordinance, right.*

-θεν, suffix meaning *place from which.*

θεός, -οῦ, ὁ or ἡ : *god, goddess.*

θεραπεύω, θεραπεύσω, etc. : *care for, attend, cure.*

θεράπων, -οντος, ὁ : *attendant.*

θερίζω, θεριῶ, etc. : *harvest, reap.*

θερμός, -ή, -όν : *hot.*

θέρμος, -ου, ὁ : *bean.*

θεσμός, -οῦ, ὁ : *law.*

θέω, θεύσομαι : *run.*

θεωρέω, θεωρήσω, etc. : *observe, watch.*

θεωρίᾱ, -ᾱς, ἡ : *observation, inspection, public spectacle* (at theater or athletic games).

θήκη, -ης, ἡ [τίθημι] : *depository, tomb, vault.*

θηριώδης, -ες : *savage, wild.*

θήσαυρος, -ου, ὁ : *treasure, treasury, store-house.*

θνητός, -ή, -όν [ἀπο-θνῄ-σκω] : *mortal, human.*

θόρυβος, -ου, ὁ : *din, noise, uproar, confusion.*

θρίξ, τριχός, ἡ : *hair.*

θυγάτηρ, -τρός, ἡ : *daughter.*

θῡμός, -οῦ, ὁ : *heart, spirit, mind, courage, anger, passion.*

θύρᾱ, -ᾱς, ἡ : *door;* αἱ θύραι : often *military headquarters, the king's court.*

θῡ́ω, θύσω, etc. : *sacrifice.*

θώρᾱξ, -ᾱκος, ὁ : *breastplate, corselet, cuirass.*

I

ἰᾶ́ομαι, ἰάσομαι, etc. : *heal.*

ἰᾱτρός, -οῦ, ὁ : *healer, physician, surgeon.*

ἰάχω, perf. ἴαχα : *shout, cry out.*

ἰδεῖν, etc., see ὁράω.

ἴδιος, -ᾱ, -ον: *own*, *personal*, *peculiar*, *private*.

ἱδρύω, ἱδρύσω, etc.: *seat*, *settle*; mid., *establish*.

ἱερο-ποιός, -οῦ, ὁ: *priest*.

ἱερός, -ά, -όν: *sacred*, *holy*; τὸ ἱερόν: *holy place*, *sanctuary*, *temple*; τὰ ἱερά: *sacrificial victims*, *sacrifices*, *omens*.

ἱζάνω (only pres. and impf.): *cause to sit*, *give a seat to*.

ἵημι, ἥσω, ἧκα, εἷκα, εἷμαι, εἵθην: *send*, *throw*; mid., *throw oneself*, *rush*, *attack*.

ἱκανός, -ή, -όν, *sufficient*, *able*, *capable*.

ἵνα, conj. adv.: *in order that* or *to*, *that*.

ἰο-στέφανος, -ον: *violet-crowned*.

ἵππ-αρχος, -ου, ὁ: *commander of horse*, *cavalry leader*.

ἱππασίᾱ, -ᾱς, ἡ: *cavalry maneuvers*, *riding about*.

ἱππεύς, -έως, ὁ: *horseman*, *cavalryman*, *knight*.

ἱππικός, -ή, -όν: *cavalry*.

ἵππος, -ου, ὁ: *horse*.

ἴσμεν, etc., see **οἶδα**.

ἴσος, -η, -ον: *equal*, *even*; *fair*, *impartial*.

ἵστημι, στήσω, ἔστησα and ἔστην, ἕστηκα, ἕσταμαι, ἐστάθην: *cause to stand*, *halt*, *place*; mid. and 2d aor. and perf. act., *come to a stand*, *halt*, *stop*.

ἱστίον, -ου, τό: *sail*.

ἵστωρ, -ορος, ὁ [οἶδα]: *judge*.

ἰσχῡρός, -ά, -όν: *strong*.

ἴσως, adv. [ἴσος]: *equally*, *perhaps*.

ἴτυς, ἴτυος, ἡ *edge* or *rim of the shield*, *shield*.

ἶφι, adv.: *bravely*, *stoutly*.

ἰχθῦς, -ύος, ὁ: *fish*.

K

καθ', see κατά.

καθ-αιρέω, see αἱρέω: *take down*, *seize*.

καθ-έζομαι, καθεδοῦμαι, etc.: *sit down*.

καθ-ήκω, see ἥκω: *come down*, *descend*; *come to*, *belong to*, *befit*.

κάθ-ημαι (pres. and impf. only): *sit down*, *be seated*.

καθ-ίζω, καθιῶ, etc.: *make to sit down*.

καθ-ίημι, see ἵημι: *let down*, *send down*.

καθ-ίστημι, see ἵστημι: *set down*, *station*, *establish*, etc.

καί, conj.: *and*, *also*, *besides*, *even* (emphasizing following word or phrase); καί . . . καί, or τε . . . καί: *both . . . and*, *not only . . . but also*.

καινός, -ή, -όν: *new*, *recent*.

καί-περ, concessive particle: *although*.

καιρός, -οῦ, ὁ: *fitting moment*, *opportune time*, *opportunity*.

κακηγορέω, κακηγορήσω, etc.: *speak abusively*, *abuse*.

κάκιστος, -η, -ον, superlative of κακός: *worst*, *basest*.

κακίων, -ον, comparative of κακός: *worse*, *baser*.

κακός, -ή, -όν: *bad*, *cowardly*, *evil*; *low born*.

κακῶς, adv.: *badly*, *ill*.

κάλαμος, -ου, ὁ: *reed*.

καλέω, καλῶ, ἐκάλεσα, κέκληκα, κέκλημαι, ἐκλήθην: *call*, *summon*, *name*.

κάλλιστος, -η, -ον, superlative of καλός: *most beautiful, lovely, noble.*

καλλίων, -ον, comparative of καλός: *more beautiful, lovely, noble.*

κάλλος, -ους, τό: *beauty.*

καλός, -ή, -όν: *beautiful, honorable, noble, favorable, fine.*

καλῶς, adv.: *beautifully, nobly, well.*

κάμηλος, -ου, ὁ, ἡ: *camel.*

κάμνω, καμῶ, ἔκαμον, κέκμηκα: *toil, work, grow weary; make with toil.*

κάρᾱ, κρᾱτός, τό: *head.*

καρδίᾱ, -ᾱς, ἡ: *heart.*

κάρπιμος, -η, -ον: *fruitful, bearing fruit.*

καρπός, -οῦ, ὁ: *fruit, produce.*

καρτερέω, καρτερήσω, etc.: *be strong, endure.*

καρτερός, -ά, -όν: *strong, steady, valiant.*

κατά, prep. with G. and A.: *down;* with G., *down from, down upon;* with A., *down along, according to, against, by.* In compounds, usually *down, along, back, against,* often with intensive force.

κατα-βαίνω, see βαίνω: *go down, descend, dismount.*

κατ-αγγέλλω, see ἀγγέλλω: *bring down word, report.*

κατ-άγω, see ἄγω: *bring down* or *back, restore.*

κατα-θνῄσκω, see ἀποθνῄσκω: *die down* or *off.*

κατ-αισχῡ́νω, see αἰσχύνω: *cover with shame, put to shame, disgrace.*

κατα-καίνω, -κανῶ, -έκανον, -κέκονα: *kill.* Poetic.

κατα-κᾱ́ω, see κάω: *burn down.*

κατά-κειμαι, see κεῖμαι: *be settled down in, established, situated.*

κατα-κόπτω, κατακόψω, etc.: *cut down, cut to pieces, slaughter.*

κατα-λαμβάνω, see λαμβάνω: *lay hands upon, seize, grasp,* so *comprehend; surprise, find on coming.*

κατα-λείπω, see λείπω: *abandon, leave behind.*

κατά-λογος, -ου, ὁ: *list, roll, catalogue.*

κατα-πηδάω, καταπηδήσω, etc.: *jump down.*

κατα-πίπτω, see πίπτω: *fall down, tumble.*

κατ-άρᾱτος, -ον: *accursed, damnable.*

κατα-σκέπτομαι, see σκέπτομαι: *inspect, examine carefully.*

κατα-τίθημι, see τίθημι: *place down, establish.*

κατα-φέρω, see φέρω: *bear* or *bring down.*

κατα-φεύγω, see φεύγω: *take refuge.*

κατα-φθίνω (pres. and impf. only): *waste away.*

κατ-εσθίω, κατέδομαι, κατέφαγον, κατεδήδοκα, κατεδήδεσμαι, κατηδέσθην: *bolt down, devour, eat up.*

κατ-έχω, see ἔχω: *hold down, hold in one's control.*

κατ-οικέω, see οἰκέω: *settle down, occupy a house;* pass., *be occupied.*

κατ-ορθόω, -ορθώσω, etc.: *set straight, make prosper.*

καῦμα, -ατος, τό: *heat.*

κᾱ́ω (καίω), καύσω, ἔκαυσα, κέκαυκα, κέκαυμαι, ἐκαύθην: *burn.*

κεῖμαι, κείσομαι: *lie, be placed.* Frequent as perf. pass. of τίθημι.

κεῖνος, -η, -ον, variant form of ἐκεῖνος.

κελεύω, κελεύσω, ἐκέλευσα, κεκέλευκα, κεκέλευσμαι, ἐκελεύσθην: *advise, bid, command, order, urge.*

κενός, -ή, -όν: *empty, vain.*

κέντρον, -ου, τό: *sharp point, goad.*

κέρας, κέρως or κέρᾱτος, τό: *horn* (of any sort), *wing* (of an army).

κέρδος, -ους, τό: *greed, gain, profit, pay, advantage.*

κεύθω, κεύσω, etc.: *cover over, hide.*

κεφαλή, -ῆς, ἡ: *head.*

κῆνος, -η, -ον, dialectic for ἐκεῖνος.

κηρός, -οῦ, ὁ: *wax.*

κῆρυξ, -ῡκος, ὁ: *herald.*

κηρῦττω (κηρῡκ-), κηρύξω, ἐκήρῡξα, κεκήρῡχα, κεκήρῡγμαι, ἐκηρύχθην [κῆρυξ]: *be a herald, proclaim.*

κῑβωτός, -οῦ, ἡ: *chest, treasure chest.*

κινδῡνεύω, κινδῡνεύσω, etc.: *incur danger, be in danger, risk.*

κίνδῡνος, -ου, ὁ: *danger, risk.*

κινέω, κινήσω, etc.: *move, set in motion.*

κλεινός, -ή, -όν: *famous.*

κλέπτης, -ου, ὁ: *thief.*

κλέπτω, κλέψω, ἔκλεψα, κέκλοφα, κέκλεμμαι, ἐκλάπην: *steal.*

κλῑνω, κλινῶ, ἔκλῑνα, κέκλιμαι, ἐκλίθην or ἐκλίνην: *bend, slope.*

κοινός, -ή, -όν: *common, general, commonplace;* τὸ κοινόν: *the commonwealth.*

κόλπος, -ου, ὁ: *fold, bay* or *gulf, bosom.*

κόμη, -ης, ἡ: *hair of the head* (usually plural).

κόρυς, -υθος, ἡ: *helmet.*

κοσμέω, κοσμήσω, etc.: *arrange, adorn, beautify; marshal troops.*

κόσμος, -ου, ὁ: *order, orderly universe; adornment.*

κρᾱνίον, -ου, τό: *upper part of head, skull.*

κρατέω, κρατήσω, etc.: *have* or *get power over, prevail, overpower, conquer, win.*

κράτιστος, -η, -ον, superlative of ἀγαθός: *most potent, best, bravest.*

κράτος, -ους, τό: *force, power, authority.*

κραυγή, -ῆς, ἡ: *shout, outcry.*

κρείττων, -ον, comparative of ἀγαθός [κράτος]: *more powerful, better, braver.*

κρεμάννῡμι, κρεμῶ, ἐκρέμασα, ἐκρεμάσθην: *hang up.*

κρίνω, κρινῶ, ἔκρῑνα, κέκρικα, κέκριμαι, ἐκρίθην: *pick out, distinguish, decide, judge.*

κριτής, -οῦ, ὁ: *judge.*

κροκόδειλος, -ου, ὁ: *crocodile.* Originally applied to the lizard. Compare *alligator.*

κρύπτω, κρύψω, etc.: *hide, conceal.*

κτάομαι, κτήσομαι, etc.: *acquire, get possession of, gain;* perfect, *possess.*

κτενίζω (pres. and impf. only): *comb.*

κτῆμα, -ατος, τό [κτάομαι]: *possession.*

κυβερνήτης, -ου, ὁ: *helmsman, pilot.*

κύκλος, -ου, ὁ: *circle, wheel.*

κύλιξ, -ικος, ἡ: *cylix, drinking cup.*

κυνέω, κυνήσω, ἔκυσα: *kiss.*

κῦριος, -ᾱ, -ον: *having authority* or *power.*

κύων, κυνός, ὁ, ἡ: *dog.*

κωλῡω, κωλύσω, etc.: *hinder, prevent.*

κώμη, -ης, ἡ: *village.*

κώνωψ, -πος, ὁ: *gnat, mosquito.*

κῶρος, -ου, ὁ: dialectic for κοῦρος· *lad, young fellow.*

Λ

λαβεῖν, etc., see λαμβάνω.

λαβύρινθος, -ου, ὁ: *labyrinth* or *winding maze.*

λαγωός, -οῦ, ὁ: *hare, rabbit.*

λαθεῖν, etc., see λανθάνω.

λαιός, -ά, -όν: *left.* Poetic for ἀριστερός or εὐώνυμος.

λακτίζω, λακτιῶ, etc.: *kick.*

λαλέω, λαλήσω, etc.: *chatter, talk, talk nonsense.*

λαμβάνω, λήψομαι, ἔλαβον, εἴληφα, εἴλημμαι, ἐλήφθην: *take, receive, get.*

λαμπαδη-φορίᾱ, -ᾱς, ἡ: *torch-carrying, torch race.*

λαμπάδιον, -ου, τό: *torch.*

λανθάνω, λήσω, ἔλαθον, λέληθα, λέλησμαι: *escape notice, elude;* with suppl. part., *do secretly;* mid., *forget.*

λέγω, λέξω, ἔλεξα, λέλεγμαι, ἐλέχθην: *say, tell, speak.*

λείπω, λείψω, ἔλιπον, λέλοιπα, λέλειμμαι, ἐλείφθην: *leave.*

λεπτός, -ή, -όν: *slender, thin.*

λευκός, -ή, -όν: *white.*

λέων, -οντος, ὁ: *lion.*

λῃστής, -οῦ, ὁ: *pirate, robber, brigand.*

λίαν, adv.: *exceedingly, very.*

λίθος, -ου, ὁ: *stone.*

λιμήν, -ένος, ὁ: *harbor, port, haven.*

λιπαρός, -ά, -όν: *oily, shiny, gleaming.*

λογίζομαι, λογίσομαι, etc.: *count, reckon, calculate, compute.*

λόγος, -ου, ὁ [λέγω]: *saying, tale, word, speech; reason; account.*

λόγχη, -ης, ἡ: *spear-point, spear.*

λοιδορέω, λοιδορήσω, etc.: *abuse, revile.*

λοιμός, -οῦ, ὁ: *pestilence.*

λοιπός, -ή, -όν [λείπω]: *left, remaining;* τὸ λοιπόν (adv. acc.): *for the future;* κ.τ.λ. (καὶ τὰ λοιπά): *etc.*

λόφος, -ου, ὁ: *hill, crest, plume.*

λοχ-ᾱγός, -οῦ, ὁ: *company leader, captain.*

λόχος, -ου, ὁ: *company* (of soldiers).

λύκος, -ου, ὁ: *wolf.*

λῡ́πη, -ης, ἡ: *grief, pain.*

λύρη, -ης, ἡ: *lyre.* Dialectic for λύρα.

λύχνος, -ου, ὁ: *light, lamp.*

λῡ́ω, λύσω, ἔλῡσα, λέλυκα, λέλυμαι, ἐλύθην: *break, destroy, loose.*

Μ

μά, intensive particle used in oaths.

μάθησις, -εως, ἡ [μανθάνω]: *learning.*

μάθος, -ους, τό [μανθάνω]: *knowledge, understanding.*

μακρός, -ά, -όν: *long, lofty, tall.*

μάλα, adv.: *very.*

μᾶλλον, adv., comparative of μάλα: *more, rather.*

μανθάνω, μαθήσομαι, ἔμαθον, μεμάθηκα: *study, learn, know, understand.*

μανίᾱ, -ᾱς, ἡ: *madness, insanity.*

μάντις, -εως, ὁ [μανίᾱ]: *seer, prophet, soothsayer.*

μάρναμαι (only pres. and impf.): *fight, struggle.* Poetic.

μάρτυς, -υρος, ὁ: *witness.*

μάτην, adv.: *idly, in vain.*

μάχη, -ης, ἡ: *battle, combat, fight.*

μάχομαι, μαχοῦμαι, ἐμαχεσάμην, μεμάχημαι: *give battle, fight,* with D.

μέγας, μεγάλη, μέγα: *great, large, loud* (of a noise).

μέγεθος, -ους, τό: *magnitude, greatness, size.*

μέγιστος, -η, -ον, superlative of μέγας: *greatest.*

μεθ', see μετά.

μεθ-ίημι, see ἵημι: *release, let go, let fly.*

μεθύσκω, ἐμέθυσα, ἐμεθύσθην: *make drunk.*

μεθύω (only pres. and impf.): *be drunk, intoxicated.*

μείζων, -ον, comparative of μέγας: *greater.*

μέλας, -αινα, -αν: *black, dark.*

μέλει, μελήσει, ἐμέλησε, μεμέληκε: *it is a care, concerns,* with D. and ὅπως clause.

μελέτη, -ης, ἡ: *practice.*

μέλλω, μελλήσω, ἐμέλλησα: *be about to, intend,* with pres. or fut. inf.

μέλος, -ους, τό: *song.*

μέν, post-pos. conj., emphasizing and contrasting the word or phrase to which it belongs with a similar word or phrase accompanied by δέ, ἀλλά, or μέντοι. Rarely to be translated.

μέν-τοι, adv.: *indeed, however, yet.*

μένω, μενῶ, ἔμεινα, μεμένηκα: *remain, await, wait for.*

μερίζω, μεριῶ, etc.: *divide, distribute.*

μέρος, -ους, τό: *share, part, rôle.*

μέσος, -η, -ον: *middle, middle of;* τὸ μέσον: *the middle.*

μεστός, -ή, -όν: *full, full of,* with G.

μετά, prep. with G. and A.: with G., *with, among;* with A., *after.* In compounds, *among, after, in quest of;* frequently also it denotes a change of position or condition.

μεταξύ, adv.: *between.*

μετ-αλλάττω, see ἀλλάττω.

μετα-νοέω, μετανοήσω, etc.: *change one's mind, repent.*

μετα-πέμπω, see πέμπω: *send after;* mid., *summon.*

μετα-τίθημι, see τίθημι: *change position, set aside.*

μέτ-ειμι, see εἰμί: *be with.*

μέτριος, -ᾱ, -ον: *measured, moderate, average*

μέτρον, -ου, τό: *measure, moderation.*

μέχρι, improper prep. with G.: *up to, until;* conj.: *until.*

μή, neg. adv.: *not.* Used instead of οὐ with imv., subjv., inf. (except in indirect discourse), and part. (when it has the meaning of a condition); also in all conditional clauses, conditional relative clauses, temporal clauses involving the subjv. or opt., purpose and object clauses (except such as are introduced by μή), and clauses expressing a wish.

μη-δέ, neg. conj. and adv.: *but not, and not, not even, nor.*

μηδ-είς, -εμία, -έν: *no one, nothing;* adjectival: *no.*

μήθ', see μήτε.

μη-κ-έτι, neg. adv.: *not again, no longer, never again.*

μήν, post-pos. intensive particle: *indeed, certainly.*

μήν, μηνός, ὁ: *month.*

μή-ποτε, neg. adv.: *not ever, never.*

μή-τε . . . μή-τε, neg. conj.: *neither . . . nor.*

μήτηρ, μητρός, ἡ: *mother.*

μητρό-πολις, -εως, ἡ: *mother city, source.*

μηχανάομαι, μηχανήσομαι, etc.: *contrive, devise.*

μηχανή, -ῆς, ἡ : *contrivance, device, machine, means.*

μία, see εἷς.

μιαρός, -ά, -όν : *foul, vile, loathsome, disgusting.*

μῑκρός, -ά, -όν : *little, small.*

μιμνῄσκω, μνήσω, ἔμνησα, μέμνημαι, ἐμνήσθην: *remind;* mid. and pass., *remind oneself, remember, recall, mention.*

μισθός, -οῦ, ὁ : *pay, reward, hire.*

μισθόω, ἐμίσθωσα, etc. : *let for pay;* mid., *let to oneself for pay, hire, engage.*

μνῆμα, -ατος, τό : *memorial, monument.*

μνήμη, -ης, ἡ : *memory, remembrance.*

μνημοσύνη, -ης, ἡ : *faculty of memory, memory.*

μόλις, adv. : *with difficulty.*

μόνος, -η, -ον [μένω] : *only, alone.*

μόσχος, -ου, ὁ : *bullock.*

μοῦνος, -η, -ον, dialectic for μόνος.

μόχθος, -ου, ὁ : *toil.*

μῡρίος, -ᾱ, -ον : *countless;* μύριοι, -αι, -α : *ten thousand.*

μωρός, -οῦ, ὁ : *fool.*

N

νᾱός, -οῦ, ὁ : *temple, shrine.* Attic νεώς.

ναυ-ηγός, -όν : *shipwrecked.*

ναῦς, νεώς, ἡ : *ship.*

ναύτης, -ου, ὁ : *sailor.*

ναυτικόν, -οῦ, τό : *fleet, navy.*

νεᾱνίᾱς, -ου, ὁ : *young man.*

νεκρός, -οῦ, ὁ : *corpse, dead.*

νέμω, νεμῶ, etc. : *distribute, apportion, assign.*

νεογνός, -όν [γίγνομαι] : *new-born.*

νέος, -ᾱ, -ον : *new, young, fresh.*

νεῦρον, -ου, τό, *sinew, bowstring.*

νή, intensive particle, used in oaths : *surely.*

νήφω (pres. only) : *be sober.*

νίζω, -νίψομαι, -ένιψα, -νένιμμαι : *wash.*

νῑκάω, νῑκήσω, etc. : *be victorious, beat, conquer, win.*

νίκη, -ης, ἡ : *victory.*

νιφετός, -οῦ, ὁ [Lat. *nix*] : *snow.*

νομίζω, νομιῶ, ἐνόμισα, etc. : *believe in, believe, regard, think,* with inf.

νόμος, -ου, ὁ : *custom, usage, law.*

νοῦς, νοῦ, ὁ : *mind;* ἐν νῷ ἔχω : *intend;* τὸν νοῦν προσέχω : *attend, pay heed.*

νύμφιος, -ου, ὁ : *bridegroom.*

νῦν, adv. : *now, at this time.*

νύξ, νυκτός, ἡ : *night.*

Ξ

ξεῖνος, -ου, ὁ, dialectic for ξένος.

ξένος, -ου, ὁ : *stranger, guest, host; hired soldier, mercenary* (soldier).

ξύλον, -ου, τό : *piece of wood.*

O

ὁ, ἡ, τό, definite article : *the;* ὁ μέν . . . ὁ δέ : *the one . . . the other;* ὁ δέ (without ὁ μέν): *but* or *and he.*

ὀβολός, -οῦ, ὁ : *obol,* an Attic coin containing about three cents worth of silver.

ὅδε, ἥδε, τόδε, demons. pron., referring to something near in time or place : *this.*

ὁδός, -οῦ, ἡ : *road, way, journey, route.*

ὀδούς, ὀδόντος, ὁ : *tooth, tusk.*

ὀδύνη, -ης, ἡ : *pain.*

ὅ-θεν, adv.: *from which place, whence.*

οἱ, see ὁ.

οἵ, see ὅς.

οἷ, see οὗ.

οἶδα, 2d perf. with pres. meaning: *know.*

οἴκα-δε, adv. [οἶκος]: *homeward.*

οἰκέω, οἰκήσω, etc.: *inhabit, have one's home, dwell.*

οἰκίᾱ, -ᾱς, ἡ: *house, home.*

οἶκος, -ου, ὁ: *house, household, family.*

οἰμώζω, οἰμώξομαι: *cry out in pain, wail.*

οἶνος, -ου, ὁ: *wine.*

οἰνο-χόος, -ου, ὁ: *wine-pourer, cup-bearer.*

οἴομαι, οἰήσομαι, ᾠήθην: *believe, suppose, think.*

οἷος, -ᾱ, -ον: *of which kind, of such kind as;* exclam., *what kind of;* οἷός τε: *of the sort that, able to.*

οἰωνός, -οῦ, ὁ: *bird of omen, omen.*

ὀκτακισ-χίλιοι, -αι, -α: *eight thousand.*

ὀκτα-κόσιοι, -αι, -α: *eight hundred.*

ὀκτώ, indeclinable numeral: *eight.*

ὀλίγος, -η, -ον; *little, small;* pl., *few.*

ὀλιγο-χρόνιος, -ον: *of short duration.*

ὀλιγώρως, adv.: *carelessly, slightingly.*

ὄλλῡμι, ὀλῶ, ὤλεσα, ὠλόμην, ὀλώλεκα or ὄλωλα: *destroy;* mid., *perish.*

ὅλος, -η, -ον: *whole, all.*

ὅλως, adv.: *altogether, as a whole, wholly.*

ὄμβρος, -ου, ὁ: *rain.*

ὁμιλίᾱ, -ᾱς, ἡ: *association, converse.*

ὄμνῡμι, ὀμοῦμαι, ὤμοσα, ὀμώμοκα, ὀμώμομαι, and ὀμώμοσμαι, ὠμόθην and ὠμόσθην: *swear, take oath.*

ὅμοιος, -ᾱ, -ον: *like, similar.*

ὁμοίως, adv.: *in like manner, similarly.*

ὁμο-λογέω, ὁμολογήσω, etc.: *say the same thing, agree, admit.*

ὅμως, adv.: *all the same, however, yet.*

ὄνειδος, -ους, τό: *disgrace, reproach, shame.*

ὄνομα, -ατος, τό: *name, noun, word.*

ὀνομάζω, ὀνομάσω, etc.: *name, call by name.*

ὄνος, -ου, ὁ: *ass, donkey.*

ὄπισθεν, adv.: *from the rear, in the rear, behind.*

ὀπισθο-φύλαξ, -κος, ὁ: *rear guard.*

ὁπλή, -ῆς, ἡ: *hoof.*

ὁπλίζω, ὥπλισα, ὥπλισμαι, ὡπλίσθην: *arm, equip.*

ὁπλίτης, -ου, ὁ: *heavy-armed soldier, hoplite.*

ὅπλον, -ου, τό: *tool;* pl., *arms, equipment.*

ὁπόσος, -η, -ον: *as many as, as much as, as great as.*

ὅποι, conj. adv.: *whither.*

ὁπόταν, conj. adv. *whenever, when.*

ὁπότε, conj. adv.: *whenever, when.*

ὅπου, conj. adv.: *wherever, where.*

ὅπως, conj. adv.: *how, that, in order that.*

ὁράω, imperf. ἑώρων, ὄψομαι, εἶδον, ἑόρᾱκα or ἑώρᾱκα, ἑώρᾱμαι or ὦμμαι, ὤφθην: *see.*

ὀργή, -ῆς, ἡ: *anger, wrath.*

ὀρέγω, ὀρέξω, etc.: *reach, stretch.*

ὄρθιος, -ᾱ, -ον: *straight up and down, steep.*

ὀρθός, -ή, όν: *erect, upright, correct, straight.*

ὅρκος, -ου, ὁ: *oath.*

ὁρμάω, ὁρμήσω, etc.: *set in motion, start, hasten;* mid. and pass., *start, rush.*

ὄρος, -ους, τό: *mountain.*

ὀρχέομαι, -ήσομαι, etc.: *dance.*

ὄρχησις, -εως, ἡ: *dancing.*

ὅς, ἥ, ὅ, rel. pron.: *who, which, that.*

ὅς, ἥ, ὅ, possessive adj. of the 3d pers. (poetic): *his, her.*

ὅσιος, -ᾱ, -ον: *sanctioned by the gods, holy, pious.*

ὅσος, -η, -ον: *how much, how great;* pl., *how many, as much (great, large, many) as.*

ὅσ-περ, ἥπερ, ὅπερ, intensive form of ὅς, ἥ, ὅ.

ὅσ-τις, ἥτις, ὅ τι: *whoever, whichever, whatever; who, which, what.*

ὀστέον, -ου, τό: *bone.*

ὅταν, conj. adv., with subjv.: *whenever, when.*

ὅτε, conj. adv.: *whenever, when, as.*

ὅτι, conj.: *that, because;* with superlatives, often used for emphasis, to denote the highest degree possible.

οὐ, οὐκ, οὐχ, neg. adv.: *not.*

οὗ, genitive of pron. of the 3d pers.

οὐ-δέ, neg. conj. and adv.: *but not, and not, nor;* as adv.: *not even.*

οὐδ-είς, -εμία, -έν: *no one, nothing;* adjectival: *no.*

οὔθ', see οὔτε.

οὐκ, see οὐ.

οὐκ-έτι, neg. adv.: *no longer, no more, never again.*

οὐκ-οῦν, (1) interrog. particle: *not then, not therefore;* (2) inferential conj.: *then, therefore.*

οὖν, post-pos. inferential particle: *so, then, therefore, accordingly.*

οὔ-ποτε, neg. adv.: *not ever, never.*

οὔ-πω, neg. adv. *not yet.*

οὐρανός, -οῦ, ὁ: *sky, heaven.*

οὔ-τε, neg. conj.: *and not;* οὔτε . . . οὔτε: *neither . . . nor.*

οὔ-τις, poetic for οὐδείς.

οὗτος, αὕτη, τοῦτο: *this;* frequently used as an emphatic personal pron.: *he, she, it, they.*

οὕτως (οὕτω usually before a conson.), adv.: *thus, so.*

οὐχ, see οὐ.

ὀφείλω, ὀφειλήσω, ὠφείλησα and ὤφελον, ὠφείληκα, ὠφειλήθην: *owe.* With infin., used to express unattainable wishes.

ὀφειλέτης, -ου, ὁ: *debtor.*

ὀφθαλμός, -οῦ, ὁ [ὄψομαι]: *eye.*

ὄφλημα, -ατος, τό: *debt.*

ὄχημα, -ατος, τό [ἔχω]: *carriage, vehicle.*

ὄψις, -εως, ἡ: *sight, spectacle.*

ὄψομαι, see ὁράω.

Π

παθεῖν, see πάσχω.

πάθος, -ους, τό [πάσχω]: *experience, treatment.*

παίγνιον, -ου, τό [παίζω]: *plaything, sport, toy.*

παιδείᾱ, -ᾱς, ἡ: *education.*

παιδεύω, παιδεύσω, etc.: *educate.*

παιδίον, -ου, τό, diminutive of παῖς: *little child.*

παίζω, παίσω, etc.: *play, sport.*

παῖς, παιδός, ὁ, ἡ: *child, boy, girl, son* or *daughter; slave.*

παίω, παίσω, etc.: *strike.*

πάλαι, adv.: *of old, in ancient times, long ago.*

πάλαιος, -ᾱ, -ον: *ancient, olden.*

πάλιν, adv.: *back, again.*

πάλλω, ἔπηλα, πέπαλμαι: *shake, toss.* Poetic.

παλτόν, -οῦ, τό: *javelin, spear.*

πάνυ, adv.: *altogether, wholly, very.*

παρά, prep. with G., D., and A.: *beside;* (1) with G., *from beside;* (2) with D., *by the side of, by, with;* (3) with A., *to the side of, alongside, past the side of;* also, *against, contrary to.* In compounds, *along, alongside, aside, beyond, past.*

παρ-αγγέλλω, see ἀγγέλλω: *pass along an order* or *message.*

παρα-βαίνω, see βαίνω: *step beyond, transgress.*

παρα-βοηθέω, see βοηθέω: *come to aid, succor.*

παρα-γίγνομαι, see γίγνομαι: *be beside, reach the side of.*

παρα-δίδωμι, see δίδωμι: *hand over to, surrender.*

παρ-αινέω: *advise.*

παρα-καθέζομαι, see καθέζομαι: *sit beside.*

παρα-καλέω, see καλέω: *summon, invite.*

παρα-κελεύομαι, mid. depon., see κελεύω: *urge along, encourage.*

παρασάγγης, -ου, ὁ: *parasang,* a Persian road measure, about 30 stades.

παρα-σκευάζω: *arrange in order* (*i.e.*, side by side), *prepare.*

παρα-στάτης, -ου, ὁ [παρ-ίστημι]: *one who stands near, comrade.*

παρα-τείνω, see τείνω: *stretch along, extend.*

πάρ-ειμι, see εἰμί: *be beside, at hand, present.*

πάρ-ειμι, see εἶμι: *go alongside* or *by.*

παρ-ελαύνω, see ἐλαύνω: *march* or *ride by* or *along.*

παρ-έρχομαι, see ἔρχομαι: *go by.*

παρ-έχω, see ἔχω: *hold out to, furnish, supply, cause; render.*

παρ-ήκω, see ἥκω: *reach the side of, arrive.*

παρθένος, -ου, ἡ: *maiden, virgin.*

παρ-ίημι, see ἵημι: *let pass, relax, omit.*

πάρ-οδος, -ου, ἡ: *pass by* or *along, passage, pass.*

πᾶς, πᾶσα, πᾶν: *all, every, entire, whole, any* (= every).

πάσχω, πείσομαι, ἔπαθον, πέπονθα: *experience, be treated, suffer.*

πατήρ, πατρός, ὁ: *father.*

πάτρη, -ης, ἡ: *fatherland, native land.*

πάτριος, -ᾱ, -ον: *ancestral, paternal.*

πατρίς, -ίδος, ἡ: *fatherland, native land.*

πατρῷος, -ᾱ, -ον: *ancestral, inherited.*

παύω, παύσω, etc.: *cause to stop, stop;* mid., *stop oneself, cease.*

πεδίον, -ου, τό: *flat country, plain.*

πεζῇ, adv.: *on foot.*

πεζός, -ή, -όν: *on foot, afoot;* ὁ πεζός: *footsoldier, infantryman.*

πείθω,* πείσω, ἔπεισα, πέπεικα and πέποιθα, πέπεισμαι, ἐπείσθην: *persuade;* mid. and pass., *be persuaded, obey,* with D.; πέποιθα: *believe, trust, be confident.*

πειθώ, -οῦς, ἡ: *persuasion.*

πειρασμός, -οῦ, ὁ, *temptation.*

πειράω, πειράσω, etc.: *test, try;* more common as pass. depon., *attempt.*

πείσομαι, see πάσχω and πείθω.

πέλας, adv.: *nearby.*

πελταστής, -οῦ, ὁ: *peltast, light-armed soldier, skirmisher.*

πέλω, πέλομαι (pres. and impf. only): *be, come to be.*

πέμπτος, -η, -ον: *fifth.*

πέμπω, πέμψω, ἔπεμψα, πέπομφα, πέπεμμαι, ἐπέμφθην: *send.*

πεντακισ-χίλιοι, -αι, -α: *five thousand.*

πεντα-κόσιοι, -αι, -α: *five hundred.*

πέντε, indeclinable numeral: *five.*

πεντε-καί-δεκα, indeclinable numeral: *fifteen.*

πεντήκοντα, indeclinable numeral: *fifty.*

πέπονθα, see πάσχω.

πέπτωκα, see πίπτω.

-περ, intensive enclit. particle.

περί, prep. with G., D, and A.: *about, around;* (1) with G., *about, concerning, for;* (2) with D, *about, in the neighborhood of;* (3) with A., literally, *about, around, in connection with, near.* In compounds, in addition to the foregoing meanings, often *over, above, beyond, exceedingly.*

περι-μάχητος, -ον: *fought about* or *over.*

πέριξ, adv.: *round about.*

περι-πατέω, περιπατήσω, etc.: *walk about.*

περι-σκοπέω, see σκοπέω: *look around at.*

περ-ισσός, -ή, -όν: *more than even, odd* (of numbers), *superfluous.*

περι-τίθημι, see τίθημι: *place around, surround with.*

πέτρᾱ, -ᾱς, ἡ: *rock.*

πηλινός, -ή, -όν: *of clay, earthen.*

πήρᾱ, -ᾱς, ἡ: *wallet.*

πιέζω, πιέσω, etc.: *press hard, oppress.*

πικρός, -ά, -όν: *bitter, painful, sharp, severe.*

πικρῶς, adv.: *bitterly, sharply, severely.*

πίμπλημι, πλήσω, ἔπλησα, πέπληκα, πέπλησμαι, ἐπλήσθην: *fill.*

πίνω, πίομαι, ἔπιον, πέπωκα, -πέπομαι, -επόθην: *drink.*

πίπτω, πεσοῦμαι, ἔπεσον, πέπτωκα: *fall; be thrown.*

πιστεύω, πιστεύσω, etc.: *put faith in, believe, trust,* with D.

πίστις, -εως, ἡ: *guarantee, pledge.*

πιστός, -ή, -όν: *faithful, trusty, loyal, reliable.*

πλᾱσίον, adv., dialectic for πλησίον.

πλάττω, πλάσω, etc.: *mold, shape, fashion.*

πλέθρον, -ου, τό: *plethron,* 100 Greek feet.

πλεῖστος, -η, -ον, superlative of πολύς: *most.*

πλείων, -ον, comparative of πολύς: *more.*

πλευρᾱ́, -ᾶς, ἡ: *rib, side.*

πλέω, πλεύσομαι, ἔπλευσα, πέπλευκα, πέπλευσμαι: *sail, travel by sea.*

πληγή, -ῆς, ἡ [πλήττω]: *blow, stroke.*

πλῆθος, -ους, τό [πίμ-πλη-μι]: *fullness, number, quantity, multitude, "the masses."*

πλήν, conj.: *except, except that;* improper prep. with G.: *except.*

πλήρης, -ες [πίμ-πλη-μι]: *full, full of,* with G.

πλησίος, -ᾱ, -ον: *near;* πλησίον (neuter) as adv.: *nearby.*

πλήττω, πλήξω, ἔπληξα, πέπληγα, πέπληγμαι, ἐπλήγην and ἐπλάγην: *strike.*

πλοῖον, -ου, τό [πλέω]: *boat.*

πλοῦς, πλοῦ, ὁ: *sailing, voyage.*

πλούσιος, -ᾱ, -ον: *wealthy.*

πλουτέω, -ήσω, etc.: *be wealthy.*

ποδωκίη, -ης, ἡ: *fleetness of foot, speed.*

πόθεν, adv.: *from where, whence, why.*

ποιέω, ποιήσω, etc.: *make, do, treat.*

ποίημα, -ατος, τό: *creation, poem.*

ποιητής, -οῦ, ὁ: *maker, creator, poet.*

ποιμήν, -ένος, ὁ: *shepherd, herdsman.*

ποῖος, -ᾱ, -ον: *of what sort.*

πολεμέω, πολεμήσω, etc.: *make war, fight.*

πολέμιος, -ᾱ, -ον: *at war with, hostile;* οἱ πολέμιοι: *the enemy.*

πόλεμος, -ου, ὁ: *war.*

πολι-ορκέω, πολιορκήσω, etc.: *besiege.*

πόλις, -εως, ἡ: *city, state.*

πολίτης, -ου, ὁ: *citizen.*

πολλάκις, adv.: *many times, often.*

πολυ-μαθής, -ές [μανθάνω]: *polymath, learned.*

πολυ-μαθίη, -ης, ἡ: *much learning, erudition.*

πολύς, πολλή, πολύ: *much, many;* οἱ πολλοί: *the majority.*

πομπή, -ῆς, ἡ [πέμπω]: *mission, procession.*

πονέω, πονήσω, etc.: *labor, toil, struggle.*

πονηρός, -ᾱ, -όν: *hard working, wretched, base.*

πόνος, -ου, ὁ: *labor, toil, suffering, travail.*

ποντο-πορέω, -πορήσω, etc.: *sail the open sea.*

πορείᾱ, -ᾱς, ἡ: *journey, way.*

πορεύω, πορεύσω, etc.: *make go;* most commonly pass. depon.: *go, advance, make one's way, journey, march.*

πορθμεῖα, -ων, τά: *ferry charges, fare.*

πορθμεῖον, -ου, τό: *ferry.*

πορθμεύς, -έως, ὁ: *ferryman.*

πορθμεύω, πορθμεύσω, etc.: *ferry, transport.*

πορίζω, ποριῶ, etc.: *furnish, provide, supply.*

πόρος, -ου, ὁ: *means of passing, ford, way; way* or *means of doing.*

πόσος, -η, -ον: *how much?*

ποταμός, -οῦ, ὁ: *river.*

πότε, adv.: *when?*

ποτέ, enclit. adv.: *sometime, once, ever.*

πότερος, -ᾱ, -ον: *which of two?* πότερον . . . ἤ: *whether . . . or?*

πότνια, ἡ, confined principally to N. and V.: *august, revered, potent.*

ποῦ, adv.: *where?*

που, enclit. adv.: *somewhere.*

πούς, ποδός, ὁ: *foot, leg.*

πρᾶγμα, -ατος, τό [πρᾱ́ττω]: *deed, fact, business;* pl., *trouble.*

πρᾱ́ττω (πρᾱγ-), πρᾱ́ξω, ἔπρᾱξα, πέπρᾱγα and πέπρᾱχα, πέπρᾱγμαι, ἐπρᾱ́χθην: *do, act, achieve, fare.*

πρᾴως, adv.: *mildly, gently.*

πρεσβύτερος, -ᾱ, -ον: *elder, older.*

πρίν, conj. adv.: *before, until.*

πρό, prep. with G.: *before, in front of, in defense of.* In compounds, in addition to foregoing meanings, *forward, beforehand.*

προ-βαίνω, see βαίνω: *go ahead, advance.*

πρό-γονος, -ου, ὁ: *progenitor, forefather, ancestor.*

προ-δίδωμι, see *δίδωμι*: *abandon, betray, give over.*

προ-έχω, see *ἔχω*: *hold forth, project, exceed.*

πρό-θῡμος, *-ον*: *eager, ready, zealous.*

προ-θύμως, adv.: *eagerly, readily.*

προ-ΐημι, see *ἵημι*: *send forth, let go, abandon.*

πρό-κειμαι, *see κεῖμαι*: *be proposed, appointed, prescribed.*

πρό-μαχος, *-ου, ὁ*: *one fighting in the front, champion, defender.*

προ-πέμπω, see *πέμπω*: *send forward* or *ahead.*

πρός, prep. with G., D., and A.: *at, by;* (1) with G., *from the presence of, from the direction of, in the sight of, with regard to;* (2) with D., *at, near, besides, in addition to;* (3) with A., *in the direction of, toward, according to.* In compounds, *toward, besides, to, against.*

προσ-άπτω, *προσάψω*: *fasten to.*

προσ-ελαύνω: *ride toward.*

προσ-έρχομαι: *approach.*

προσ-ευχή, *-ῆς, ἡ*: *prayer, supplication, vow.*

προσ-εύχομαι, see *εὔχομαι*: *pray to, vow to, supplicate.*

πρόσ-θεν, adv.: *from the front, in the front, before, sooner.*

προσ-λαμβάνω, see *λαμβάνω*: *take besides.*

προσ-πίπτω, see *πίπτω*: *fall upon, fall in with, befall.*

προσ-τίθημι, see *τίθημι*: *put upon, attribute, add;* mid.: *join, agree with.*

προσ-φέρω, see *φέρω*: *bring to, apply;* mid., *bear* or *conduct oneself toward, behave.*

πρότερος, *-ᾱ, -ον* [*πρό*]: *earlier, former; πρότερον*, adv.: *formerly.*

προ-φέρω, see *φέρω*: *bring forth, produce.*

πρώην, adv.: *recently.*

πρῶτος, *-η, -ον* [*πρό*]: *first, foremost; πρῶτον*, adv.: *at first.*

πτέρυξ, *-υγος, ἡ*: *wing.*

πύλη, *-ης, ἡ*: *gate;* pl., *pass.*

πυνθάνομαι, *πεύσομαι, ἐπυθόμην, πέπυσμαι*: *inquire, learn* (by inquiry).

πῦρ, *πυρός, τό*: *fire.*

πῡρο-φόρος, *-ον*: *wheat-bearing.*

πωλέω, *πωλήσω*, etc.: *sell.*

πῶς, adv.: *how?*

πως, enclit. adv.: *somehow, in any way, I suppose.*

Ρ

ῥᾴδιος, *-ᾱ, -ον*: *easy.*

ῥᾳδίως, adv.: *easily.*

ῥᾷστος, *-η, -ον*: *most easy.*

ῥᾴων, *-ον*: *more easy.*

ῥέω, *ῥυήσομαι, ἐρρύηκα, ἐρρύην*: *flow.*

ῥήγνῡμι, *ῥήξω*, etc.: *break.*

ῥῆμα, *-ατος, τό*: *word, saying.*

ῥήτωρ, *-ορος, ὁ*: *speaker, orator.*

ῥίπτω, *ῥίψω, ἔρρῑψα, ἔρρῑφα, ἔρρῑμμαι, ἐρρίφθην* and *ἐρρίφην*: *hurl, throw, cast aside.*

ῥύομαι, *ῥύσομαι*, etc.: *protect, shield, save.*

Σ

σάλπιγξ, *-γγος, ἡ*: *trumpet.*

σάρξ, *-κός, ἡ*: *flesh.*

σατράπης, *-ου, ὁ*: *satrap*, a Persian official, *governor.*

σε-αυτοῦ, *-ῆς*, reflexive pron. of the 2d pers.: *of yourself.*

σέβασμα, *-ατος, τό*: *something revered, holy image.*

σεισμός, -οῦ, ὁ: *earthquake.*

σελήνη, -ης, ἡ: *moon.*

σημαίνω, σημανῶ, etc.: *give a signal, signify, betoken, make known.*

σημεῖον, -ου, τό: *sign, token, mark, signal.*

σήμερον, adv.: *today.*

σίδηρος, -ου, ὁ: *iron, steel, iron* or *steel weapon.*

σῑγή, -ῆς, ἡ: *silence.*

σῖτος, -ου, ὁ: *grain, food.*

σκαιός, -ᾱ́, -όν: *left, left-handed, awkward.*

σκάφη, -ης, ἡ: *bowl, tub.*

σκέλος, -ους, τό: *leg.*

σκέπτομαι, σκέψομαι, etc.: *observe closely, look to see, see to it, inquire, consider.*

σκηνή, -ῆς, ἡ: *tent, booth, "stage."*

σκιᾱ́, -ᾶς, ἡ: *shadow, shade.*

σκοπέω (only pres. and impf.): *look to see, see to it, inquire, consider.*

σκώπτω, σκώψω, etc.: *scoff, jest at, make fun of.*

σός, -ή, -όν: *thy, thine.*

σοφίᾱ, -ᾱς, ἡ: *wisdom.*

σοφός, -ή, -όν: *wise.*

σπένδω, σπείσω, ἔσπεισαν: *pour drink offering, libation;* mid., *make a treaty.*

σπεύδω, σπεύσω, etc.: *hurry, hasten, be in earnest.*

σπήλαιον, -ου, τό: *cave.* Compare Latin **spelunca.**

σπονδή, -ῆς, ἡ [σπένδω]: *libation;* pl., *treaty, truce.*

σπουδαῖος, -ᾱ, -ον: *earnest, zealous, serious, weighty.*

σπουδή, -ῆς, ἡ [σπεύδω]: *earnestness, zeal, haste.*

στάδιον, -ου, τό, pl. either στάδιοι or στάδια: *stadium, stade* (100 Greek feet).

σταθμός, -ου, ὁ [ἵστημι]: *stopping-place, stop, day's march.*

στάχυς, -υος, ὁ: *ear of grain.*

στέλλω, στελῶ, ἔστειλα, ἔσταλκα, ἔσταλμαι, ἐστάλην: *arrange, equip, send.*

στενός, -ή, -όν: *narrow.*

στένω (only pres. and impf.): *groan.*

στέφανος, -ου, ὁ: *crown, wreath.*

στοιχέω, στοιχήσω, etc.: *go in a line, stand beside* a person *in battle.*

στόμα, -ατος, τό: *mouth, van* (of an army).

στράτευμα, -ατος, τό: *army.*

στρατεύω, στρατεύσω, etc.: *make a campaign;* more common in the mid.

στρατ-ηγέω, στρατηγήσω, etc.: *be general, command.*

στρατ-ηγός, -οῦ, ὁ [ἄγω]: *army leader, general.*

στρατιᾱ́, -ᾶς, ἡ: *army.*

στρατιώτης, -ου, ὁ: *soldier.*

στρατο-πεδεύω, στρατοπεδεύσω, etc.: *encamp;* more common in the mid.

στρατό-πεδον, -ου, τό: *camp-ground, encampment, camp.*

στρέφω, στρέψω, ἔστρεψα, ἔστραμμαι, ἐστράφην: *turn, twist.*

σύ, σοῦ: *thou, you.*

συγ-γενής, -ές [γίγνομαι]: *of the same family, related.*

συλ-λαμβάνω, see λαμβάνω: *seize, arrest.*

συμ-βόλαιον, -ου, τό [βάλλω]: *mark, sign, symbol; agreement.*

συμ-βουλεύω, see βουλεύω: *counsel, advise;* mid., *consult with.*

σύμ-βουλος, -ου, ὁ: *adviser.*

σύμ-μαχος, -ου, ὁ: *helper in battle, ally.*

συμ-πέμπω, see πέμπω: *send with.*

συμ-ποδίζω, συμποδιῶ, etc.: *hobble, shackle.*

συμ-πολεμέω, see πολεμέω: *join in war, fight on the side of.*

συμ-φιλοσοφέω, συμ-φιλοσοφήσω, etc.: *philosophize with.*

σύν, prep. with D.: *with, along with, with the help of.* In compounds, *together, altogether, with, completely.*

σύνεσις, -εως, ἡ [συν-ίημι]: *intelligence, understanding.*

συν-τίθημι, see τίθημι: *place together*; mid., *agree on, make an agreement.*

συ-σπεύδω, συσπεύσω, συνέσπευσα, etc.: *join in showing haste* or *zeal.*

σφίσι, see οὗ.

σχημάτιον, -ου, τό: *figure, dance step.*

σχίζω, ἔσχισα, ἐσχίσθην: *split.*

σχολάζω, σχολάσω, etc.: *be leisurely* or *slow.*

σχολή, -ῆς, ἡ: *leisure, slowness, free time* for anything.

σῴζω, σώσω, etc.: *save, bring safely, rescue.*

σῶμα, -ατος, τό: *body, person, life.*

σωτήρ, -ῆρος, ὁ: *savior.*

σωτηρίᾱ, -ᾱς, ἡ: *salvation, safety.*

σώ-φρων, -ον: *sound minded, sensible, temperate, chaste.*

T

ταί, dialectic for αἵ.

τάλαντον, -ου, τό: *a talent*, a weight of coin equivalent to about $1080.00.

ταξί-αρχος, -ου, ὁ: *division commander, taxiarch.*

τάξις, -εως, ἡ: *order, arrangement, line of battle, position, division.*

τάττω, τάξω, ἔταξα, τέταχα, τέταγμαι, ἐτάχθην: *arrange, order, post, station.*

τάφος, -ου, ὁ [θάπτω]: *burial, grave, tomb.*

τάφρος, -ου, ἡ [θάπτω]: *trench, ditch.*

τάχα, adv.: *quickly, soon, perhaps.*

ταχύς, -εῖα, -ύ: *quick, swift, rapid.*

τε, enclit. conj. commonly paired with καί: *and.*

τέγγω, τέγξω, etc.: *wet, moisten, soften.*

τέθνηκα, etc., see **ἀπο-θνῄσκω.**

τείνω, τενῶ, ἔτεινα, τέτακα, τέταμαι, ἐτάθην: *stretch, strain, be tense; extend, reach; hasten.*

τεῖχος, -ους, τό: *wall, fortification.*

τέκνον, -ου, τό: *child, offspring.*

τελευτάω, τελευτήσω, etc.: *end, finish, die.*

τελευτή, -ῆς, ἡ: *end, death.*

τέλος, -ους, τό: *end, completion, goal*; A. used as adv.: *finally.*

τέμνω, τεμῶ, ἔτεμον and ἔταμον, τέτμηκα, τέτμημαι, ἐτμήθην: *cut.*

τερπνός, -ή, -όν: *delightful, enjoyable, pleasant.*

τετταράκοντα, indeclinable numeral: *forty.*

τέτταρες, -α: *four.*

τέχνη, -ης, ἡ: *art, craft, skill; profession* or *calling.*

τῇδε, adv.: *here.*

τίθημι, θήσω, ἔθηκα, τέθεικα, τέθειμαι, ἐτέθην: *put, place, set.*

τιθήνη, -ης, ἡ: *nurse.*

τίκτω, *τέξομαι, ἔτεκον, τέτοκα* : *beget, give birth, produce.*

τῑμάω, *τῑμήσω*, etc.: *honor, reward, pay.*

τῑμή, -*ῆς*, *ἡ* : *value, price, honor.*

τίμιος, -*ᾱ*, -*ον* : *precious, costly.*

τῑμ-ωρέω, *τῑμωρήσω* : *avenge;* mid., *exact vengeance, punish.*

τίς, *τί*, G. *τίνος*: *who? which? what?* neuter as adv.: *why?*

τις, *τι*, G. *τινός*, enclit.: *a, an, any, some.*

τιτρώσκω, *τρώσω*, etc.: *wound.*

τοι, enclit. particle developed out of the D. of 2d pers. pron.: *let me tell you, I assure you, indeed,* etc.

τοιήδε, dialectic for *τοιάδε*, see *τοιόσδε.*

τοί-νυν, post-pos. adv.: *therefore, then, so.*

τοιόσ-δε, *τοιά-δε*, *τοιόν-δε* : *such, such as follows.*

τοιοῦτος, *τοιαύτη*, *τοιοῦτο* : *of such sort, so fine.*

τόξον, -*ου*, *τό* : *bow.*

τόπος, -*ου*, *ὁ* : *place.*

τοσοῦτος, *τοσαύτη*, *τοσοῦτο* : *of such size* or *quantity, so large, so much;* pl., *so many.*

τότε, adv.: *at that time, then.*

τράπεζα, -*ης*, *ἡ* : *table.*

τραυματίᾱς, -*ου*, *ὁ* : *wounded man.*

τρεῖς, *τρία* : *three.*

τρέπω, *τρέψω*, *ἔτρεψα* and *ἔτραπον*, *τέτροφα*, *τέτραμμαι*, *ἐτράπην* and *ἐτρέφθην* : *turn.*

τρέφω, *θρέψω*, *ἔθρεψα*, *τέτροφα*, *τέθραμμαι*, *ἐτράφην* and *ἐθρέφθην* : *nourish, keep* (of animals), *support, rear.*

τρέχω, *δραμοῦμαι*, *ἔδραμον*, *δεδράμηκα*, *δεδράμημαι* : *run.*

τριᾱ́-κοντα [*τρεῖς*], indeclinable numeral : *thirty.*

τριᾱ-κόσιοι, -*αι*, -*α* : *three hundred.*

τρι-ήρης, -*ους*, *ἡ* : *trireme, war vessel* with three banks of oars.

τρισ-καί-δεκα, indeclinable numeral: *thirteen.*

τρισ-χίλιοι, -*αι*, -*α* : *three thousand.*

τρί-τος, -*η*, -*ον* : *third.*

τρόπος, -*ου*, *ὁ* : *turn, "bent," direction, manner, character, way.*

τροφή, -*ῆς*, *ἡ* [*τρέφω*]: *nurture, support, food.*

τυγχάνω, *τεύξομαι*, *ἔτυχον*, *τετύχηκα* : with G., *hit, attain;* with suppl. part., *happen.*

τύραννος, -*ου*, *ὁ* : *king, tyrant,*

τυφλός, -*ή*, *όν* : *blind.*

τύχη, -*ης*, *ἡ* : *chance, lot, fate.*

Υ

ὑγίεια, -*ᾱς*, *ἡ* : *health.*

ὕδωρ, *ὕδατος*, *τό* : *water.*

υἱός, -*οῦ*, *ὁ* : *son.*

ὕλη, -*ης*, *ἡ* : *wood, woods, material.*

ὑμεῖς, see *σύ*.

ὑμέτερος, -*ᾱ*, -*ον* ; *your, yours,*

ὑπ-ακούω, see *ἀκούω* : *listen to, heed.*

ὑπ-άρχω, see *ἄρχω* : *subsist, be to begin with, be.*

ὑπέρ, prep. with G. and A.: *over;* (1) with G., *over, above, in behalf of;* (2) with A., *over, above, beyond.* In compounds, *over, above, in behalf of, exceedingly.*

ὑπερ-κύπτω, *ὑπερκύψω*, etc.: *peer over, lean over.*

ὑπέρ-τατος, -*η*, -*ον* : *uppermost, most high* or *exalted.*

ὑπ-ηρέτης, -*ου*, *ὁ* : *servant, attendant.*

ὑπ-ισχνέομαι, *ὑποσχήσομαι*, *ὑπεσχό-*

μην, ὑπέσχημαι [ἔχω]: *undertake, promise, profess.*

ὑπό, prep. with G., D., and A.: *under;* (1) with G., *under, from under, from, by, because of;* (2) with D., *under, beneath, at the foot of;* (3) with A., *under, down under.* In compounds, *under, secretly;* also with diminutive value.

ὑπο-δέχομαι, see δέχομαι: *receive, welcome.*

ὑπο-ζύγιον, -ου, τό: something *under-the-yoke, pack animal, beast of burden.*

ὑπο-λαμβάνω, see λαμβάνω: *undertake.*

ὑπο-μένω, see μένω: *remain under, endure.*

ὑπο-μιμνήσκω, see μιμνήσκω: *remind, suggest.*

ὑπο-πίπτω, see πίπτω: *fall at the feet of, cringe, fawn.*

ὑπ-οπτεύω, ὑποπτεύσω, etc.: *look underneath, suspect.* Compare Lat. **su(b)-spicio.**

ὑστεραῖος, -ᾱ, -ον: *later, following, second, next;* τῇ ὑστεραίᾳ (ἡμέρᾳ): *next day.*

ὕστερος, -ᾱ, -ον: *later.*

Φ

φαίδιμος, -η, -ον: *gleaming, glorious.*

φαίνω, φανῶ, ἔφηνα, πέφαγκα or πέφηνα, πέφασμαι, ἐφάνην and ἐφάνθην: *shed light, show;* mid. and pass., *show oneself, appear, be seen.*

φάλαγξ, -γγος, ἡ: *line of battle, phalanx.*

φανερός, -ά, -όν [φαίνω]: *manifest, visible, apparent.*

φάρμακον, -ου, τό: *drug, poison.*

φείδομαι, φείσομαι, etc.: *spare, be sparing of.*

φέρω, οἴσω, ἤνεγκα and ἤνεγκον, ἐνήνοχα, ἐνήνεγμαι, ἠνέχθην: *bear, bring, carry, endure.*

φεύγω, φεύξομαι and φευξοῦμαι, ἔφυγον, πέφευγα: *flee, be in exile;* (legal) *be defendant.*

φημί, φήσω, ἔφησα: *say, say yes.*

φθάνω, φθήσομαι, ἔφθην and ἔφθασα: *anticipate, outstrip, beat,* with suppl. part.

φθείρω, φθερῶ, ἔφθειρα, ἔφθαρκα, ἔφθαρμαι, ἐφθάρην: *destroy, ruin, corrupt.*

φιλ-αργυρίᾱ, -ᾱς, ἡ: *love of money, greed.*

φιλέω, φιλήσω, etc.: *love;* with infin., often, *be likely to.*

φίλημα, -ατος, τό: *kiss.*

φιλίᾱ, -ᾱς, ἡ: *affection, friendship, love.*

φίλιος, -ᾱ, -ον: *friendly.*

φίλ-ιππος, -ον: *fond of horses, horse-lover.*

φιλο-μαθής, -ές [μανθάνω]: *fond of learning, studious.*

φιλό-οινος, -ον: *fond of wine.*

φίλος, -η, -ον: *friendly, dear; own.*

φιλό-σοφος, -ου: *fond of wisdom, philosopher.*

φιλο-ψυχέω, φιλοψυχήσω, etc. [ψυχή]: *be fond of life.*

φοβερός, -ά, -όν: *frightful, fearful; timid.*

φοβέω, φοβήσω, etc.: *frighten;* as pass. depon., *be frightened, fear.*

φόβος, -ου, ὁ: *fright, dread, fear.*

φρήν, φρενός, ἡ: *mind, heart.*

φρονέω, φρονήσω, etc.: *use one's*

mind, think; be minded, with adv. or cogn. A.

φρόνημα, -ατος, τό: *thought, pride.*

φροντίς, -ίδος, ἡ: *anxious thought, pondering, worry.*

φυγάς, -άδος, ὁ [φεύγω]: *fugitive, exile.*

φυγή, -ῆς, ἡ: *flight, exile, rout.*

φυλακή, -ῆς, ἡ: *garrison, guard, guard duty.*

φύλαξ, -ακος, ὁ: *a guard.*

φύλ-αρχος, -ου, ὁ: commander of a tribal division, *phylarch.*

φυλάττω, φυλάξω, etc.: *guard, watch for* or *over.*

φύσις, -εως, ἡ: *nature.*

φῡ́ω, φύσω, ἔφῡσα and ἔφῡν, πέφῡκα: *produce, grow, be born.*

φωνεύσᾱς, G. sing. fem. of pres. part. (dialectic) of φωνέω, *speak.*

φωνή, -ῆς, ἡ: *speech, language, voice.*

Χ

χαλεπαίνω, χαλεπανῶ, ἐχαλέπηνα, ἐχαλεπάνθην: *be angry, be severe, behave angrily.*

χαλεπός, -ή, -όν: *hard, difficult, harsh, severe.*

χαλεπῶς, adv.: *hardly, harshly.*

χαρακτήρ, -ῆρος, ὁ: *stamp, impression, character.*

χαρίεις, -εσσα, -εν: *full of charm* or *grace, graceful.*

χαρίζομαι, χαριοῦμαι, etc.: *do a favor, be gracious toward.*

χάρις, -ιτος, ἡ: *grace, gratitude, favor;* χάριν ἔχω: *feel grateful to,* with D.

χάσμα, -ατος, τό: *chasm.*

χεῖλος, -ους, τό: *lip, edge.*

χείρ, χειρός, ἡ: *hand, arm.*

χείριστος, -η, -ον, superlative of κακός: *worst.*

χειρο-νομέω, χειρονομήσω, etc.: *move the hands, gesticulate.*

χειρο-ποίητος, -ον: *hand made, artificial.*

χειρο-τονέω, χειροτονήσω, etc. [τείνω]: *stretch* or *raise the hand* (in voting), hence *elect* or *vote.*

χείρων, -ον, comparative of κακός: *worse.*

χθών, χθονός, ἡ: *earth, ground.*

χίλιοι, -αι, -α: *one thousand.*

χιών, -όνος, ἡ: *snow.*

χορδή, -ῆς, ἡ: *cord, string.*

χράομαι, χρήσομαι, etc., mid. depon.: *use, treat,* with D.

χρή, χρήσει: *be necessary, fitting.*

χρῆμα, -ατος, τό [χράομαι]: *something used, thing;* pl., *things,* i.e., *property, wealth, money.*

χρῆν or ἐχρῆν, see χρή.

χρήσιμος, -η, -ον: *useful.*

χρηστός, -ή, -όν: *usable, good, excellent.*

χροιᾱ́, -ᾱς, ἡ: *color, complexion.*

χρόνος, -ου, ὁ: *time, period.*

χρῡσοῦς, -ῆ, -οῦν: *golden.*

χρῡσίον, -ου, τό: *gold piece, gold, money.*

χρῡσός, -οῦ, ὁ: *gold metal, gold.*

χρῶμα, -ατος, τό: *color.*

χωλός, -ή, -όν: *lame, maimed, crippled.*

χώρᾱ, -ᾱς, ἡ: *place, land, country.*

χωρίον, -ου, τό: *place, spot, stronghold.*

Ψ

ψάμμος, -ου, ὁ or ἡ: *sand.*

ψαμμώδης, -ες: *sandy.*

ψευδής, -ές : *false; τὰ ψευδῆ : falsehoods, lies.*

ψεύδω, ψεύσω, ἔψευσα, ἔψευσμαι, ἐψεύσθην : *deceive;* mid., *lie, cheat.*

ψῡχή, -ῆς, ἡ : *soul, spirit, life.*

Ω

ὦ, interjection, usual in direct address : *O!*

ὧδε [ὅδε], adv. : *thus, as follows.*

ὠθέω, ὠθήσω, etc. : *push, crowd, jostle.*

ὠνέομαι, ὠνήσομαι, ἐπριάμην : *purchase, buy.*

ὥρᾱ, -ᾱς, ἡ : *time, period, hour, season.*

ὡραῖος, -ᾱ, -ον [ὥρα] : *at the right season, seasonable.*

ὡς, conj. adv. : *as, as if, when, how, that, because;* with superlatives for emphasis, to express the highest degree possible.

ὥσ-περ, adv. : *just as, even as, as if.*

ὥσ-τε, conj. adv. : *so as, so that.*

ὠφελέω, ὠφελήσω, etc.: *aid, help, benefit.*

ὠφέλιμος, -η, -ον : *helpful, useful, beneficial.*

ENGLISH-GREEK VOCABULARY

In the Greek-English vocabulary will be found more extended information about the Greek words given here.

A

able : δυνατός, -ή, -όν; ἱκανός, -ή, -όν.
able, be : δύναμαι.
about : ἀμφί, with A.; περί, with G., D., and A.
absent, be : ἄπ-ειμι.
accordingly : οὖν.
account of, on : διά, with A.
addition to, in : πρός, with D.
admire : θαυμάζω.
advise : συμ-βουλεύω.
afraid, be : δέδοικα, φοβέομαι.
after : μετά, with A.
again : ἔτι, πάλιν.
agree, make an agreement : συν-τίθεμαι.
aid : ὠφελέω.
all : πᾶς, πᾶσα, πᾶν.
all-the-same : ὅμως.
ally : σύμ-μαχος, -ου, ὁ.
along : κατά, with A.
already : ἤδη.
also : καί.
always : ἀεί.
ancient : ἀρχαῖος, -ā, -ον.
and : δέ, καί.
angry, be : χαλεπαίνω.
announce : ἀγγέλλω.
another : ἄλλος, -η, -ο.
any, anybody, anything : τις, τι.
appear : φαίνομαι.
appoint : ἀπο-δείκνῡμι.
archon : ἄρχων, -οντος, ὁ.
arise (= take place) : γίγνομαι.
arm (verb) : ὁπλίζω.
arms (of war) : ὅπλα, -ων, τά.
army : στράτευμα, -ατος, τό; στρατιά, -ᾶς, ἡ.
arrange : τάττω.
arrive : ἀφ-ικνέομαι.
art : τέχνη, -ης, ἡ.
as, as if : ὡς.
as (with superl.) : ὅτι, ὡς.
as follows : ὧδε.
ashamed, be : αἰσχύνομαι.
ask (a question) : ἐρωτάω.
ask for (a favor) : αἰτέω.
as possible : ὅτι or ὡς with superl.
at : ἐπί, with D.; κατά, with A.; παρά, with D.
Athenian : Ἀθηναῖος, -ā, -ον.
Athens : Ἀθῆναι, -ῶν, αἱ.
attack : ἐπι-τίθεμαι.
attempt : πειράομαι.
away from : ἀπό, with G.

B

back : πάλιν.
bad : κακός, -ή, -όν.
barbarian : βάρβαρος, -ου, ὁ.
battle : μάχη, -ης, ἡ.
be : γίγνομαι, εἰμί.
beast of burden : ὑπο-ζύγιον, -ου, τό.
beat : παίω.
beautiful : καλός, -ή, -όν.
because : ἐπεί.
because of : διά, with A.; ὑπό, with G.
become : γίγνομαι.
before (conj.) : πρίν.

before (prep.): πρό, with G.
begin : ἄρχω.
behalf of, in : ὑπέρ, with G.
besiege : πολιορκέω.
best, it seems : δοκεῖ.
bird : ὄρνῑς, -ῑθος, ὁ or ἡ.
boat : πλοῖον, -ου, τό.
body : σῶμα, -ατος, τό.
both . . . and : καί . . . καί, τε . . . καί.
bow : τόξον, -ου, τό.
boy : παῖς, παιδός, ὁ.
brave : ἀγαθός, -ή, -όν.
bravery : ἀρετή, -ῆς, ἡ.
breadth : εὖρος, -ους, τό.
break : λύω.
breastplate : θώρᾱξ, -ᾱκος, ὁ.
bridge (noun): γέφῡρα, -ᾱς, ἡ.
bridge (verb): ζεύγνῡμι.
bring : ἄγω.
brother : ἀδελφός, -οῦ, ὁ.
burn : κάω or καίω.
but : ἀλλά, δέ.
buy : ἀγοράζω.
by : κατά, with A.; παρά, with D.; ὑπό, with G.

C

call : καλέω.
camp : στρατόπεδον, -ου, τό.
campaign, make a : στρατεύω (usually in mid.).
canal : διῶρυξ, -υχος, ἡ.
capable : ἱκανός, -ή, -όν.
captain : λοχᾱγός, -οῦ, ὁ.
capture : αἱρέω.
captured, be : ἁλίσκομαι.
carry : φέρω.
cart : ἅμαξα, -ης, ἡ.
cattle : βοῦς, βοός, ὁ and ἡ.
cause : παρ-έχω.
cavalry : ἱππεῖς, -έων, οἱ.
cease (intrans.): παύομαι.
certain, a : τις, τι.
chariot : ἅρμα, -ατος, τό.
child : παῖς, παιδός, ὁ and ἡ.
choose : αἱρέομαι.
circle, in a : κύκλῳ.
citizen : πολίτης, -ου, ὁ.
city : πόλις, -εως, ἡ.
clever : δεινός, -ή, -όν.
collect : ἀθροίζω.
come : ἔρχομαι; **come away** : ἀπ-έρχομαι.
command (verb): κελεύω.
command of, in : ἐπί, with D.
commander : ἄρχων, -οντος, ὁ.
common : κοινός, -ή, -όν.
company (of soldiers): λόχος, -ου, ὁ.
compel : ἀναγκάζω.
conduct : ἄγω.
confident, be : πέποιθα.
consider well : ἐν-θῡμέομαι.
contrivance : μηχανή, -ῆς, ἡ.
country : χώρᾱ, -ᾱς, ἡ.
courage, have : θαρρέω.
cowardly : κακός, -ή, -όν.
cross : δια-βαίνω.
crossable : δια-βατός, -ή, -όν.
crown : στέφανος, -ου, ὁ.
cut : τέμνω.
cut to pieces : κατα-κόπτω.
Cyrus : Κῦρος, -ου, ὁ.

D

danger : κίνδῡνος, -ου, ὁ.
danger, incur : κινδῡνεύω.
day : ἡμέρᾱ, -ᾱς, ἡ.
day's journey or march: σταθμός, -οῦ, ὁ
dead, be : τέθνηκα.
death : θάνατος, -ου, ὁ.
death, put to : ἀπο-κτείνω.
deceive : ἐξ-απατάω, ψεύδομαι.
decide : κρίνω.
deed : ἔργον, -ου, τό.

defeated, be : ἡττάομαι.
delay : μέλλω.
deliberate : βουλεύομαι.
demand : ἀξιόω, ἀπ-αιτέω.
depart from : ἀπ-αλλάττομαι.
deprive : ἀπο-στερέω, ἀφ-αιρέω.
desire : δέομαι, ἐθέλω, ἐπι-θῡμέω.
desolate : ἔρημος, -η, -ον.
destroy : ἀπ-όλλῡμι, λύω.
die : ἀπο-θνήσκω.
difficulty : ἀ-πορίᾱ, ᾱς, ἡ.
difficulty, be in : ἀ-πορέω.
disclose : ἐπι-δείκνῡμι.
dishonor : ἀ-τῑμάζω.
do : ποιέω, πράττω.
door : θύρᾱ, -ᾱς, ἡ.
down from : κατά, with G.; **down along** : κατά, with A.
draw up : τάττω.
drink : πίνω.
during : indefinite time, G.; duration, A.

E

each : ἕκαστος, -η, -ον.
easy : ῥᾴδιος, -ᾱ, -ον.
eight : ὀκτώ.
enemy : πολέμιοι, -ων, οἱ; **personal enemy** : ἐχθρός, -οῦ, -ό.
enlist : ἀθροίζω.
enraged, be : χαλεπαίνω.
entire : ὅλος, -η, -ον; πᾶς, πᾶσα, πᾶν.
escape notice : λανθάνω.
every : πᾶς, πᾶσα, πᾶν, see **each**.
everything : πάντα.
evident : δῆλος, -η, -ον.
exile : φυγάς, -άδος, ὁ.
expect : ἐλπίζω.
express : ἀπο-δείκνῡμι.

F

faithful : πιστός, -ή, -όν.
fall : πίπτω.
false : ψευδής, -ές; **falsehoods** : τὰ ψευδῆ.
fare ill or **well** : κακῶς or καλῶς πράττω.
fast : ταχύς, -εῖα, -ύ.
father : πατήρ, πατρός, ὁ.
fatherland : πατρίς, -ίδος, ἡ.
favorable : καλός, -ή, -όν.
fear (noun) : φόβος, -ου, ὁ.
fear (verb) : δέδοικα, φοβέομαι.
fearful : φοβερός, -ά, -όν.
few : ὀλίγοι, -αι, -α.
fight : μάχομαι.
fill : πίμπλημι.
find : εὑρίσκω, κατα-λαμβάνω.
fine : καλός, -ή, -όν.
fire : πῦρ, πυρός, τό.
first : πρῶτος, -η, -ον; (adv.), πρῶτον.
fish : ἰχθύς, -ύος, ὁ.
fitting moment : καιρός, -οῦ, ο.
five : πέντε.
flee : φεύγω.
flight : φυγή, -ῆς, ἡ.
foes : πολέμιοι, -ων, οἱ.
follow : ἕπομαι.
follows, as : ὧδε.
food : σῖτος, -ου, ὁ.
for (conj.) : γάρ.
for (prep.) : ἐπί, with D. and A.; περί, with G.
force : δύναμις, -εως, ἡ; κράτος, -ους, τό, βίᾱ, -ᾱς, ἡ.
foreigner : βάρβαρος, -ου, ὁ.
formation : τάξις, -εως, ἡ.
former (adj.): πρότερος, -ᾱ, -ον.
former, the : ὁ μέν, ἡ μέν, τὸ μέν.
formerly : πρότερον.
four : τέτταρες, -α.
free : ἐλεύθερος, -ᾱ, -ον.
freedom : ἐλευθερίᾱ, -ᾱς, ἡ.
frequently : πολλάκις.
friend : φίλος, -ου, ὁ.
friendly : φίλιος, -ᾱ, -ον.

friendship : φιλίᾱ, -ᾱς, ἡ.
frightful : φοβερός, -ά, -όν.
from : ἀπό, ἐκ, παρά, with G.
fugitive : φυγάς, -άδος, ὁ.
full, full of : μεστός, -ή, -όν.
future, for the : τὸ λοιπόν.

G

garrison : φυλακή, -ῆς, ἡ.
gate : πύλη, -ης, ἡ.
gather : ἀθροίζω.
general : στρατηγός, -οῦ, ὁ.
get together : συν-άγω.
gift : δῶρον, -ου, τό.
give : δίδωμι ; **give back** : ἀπο-δίδωμι.
give battle : μάχομαι.
give signal : σημαίνω.
gladly : ἡδέως.
go : εἶμι, ἔρχομαι ; **go by** : πάρ-ειμι, παρ-έρχομαι.
god : θεός, -οῦ, ὁ.
gold : χρῡσίον, -ου, τό ; χρῡσός, -οῦ, ὁ.
good : ἀγαθός, -ή, -όν.
grain : σῖτος, -ου, ὁ.
grateful, feel : χάριν ἔχω.
great : μέγας, μεγάλη, μέγα.
greatly : μεγάλως.
Greece : Ἑλλάς, -άδος, ἡ.
Greek (adj.) : Ἑλληνικός, -ή, -όν.
Greek (noun) : Ἕλλην, -ηνος, ὁ.
guard (noun) : φυλακή, -ῆς, ἡ ; φύλαξ, -ακος, ὁ.
guard (verb) : φυλάττω.
guest : ξένος, -ου, ὁ.
guide : ἡγεμών, -όνος, ὁ.

H

halt : ἵστημι, τίθεμαι τὰ ὅπλα.
hand : χείρ, χειρός, ἡ.
happen : τυγχάνω.
harbor : λιμήν, -ένος, ὁ.
hard : χαλεπός, -ή, -όν.
harm, do : βλάπτω, κακῶς ποιέω.
harm, suffer : κακῶς πάσχω.
hasten : σπεύδω.
have : ἔχω.
hear : ἀκούω.
heavy-armed soldier : ὁπλίτης, -ου, ὁ.
height : ἄκρον, -ου, τό.
Hellespont : Ἑλλήσποντος, -ου, ὁ.
help : βοη-θέω, with D.
her : oblique cases of αὐτή.
herald : κῆρυξ, -ῡκος, ὁ.
here : ἐνταῦθα.
hill : λόφος, -ου, ὁ.
him : oblique cases of αὐτός.
himself, of : ἑαυτοῦ.
honor (noun) : τῑμή, -ῆς, ἡ.
honor (verb) : τῑμάω.
hope : ἐλπίς, -ίδος, ἡ.
hoplite : ὁπλίτης, -ου, ὁ.
horse : ἵππος, -ου, ὁ.
horseman : ἱππεύς, έως, ὁ.
hostile : ἐχθρός, -ά, -όν ; πολέμιος, -ᾱ, -ον.
hour : ὥρᾱ, -ᾱς, ἡ.
house : οἰκίᾱ, -ᾱς, ἡ.
how (inter.) : πῶς.
how (rel.) : ὅπως.
how much (inter.) : πόσος, -η, -ον.
however : δέ, μέντοι, ὅμως.
hurl : βάλλω, ἵημι.

I

I : ἐγώ.
if : εἰ, ἐάν, ἤν.
ill (adv.) : κακῶς.
immediately : εὐθύς.
impassable : ἄ-πορος, -ον.
impossible : ἀ-δύνατος, -η, -ον or οὐκ ἔξ-εστι.
in : ἐν, with D.
in addition to : πρός, with D.
in charge of : ἐπί, with D.

incur danger : κινδῡνεύω.
in order that : ἵνα, ὅπως, ὡς.
indeed : δή.
infantryman : πεζός, -οῦ, ὁ.
inferior : ἥττων, -ον.
inflict (punishment) : ἐπι-τίθημι.
injure : ἀ-δικέω, βλάπτω, κακῶς ποιέω.
inquire : ἐρωτάω, πυνθάνομαι.
instead of : ἀντί, with G.
intend : μέλλω, ἐν νῷ ἔχω.
into : εἰς, with A.
itself : αὐτό, -οῦ.

J

javelin : παλτόν, -οῦ, τό.
journey : πορείᾱ, -ᾱς, ἡ.
judge : κρῑ́νω.
just : δίκαιος, -ᾱ, -ον.
justice : δίκη, -ης, ἡ.

K

kill : ἀπο-κτείνω.
king : βασιλεύς, -έως, ὁ.
know : γιγνώσκω, οἶδα.

L

lack : ἀ-πορέω, δέομαι.
land : γῆ, γῆς, ἡ.
large : μέγας, μεγάλη, μέγα.
later : ὕστερος, -ᾱ, -ον.
latter, the : ὁ δέ, ἡ δέ, τὸ δέ.
law : νόμος, -ου, ὁ.
lead : ἄγω, ἡγέομαι.
leader : ἡγεμών, -όνος, ὁ.
learn : μανθάνω, πυνθάνομαι.
leave : λείπω.
leisure : σχολή, -ῆς, ἡ.
let go (= dismiss) : ἀφ-ίημι.
letter : ἐπιστολή, -ῆς, ἡ.
lie : ψεύδομαι.
line (of battle) : τάξις, -εως, ἡ.
little : ὀλίγος, -η, -ον.
long : μακρός, -ά, -όν.
longer (adv.) : ἔτι.
look : βλέπω.
look to it : σκοπέω.
love : φιλέω.
loyal : εὔ-νους, εὔ-νουν.

M

majority, the : οἱ πολλοί.
make : ποιέω.
make a campaign : στρατεύω.
make plain : δηλόω.
make war : πολεμέω.
man : ἀνήρ, ἀνδρός, ὁ; ἄνθρωπος, -ου, ὁ.
many : πολύς, πολλή, πολύ.
march : ἐλαύνω, πορεύομαι.
march by : παρ-ελαύνω.
market : ἀγορά, -ᾶς, ἡ.
master : δεσπότης, -ου, ὁ.
mercenary : ξένος, -ου, ὁ.
messenger : ἄγγελος, -ου, ὁ.
might : κράτος, -ους, τό.
money : χρήματα, -ων, τά.
month : μήν, μηνός, ὁ.
monument : μνῆμα, -ατος, τό.
more (adv.) : μᾶλλον.
mother : μήτηρ, μητρός, ἡ.
mountain : ὄρος, -ους, τό.
much : πολύς, πολλή, πολύ.
multitude : πλῆθος, -ους, τό.
must : δεῖ, ἀνάγκη ἐστί, χρή; often verbal in -τέος.
my : ἐμός, -ή, -όν.
myself, of : ἐμ-αυτοῦ, -ῆς.

N

name : ὄνομα, -ατος, τό.
near : ἐγγύς; πρός, with D.
necessary : ἀναγκαῖος, -ᾱ, -ον.
necessary, it is : δεῖ, ἀνάγκη, χρή.

neither . . . nor : οὔ-τε . . . οὔ-τε.
next : ὑστεραῖος, -ᾱ, -ον.
night : νύξ, νυκτός, ἡ.
no longer : οὐκ-έτι or μη-κ-έτι.
no one : οὐδ-είς, οὐδε-μία, οὐδ-έν (μηδ-είς).
noise : θόρυβος, -ου, ὁ.
not : οὐ, οὐκ, οὐχ (μή).
not yet : οὔ-πω.
now : νῦν.
number, great : πλῆθος, -ους, τό.

O

oath : ὅρκος, -ου, ὁ.
obey : πείθομαι.
old man : γέρων, -οντος, ὁ.
on : ἐπί, with G., D., and A.
on account of : διά, with A.
once (adv.) : ἅπαξ, ποτέ.
once, at : εὐθύς.
one : εἷς, μία, ἕν; τις, τι.
one another, of : ἀλλήλων.
only : μόνος, -η, -ον.
opponents : ἐν-αντίοι, -ων, οἱ.
or : ἤ.
orator : ῥήτωρ, -ορος, ὁ.
order : κελεύω.
order that, in : ἵνα, ὅπως, ὡς.
other : ἄλλος, -η, -ο.
others : see *some*.
ought : δεῖ, χρή.
out of : ἐκ, ἐξ, with G.
outcry : θόρυβος, -ου, ὁ; κραυγή, -ῆς, ἡ.
owe : ὀφείλω.
ox : βοῦς, βοός, ὁ.

P

palace : βασίλεια, -ων, τά.
parasang : παρασάγγης, -ου, ὁ.
park : παράδεισος, -ου, ὁ.
part : μέρος, -ους, τό.
pass : πύλαι, -ῶν, αἱ.
passable : δια-βατός, -ή, -όν.
pay (noun) : μισθός, -οῦ, ὁ.
pay (verb) : μισθόω.
pay back : ἀπο-δίδωμι.
peace : εἰρήνη, -ης, ἡ.
peltast : πελταστής, -οῦ, ὁ.
perceive : αἰσθάνομαι.
perish : ἀπ-όλλυμαι.
permit : ἐάω.
perplexed, be : ἀ-πορέω.
persuade : πείθω.
phalanx : φάλαγξ, -γος, ἡ.
pillage : δι-αρπάζω.
place : τόπος, -ου, ὁ; χωρίον, -ου, τό.
place, take : γίγνομαι.
plain (adj.) : δῆλος, -η, -ον.
plain (noun) : πεδίον, -ου, τό.
plain, make : δηλόω.
plan (noun) : βουλή, -ῆς, ἡ.
plan (verb) : βουλεύω.
pleased, be : ἥδομαι.
plethrum : πλέθρον, -ου, τό.
plot : ἐπι-βουλή, -ῆς, ἡ.
plot against : ἐπι-βουλεύω.
plunder : ἁρπάζω.
possible, it is : ἔξ-εστι(ν), ἔστι(ν).
post : τάττω.
prepare : παρα-σκευάζω.
present, be : πάρ-ειμι.
prevent : κωλύω.
proceed : πορεύομαι.
profit : κέρδος, -ους, τό.
promise : ὑπ-ισχνέομαι.
province : ἀρχή, -ῆς, ἡ.
provisions : ἐπιτήδεια, -ων, τά.
punish : τῑμ-ωρέομαι.
punishment : δίκη, -ῆς, ἡ; **inflict punishment** : δίκην ἐπι-τίθημι.
pursue : διώκω.
put : τίθημι.

put to death : ἀπο-κτείνω.
put together : συν-τίθημι.

Q

queen : βασίλεια, -ᾱς, ἡ.
quick : ταχύς, -εῖα, -ύ.
quickly: ταχέως.

R

rank : τάξις, -εως, ἡ.
rapid : ταχύς, -εῖα, -ύ.
rapidly : ταχέως.
reach : ἀφ-ικνέομαι.
rear, in the : ὄπισθεν.
receive : δέχομαι, λαμβάνω.
regard : νομίζω.
regard to, with : περί, with G.
release : ἀφ-ίημι.
remain : μένω or εἰμί.
remember : μέμνημαι.
reply : ἀπο-κρίνομαι.
report : ἀγγέλλω.
rest of, the : ὁ ἄλλος, etc.
result that, with the : ὥστε.
ride : ἐλαύνω ; **ride by** : παρ-ελαύνω.
right : δεξιός, -ά, -όν.
rise : ἀν-ίσταμαι.
river : ποταμός, -οῦ, ὁ.
road : ὁδός, -οῦ, ἡ.
rout : εἰς φυγὴν τρέπω.
ruler : ἄρχων, -οντος, ὁ.
run (noun) : δρόμος, -ου, ὁ.
run (verb) : τρέχω.
rush : ἵεμαι.
rush into : εἰσ-πίπτω (εἰς and A.).

S

sack : δι-αρπάζω.
sacred : ἱερός, -ά, -όν.
sacrifice, offer : θύω.
sacrifices : ἱερά, -ῶν, τά.
safe : ἀ-σφαλής, -ές.
safely : ἀ-σφαλῶς.
safety : σωτηρίᾱ, -ᾱς, ἡ.
sail : πλέω.
same : αὐτός, -ή, -ό.
same time, at the : ἅμα.
satrap : σατράπης, -ου, ὁ.
save : σῴζω.
say : λέγω, φημί.
sea : θάλαττα, -ης, ἡ.
seated, be : κάθ-ημαι.
second : δεύτερος, -ᾱ, -ον.
see : ὁράω.
see to it : σκέπτομαι, σκοπέω.
seem, seem best : δοκεῖ.
seer : μάντις, -εως, ὁ.
seize : ἁρπάζω.
self : αὐτός, -ή, -ό.
sell : πωλέω.
send : πέμπω.
set forth or out : ὁρμάομαι.
seven : ἑπτά.
shameful : αἰσχρός, -ά, -όν.
share : μέρος, -ους, τό.
ship : ναῦς, νεώς, ἡ.
short : βραχύς, -εῖα, -ύ.
shout : κραυγή, -ῆς, ἡ.
show : φαίνω.
signal, give a : σημαίνω.
silence : σῑγή, -ῆς, ἡ ; **in silence** : σῑγῇ.
silver : ἀργύριον, -ου, τό.
since : ἐπεί, ἐπειδή.
six : ἕξ.
slowly : σχολῇ.
small : μῑκρός, -ά, -όν.
so : οὕτω, οὕτως.
so much : τοσοῦτος, -η, -ο.
so that : ὥστε.
soldier : στρατιώτης, -ου, ὁ.
some, somebody, something : τις, τι.
some . . . others : οἱ μέν . . ., οἱ δέ . . . .

son : υἱός, -οῦ, ὁ.
speak : λέγω.
spear : δόρυ, δόρατος, τό.
speech : λόγος, -ου, ὁ.
speed, at full : ἀνὰ κράτος.
spend : δαπανάω.
spot : χωρίον, -ου, τό.
spring : πηγή, -ῆς, ἡ.
stade : στάδιον, -ου, τό.
stadium : στάδιον, -ου, τό.
stand (trans.) : ἵστημι.
start (trans.) : ὁρμάω.
steal : κλέπτω.
stealth, by : use λανθάνω.
steep : ὄρθιος, -ā, -ον.
still : ἔτι.
stone : λίθος, -ου, ὁ.
stop (trans.) : παύω.
stranger : ξένος, -ου, ὁ.
strike (a blow) : παίω.
strong : ἰσχῡρός, -ά, -όν.
struggle : ἀγών, -ῶνος, ὁ.
suffer : πάσχω ; **suffer harm** : κακῶς πάσχω.
sufficient : ἱκανός, -ή, -όν.
summon : μετα-πέμπομαι.
supply : παρ-έχω.
support : τρέφω.
suppose : οἴομαι.
sure, to be : μήν.
suspect : ὑπ-οπτεύω.
swear : ὄμνῡμι.
sweet : ἡδύς, -εῖα, -ύ.
swift : ταχύς, -εῖα, -ύ.
swiftly : ταχέως.

T

table : τράπεζα, -ης, ἡ.
take (= seize): αἱρέω, λαμβάνω.
take care of : ἐπι-μελέομαι, with G.
talk : λόγοι, -ων, οἱ.
tax ; δασμός, -οῦ, ὁ.
teach : διδάσκω.
tell : λέγω.
ten : δέκα.
tent : σκηνή, -ῆς, ἡ.
terrible : δεινός, -ή, -όν ; φοβερός, -ά, -όν.
than : ἤ.
thankful, feel : χάριν ἔχω.
that (conj.): ὅτι ; (= in order that): ἵνα, ὡς ; (= so that): ὥστε.
that (dem. pron.): ἐκεῖνος, -η, -ο.
that (rel. pron.): ὅς, ἥ, ὅ.
the : ὁ, ἡ, τό.
then : εἶτα.
thence : ἐντεῦθεν.
there : ἐκεῖ, ἐνταῦθα.
there, from : ἐντεῦθεν.
therefore : οὖν.
thereupon : ἔπ-ειτα.
think : νομίζω, οἴομαι.
this : ὅ-δε, ἥ-δε, τό-δε ; οὗτος, αὕτη, τοῦτο.
thousand : χίλιοι, -αι, -α.
Thracian : Θρᾷξ, Θρᾳκός, ὁ.
three : τρεῖς, τρία.
through : διά, with G. and A.
throw : βάλλω, ἵημι.
time : χρόνος, -ου, ὁ.
to : εἰς, ἐπί, παρά, πρός, all with A.
together with : ἅμα.
toil : πονέω.
tomb : τάφος, -ου, ὁ.
touch : ἅπτομαι, with G.
transgress : παρα-βαίνω.
treat well : εὖ ποιέω.
treaty : σπονδαί, -ῶν, αἱ.
tree : δένδρον, -ου, τό.
trench : τάφρος, -ου, ἡ.
trireme : τριήρης, -ους, ἡ.
trouble . πράγματα, -ων, τά.
truce : σπονδαί, -ῶν, αἱ.
true : ἀληθής, -ές.
trumpet : σάλπιγξ, -γγος, ἡ.

trust : πιστεύω.
try : πειράομαι.
turn : τρέπω.
twenty : εἴκοσι; **twenty-one** : εἴκοσι καὶ εἷς; **twenty-six** : εἴκοσι καὶ ἕξ.

U

uncrossable : ἀ-διά-βατος, -ον.
under : ὑπό, with G., D., and A.
unjust : ἄ-δικος, -ον.
unless = *if not.*
until : μέχρι, πρίν.
use : χράομαι, with D.
useful : ὠφέλιμος, -η, -ον.

V

van (of an army): στόμα, -ατος, τό.
vengeance, exact : τῑμ-ωρέομαι.
vexed, be : ἄχθομαι.
victory : νίκη, -ης, ἡ.
view : σκέπτομαι.
village : κώμη, -ης, ἡ.
vow : εὔχομαι.
voyage : πλοῦς, -οῦ, ὁ.

W

wagon : ἅμαξα, -ης, ἡ.
wall : τεῖχος, -ους, τό.
want : δέομαι, with G.
war : πόλεμος, -ου, ὁ.
war, carry on : πολεμέω.
warlike : πολεμικός, -ή, -όν.
waste (time): δια-τρίβω.
water : ὕδωρ, ὕδατος, τό.
well, be or **go** : εὖ γίγνομαι.
well-disposed : εὔ-νους, εὔ-νουν.
when : ἐπεί, ἐπειδή, ὅτε.
whenever : ἐπεί, ἐπάν, ἐπειδάν, ὅταν.
where (inter.): ποῦ.
whether : εἰ.
while : ἕως.
who, which, what (inter.) : τίς, τί.
who, which, what (rel.): ὅς, ἥ, ὅ.
whoever, whichever, whatever : ὅσ-τις, ἥ-τις, ὅ τι.
whole : ὅλος, -η, -ον; πᾶς, πᾶσα, πᾶν.
why (inter.): τί.
width : εὖρος, -ους, τό.
wife : γυνή, γυναικός, ἡ
willing, be : ἐθέλω.
willingly : ἑκών, -οῦσα, -όν.
win : νῑκάω.
wine : οἶνος, -ου, ὁ.
wing (of an army): κέρας, -ᾱτος, τό.
wisdom : σοφίᾱ, -ᾱς, ἡ.
wise : σοφός, -ή, -όν.
wish : βούλομαι, ἐθέλω.
with : μετά, with G.; σύν, with D.; ἔχων.
within : (of time) use G.
without : ἄνευ, with G.
woman : γυνή, γυναικός, ἡ.
wonder : θαυμάζω.
wood : ξύλον, -ου, τό.
work : ἔργον, -ου, τό.
worsted, be : ἡττάομαι.
worthy : ἄξιος, -ᾱ, -ον.
wound : τιτρώσκω.
write : γράφω.
wrong, do or **be in the** : ἀ-δικέω.

Y

year : ἔτος, -ους, τό.
yearn : ἐπι-θῡμέω.
yet : ἔτι, μέντοι; **not yet** : οὔ-πω.
you : σύ.
young : νέος, -ᾱ, -ον.
your (pl.): ὑμέτερος, -ᾱ, -ον.
yourself, of : σε-αυτοῦ, -ῆς.

Z

zeal : σπουδή, -ῆς, ἡ.
zealously : προ-θύμως.

INDEX

(References are to sections, except where otherwise noted. Roman numerals refer to sections in the Introduction.)

A

W